WHAT IS SOUL?

WHAT
IS
SOUL?

WOLFGANG GIEGERICH

Routledge
Taylor & Francis Group

LONDON AND NEW YORK

First published 2012 by Spring Journal Books

Published 2020 by Routledge
2 Park Square, Milton Park, Abingdon, Oxon OX14 4RN
52 Vanderbilt Avenue, New York, NY 10017

Routledge is an imprint of the Taylor & Francis Group, an informa business

British Library Cataloguing-in-Publication Data
A catalogue record for this book is available from the British Library

Library of Congress Cataloging-in-Publication Data
A catalog record has been requested for this book

ISBN: 978-0-367-47717-2 (hbk)
ISBN: 978-0-367-47718-9 (pbk)
ISBN: 978-1-003-03614-2 (ebk)

Cover design and typography by:
Northern Graphic Design & Publishing
info@ncarto.com

Dedication

For Greg Mogenson

in gratitude for the experience over many years
of a kindred spirit,
a truly psychological sensitivity, and
productive collaboration

Contents

Prefatory Note

For the main part this book was written during 2009, with some additions in 2010. It was finalized in the Spring of 2011. An early version of portions of the text was presented orally at the C.G. Jung Institute Zürich during the summer semester 2009. The first chapter was discussed in one part of a seminar for a group of Japanese Jungian analysts, which I conducted in Berlin in August 2011.

What is Soul? was first published by Spring Journal Books, New Orleans, Louisiana, in its "Studies in Archetypal Psychology Series" edited by Greg Mogenson. After Spring Journal Books terminated operations it found a new home with Routledge. This new edition is unaltered except for minor corrections.

W.G.

Sources and Abbreviations

For frequently cited sources, the following abbreviations have been used:

CW: Jung, C. G. *Collected Works.* 20 vols. Ed. Herbert Read, Michael Fordham, Gerhard Adler, and William McGuire. Trans. R. F. C. Hull. Princeton: Princeton University Press, 1957-1979. Cited by volume and, unless otherwise noted, by paragraph number.

GW: Jung, C. G. *Gesammelte Werke.* Zürich and Stuttgart (Rascher) now Olten and Freiburg i:Br: Walter-Verlag, 1958 ff. Cited by volume and, unless otherwise noted, by paragraph number.

Letters: Jung, C. G. *Letters.* 2 vols. Ed. Gerhard Adler. Bollingen Series XCV: 2. Princeton: Princeton University Press, 1975.

MDR: Jung, C. G. *Memories, Dreams, Reflections.* Rev. ed. Ed. Aniela Jaffé. Trans. Richard and Clara Winston. New York: Vintage Books, 1965. Cited by page number.

What Is Soul?

Showing a complete lack of psychological conscience, Jungians after Jung (with only James Hillman and a very few others as exceptions) merely acted out Jung's psychology in various ways. Armed with Jung's and, partially, Freud's theoretical ideas as their model, they usually went directly, just like that, to the psychic material to be studied. They interpreted dreams, studied cases, developed theories, applied psychological concepts to ancient myths and works of literature, and applied myths and psychodynamic theories to personal biographies and pathologies. They were given over to the *object* before them, be it in the form of experiencing and observing it or in the form of theorizing about it, without wasting a thought on the *subject*, on what they themselves as observing or theorizing consciousness are doing, and on what justification there is, if any, for such a thing as psychology in the first place. What makes a psychology psychological? How do our individual assumptions and statements in psychology tie in with the whole of psychology as well as with modern reality around us? In what sense can we speak of a soul? Actually, these questions ought to be answered before one goes to work in psychology. Psychology, one of whose jobs it is to make conscious, first of all ought to be conscious of itself.

The fact, however, is that psychology is decidedly special. Other than in the sciences, which have a separate theory of science or epistemology outside themselves that at least logically precedes them (although in practice it usually comes later), the nature of psychology is such that, like life, there is no possibility of going back before or outside of it. Psychology and life have in common that they have to resort to what has been called "piecemeal engineering." Just as a ship on the ocean that has been damaged by a storm confronts the sailors with the double task of continuing to steer it ahead *while* repairing the damage with whatever means they have on board, so life and psychology confront us with a double task. There is no dry dock for us. Life and psychology are always already ongoing. We cannot first develop an insight into what life is about and how it should be lived and only then begin to live. While in the process of living life we have to try to make sense of it, and our actually lived life is itself our answer to the question of what sense to make of life. Both aspects are inseparable. By the same token, we cannot first acquire a clear concept of soul and only then begin to do psychology. This would be simply impossible. Why? Because the thinking about the soul would already be a psychological act. The reflection of life is an integral part of our living life itself. Becoming conscious of what a true psychology ought to be and what soul is *is* in itself an integral part of doing psychology.

Those questions about psychology and the soul therefore always, and each time anew, ought to accompany every *particular* psychological investigation or interpretation, because the question about soul and psychology is an ongoing question *inherent* in psychology itself. Like life, psychology is a doing and self-reflection at one and the same time. Those large questions should implicitly be kept alive in all the daily and nitty-gritty psychological work we are doing—as this work's own soul, its inspiration. But generally they are of no interest and concern to psychologists who prefer to focus straightforward on the object, on what happens, how to interpret and how to treat it. Having their true home in the practitioner's consulting room and perhaps aiming for people's as well as their own self-actualization or individuation or for the quest for meaning, most Jungians have no use for them. The concept of soul and the soul's existence are literally pre-supposed, blindly taken for granted; for their basic psychological framework one simply relies on Jung and other theorists. The reality of the soul seems to be a matter of course in this thinking; the term soul is simply used as a ready-made. If the need for some explanation is felt at all, it is thought sufficient to fall back on a few clichéd definitions given by Jung about psyche, soul, anima, and self so that psychology itself, the doing of psychology, is free of this question and can simply go to work without further ado. This means that, as the Bible put it, "they know not what they do," or rather, and more appropriately considering the special requirements of psychology, their *doing* does not know what it is doing; their doing is not in itself self-reflective. They want to have its reflection outside of it, in the antecedently given teachings of the great master, be it Jung or be it Freud, Winnicott, Kohut, and so on. And because there is generally no sense of a personal *responsibility* on the part of the Jungians for the question of soul and what psychology is and because psychology therefore inevitably turns into a mere ideology catering to popular demand, the designation "psychology of the *unconscious*" for what has become of Jungian psychology is most appropriate, if we take the genitive as a subjective one.

There is another reason why the answer to the question of what the soul is cannot be placed at the beginning of psychology. It is a question of which the field of psychology in its entirety with all its ongoing research would be the answer, much like the question what nature in the sense of the natural sciences is is the whole content of all open-ended scientific research. The answer to the question about the soul could only be given once this field had attained its ultimate completion and conclusion through its having successfully studied everything there is to know within its own precinct. But apart from the fact that such a completion is utopian, it means that the answer to the question what "soul" is can neither have the form of one sentence, or of a series of sentences (because it comprises the sum total of all findings and insights about thousands of details gained in the course of psychology's efforts), nor can it be placed, as a definition, at the beginning of psychology and precede psychological research (because the "definition" of "soul" can only be psychology's end result).

But inasmuch as in the Jungian tradition of psychology we talk about the soul we must be able to give at least some account of what we mean by this word.

CHAPTER 1

The *Concept* of Soul

E ven prior to our having completed psychological research we must explicitly articulate what our concept of soul is that in fact implicitly informs and is at work in our doing psychology. We must make ourselves conscious of what precisely we mean by soul, in order to be able to determine which elements of the multifarious phenomenology of life belong to the field of psychology and which not. We must be able to designate a definite border that separates what is a possible topic of psychology from what needs to be excluded from it. Undoubtedly it is our responsibility to get our ideas straight before we get to work or continue to go to work.

1.1 PSYCHOLOGY WITH OR WITHOUT SOUL?

Academic psychology and most schools of psychotherapy do not use, or rather systematically avoid, the concept soul. One talks instead, for example, about "the psyche," about the "behavior of the organism," or about "what goes on inside people" as "the subjective aspect of human life," but not about the soul. The word soul is "left to the poets" (and musicians: "Soul") or in colloquial language survives as a *façon de parler* reserved for certain sentimental or romantic moments. From religion and theology, formerly the true home of the concept of soul, this word seems to have disappeared. Under these circumstances it is a unique feature of Jungian psychology that it makes serious use of the term soul. This is easier to see in Hillman's work with its emphasis on soul-making than in Jung's, at least if one has to rely on the English version of Jung's *Collected Works*. But in the original German texts, Jung commonly speaks of soul, too. It is true, he also uses "psyche," sometimes psyche and sometimes soul, but usually interchangeably, although occasionally with a terminological distinction. The translator of the English *Works*, however, does not follow Jung's diction. Instead, most of the time he substitutes for Jung's word "soul" the more scientific sounding word "psyche."

Jung not only makes use of the term soul, but also explicitly opts for a "'psychology with soul,' that is, a psychology [*Seelenlehre*] based on the hypothesis of an autonomous mind [*Geist*]" (*CW* 8 § 661, transl. modif.). I had to modify the translation because the English *CW* text characteristically renders Jung's German phrase "Psychologie mit Seele" as "psychology *with* the psyche," which in this case is a fatal mistake. While in other cases when the word "psyche" is substituted for "soul," the damage may not be so great, here it means that the whole point that Jung wants to make is missed. I suspect that the translator's strange misunderstanding is above all due to ideological prejudices: he wants to "improve" Jung in the direction of a positivistic science where soul has no place. However, the fault is not only the substitution of psyche for soul. No, Jung's specific message is completely distorted. The first problem of this wrong translation is the definite article. What Jung is concerned with here is not "the psyche" (nor "the soul") as an object or real, but the traditional *term* and *concept* "soul." His question is whether psychology, the way it wants to define itself, has to rid itself of the term "soul" in order to become scientific, or whether it can rather retain it. The second problem of this rendering is that by saying "psychology *with* the psyche" and putting the word "with" in italics, the wording by the translator of Jung seems to suggest that the issue Jung addressed himself to was whether psychology wants to work *with* or *against* the psyche, which is of course a non-issue.

Jung's phrase "psychology with soul" is not his own free invention, but a citation, or rather his response to a much-quoted dictum by Friedrich Albert Lange in his influential *Geschichte des Materialismus* (1866, second edition 1873–75), which, for example, had been very important for Nietzsche. Lange had boldly spoken up in favor of a "psychology without soul." And a few paragraphs before his own plea for a "psychology with soul," Jung himself had cited the opposite phrase, "psychology without soul" (§§ 658 and 660, transl. modified, because, typically, the *CW* have again "psychology without the psyche,"[1]) to which he objected.

Jung was well aware of how scandalous his opting for a psychology with soul was. Having in § 660 pointed out that "Nobody could dare nowadays to found a scientific psychology on the assumption of an autonomous soul independent of the body" (transl. modif.), he immediately adds in § 661 the comment to his plea for a "'psychology with soul,' that is, a psychology [*Seelenlehre*] based on the hypothesis of an autonomous mind [*Geist*]," the following statement: "The unpopularity of such an undertaking must not put us off ..." (transl. modif.). In my *The Soul's Logical Life* I already quoted a comment from a letter by Karl Kerényi in which the latter stated, "Jung wrote me ... citing an alchemist, '*maior autem animae pars extra corpus est*' and he really meant it. He stands out as the only one among his colleagues—at least I have not found a second one among the not confessionally bound psychologists—, who firmly believed in the existence of the soul."[2] The issue at stake in the opposition between the conception of psychology as a "psychology without soul" versus a "psychology with soul" is whether there is an autonomous soul independent of the body or not.

Jung's unique and ultimately truly scandalous position is scandalous because Lange's idea of a "psychology without soul" was by no means far-fetched and arbitrary, not merely one possible thesis, not his idiosyncratic choice, but fully justified. It simply corresponded to the state of affairs, to the best insight available. All Lange had done was to honestly and conscientiously draw the necessary consequences

---

[1] Also in *CW* 11 § 490, however with the indefinite article ("psychology without a psyche"), § 507, where Jung's "psychologies without soul" is rendered as "psychology without the psyche." An exception, however, is § 649, which has "psychology without the soul," which would be correct if it did not contain the (definite) article.

[2] Letter of December 18, 1961 to C. J. Burckhardt. My translation. Quoted in Karl Kerényi, *Wege und Weggenossen*, vol. 2, München (Langen Müller) 1988, p. 487, note 355. In this note the word, *pars*, had been omitted by mistake from the alchemical dictum, but was reinserted by me. The Latin phrase means, "the larger part of the soul, however, is outside of the body." Jung's letter is dated 12 July 1951 (*Letters 2*, p. 19). On the greater part of the soul being outside the body cf. *CW* 12 §§ 396, 399, and 562.

of the historical development of human knowledge concerning the notion of soul. In the history of the soul, not only the notion of God, but also that of its human counterpart, the notion of the soul itself, had slowly dissolved into thin air. When in the second half of the 19th century Nietzsche proclaimed the death of God and Lange the demise of the soul, they did not merely present their personal and debatable views. They rather were, we might say, the mouthpiece of the objective psyche. They gave expression to what had in fact become of God and the soul, respectively, in the course of the soul's historical opus.[3]

As late as the Baroque age, the old concept of the soul as an immaterial substance that was the true core of the human person and the guarantor of man's hope for immortality (for eternal salvation) had still remained undisputed, both in standard philosophical and in orthodox theological thinking as well as, all the more so, in popular belief. But in contemporary philosophy, in the new thinking of Descartes, Spinoza, and Hobbes, a shift away from that notion of soul had occurred, which helped to base man's self-understanding instead on the new notion of *subjectivity*. Descartes stated: "*En sorte que ce moi, c'est-à-dire l'âme par laquelle je suis que je suis, est entièrement distincte du corps ....*"[4] From the phrase "The I, that is to say, the soul through which I am what I am" we see that the soul is identified as the I and as such is that which gives persons their personal identity. The empirical philosophy of Locke and the radical thought of David Hume raised explicit doubts about the soul substance. According to Hume not only the idea of immortality but also that of God and other transcendent notions not born out by empirical experience are theoretically illicit, having at most a possible validity in subjective faith. The soul, just as the I for that matter, is not a substance, not anything identical. Rather, it is a bundle of continually changing feelings and representations. Kant had to concede that theoretical reason was not allowed to entertain these transcendent ideas (including that of the immortality of the soul), although he was able to rescue them in the sphere of practical reason.

---

[3] Cf., Jung: "When Nietzsche said 'God is dead,' he uttered a truth which is valid for the greater part of Europe. People were influenced by it not because he said so, but because it stated a widespread psychological fact. ... [Nietzsche's pronouncement] has, for some ears, the same eerie sound as that ancient cry which came echoing over the sea to mark the end of the nature gods: 'Great Pan is dead.'" (*CW* 11 § 145).

[4] René Descartes, *Discours de la méthode* IV, 2.

Something very new during the 18th century was also that
Shaftesbury developed his theory of the "moral sense," an inner sense
of man with moral and aesthetic qualities. In light of this, Rousseau
was most momentous for this fundamental historical shift, above all
with his *Discours sur l'inégalité* of 1755. The result of this development
was that the determination of man was no longer placed in his reason,
in the *ratio* (the understanding), but in his *sentiment*, his sense and
sensibility, to which corresponded a strong and widespread popular
movement that caused a whole historical period to be called the epoch
of *Empfindsamkeit* (or the age of Sentimentalism, cf., for example,
Laurence Sterne's *A Sentimental Journey*). The emergence of
Sentimentalism involved above all a change of focus. The traditional
observation of the world was now complemented, if not replaced, by
self-observation (Niklas Luhmann characterized the latter as
"observation of the second degree"). This second-order observation led
to the discovery of the senses and the body in general (one's body
sensations and reactions) as media through which reality was to be
experienced and assessed. What was going on "in me" had all of a
sudden become worth mentioning, indeed essential. In religion
Sentimentalism had been preceded and also experientially underpinned
by the Protestant movement of Pietism which aimed for a very personal
inner spiritual piety and the scrupulous exploration of one's conscience.
So it is not surprising that for Johann Joachim Spalding, a protestant
theologian of the German Enlightenment of the 18th century, the seat
or organ in man of religion, too, was no longer the soul, but human
sensibility (*Empfindsamkeit*).[5] In other words, what used to be the soul
became psychologized in a modern sense (that is to say, subjectivized,
privatized, personalistic). For Schleiermacher (in his 1799 *Addresses
on Religion*) "Religion ... is neither a metaphysic, nor a morality [as
for Kant], but above all and essentially an intuition and a feeling."
Religion is "the sense and taste for the infinite." In a later work
Schleiermacher declared that the basis of religion was the feeling of
absolute dependence. Sense, taste, feeling. We see here how religion
is now seen as rooted in empirical man as individual, in his physical

[5] Walter Sparn, "Fromme Seele, wahre Empfindung und ihre Aufklärung. Eine
historische Anfrage an das Paradigma der Subjektivität," in: *Subjektivität im Kontext.
Erkundungen im Gespräch mit Dieter Henrich*, ed. by Dietrich Korsch and Jörg Dierken,
Tübingen (Mohr Siebeck) 2004.

nature, be it his feelings (accessible only through his body awareness) or, as in the case of other thinkers, in his ideas (representations, beliefs). During the latter half of the 18ᵗʰ century Georg Christoph Lichtenberg had already laconically established the demise of the soul: "One still says soul the way one says *thaler*, after the minted *thalers* have long disappeared." Already then "soul" had become a fossilized relic of the past.

Our understanding of these changes is hampered by our usual egoic prejudices. We think that just as our opinions so, too, what philosophers said is their subjective views and as such up for discussion. But much like myth thousands of years ago, so in later ages great philosophy and great art are the expression or self-articulation of the inner truth of the particular historical locus to which they belong. Philosophy, Hegel stated, is *its* time grasped in thought. Ultimately, in its core, it is the soul's speaking about itself at one moment of its ongoing life—through the human philosopher as its mouthpiece, so to say. In exactly this sense Jung, too, had viewed Nietzsche's dictum about the death of God as something that was "a truth which is valid for the greater part of Europe" "because it stated a widespread psychological fact" (*CW* 11 § 145).

The shift mentioned concerning the determination of man from *ratio* (the understanding) to *sentiment* had already amounted to a translocation of the essential *standpoint* from which to conceive of God and the world, a translocation away from universal and public knowledge to personal human feeling. With respect to this fundamental historical change, we could speak of an anthropological turn, a turn which is perhaps best exemplified in the fact that for Kant the three fundamental questions of philosophy formulated by him come together in the one fourth question, "what is man?," and that all of the three questions have to be regarded as belonging to anthropology.[6] *Before* this fundamental shift, religion had not been seen in terms of and from the point of view of finite man and his personal feelings and not as human ideas either, but as a quasi cosmic or metaphysical truth. Man had been viewed in the light of those truths and not, the other way around, religion in the light of human emotional needs, tastes, views, and fantasies. Metaphysical truths were

---

[6] Immanuel Kant, *Logik* (Jäsche), A25.

"objective," infinite truths, they were not finite human *ideas*, ideas that humans *come up with* and that may or may not be accepted by them. They either came to man, philosophically, through the *lumen naturale*, the natural light of the *mens humana* (the human mind, *Geist*), or religiously through revelation. The natural light of the *mens* shone for everybody. What was seen in it did not come from within man, as subjective opinions, but was universal and objective, much as the external light of the sun. Man could know about the infinite because something infinite was present and active in him, his immortal soul, on the one hand, and because, on the other hand, the natural light, much like the light of the sun in the physical world, guaranteed that his seeing was the seeing or insighting of something real, a true substance.

But by the time of Kant this had radically changed. For him it now appeared that metaphysics had entertained a mere pseudo-knowledge. So-called metaphysical truths were mere thought-things (*entia rationis*), we could say figments of the mind, that human reason had entertained and believed in precisely without guarantee that anything real corresponded to them. It was this real radically new situation that made it necessary for Kant to undertake the work of his great critical examination of "pure reason," where "reason" is by no means the same as the metaphysical *mens*, but already anthropological, a property or faculty of the human being. With Kant the old metaphysic of soul had once and for all been replaced by the (however still idealistic) theory of subjectivity, but by the time of Hegel's death even this theory had come to an end. The *mens humana* as well as the subjectivity in the sense of Kant and his idealistic followers were a logical *universal*. Despite the anthropological shift that had become explicit in Kant, they were nevertheless not fundamentally individual, each person's private possession, the way our body is (whether we are tall or short, thick or thin, strong or weak, etc.). My *brain* is *my* brain. But in the situation of metaphysics, the *mens humana* was not analogously each empirical person's attribute. It was the other way around. An individual person *participated* in the universal *mens*, or, later, in Kant's "pure reason." Kant[7] distinguished man as empirical

---

[7] Immanuel Kant, *Grundlegung zur Metaphysik der Sitten*, BA 66 f, *Critique of Practical Reason*, A155.

person from "the humanity in the person,"[8] "the idea of humanity considered wholly intellectually," or, which is the same, from the *Persönlichkeit* (Personality), which, belonging to the intelligible or supersensible world, is free from and independent of the mechanism of the whole nature. The person, although part of the sensible, material world, is nonetheless at the same time subject to the pure moral laws given to it by its own reason and *ipso facto* to its own Personality.

In the modern situation beginning with the 19th century, however, to honestly think such a universal had become an impossibility. The only real that was now imaginable concerning the idea of man and human nature was the physically existing individual human being, man as biological body. Already Arthur Schopenhauer insisted, in contrast to Kant's still universal "consciousness-as-such," that "only the individual, but not the human race has real, immediate unity of consciousness. ... in the human race only the individuals and their life is real, the nations and their life are mere abstractions."[9] Philosophy "necessarily demands something absolutely immediate for its starting point: such a thing, however, is only what is given to *self-consciousness*, the inner, the *subjective*."[10] This is worlds apart from the thinking of German Idealism and its subject-object. It marks the beginning of the radically new and incompatible stance of modernity over against the entire historical tradition of metaphysics from Plato, if not Heraclitus, to Hegel. If now there was to be a concept with which one might hope to (of sorts) transcend the idea of the atomic individual as the exclusively real, all one could now come up with was the idea of the "collective," that is, of an aggregation of atomic individuals. A true universal like the *mens* or "subjectivity" in the early-modern period of metaphysics had simply become utterly implausible and unacceptable, indeed *unthinkable*. In other words, the thinking of modernity had inevitably become a *naturalistic* anthropological

---

[8] Kant speaks of "the Humanity *in* your person as well as *in* the person of any other human being" (my ital.). It is one and the same (universal) Humanity in all, and this Humanity is *das vernünftige Weltwesen überhaupt* (which has been translated as "rational being in general as pertaining to the world").

[9] Arthur Schopenhauer, *Die Welt als Wille und Vorstellung* II, ch. 38, in: *idem, Werke in fünf Bänden*, ed. L. Lütkehaus, vol. 2, Zürich (Haffmans) 1988, pp. 514 f. (My transl.)

[10] *Ibid.*, II, p. 366. (My transl.)

thinking, be it in the style of Feuerbach, who explicitly stated that "the metaphysical and ontotheological determinations have truth and reality only when they are reduced to psychological or rather anthropological determinations"[11] and for whom therefore "God" is ultimately nothing else but the projected and hypostatized inner nature of man himself, imagined as freed from all real individual limitation, or be it in the "existentialist" style of Kierkegaard, whose thinking about religion starts out from the idea of the isolated individual in its loneliness and its very personal experiential, existential relation to God, or be it, and this especially, in the style of scientific psychology, with its idea of the psyche as located in the brain or in instincts or hormones, etc., at any rate in the biological human organism as its substrate. And as we all know, after a brief interlude of a more introspective psychological tendency in the 20th century, much present thinking at the beginning of the 21st century about "psychological" matters once more centers positivistically around the brain (and to some extent also around genes). But even introspective depth-psychological orientations in no way left the anthropological foundation, i.e., the idea of the physical individual as the indispensable substrate of the psyche. Jung, too, following Schopenhauer, repeatedly stressed *for psychology* that the individual was "the only real carrier of life"[12] and that therefore the individual had to be the locus of any psychological transformation and any change of consciousness.

The upshot of all this is that the inherited notion of *soul* in our Western tradition intrinsically belongs to metaphysics and is incompatible with an anthropological, naturalistic thinking. And inasmuch as all *modern* thinking about the issues that we are here interested in is inevitably anthropological and naturalistic and as the very concept of modern psychology is rooted in the anthropological concept of man as a piece of positivistically

---

[11] Ludwig Feuerbach, *Grundsätze der Philosophie der Zukunft* (1843), § 6, my translation.
[12] E.g., *Letters 2*, p. 286, to Böhler, 8 Jan 1956. Cf. *CW* 10 § 498 ("the true carrier of reality", transl. modif.). Biologically this is a truism. But as a psychological dogma it is, due to its positivistic and existentialist prejudice, untenable. In psychology we are not concerned with life, but with soul, or, to put it another way, not with biological life, natural life, but with the soul's life, with Mercurial life. *Vita nostra non est vita vulgi.*

imagined nature and a product of biological evolution, it is clear that there is no place for the traditional notion of soul in psychology. Modern psychology can be concerned with the feelings, emotions, wishes, desires, drives, ideas, experiences, traumas, symptoms, dreams, etc., of natural, empirical, finite man, bodily existing man, man as positive fact. It cannot entertain the notion of an immaterial soul substance as the infinite, divine core of man, the deepest source of his religion, and the foundation of his hope for immortality. And so we now have a clearer understanding why Jung's opting for a "'psychology with soul,' that is, a psychology based on the hypothesis of an autonomous mind" is scandalous. How can he dare to entertain the idea of an *objective* soul and insist that the larger part of the soul is outside the body, i.e., precisely *not* anthropological—*without* becoming guilty of reverting to metaphysics? Especially, since he had otherwise his firm basis in the stance first expressed by Schopenhauer.

Let me drive home a bit more the essential insight in the unlikelihood, if not impossibility, of a concept of soul in our modern situation by means of another, though related, reflection. The soul had always been considered to be the one part of a duality, the body-soul pair, which together made up the essence of human existence. In the archaic situation, the soul was that aspect of the human being that after death joined the ranks of the venerated, near-divine ancestors in the underworld. For the Homeric Greeks the soul had of course been reduced to the pale melancholy "shades" in Hades, but nevertheless remained immortal. Later, in the Christian tradition, the soul was essentially (I already hinted at this) what people's vital concern for "eternal salvation" and the fear of "eternal damnation" circled around. In other words, the soul was the otherworldly immortal aspect that had its true place only in a hereafter or the beyond and not in this empirical world.[13] By contrast, the human body was the visible, empirical but mortal, perishable aspect of man. The

---

[13] The beyond was, however, present already here in this life (1) in *initiation* experiences for the individual (who in Christianity was replaced by the *ecclesia* as the human, earthly counterpart of the divine, which meant that initiation became obsolete in Christianity) and (2) in ritual and in cult-images, cult-places, and cult-objects for the social group.

body-soul pair thus meant that human existence as a whole was comprehended as a *coniunctio oppositorum*, as the contradictory unity of mortal and immortal, finite and infinite, human, all-too-human and divine, temporal and eternal.[14]

But since in the modern world, the way it is logically constituted, the beyond and the hereafter simply dropped out from the world conception and lost all credibility, nay, all realness, modernity also necessarily had to lose the soul. The term became meaningless, a stray and spurious foreign body with no foundation. A mere relic of the past. Without the cosmic realness of the realm of the ancestors and without the metaphysical reality of heaven and hell as the true places of the soul, the talk about soul is phony. Still using it would be a dressing oneself (or one's experiences) with borrowed plumes. We moderns have no right to the term soul. In a world for which human existence is only a positivistic fact and man only finite and the product of biological evolution, etc., there is no room for the term soul. Of the original body-soul pair, only its one side, the body, has remained. The body or the human organism may of course have a psyche in the Aristotelian sense, i.e., it may exist as active self-performance through which it maintains the intactness of its internal organization and individuality and it may have psychic functions like feeling, imagining, remembering, thinking, seeing, desiring, just as it has the physical functions of walking and eating. But it is strictly incompatible with the idea of a soul.

So once again we have to ask, how could Jung nevertheless return to the term soul? Is a "psychology with soul" possible today? Did Jung's return to it mean that he reverted, regressed, to the long-superseded metaphysical world-view, merely indulging in a nostalgic longing? Or is there indeed some reason why his use of "soul," and if we

---

[14] We have to contrast this with a very different view of body and soul, namely the Aristotelian-Thomistic one. According to it, like any other living creature so man, too, is seen as a primary, irreducible unity. The soul is not a separate entity, an object, not a part, an organ, a condition, or quality of the organism, but what makes a living human being *as a whole* be what it is. It is its very own life principle, the principle of its self-organization, self-constitution, self-formation, and thus tied to its individuality. Soul is not to be conceived according to the model of a thing, but is the complex whole of a living being's constituting and maintaining its individuality through its own active self-performance. Here, the "soul" can be distinguished from the body or biological organism only on the *conceptual* level, only in thought, not on the level of the pictorial imagination, let alone on that of phenomenology.

follow him in this, why *our* use of "soul," is legitimate, after all? For our interest here is of course less a historical one, a question about Jung and whether he was right, but much rather a systematic one, the general question of whether "soul" can have a legitimate place in psychology today.

The issue of legitimacy is one question in this context. There is also a second one. Why, for what good, would we want to retain the term soul in the first place? What is the benefit of the word soul? Is it needed? Is it indispensable? What is it that only it can contribute to the self-constitution of psychology?

Would it not in fact be simpler, better, and even more correct to insist on a "psychology with psyche" rather than one "with soul," especially inasmuch as the word "psychology" itself quite obviously contains the word "psyche" and not "soul"? Not at all. "Psychology" is merely the Greek or Latinized academic word for the traditional study or doctrine "which treats of the Soul" or "searches out man's Soul," as the old definitions go. The word psychology, properly translated, means "logos [account] of the soul." The use of "psyche" instead of "soul" is a *new* import into scientific language, an artificial and abstract *technical term* and is clearly inspired by the wish that arose during the 19th century to avoid the traditional word and to cleanse psychology from all the above-mentioned metaphysical, religious overtones and feeling associations and implications of this word: to sterilize psychology. Or, to put it positively, it is inspired by the wish to get the subject of psychology *a priori* into a scientific, positivistic straightjacket. With the word "psyche," let alone with phrases like "the behavior of the organism," psychology is from the outset "taken prisoner for" the theoretical positivism, practical-technical operationalism, and naturalism of science.

By defining psychology with the term psyche you also have *a priori* decided that psychology is limited to meaning a "part" or one "aspect" of the human being, in contradistinction to its other parts, such as the body or reason. "Psyche" integrates the soul into the scientific notion of the natural world at large. In order to arrive at "psyche," from out of the whole of the natural world, you first have to isolate that element called man and then in man you again divide the entire reality of man into different parts, one of which is psyche.

Thus the notion of psyche is inalienably tied to the notion of man as its ontic substrate. The term "psyche" makes psychology inevitably, but unwittingly, fundamentalistic. Psychology becomes a *Fach*, a specialist field of study of one compartment of the completely compartmentalized scientific notion of reality as such. "Psyche" (and even more so "behavior of the organism") is a prejudgment, the axiomatic curtailment of the *fundamental openness* of the question of what that particular reality is that psychology is about. In addition to underlaying the "psyche" with a substrate ("man" as existing entity) and to the absorption of it into the idea of positive-factually existing nature, the prejudgment lies also in the whitewashed neutrality of the word "psyche." Its strategic purpose is, as already indicated, to exclude any feeling-tones, any traditional cultural associations that come with "soul." We must be grateful to Fr. A. Lange for his term "psychology without soul" because it innocently lays open this manipulation and the problem behind this move away from soul.

"Psyche" as an artificial term is a construct. It is construed precisely in reaction and opposition to the traditionally given term "soul." As such it is the reflection of a disruption of tradition, and a systematic negation, rejection, exclusion of it. Psychology conceived as a science wants to begin with a fresh start, a start all of its own. This also means that *it* wants to be the one that determines what is admitted and what not. With "psyche" the object of psychology has, in its most general outline, been *preformed* in advance by psychology itself, *preformed*, of course, in a negative way, by *avoiding* any feeling-tones and cultural associations. Such a psychology does not simply study what is given to it and how it is given. Paradoxically, the strategic move to eliminate all prejudice and thus start with an empty term itself amounts to a radical prejudice by depriving psychology, if it is thus conceived, of its necessary fundamental openness, which ought to be an openness that is capable of *fearlessly embracing all prejudices*. Nothing must be *a priori* excluded or avoided.

A "psychology with soul," by contrast, leaves the subject to be studied completely open. It lets its subject-matter be the way it shows itself, the way it comes of its own accord. It lets its subject-matter be *given* to itself by tradition and by the real phenomenology in ordinary daily life. It lets this phenomenology and the traditional, "natural-language" sense of what we mean by soul decide what belongs and what not. It does not *a priori* approach the phenomena with a filter of its own making, depth-psychologically speaking with a defense. This is already one tremendous benefit of the term soul.

When it comes to psychology, you obviously have to make a choice. Either you insist on the strict scientific form of psychology and then you necessarily have to get rid of "the soul" and use some scientifically better-suited substitute concept *instead*, or you choose to "rescue (or preserve) the phenomena" (*sôzein ta phainomena*), that is in our case: the fundamental openness of what "soul" means and the infinity of "the soul" and *ipso facto* forego the possibility of construing psychology as an (ultimately positivistic) science. In the second case the field is wide open. What soul is, is precisely not prejudged.[15] What it is remains to be seen. The fact that you have to choose between either the scientific form of psychology or the uncurtailed object of psychology and, conversely, between either the avoidance of "soul" or the renouncement of the scientific nature of psychology is already one of the distinguishing marks of the subject-matter of psychology. In no other field will you be confronted with the necessity of such a choice.

Furthermore, we can ask, how can we call our field psychology if we give up the notion of soul? Is there not *objectively* inherent in the name psychology a claim that it has to be about the soul? I already pointed to the fact that the old definitions of the word psychology are the field "which treats of the Soul" or "searches out man's Soul." Of course, Friedrich Albert Lange had already anticipated this question. He said, "But does not the very name of psychology mean *science of the soul*? How could a science be conceivable for which it seems to be doubtful that it has *an object at all*?" And he also provides his answer. For him this question is

---

[15] By opting for "the soul" we of course also commit a prejudgment; but the point is that the content of this prejudgment is precisely the unprejudiced openness of what "soul" means.

a nice little example of the confusion of name and object [*Sache*].
The name for a large, but by no means clearly delimited group
of phenomena has come down to us. This name stems from a
time when our present-day demands on a science did not yet
exist. Should one dismiss it simply because the object of the
science has changed? This would be impractical pedantry. Let
us therefore not hesitate to posit a psychology without soul! The
old name [i.e., "psychology"] is still usable as long as there still
remains here something to be done that is not completely taken
care of by one of the other sciences.[16]

In other words, the fact that the name psychology contains the
notion of soul in his opinion neither commits us to this notion nor
disqualifies this name of the field once and for all. Name and object,
this is Lange's argument, are separable. If the old object, soul,
referred to by the name psychology has disappeared because under
the conditions of a strictly scientific thinking it is untenable, the
name has become free, sort of public domain, so that if there are
certain phenomena that clearly do not fall into the competence of
other fields, there is no good reason why we could not use this old
name for the scientific study of these phenomena.

Three things are particularly noteworthy in this view and can be
learned from it.

1. Science (in the modern sense) and soul are incompatible. If
science, then no soul. If soul, then no science. With this assessment
we can agree without reserve.

2. The particular object that this new scientific psychology without
soul studies is only the leftovers, that remainder of reality that is left
when all the other sciences have staked their own claims. The object
of psychology is what the other sciences have no use for and cannot
do anything with. This view needs to be called into question.

3. Lange proceeds from the assumption that when the
metaphysical soul has become obsolete, we are simply left with
nothing, just as when phantasms like, for example, the griffin or the
Martians are seen through as such, nothing remains. The soul dissolved
into thin air. Only the word stayed alive in language for a while as a

---

[16] Lange, *Geschichte des Materialismus*, (second edition) 1873–75, p. 822f., cited
from the edition of this work edited by D.A. Ellissen, Leipzig (Reclam) no date, vol. 2,
p. 474. My transl.

relic of the past, but completely detached from any referent and any specific meaning, an empty label ready to be attached to whatever object you like. This is in my opinion also a mistake.

With the disappearance of the *metaphysical concept* and definition of the soul the soul itself did not also disappear. It merely underwent a form change. It entered a different logical status. It is a positivistic fallacy to think that the negation of the metaphysical soul led simply to nothing at all, so that psychology lost its object altogether. Of course psychology is about the soul and not merely about the leftovers of the other natural sciences, not only about what can be positivistically discerned about the behavior of the human organism. Jung stated: "Psychology, however, is neither biology nor physiology nor any other science[17] than just the knowledge of the soul" (*CW* 9i § 63, transl. modif.). What has become impossible since the demise of metaphysics is merely to conceive of the soul as an immaterial substance, an existing entity.

At one point Mephistopheles in Goethe's *Faust* said that the word "devil" has long become part of the fairy-tale world, but that for people this change did in no way mean a change for the better because although mankind is thus freed of *the* Evil One, evil ones [and we might add: evil itself] nevertheless have remained in the world just the same. The personified or mythological figure disappeared; it has indeed become pretty much impossible for a modern person and even for theology to still believe in the devil, but the phenomenal reality that was his area of competence (lies, temptation, evil thoughts, desires, deeds, and crimes) still exists as before. In a similar way we could say that with the death of metaphysics the soul moved from the sphere of ontology to that of logic, without thereby losing any of its reality.

The persistence of this, the soul's reality, through the form change from ontology to logic can be discerned in the rise of modern psychology. What ultimately had made psychology so attractive to many people at the end of the 19th and the beginning of the 20th centuries is the (of course usually unacknowledged, if not systematically denied) promise of learning the secret of the soul. The desire to get to know and understand the soul is the secret driving motivation behind the existence of the whole field, even if the field

---

[17] Today it would be timely to add to this list, above all, neuroscience.

itself avoided the word soul. It amounts to a deception and self-deception to pretend that what people wanted to know through psychology was the dry facts established through tests, statistical evaluation of opinion polls, and experiments. Even the very people who developed experimental psychology, who introduced statistics into psychology, who invented tests and all the other devices of academic psychology were secretly, maybe even unbeknownst to themselves, driven by the hope of in this way getting at a reality of an entirely different order than what they were immediately working on, namely at the truth of the soul. This is what inspired the passion behind their research. Just as nowadays what inspires much of the neuroscientific research is the hope to become able to pin down the "ghost in the machine," to finally catch the spirit Mercurius.

The notion of a "psychology without soul" is structurally deceptive and dishonest. In the *word* psychology it *unconsciously* keeps that promise alive, but with the two following words "without soul" it explicitly denies its commitment to the soul. Through this expulsion of the notion of soul it makes it *a priori* impossible to fulfill this promise; by not putting its cards on the table, by not openly owning up to what it in truth wants to achieve, it systematically frustrates its own project. It plays with itself the tantalizing game that people sometimes play with dogs: they hold a sausage above the dog's head and when it jumps for it, they pull it away. Psychology fools itself about its own real interest, its own real subject-matter. We can also, like Freud, remember the image of Moses reached by the promise of the Holy Land, but *a priori* prohibited and prevented from ever reaching it.

To construe a psychology without soul is as absurd as would be a biology that had given up the notion of life. We cannot simply pretend to do psychology while in reality doing something else. *Psychologically*, the field of psychology and the name of psychology make a demand on us, indeed, they always already have made this demand, regardless of whether we are conscious of it and own up to it or not. They have a real echo in us. The concern for soul has not disappeared. We cannot get away from the soul by simply throwing the notion of it overboard and instead devoting ourselves to observable empirical facts. Our first question had been the general one of whether "soul" can have a legitimate place in psychology today. Now it turns out that this question at the same time amounts to the second question of whether there can be true psychology, a psychology that deserves its name.

So we have arrived at a dilemma. On the one hand, inasmuch as psychology is a *modern* field of study and as such is grounded on the truth of modernity, it inevitably starts out as a psychology without "soul." How then can the notion of soul come back into a field into whose very definition soul-lessness is built, and come back into it precisely as its root metaphor? How can this be without psychology's getting phony, kitschy, nostalgic—or ideological, on account of the absolute contradiction of "soul" and the truth of the age? But conversely: how can we want to do psychology if we have renounced the notion of soul? It would be unreasonable and irresponsible to construe a psychology without soul. There is really no way around Jung's statement, "Psychology, however, is neither biology nor physiology nor any other science than just the knowledge of the soul" (*CW* 9i § 63, transl. modif.).

One might want to see this terrible dilemma as our Scylla and Charybdis. But *that* image would suggest that we would have to try and see how to get somehow through these two monsters in between them, in other words, how to avoid them. But sneaking past them is precisely not the solution. Rather, we have to give both of them their due. They are not monsters, not dangers to be avoided by us, but our teachers, helpers. Precisely in their simultaneity—and Scylla and Charybdis always appear together—that is, in their negating each other, they show us the way.

The "psychology without soul" prevents us from ontologizing the soul as an existing mysterious entity. The soul must not be positivized. It does not exist. But this does not at all mean that it is simply nothing, a word to be struck off from our vocabulary. Paradoxically, the argumentation of Fr. A. Lange itself stays stuck in the metaphysical, ontologizing mode of thinking that it wants to depart from. That he has to eliminate the soul altogether indicates the fact that he unwittingly still holds on to the very ontologized notion of soul; that he construes the soul as an entity or substance, reifies it. He shares this with the metaphysical belief in the soul as a substance. His focus is the same. The only difference between metaphysics and Lange's position is that the former affirms the idea of a substantial soul, while the latter denies it. It is as a matter of course that for us the soul is not a positive fact, an entity, or substance. As long as you view it as a positively existing entity, you have to dismiss it. This is why we have to say that Lange directs the negation against the *object* soul rather than against the metaphysical style of thinking, the concretistic hypostatizing conception in his own mind. By acting the negation out upon the object as the latter's cancellation or elimination, the old *logic* of consciousness itself gets away unscathed. The soul (as a *content* of consciousness) has to bear the full brunt of the negation. Lange operates on the semantic level (surgical removal of this content) and thereby protects and rescues the life of the same old structure of thought, the syntax of consciousness that he shares with metaphysics. To be sure, by having rid himself of the object of metaphysics, his thinking is no longer metaphysical. But because he only negated the metaphysical object while retaining the thinking in terms of thing-like entities, his thinking has become positivistic. Positivism is, as it were, a metaphysical thought-style deprived of the metaphysical world dimension belonging to it, deprived especially of the metaphysical world's foundation in God. The negation is half-hearted and external. It does not come home to thought itself.

If, however, the negation is allowed to go all the way, it imparts itself on the logic of consciousness and is integrated into its own style of thinking. The *logic* of the metaphysical substance then suffers a sublimation, distillation, a *determinate* negation, rather than its wholesale annihilation (elimination). The soul, instead of being dismissed, has in itself become logically negative. This is the effect and achievement of our Charybdis.

Therefore, let me here stress this once more, we are not positing or ontologizing the soul as a hypostasis after all. We do not conceive it as a thing-like object, a natural being or essence, a metaphysical substance, an entity, "the ghost in the machine." It is not set up by us as a subject and invisible agent or stage director behind the scene. Nor is it viewed as a component or compartment of man and as having a substrate (such as the body, the human organism). We do not even say, "there is such a thing as soul," "soul exists." The use of the definite article (our speaking of "the soul") must therefore not be taken literally. It seems to imply that a factual existence of the soul is posited and that it is set up as a substance. We must therefore always keep in mind that the talk of "the soul" is figurative speech, merely part of the *rhetoric* of psychology. It is a mythologizing, almost personifying, manner of speaking. When using it, we always have to imagine quotations marks around the expression. This means that we are required to *think* when we use the phrase, have to use it thinkingly, in other words, we must not fall for the seductive force (Jung: "suggestive power" *CW* 7 § 269) of the mythological personification.[18] If we took it literally and nailed it down to what it *says*, the wording "the soul" would be incorrect, even illegitimate. We use it nonetheless because we are speaking, expressing ourselves, in language, and because the use of nouns conforms to the structure of our language. Our language proceeds from the idea that there is a subject of which something is stated in the predicate. It would be far too cumbersome to always express oneself correctly here (psycho-politically correct), because this would make an unidiomatic use of language or constant qualifications and warnings necessary. Political correctness always wants to solve the problems it finds externally and *mechanically*, by substituting "correct" names for "bad" ones. An exchange of labels. Psychology, by contrast, must put the burden of "correctness" on the mind, its having to provide the proper understanding for the same old names it uses, thereby following the ways of language itself which has always put new wine (new meanings) into old bottles (old words).

The gift to us of the idea of a psychology without soul is that it protects us from ontologizing or reifying the soul as a second entity besides the body. And conversely, the gift to us of our Scylla, i.e., the

---

[18] Personification is inherent in mythology. But it is interesting to note that when imagining the soul, mythology—despite its inevitable personifying and substantiating style—nevertheless precisely tries to imagine the soul as insubstantial: as a cold breath, as a bloodless shade, as invisible, incorporeal, underworldly, ghostly. The semantic content of the soul images, with its attributes "*in*-visible, *in*-corporeal, blood-*less*," does its best to negate what the syntactical form of personifying and substantiating suggests. But of course, even a ghostly soul that can effortlessly penetrate stone walls remains nevertheless inescapably substantiated, a kind of breath-*body*. A semantic negation (the negation of the content of a statement) can never successfully undo what is established by the underlying and encompassing syntactical form of the statement, the imaginal form of consciousness. (Here, as Greg Mogenson reminds me, we could compare Freud's paper "On Negation," along with this well-known statement from another context, "the unconscious knows no negation." Expressing this as a rule, Freud locked his sense of psychology into the perduring, positivized realm of the semantic negation, the merely semantically negated un-ness of the unconscious.)

old metaphysical notion of the soul, is that it allows us to preserve the phenomenon that we as psychologists are truly interested in, namely the notion of soul with (1) its sense of value, importance, indispensability, (2) with its sense of mystery and otherworldliness (even if of course only a metaphorical otherworldliness), (3) with the fact that it makes a claim on us, immediately involving our subjectivity, our deepest essence, and (4) as something without substrate and not identical with any functions of the biological organism. The old metaphysical sense of soul urges us not to throw all these aspects intrinsic to both the notion of soul and to our interest in psychology overboard and thereby betray our own actual purpose and what objectively the true purpose of the field of psychology is. It teaches us not to let the scandalousness of such an idea scare us away from the idea of a psychology with soul "based on the hypothesis of an autonomous mind."

If we take both our Scylla and our Charybdis together, we arrive at the idea of a logically negative autonomous or objective soul, where "negative," on the one hand, and "autonomous or objective," on the other hand, seem contradictory. Jung's and alchemy's idea that the major "part" of the soul is outside the body can now be understood to mean for our modern psychology that its notion of soul has logically cut itself loose from, and made itself totally independent of, the traditional body-soul pair and thus also from/of the human being as substrate personality altogether. Soul has become *sui generis*. For this reason and in this sense Jung called it the *objective* or *autonomous* soul.

Earlier we asked whether there could legitimately be a psychology with soul during our modern age. But we have to realize that it is precisely *only* in our modern age that there can be a psychology with soul, because in former ages there was no need for psychology in our sense at all. As long as there were ancestors as a constituent part of man's world conception and experience, as long as there existed heaven and hell and an immortal soul, you had mythology, cosmology, religion, metaphysics, but did not need any psychology (in our sense). As already Jung pointed out repeatedly (e.g., *CW* 10 §§ 158–61), it is the loss of religion and metaphysics in modernity that is the condition of the possibility as well as the necessity of psychology as an empirical discipline.

A famous dictum of Aristotle is that there are multiple meanings of how the term "being" is used (*to on ... legetai pollachôs*, Met. 1026 a 33f.). Analogously I want to state that in our psychological discourse the term "soul," too, has several meanings; what is meant by it has several facets depending on the situation or context. We must not think of "soul" in the manner of a scientific technical term that has, or at least is ideally supposed to have, one fixed, always identical definition, all the more so as it does not refer to a subsisting entity. Psychological language is like the natural language of daily life as well as of poetic literature, a living language whose words are pregnant with a whole range of potential meanings. To mention, in advance and only in passing, a few examples to be discussed later, there is a difference between

- soul in a very general sense as a whole dimension or status of existence, the "world" of the mind, in contrast to natural, positive-factual being, and
- soul in the sense of the soul of and in the Real, i.e., the mercurial logical life stirring within the real developments,
- the soul as subjectivity and self-relation,
- soul manifesting as particular phenomena, i.e., certain motifs, symbols, narratives, symptoms, and teleological interests in contrast to other ones that are "not soul,"
- soul as a particular ("soulful") style of approach, a way of seeing.

There is also a difference between speaking about the soul in the context of modern individual life as it is, for example, revealed in personal analysis, on the one hand, and speaking about the soul in the wholly other context of the soul's *opus magnum*, its historical process, on the other.

But before we can go into the specific meanings of "soul," we have to dwell a little longer with what the term "soul" *in its most general sense* can mean for us.

1.2 THE CORPSE AND LIFE

To give us a first idea of what the notion of a logically negative, but objective soul could mean, I return to my statement that "To construe a psychology without soul is as absurd as would be a biology that had given up the notion of life." The concept of life in its biological sense is more easily accessible and may serve us both as a backdrop and as an analogy to the problem of soul and thus also as a bridge to it. We may avail ourselves of the example of "life" in our context with all the more justification as at those times when the soul was seen as the one side of the body-soul tandem, the soul itself was usually, both in popular belief as well as in philosophy and theology, identified with life, the life principle, the principle of self-movement.

In listing and discussing major factors of biological evolution, Hubert Markl, a biologist, named as one of those factors "the mortality of all living beings, their metastable shorter or longer dance upon the lifeless, into which they must return."[19] This is a most illumining metaphor. Life as such is a dance. A movement, nothing more. And a movement *on* the lifeless, using it as a "base," so to speak. Life is obviously real, but nevertheless nothing ontological, not "something," a subsisting entity. It is invisible and intangible. True, we can see and touch living *beings, organisms*, and see that *they* are alive. But living organisms and their life must be distinguished. The latter we cannot see. What makes a living being visible and tangible is precisely its lifeless material aspect, the fact that in it life *happens upon the existing lifeless substrate* as its base. Only its lifeless matter, ultimately the corpse that it is, is "ontological." *It* exists indeed; *it* is a real substrate for all the processes that go on with it. But life itself is only the miracle of a dance that makes the corpse be alive.

Markl is not right in saying that it is the organism's and living beings's dance. No, the dance he has in mind is going on even when the living being is completely at rest, asleep for example. Life is that dance that makes the living beings alive and turns them into organisms in the first place. Life, we might say, is only the frivolous movement of a dance, only the self-sufficient movement as such with no moving subjects or agents who do the moving: a dance *without* a dancer. It is precisely not the organism that does the dancing. It is the other way around.

---

[19] Hubert Markl, "Vom Nutzen der Vergängnis, der Knappheit und des Zufalls," FAZ 35, 11. Feb. 2009, p. N 3, my transl. (The *dance* upon the lifeless can be contrasted with Freud's ideas from *Beyond the Pleasure Principle* about life as the detouring of the path to death, his view that even the pleasure principle might have to be seen as being a function of the death drive.)

A dance is airy, playful, light. The dance of life does not solidify or congeal into an existing result, into an entity or being in its own right, which is also why it is called metastable; it only manifests in something lifeless that only through it, through the dance of life, comes alive and turns into an organism. It is only an ongoing process that lasts for as long as it lasts. Life is logically negative.

The meaning of "logically negative" can easily be demonstrated. When in our age of organ transplantation, a surgeon opens the body of a dead accident victim and takes out certain vital organs, he has them as *positive*-factual objects and can use them for other patients. Similarly, when I take someone's purse, I have it. However, when someone, as we are used to say, "takes" another person's life, he does not come into the possession of this life at all, and not because it was something so extremely subtle and invisible that it slipped through his fingers, but simply because there really *is* and *was* NOTHING in addition to the now lifeless body in the first place. Nothing escaped. The living organism is not a compound of *two* different positive substances, the lifeless body plus "the life" that animates it. There is only one positive substance, the body. When it dies, it does not lose anything; it merely *ceases* to live, that is, to *perform* the *activity* of living, much like a runner after reaching his goal ceases to run, but does not lose a substance called "running." Dying is the organism's stopping to *do* something, namely to keep itself alive, rather than its being deprived of something. Because life is really nothing, and yet utterly real, it is logically negative.

The mortality of all living beings that Markl emphasized is far more than the fact that every creature has to die sooner or later. *That* is nothing special. Lifeless things, too, do not last forever; we are even told that stars "die." But they are not mortal. They do not suffer death, and they are not truly "dead" either. The invention of death in the true sense is the beginning and the *sine qua non* of life. Life and death are not undialectical, i.e., mutually exclusive, opposites. Death is the very basis of life. Without death, that is, without the capacity to die, no life. I take the mortality of all living beings to be the biological expression of life's logical negativity, negativity's itself becoming positive. As a not-positive-factual and thus logically negative dance, life has its mortality *in itself* as its own permanent logical and life-giving character. This mortality and life's constant overcoming of it and its never minding its having to die is what makes life a *dance* upon the lifeless in the first place rather than one of all the *literal* movements and processes that go on in lifeless nature—for example, the tectonic movements in and under the crust of the earth or the chemical changes in the suns and the gravitational pull of black holes in the universe. Maybe it would not be totally wrong to call life itself the true Dance of Death.

From the point of view of lifeless matter, life is, if I may say so, an impertinence. Instead of, like a stone for example, just passively lying there and letting itself be exposed to all sorts of external influences, to temperature changes, to pressure and external impact, to gravity and all sorts of rays, life all of a sudden and out of the blue has the nerve to push off from material, physical being, to rise up and to begin "to dance," to subdue the lifeless to its rule and integrate it as a sublated moment to its self-organization. Life makes what only through it is an organism insist on being its own center, and circling around *itself* as this center. It makes it exist as self-interest, an irresistible *will* to live: it impels the organism to feel the need to nourish *itself*, to mark off *its own* territory and defend it against others, to fight for *its own* survival, it gives it its drive to reproduce *itself*. Compared to a stone that modestly and obediently just sits there and, without a center of its own, is seamlessly integrated into the play of forces in the universe as a whole, life's uprising is absolutely impudent, selfish, arrogant behavior above the level of mere lifeless being.

So in life we have something that, as a dance, is thoroughly negative, without any positive existence of its own. And yet it is obviously something very real and powerful. The fact that it is invisible and intangible does not make it a substance in the metaphysical sense. In addition, life is and remains a mystery and a truly autonomous reality, but our making such a statement does not either turn us into metaphysicians, because life is simply an evident and undeniable reality. In entertaining the concept of life we stay fully down to earth. We are not drifting off into spheres of spurious speculation.

1.3 SHARED MEANINGS. OR: LIFE AND THE SOUL

From here coming back to the concept of soul I would like to state that the soul is, as it were, a dance to the power of two: the dance not upon the lifeless, but on biological life, which itself is, as we have seen, a dance, the dance upon the lifeless. Within and out of the dance as which natural life *is*, all of a sudden and out of the blue another dance commences, the life of the soul. It is clear that I am speaking here about the soul in the sense of a whole dimension or status, the soul as the "world" of the mind or mindedness.

In contrast to the hallowed old Aristotelian tradition that identified the soul precisely with the life principle, as a modern psychologist I make, as can be seen, a fundamental distinction between natural life here and soul there. If in the present context we mean by "nature" above all the sphere of biological life that gives to the living beings their powerful drive for survival, the soul is something fundamentally new, and precisely *contra naturam*. Just as life had pushed off from lifeless being, so, within the sphere of biological life, "the soul" suddenly has the nerve to rise up and go beyond biological life, pushing off from it to something unheard of before, an utterly new dimension. It has the audacity not to be content to simply be alive, but impudently dares to have *ideas* about the world and about life itself, to insist on giving life a *telos* or *purpose*, on *interpreting* and trying to *understand* what is and what happens; it insists on *thinking*, on entertaining *fantasies* and inventing *stories*, having *memories*, perceiving the things of the world as coherent shapes and figurations; it insists on entertaining *images* and seeing *person-like figures* in what there is and happens, and on connecting *meanings* with events and things. Furthermore, the soul makes us develop a sense of self, relate to ourselves, reflect about ourselves, and of course also comprehend and establish ourselves as "I." It forces us to have a sense of *beauty* and symmetry as well as ugliness and disgust, a sense of right and wrong and of *law*, of absolute *taboos*, and it forces us to know about, and feel committed to, *ideals*, ideals which in extreme cases may make a human being even stake his very life on them.

Just as natural life is above the level of the lifeless, the life of the soul is above the level of life, of the human organism. Biological life is sublated material existence, the physical body is a sublated moment within life. Life uses matter for its ends and purposes. In an analogous way, the soul uses the living organism to serve its, the soul's, ends and purposes. Especially the last example of a person's most precious ideals for which he may stake his life—people have been known to die for their king and country, for their religious faith, for their communist ideals, etc.—demonstrates that biological life is merely a sublated moment in "the soul," instrumentalized by it. Proklos (Comm. on *Alcibiades I*) already presented as the true Platonic definition of man the phrase, *psychê sômati chrômenê,* man is the soul utilizing the body. Indeed, according to Plato (*Timaios* 34 b-c), soul is the body's queen (*despotin*); the body is only an instrument for affecting the ends of the soul, for giving it a *real* presence in empirical reality, sort of "bringing it down to earth." In Kant, as we had already seen, towards the end of the epoch of classical metaphysics, the same logic was still at work when he comprehends the person, being part of the material world, nevertheless as being subject to its own Personality, which belongs to the supersensible or intelligible world. And Hegel, now really at the end of this epoch, pointed out that

> it is rather the nature of spirit, in a much higher sense than it is the character of the living thing in general, not to receive into itself another *original* entity, or not to let a cause continue itself into it but to break it off and to transmute it. ... It has become a common jest in history to let great effects arise from small causes .... Such a so-called cause is to be regarded as nothing more than an *occasion,* an *external stimulus,* of which the *inner spirit* of the event had no need, or could have used a countless host of other such in order to begin from them in the sphere of Appearance, to disengage itself and give itself manifestation. The reverse rather is true, namely, that such a petty and contingent circumstance is the occasion of the event *only* because the latter has determined it to be such.[20]

The soul is *causa sui,* its own cause. It produces itself. Already Plato conceived of the soul (*psychê*) as that which moves itself (*to hayto kinoyn, Phaidros,* 245 c 7). The things of nature including our bodily reality are all moved by something that is external to themselves. Everything has a cause, i.e., is the effect of a cause. The sun warms the stone. The soul, however, and to a lesser degree already life in a biological sense, is not moved by something outside itself. The soul has its causes within

---

[20] *Hegel's Science of Logic,* transl. by A. V. Miller, Atlantic Highlands, NJ (Humanities Press International, 1990), p. 562.

itself. It IS interiority. This is why the soul is fundamentally *contra naturam*. In the imaginal language of alchemy we could say that the matter, which is not itself soul but something positive, is moved, from within itself, by the spirit Mercurius stirring in it.

Ideas, thoughts, interpretations, meanings, fantasies, values are nothing visible and tangible. They are nothing ontological. They are just air, and up in the air. They are, if I may say so, in the literal sense utopian, having *oy topos*, no place—being nowhere. The soul is "life" per se and not a living being, and as such becomes accessible to us only in what it produces, in the said meanings, interpretations, ideas, fictions, values, etc. And because what the life of the soul is about has the character of meanings, interpretations, ideas, etc., it is essentially noetic or logical life, Mercurial[21] life—mindedness, the sphere of intelligibility.

This is why Jung, despite his positivistic Schopenhauerian insistence on the individual as the exclusive carrier of (psychic) life, nevertheless also insisted on basing psychology "on the hypothesis of an autonomous mind," and why he could do so without reverting to a "metaphysical" stance during a post-metaphysical age, which, if he had reverted to it, would necessarily have meant simulated, phoney metaphysics. The soul's logical life is truly autonomous because it is irreducible. Meanings and values cannot be derived from biological, let alone from physical, factors. They are not caused by external conditions. On the contrary, they may at times integrate all such natural factors into their autonomous designs and purposes as their sublated moments and instruments.

The meanings of words and sentences, for example, are not rooted in our body, not located in the brain. They do not come out of ourselves. The meaning of a word like "peace" or "democracy" or "home" or "rose" or "awful" is nobody's private property. Meanings are not like life in nature. Concerning life, it does make sense to speak of *my* or *your* life, of the life of a cow or lion, because here we are concerned with literal life. People can take other people's life. But meanings exist only as something that is *shared* and because it is shared. However, not shared the way husband and wife share one bed or how

---

[21] "Mercurius is the Logos become world" (*CW* 13 § 271). "Mercurius non vulgi id est philosophorum" (*CW* 9ii § 240). He has a "pneumatic nature" (*CW* 9ii § 371).

two people may share one sandwich. In those latter cases, sharing means that each of the two people gets one half of the sandwich or the bed. The more children share one birthday cake, the more shareholders hold a share in a given company, the smaller the portion that they get of the cake or own of the company. But in the case of meanings, all the people (and they may count millions) who share a given meaning, say the idea of democracy, each get the full meaning, all of it undivided. Why? Because there *is nothing* that could be divided. Meanings are logically negative, *oy topos* (nowhere), just "air." They do not exist as entities. And you cannot divide what does not exist.

We are driven here to recognize that there are two fundamentally different, indeed reversed senses of sharing. The ordinary sense means sharing an already given object or entity. The object comes first and only then may it be shared or not. This sharing is inevitably reductive or diminutive in the old sense of "making smaller." In the case of meanings we have a sharing that, by contrast, is essentially productive. This sharing is essentially *Mit-teilung* ("im-parting"), where nothing gets lost or diminished.

Only by virtue of their being shared does such a thing as "meanings" exist in the first place. Here it is precisely the sharing that produces, generates that which is shared. But to avoid misunderstandings that easily might arise from the formulations used by me so far, I must stress that the sharing that we are concerned with here is not to be understood as the literal empirical behavior of sharing in positive-factual reality, not a *psychic* act, for example by means of actual verbalizations. It is not *people's* sharing, not a sharing on the social level and in a social sense at all. No, the only act by humanity in the area referred to with the phrase "shared meanings" is its logical, *psychological* rise (or rather, inasmuch as it is a priori, its having risen) to the objective *level* of sharedness, the level of *universals*. Human beings are characterized by their awareness of, and working with, something that is *a priori* constituted as, and thus comes as (logically, not necessarily factually), shared conceptions that therefore belong to the *generality* (in contrast to screams of pain and the like, which are totally subjective and private utterances, even if they in certain cases might be meant to elicit help or sympathy from others, in other words, employed as signals). Therefore, instead of "sharing" we had better speak of the meaning's *sharedness*. There is no empirical doing. This sharedness is a logical status, an objective and inherent character, of the meanings themselves, their always already "having been" shared (perfect tense!). If they come as always already "having been" shared, it follows that, empirically speaking, there has never been an event of sharing. They don't need our sharing them for their own being shared. The latter is not a happening in time. According to their logical form, meanings are universals, and inevitably so. They belong to the generality (and to the sphere of intelligibility) regardless of whether on the behavioral and social level they are in fact communicated and generally accepted or not. Provided we want to retain the word form "sharing" at all, we could call this sharing that constitutes meaning "absolute sharing," because it is not dependent on people or on an actual performance of an act of sharing. Even meanings (concepts, ideas) that are accepted only by the one single individual who entertains them, and even meanings that are kept absolutely secret, nevertheless *qua* meanings come as on principle shared meanings.

Another way of indicating the special nature of the status of sharedness is to contrast "shared meanings" with ordinary sharing in the sense of communication between people. In the latter type of literal sharing, there are "two" elements: first a content, idea, or meaning (which is to be shared) and then the act of an actual sharing of this content. In the case of what we are here concerned with, by contrast, there is only one single "thing." Sharedness IS what constitutes that which we call "meanings" in the first place. And meaning IS in itself sharedness, generality, universality, and so it is independent of in fact being externally shared by people in social reality, much like "2 x 2 = 4" IS meaningful, IS true, even if people don't understand it or know it. Any secondary and literal sharing (in the social sense) of ideas or feelings presupposes the *a priori* sharedness of these contents as the latter's intrinsic character. Conversely, the moment a meaning would lose its intrinsic sharedness it would also cease being a *meaning* and would be reduced to a natural fact or event. A simple experiment shows this. If you quickly repeat a word one hundred times, the sound in its natural physicality becomes so prominent that you lose the connection to the *word as* meaning. You have momentarily dropped down from the level of sharedness and generality to that of individual fact (sound, noise).

Whereas the dividing inherent in the ordinary act of sharing leads to ever smaller pieces, "division" in the realm of meanings is fundamentally augmentative. It has the form of introducing distinctions, differentiations, and thus means generating new meanings. Concepts, ideas, words get deeper, more and more substantial, more filled with concrete, detailed meaning. The vocabulary and the repertoire of notions, ideas, feelings, and potential experiences available in a culture get ever richer and more diversified. An enormous multiplication.

This is the basis of human culture and its historical development. Because culture is *a priori* based on shared meanings and not on what comes out of each human organism in its individuality, later generations can build on what earlier generations created. The work of cultural evolution can be continued. This would be impossible if the individual organisms were the source of culture. Because then each individual and each new age would have to start all over again from scratch. (This is why I cannot accept Aristotle's definition of the soul [*psychê*] as life principle for the concept of the soul in our sense and have to distinguish soul from psyche ["psychological difference"].) Those who will be scientists, scholars, artists, and philosophers enter the cultural process at the cultural level reached to date and take the baton from their forerunners and carry it further, as expressed in the widely used metaphor, dating back to the Middle Ages, of being able, even if one is a dwarf, to see farther because one is standing on the shoulders of giants. This historical continuity is only possible because the cultural process happens on the level of sharedness or of the generality *above* the heads of individual human beings.

But of course, this also means that the whole of culture is a building of castles in the air. The new generations that build on what has been established by previous ones are not even, as the Biblical "foolish man," building the new (or remodeled, expanded, higher rising) house of culture on sand, but much worse, on something that is essentially up in the air, *oy topos*, because everything, its foundation as well as what the new contributions are added on to, exists only in the sharedness or generality, that is to say, in the *absolute negativity* of the objective soul. Cultural progress does not have any positive-factual base as a sure foundation for its "building up."

The prime paradigm of the realm of shared meanings is of course language. My mother tongue is, as already this designation suggests, not inborn. It is "my mother's" tongue, and I have to learn it from her and from other speakers. It is not their property either. But a language does not either objectively exist in dictionaries and grammar books, which merely record certain abstracted aspects of it. It exists only in the sharing, as something shared, and the term mother tongue points directly to its sharedness. It is *fundamentally* a "common" (in the sense of how a village green was a common), an *Allmende*, but other than the village green, which theoretically could just as well be parceled out to each villager as their private property, the common as which language *is* has no material presence and is without limitation as to size or quantity. Sharedness is an instance of absolute logical negativity. Language and similarly culture do not belong to anybody, and yet to all. Despite empirically being particulars (there are many languages, different cultures) and *as* particulars, logically, according to their inner logical form, they are universals: *concrete* universals. Meanings exist above the heads of people who entertain them, in the shared, communal language and culture of a social group. *Maior autem animae pars extra corpus est*, Jung had said citing an alchemist, and *we* have to understand this idea from what I just explained, regardless of whether or not this exactly coincides with what Jung himself had in mind with this Latin sentence (which it possibly does not).

It seems that shared meanings, and thus "soul" in our sense, exist only for human beings. Animals cannot speak. They do not penetrate to the sphere of shared meanings that exist "above their heads." Just as our human moaning, weeping, or shouting for joy, their sounds are merely the organism's own fundamentally private behavior. It is true, they can utter cries and sounds and may betray what we call body language. And their sounds and body language may, in addition to being a strictly personal self-expression, also function for other animals of the same species as signals to perform certain behaviors. This may give us the impression that they are communicating with each other. But apart from the fact that animal sounds are mostly genetically rooted, inflexible, fixed, they are never intentionally *addressed* at others, do not *mean* other individuals, and do not convey meanings; they never in themselves transcend their possible signal quality so as to turn them into fundamentally or a priori common, *communal* contents: universals. There is no sharing of a meaning as a common one when the other animals hear and react to the sounds. The sounds, if they function as signals, merely induce fixed more or less automatic reactions. They are at most signs in the strict sense. They function much like, for example, sunrise and sunset that also signal to certain species that it is time to become active or to go to sleep, although sunrise and sunset are merely physical events and not intentionally addressed by the sun to the individuals of those species for the purpose of asking them to become active or to go to sleep. There is no communication. They are merely factual happenings without the least intentionality. Only because certain animals are programmed to react to sunrise and sunset in a specific way do they function as signals. Day-active animals cannot decide to sleep in today and only get up at noon.

Since some animal species live in social groups, all the members of the group may "understand" all the signals relevant to them in the same way. But nevertheless, they do not share this understanding as a common meaning in the sense of our "absolute sharing." Each individual animal uttering cries or showing something through its body language stays all alone with its utterance on its side, and each individual reacting to the experienced signal likewise stays alone, completely enclosed within itself, which may be comparable to how in the case of an influenza epidemic, although all of the infected people suffer from the same type of influenza, the latter is not shared, but is each individual's very own illness. Each is a separate particular *case* of something *abstractly* general, much like each individual organism is a separate particular case of the species to which it belongs, but there is no rising to the level of sharedness.

An isolated human individual would necessarily exist without meanings. If it grew up in total isolation from other human beings, it would inevitably have to be an idiot; if the isolation were not total, it would lead at least to mental retardation, because the individual would share only a rudimentary set of meanings, i.e., of words, ideas, feelings, everything being very abstract and with only the crudest distinctions and no subtle differentiations. Because meanings *are* fundamentally shared meanings, an isolated individual could not make up meanings all by himself.[22] There cannot be a private language (Wittgenstein).

Aristotle defined Man as *zôion logon echon*, as the animal that has logos (which can mean mind, reason, speech). After what we just discussed, we could translate Aristotle's definition as, Man is the animal that has the capacity to become aware of and participate in shared meanings, the animal that lives in and with shared meanings and to whom those meanings in fact *mean* something—in other words, the animal that can *think*. Aristotle's other definition of Man as *zôion politikon* ("animal to whose nature it belongs to be a member of a *polis*") could be taken to mean basically the same thing as the first definition, inasmuch as logos presupposes community, an existence—of course not in a herd or "collective" as an aggregation of individuals, but—in a community as the *fundamental sharedness* of meanings, that is to say, in what we call mind, mindedness, or soul.

Shared meanings precede the individual,[23] as can be seen from language, which always already has a long history before individuals begin to speak and always needs to be learned by each child. In this sense meanings are *extra corpus* and a priori. But this a priori must not be literalized and hypastatized, as if meanings existed like metaphysical substances, much like Platonic ideas, in a *hyperoyranios topos*, a supercelestial place, or as archetypes-in-themselves in a mysterious collective unconscious, or as Descartes's free-floating

---

[22] This is not contradicted by the fact that hermits, poets, thinkers, religious men, as persons who had grown up in a community and had already fully absorbed its shared meanings that live in its language and cultural life, may perhaps at times find it helpful to withdraw into seclusion to give birth to what they have gone pregnant with on account of their experience in this culture. Robinson Crusoe in his period of absolute solitude was psychologically not alone. The difference that we have to be aware of here is that between a primordial (and total) isolation, on the one hand, and a seclusion in adult life. The latter seclusion is precisely not a total isolation, because the mature adult can stay in communion (in a true internal *dialogue*) with the already experienced forces active in his age as well as with contemporary or former minds (present to him in his memory of their teachings or productions).

[23] Even when through a great innovator entirely new shared meanings come into the world, so that for that innovator they do not literally precede him (they, after all, come into the world only through him), they nevertheless precede him logically. He does not fabricate them. They emerge in him. *They* have made him the place of their appearance. Their sharedness is their intrinsic logical character, so that they emerge in him *as* shared meanings that a priori transcend him as empirical individual. It is not to be confused with any secondary factual sharedness due to their empirical publication.

subjectivity as *res cogitans*. Of course, we could also precisely retain the idea of the *hyperoyranios topos*, provided we see in it, rather than ourselves literalizing it, one way to formulate what I called the *oy topos* of sharedness and generality, a space that is totally "out of this world," out of positive-factual reality. At any rate, there is not a pre-existing treasury of meanings, ideas, and images nor of forms into which one merely taps or across which one could stumble, the way the collective unconscious in Jung and "the imaginal" in archetypal psychology is imagined. Meanings are not available like ready-mades, not natural facts. They are not discovered the way unknown continents, the sources of the Nile river, distant stars, and viruses can be discovered. Meanings are *generated* within and by a concrete language, or a specific cultural community and are thus a posteriori. So we arrive here at the contradictory notion of something that *as* a priori is nevertheless a posteriori.

For those who need a visual aid to understand the *extra corpus* nature of meanings and of the progress of culture, I offer the image of the building of medieval cathedrals. It took decades or even centuries to build them. Generation after generation of stone masons and construction workers step by step continued the work. Who they as persons and subjects were is for the most part forgotten. They did the work. However, not they but the work itself in its objectivity is what counts. The objective project of the continuously ongoing building of the cathedral spanned across all the individuals and indeed all the generations of workers through which it slowly came into existence. Much as the task of completing the cathedral is *outside* of and, as a vision and project, *above* the architects and workers, having its own telos within itself (for the realization of which the workers are merely used), so the sphere of meanings and culture are "objective" and "autonomous" in Jung's sense: *extra corpus*.

Who, then, generates those shared meanings? I already pointed out that they do not stem from people in their subjectivity and individuality (not out of the human organism), and I also denied that they have a separate *a priori* existence as entities, be it concretistically in dictionaries or metaphysically as hypostases. The answer to our question can, therefore, only be that the shared meanings generate themselves. They are autogenetic, autopoietic. Heidegger said, *Die*

Sprache spricht, "it is language that speaks." Meanings cannot be
arbitrarily invented *ad libitum.* They have their own inner necessity
and force, their logic, which alone gives them their unquestionable
conviction and makes their true sharedness or logically universal
character possible. The process of cultural development is the self-
unfolding and self-differentiation of the sphere of shared meaning. This
is what we mean by the soul's logical life.

Another possible illustration of the soul as logical negativity is
sandplay therapy. In a sandplay picture it is quite obvious that (a)
the sand and the toy figures as well as the whole constellation of
the figures do not mean what they immediately are: sand and toy
figures, etc. They negate themselves and mean something else, some
other, something that is not positively present. But (b) they also
do not, as *signs* would do, point away from themselves to some
external referent, something empirically existing somewhere else;
no, they self-sufficiently dwell with and in themselves and point
to their own internal negativity or depth, which is their actual
meaning. And (c) that which they point to has a presence and
reality *only* in the visible sandplay picture. In the context of such
a therapy, the patient gets into contact with his soul *only* through
creating the sandplay picture and in the process of creating it. The
production of the sandplay is the creation of "the soul." There is
not a mysterious soul as a substance *behind* the process of making
the sandplay as the actual "author" of the sandplay. No, the
sandplay is itself its own author and within itself creates "the soul."
We need to read Jung's references to the psyche as a treasure house
of images in the light of this criticism.

Just as Jung had said about great art: In the last analysis *das
Wollende in ihm* (that which wills in him [the artist], i.e., the driving
force, the creative impulse, in him) is the work of art itself and not he,
the human being as person (*GW* 15 § 157). The as yet still uncreated
work creates itself, *it* is its own true author. Mythologically speaking
we can say: it "chooses" the human author, in order to become born
through him. The future (the finality) is the origin, the beginning.
Jung, for once, in this passage, does not posit anything external to the
produced work of art as the author of it, neither the man, nor "the
unconscious," nor "psyche." No, the soul is internal to the work. It

does not exist prior to the work, but only comes into being through the process of creating the work.

Where the soul does not stir, where it does not produce (feelings, ideas, symptoms, dreams, works of art or culture ...), *there simply is no soul*. I will come back to this aspect in the next chapters on the soul as self-production and actuosity (1.4) and on the fundamental temporality of the soul (1.5).

If the true "author" of a cultural work is what is still in the future, we see again how the soul is logically negative (and uroboric). For the future does not yet exist. It precisely has no positive presence. And yet *it* is the driving force and as such a powerful reality. "The soul," in other words, is logical negativity *as* a real power. Absolute negativity does not mean nothing at all. It means the realness of what in itself (in its nature or essence) is logically negative.

The contradictory unity of *a priori* and *a posteriori* is essential. The "*a posteriori*-ness" means that there is no *a priori* master plan or design. The soul's logical life follows the rules of trial and error. Jacob Burckhardt spoke of *der Geist als Wühler*, the Spirit as a burrowing spirit. The spirit *is* a burrowing. It is a trying to free and advance itself, availing itself, as it were, of any available opening or opportunity to get ahead. We can here to some extent hark back to what we heard from Hegel above when he talked about the common idea that a petty cause can produce a great event, namely that "Such a so-called cause is to be regarded as nothing more than an *occasion*, an *external stimulus*, of which the *inner spirit* of the event had no need, or could have used a countless host of other such in order to ... give itself manifestation." Alchemy similarly spoke of the Mercurius as an agitating spirit stirring within the prime matter (*prima materia*). It is, the alchemists thought, imprisoned in the matter, so to speak under the surface, and thus invisible, a "ghost" hidden deep inside the opaque matter, but as a spirit or ghost it has its own internal dynamic and intentionality. This idea of an almost subversive stirring from underneath is obviously in contrast to any idea of a teleological master plan that is to be consistently realized step by step. The Mercurius does not have a master plan for itself. It only has, or rather is, a dark urge, an unclear impulse and gropingly tries every possible avenue that by chance opens itself to it. So we have here the unity of *teleology* and *contingency*. No preordained linear progress. Alchemy spoke of fermentation.[24] Much as in our present understanding of biological evolution, it is a life that includes many trials and errors, impasses, regressions. Because the soul's teleological striving is intrinsically tied to contingency, we can understand why pathology is very important to the soul's life: it is often *the first immediacy of a new stage of development.* What is actually intended first appears in distorted form.

It is of course essential that we do not think that we could substantiate and positivize the spirit Mercurius, merely because alchemy used an imaginal, personifying style of thinking. He is not a literal ghost, not even anything subsisting independently from the matter. And he is also not one and the same "individual" that, as an overall reality, merely happens to be at work in every phenomenon. He is only the intrinsic depth and fundamental negativity of *each* prime matter *itself,* its own inner teleological impulsiveness, its actuosity[25]—its soul, the soul in the Real, Hegel's "inner spirit of the event." No mystifications!

A given historical locus with its internal unresolved contradictions—for example the contradictions between the actual ideas prevailing in society, on the one hand, and the already changed actual conditions in social life and material reality, on the other hand—demands a progression to new meanings. We may think here of all those situations where the real conditions of life (the actual way of how life is lived) have changed (for example, through technological advances such as through the move from hunting and food-gathering to agriculture, through the move from the handicraft to the industrial mode of production, through the introduction of computers, television, cell phones, GPS, the world wide web), but where the mindset and the categories—the meanings—with which this new situation is perceived are still the ones of the previous, now obsolete

---

[24] The notion of fermentation, to which we could add putrefaction, corruption, mortification, incineration, *solutio,* pulverization, etc., can remind us of the fact that not only the matter's inner mercurial spirit is negative, but that also the soul's progressive development itself is a fundamentally negative one, a development to *higher* degrees of differentiation through a *downward* decomposition movement—and thus anything but an undialectical upwards movement. I call this paradoxical type of process and progress "absolute-negative interiorization." Another term that comes to mind is: recursive progression.

[25] See below ch. 1.4.

cultural status. Real meanings are always necessitated and determined by the actual situation, the new historical locus. The history of the soul is grounded in, and has its measure in, reality, in actually lived life, how it is in fact organized in a specific culture at a given time. What the response to the actual situation will be, what new meanings will come up, is unpredictable, just as it is unpredictable whether the new acquisitions will be optimal solutions or, rather, poor, maybe even pathological ones.

This is also why there are many different languages, many culturally different forms of art, religion, philosophy, many different cultural responses to what life is about, etc. If there were a master plan, there would only be one single language.

This is the one side. The other, *a priori*, side means that in all this burrowing and stirring from beneath there is nevertheless a determinate logic, a longing and telos, a fact which is actually already implied in the word burrowing. The whole point or intentionality of the soul's logical life is that "the soul" wants to become real in empirical life; it wants to have an affirmative presence in consciousness; more than only in subjective consciousness: it wants to be objectively *born* into the world. Through this self-representation it wants to become real and explicit to itself. And to become real in the world means more than simply entering the world. The soul also wants to unfold and display its full reality in the empirical world and real life. It wants to represent itself in its whole circumference, in all its possible forms and stages of refinement. This aiming for the completion of its self-representation, for its self-display in its fullness, is what gives to the soul its fundamental process and *opus* character (*opus* in the alchemical sense, but applied to the history of the soul). It is and happens as the ongoing *opus magnum*.

On the way to its ever fuller self-unfolding, the soul pushes off from a given historical situation of itself, and it does so predominantly by means of a determinate negation or sublation of the status quo, in order to adapt to the changes encountered. The fact that it is a determinate negation of the prevailing situation gives to the soul's response to this situation, or to its move beyond it, its logical consistency, although the precise form that the negation and thus the response may take is, due to the *a posteriori* and contingency character of the process, always unforeseeable. Thanks to the contradictory unity of *a priori* and *a posteriori* in the process of the soul's life, necessity and logical consistency, on the one hand, and freedom, fundamental openness, fortuitousness, and thus unpredictability, on the other hand, go together in the soul's development.

Meanings are logically negative. But as I pointed out, that does not imply that they are nothing. In fact, they are utterly real and most powerful realities. They are responsible for wars, murders, delusions and compulsions, but also for deep feelings of love and the most sublime works of art, poetry, philosophy, for complex forms of the organization of society, for rituals, in short for culture in general.

1.4 THE SOUL AS SPEAKING AND PRODUCTION

It is only over the millennia that biological life is productive, namely in the evolution of new species. But on the level of individual existence, biological life rather shows its productivity merely in *re*production (production of more of the same), in the multiplication and substitution of the individuals. The soul's logical life or what Jung called the autonomous mind, by contrast, is essentially productive, in fact ongoing production (without a producer). It is self-expression, self-representation, self-portrayal. In this sense it is, both in a literal and in a generalized sense, *speaking* as such (a speaking, however, without a speaker). This is what Plato hinted at when he spoke of the soul's soliloquy, but soliloquy not as a monologue, rather as a dialogue that the soul engages in with itself. It is a soliloquy whose only topic is *itself*, its own inner logic and nature (cf. *Sophistes* 263e: *entos tês psychês pros haytên dialogos aney phonês ...*; and *Theaitetos* 189e: *logon hon aytê pros haytên hê psychê diexerchetai*). The soul is fundamentally a linguistic reality. As self-representation, the soul in all its countless and most variegated forms of expression has no other topic but itself, its own truths. As self-relation it is also self-referential. Accordingly Jung stated, "In myths and fairytales, as in dreams, the soul speaks about itself, and the archetypes reveal themselves in their natural interplay, as 'formation, transformation / the eternal Mind's eternal recreation'" (*CW* 9i § 400, transl. modif.). Another statement of his, although it makes a different point, also confirms the view of the soul's self-relation. "We should never forget that in any psychological discussion we are not making statements *about* the psyche, but the psyche is inevitably expressing itself" (*CW* 9i § 483, transl. modif.). And again: "It is not the personal human being who is making the statement, but the archetype is expressing itself in it" (*MDR* p. 352, transl. modif.). The soul, it needs to be stressed again and again, does not speak about us[26] and, other than life, has no interest in us and our well-being. Nor does it speak about the world and the things and events in this world. Or, in apparently speaking about them, it in truth only speaks about itself (which is of course an easy source of serious misunderstandings). It is, after all, *contra naturam*.

Everything of psychological relevance is ipso facto a "symbol." It is a symbol for something negative, irrepresentable, for *its own* inner depth, inner infinity. This, and nothing else, is "the soul." *Transformations and Symbols of the Libido*, the title of Jung's early main work, in some way expresses precisely this idea: The "libido" transforms itself constantly and thus crystallizes in ever different symbols; but as we know, libido for Jung no longer means sexual libido; he said it means abstract psychic energy in a quantitative sense (degrees of intensity) and not a *dynamis*, a force; in truth it can basically be considered as his early word for the irrepresentable soul in its logical negativity and as *opus* or productive process, a word that, to be sure, still suggests a positive substance or entity, but is expressly stated to mean something non-objectual. Today we could reformulate Jung's early title as *Transformations and Symbols of the Soul's Logical Life*.

With Aristotelian terms used by Wilhelm von Humboldt to discuss the nature of language we can say that the soul is *energeia* (en-*erg*-eia), the need to express itself and give itself an objective presence. As such it produces *erga* (erg-a, plural of erg-on), works, the works of culture (as well as, in individual people, dreams and psychopathological symptoms and, of course, speech in general), in which this the soul's self-articulation becomes visible or audible and in which the soul realizes itself. As ongoing production process without a producer, without a subject or substance as origin or cause *behind* the production, without an agent or author *who* produces, it *is* its products, its results.

---

[26] Remember the above quotations: "In myths and fairytales, as in dreams, the soul speaks about itself, and the archetypes reveal themselves in their natural interplay, as 'formation, transformation / the eternal Mind's eternal recreation'" (*CW* 9i § 400, transl. modif.). "We should never forget that in any psychological discussion we are not making statements *about* the psyche, but the psyche is inevitably expressing itself" (*CW* 9i § 483, transl. modif.).

It becomes real only in and through its products, its results. The soul *makes* itself (I called it autogenetic, autopoietic); it first (and exclusively) comes into being in what it produces in its "speaking." Pure self-expression, self-manifestation, but, because "pure" self-manifestation, a self-manifestation without a "self" that exists prior to its manifestation. Self-expression as self-*production*. And this is also why *what* it produces is only the soul *itself* and not some other, in contrast to human productions, where the maker and the work he has made are two different realities.

Availing ourselves of a term of medieval philosophers, we could say that the soul is *actuosity*. This term comes from Latin *actuosus*, a rare word meaning "full of movement, life, abounding in action." The medieval philosophers used it to distinguish the nature of the Biblical God as a *living, active* God from other attributes often assigned to him, attributes like "supreme being," "*summum bonum*," the "Eternal," which were all modeled on the metaphysics of substance and its ideal of static immobility and duration. God IS *vita* (life), life as such; he is not merely a highest being who, like all living organisms in the empirical world, happens to have the nature of being *alive*. And this *vita* was comprehended as *actuositas*.

When I say that the soul is actuose, this is to emphasize once more that it is not to be thought of as a substance, an existing entity or being, but as ongoing enactment or performance. As I pointed out: there is not such a thing as the soul. Soul is in itself pure actuosity, an actuosity without an existing agent as the author of this activity. It is the activity of self-generation, self-constitution, self-relation, self-reflection, self-representation (symbol formation, expression, production), self-negation, the whole dialectical process described above. It *is* process and life with no substrate or carrier of this life behind it. Human beings and human societies are not the substrate for this life! They are only the stage upon which this actuosity that we call "the soul" appears, the place where it happens: where the soul thinks itself, where dreams and insights and emotions and symptoms appear, where works of art are generated.

Returning to the Aristotelean distinction between *energeia* and *erga*, it is obvious that the *erga*, be they works or symbols (symbolic representations), are always objectified, materialized. To be this (namely, objectified products) is their purpose as *expressions* of the soul. Other than the soul itself as *energeia* and thus as absolute negativity, they have indeed an independent and external existence as objects. In other words, they are ontologized. They have become positive existence. This is, as a matter of course, highly problematic. What is positive can easily become positivized. The moment you get *erga*, objectified representations of the soul, they can appear to be dead objects and ossified, formalistic routines—merely external and objective. This is what Schiller pointed to in his distich entitled "Language."

> Why can the living mind not appear to the mind?
> The moment the soul *speaks*, it is, alas!, no longer the *soul* that is speaking.[27]

In its speaking, its expressing and representing itself, so this argument goes, the soul completely loses itself, loses its life.[28] It has become real, but precisely as what it is not. For the soul to be born into the world would of course mean to be born *as negative presences*! But symbols and cultural works are undoubtedly positive.

From the insight into the positivity of all symbolizations and empirical representations of the soul we can understand why the fight that so often arises among Jungians between a clinical or a symbolical orientation, is based on a misunderstanding. It does not make sense to set these two realms up in opposition to each other because they both share the same virtues and problems, only in different ways. Both display a part of the total phenomenology that can be of psychological interest; both are, from a psychological point of view, in themselves symbolic, even the clinical. But both are in practice usually positivized, taken at face value, as being identical with themselves and immediately meaning themselves (instead of merely meaning its internal irrepresentable other). Neither the positivized clinical, nor the positivized symbol are subject-matters of psychology because both have then been deprived of the soul: of their internal absolute negativity, their inner depth and infinity. The fight between these two extremes

---

[27] Fr. Schiller, Xenien und Votivtafeln. "Sprache. Warum kann der lebendige Geist dem Geist nicht erscheinen? *Spricht* die Seele, so spricht ach! schon die *Seele* nicht mehr."

[28] Apart from the fact that in this distich the metaphysical logic of the soul as substance or acting subject behind the speaking seems to be at work, it is also undialectical, i.e., one-sided. Nevertheless, it is helpful for our discussion.

is the fight between "inimical brothers": reductionism (the positivized "clinical") and mystification (the positivized "symbolic" and "numinous"). Reductionism sticks to the manifest, factual, and technical aspect of phenomena, whereas mystification starts out from the negative moment inherent in a phenomenon seen as symbol, but, isolating it, gives it independent reality: it turns precisely the negative moment itself into a positivity! (*Vide* only the fuss often made about mandala symbolism).

Just as we do not see life itself as a separately existing metaphysical substance—for example, in the substantial form of a breath or vapor that leaves the living being at death, the way it was imagined in archaic times—and just as we become aware of biological life only indirectly via the behavior (self-movement) of living beings, so—even more so—the soul is for us not a metaphysical substance or entity. *The soul, after all, does not exist.* We always have to keep this in mind. Compared to lifeless matter, the realm of shared meanings is even more airy and frivolous than natural life. The difference between natural life and the soul's life and the latter's heightened airiness comes out most clearly in the fact that natural life at least gives itself a positive-factual presence and physical reality in living organisms, whereas the soul does not have an equivalent form of realization. The very point of the life of the soul is that it does not express itself in *existing souls* as absolute-negative presences, the way biological life expresses itself in living beings, but only in primarily dead works and letters. Markl could speak of the life of living beings as their *metastable* dance upon the lifeless. I called the soul's life a dance to the power of two. It is a dance to the power of two because it is not even metastable, let alone stable. Its dance does not in a natural way embody itself as some sort of soulful *being* or entity the way the dance of life embodies itself in plants and animals. The dance as which the soul is does not embody itself at all as dance. A living being is unambiguously, obviously alive for the duration of its life. And living beings reproduce themselves, that is, produce new living beings of the same species. Those new beings clearly manifest *life* and give life an objective reality, a natural existence. Not so the soul. It has no existence at all. And all it produces is "corpses": dead letters, music scores, symbolic signs, ceremonial routines, dogmas, works of art, sterile institutions that are primarily dead things. In this sense, Schiller was absolutely right. We could say: biological life exists, and openly presents its life, *intra corpus*. By contrast, the fact that the soul, according to Jung, is fundamentally *extra corpus* must also be comprehended as pointing to the fact that it does neither have, nor give to its productions (the shared meanings), any bodily reality at all. The soul does not "materialize" *as living soul*, i.e., as negative presence.

This is a crucial point, but it seems to be contradicted by the fact that we have numerous "documents of the soul," dream diaries, deep poems, wonderful Greek temples and Gothic cathedrals, magnificent paintings, statues, and uplifting works of music, furthermore sacred books and holy dogmas, splendid rituals, innumerable myths, and wonderfully deep symbols, and so on. Are they not all embodiments of soul? Why do people pay as much as 40 million dollars for certain paintings? For corpses? Are not all the works of culture ways how the soul's life objectively crystallizes for us?

Only at first glance can these questions be answered in the affirmative. Yet, for a deeper understanding, the answer must be, no.

1.5 THE CORPSE AND THE PERCEIVING MIND AND THE SOUL AS SUBLATED "CORPSE"

Although doubtlessly the sacred books of the great religions record soul experiences of greatest importance, the sacred books themselves are not an actual bodily presence of soul the same way that a living tree or tiger is a bodily presence of natural life. Those books as such are in themselves dead objects, soulless matter. They only *become* events of soul if there is an understanding mind and a feeling heart that reads and appreciates them, and only through such a mind and heart. The acoustic sounds of words and sentences are something physical. But they become a moment of soul only if there is a mind that pushes off from the sounds and thereby in itself creates the corresponding meanings. Music is certainly an expression of soul. But music scores are not themselves music. They are merely an instruction or sensory memory aid for musicians. Music exists only in the actual event of being played and heard by a musically receptive consciousness and only for the duration of its resounding (be it a literal resounding or a reverberation in the mind). In other words, the soul as *energeia* does not appear at all in space, not in a thing-like manner, embodied, but *only in time*. It is essentially performative. The life of the soul, rather than being metastable and having a natural existence, is totally ephemeral. Even its very form of realization and actualization is incorporeal, unnatural, fundamentally sublated, distilled, vaporized: momentary act. It is only in the doing: in the act or process of awareness, feeling appreciation, thinking comprehension. In the soul, the dance as logical negativity, which on the level of biological life still congealed into living *beings*, positively existing *entities*, has truly come home to itself. It is really just a *dance* with no dancers, nothing but a dance. It is and stays logically negative, exclusively negative, not even metastable.

When the moment of understanding, of deep feeling, of poetic or musical appreciation is over, the soul is gone and only a dead thing, a music score, the dead letters of a printed book, a canvas full of paint, remains. What in the case of soul does get embodied is only its one sublated moment: the corpse, the produced work as a dead record, the words in the sense of "words, words, words," the letter, not the animating spirit. It only *seems* that all the works of culture that often appear in indestructible stone or bronze or in a poetic *monumentum aere perennius* ("a monument more lasting than bronze," Horace) are the objective manifestation of soul, because we *a priori* apperceive them from the point of view of the mind capable of appreciating them. But they themselves are and stay only its corpse (from the Latin, *corpus*) that, if the soul is to come to life, needs to be awakened through the act of appreciation: *extra corpus*! It is an act that does not happen *in* them the way biological life happens in the body, in the living organisms. The printed book stays a printed book (black ink on white paper); the canvas, a canvas. *They* do not start to move or change. They are mere insinuating signs that need *our* soul-*making*, that is, *our* negating them, our pushing off from them into the *extra corpus* sphere of shared meanings indicated by them, our inwardizing them into their absolute negativity. Only in the understanding, appreciating, feeling mind, and not in the cultural *erga* themselves, can the soul be really born into the world *as negative presences*. Soul itself is fundamentally—and this means inescapably—temporary, fleeting.

And this is why language, which itself uses as its signs the most fleeting things, absolutely momentary things, namely sounds, is perhaps the most fitting expression of soul.

But having given a strong expression to the irrevocably performative nature and fleetingness of the soul and having put down the objective works of culture as dead objects, as the soul's mere corpses, we now have to rehabilitate, as it were, the notion of corpse in its significance for the life of the soul. Here we merely have to remember that "soul" originally referred to the dead souls. For Homer the *psychê* comes into play only after a person's death. I submit that what originally gave birth to the notion of soul, to the notion of the living dead in the underworld and to the idea of the ancestors in the first place was the very real sight of a *corpse*. It was precisely not the living person (with its emotions, will, desires) that inspired the idea of a soul. "Soul" is dependent on corpses. They *are* the inspiration. The idea of soul had its origin and place historically in the cult of the dead and mythologically in the underworld. Departedness, the death of natural, biological life, is intrinsic to soul. It is its constitutive nature. Just as the invention of death (the capacity to die in the true sense) was the beginning of life, so the dead body—the visible death of biological life—is the beginning of soul.

And the idea of the dead souls was, conversely, the birth of man as a *human* being. Humans are humans through the fact that they, as I can say availing myself of a Jung quote which expresses this idea in a mythological idiom (*MDR* p. 333, transl. modif.), are "more than autochthonous *animalia* sprung from the earth, but as twice-born ones ha[ve] their roots in the deity itself." With the concept of "the deity itself" Jung refers of course to a much later cultural epoch, the time of Christianity. For the primordial situation that we are concerned with we should say: in the ancestors, in the *spirits* of the dead. As *humans* we live primarily in words, ideas, images, not in the body. We are not *grounded* in the earth, but *hanging* on the sphere of insubstantial shared meanings up in the air. This is why mythologically man was often imagined as an "*arbor inversa*," a tree that has its roots in the sky and its treetops in the earth (*CW* 13 §§ 410 ff.).

Early man had *his* soul *extra corpus*, that is, not in himself, but outside of himself in the ancestors. Later he had his soul predominantly in the gods, and still later the Christians had their soul in Christ.[29]

When I said the corpses are the inspiration, what does inspiration mean here? We should not imagine that the sight of the corpse served as a stimulus to free fantasizing, to "imagining things." Then we would be guilty of a *petitio principii*. Imagination becomes possible only once the realm of soul has already been established and become enriched by numerous differentiations of the primordial "inspiration." The primordial notion of soul inspired by the sight of a corpse *is* merely the determinate negation of the corpse. The soul in its first immediacy is nothing but the sublated corpse, in other words, the negation of the negation of life (which itself is the negation of "death," death in the sense of the *lifelessness* of matter). The soul is not an additional reality, not an Other, in addition to the corpse. If we thought along such lines, we would be back at a mythological or metaphysical soul as a substance in its own right, back at the "body plus soul" concept, where it would make little difference whether the soul substance were assumed to in fact exist or to exist only as an image, a fantasy. There is only one thing, the corpse which within itself is negated. The soul, I stressed, does not exist at all, neither literally nor imaginally. It is nothing but the product or result of a logical act of negation that opens up the space of logical negativity. It IS the negated corpse, its having absolute-negatively been inwardized into its concept or truth as the negation of life. Only on the basis of the determinate negation of the corpse and within the thereby established logical space of negativity can fantasy begin. All imagining takes place "*within*" the sublated corpse, not beyond, not outside of it.

Archaic thinking (and not only it) is characterized by the fact that it tends to substantiate and personify. Thus for archaic man there were probably two different realities, the corpse and the soul as a separate immaterial substance, as the ancestors, the living dead, or the shades in the underworld, etc. But we must not fall for this substantiating

---

[29] Things are, of course, much more complicated. The ordinary people of a tribe or nation also had their *communal* soul in the shaman, the king, Pharaoh. Individuals had their *personal* soul in certain objects, a man, for example, in his sword or spear, or staff, a woman in Japan in her sewing box, etc. Military units had their *group* soul in their banner .... But in the present context we are only concerned with the soul *as* soul, the very *concept* of soul *kat' exochen*.

style of thinking. On the contrary, we have to realize that the idea of the ancestors IS in itself nothing else but the (pictorially imagined) absolute negation of the dead bodies.

If the corpse is the inspiration, "inspiration" boils down to mean the incitement to negate and sublate the corpse. However, the corpse as such, as positive fact, is not the empirical cause and origin of the notion of soul. If it were the corpse itself that produced the soul, then apes who certainly also see corpses of their own kind would also have a notion of soul in contradistinction to body. The soul cannot be reduced to the corpse as fact. The first cause and origin of soul is the soul itself. Soul, as I have said, is autogenetic. It makes itself, and its making takes place within the sphere of soul. However, in order to have made itself for the first time, in the primordial act of soul-making, it was dependent on the corpse as an *Anhalt* (a sensual, visual aid and, so to speak, catalyst). But as this *Anhalt*, the corpse is not "nothing but" empirical fact, "nothing but" a positivity. There is no natural transition from nature to soul. Rather, that corpse that comes into play in the soul's autogenesis is the corpse as it is already apperceived by the soul, soulfully, on the—as yet still implicit (*ansichseiend*)—level of absolute negativity, or, to put it yet another way: the corpse not as a fact of nature, but *already* as an element of culture (even if early on it was culture in its most rudimentary form). Otherwise it could not function as sensual aid. The corpse *per se*, in its nakedness, i.e., reduced to its positivity, could not be the inspiration. By extension, we can say here in general that that literal and that positive-factual that we as humans become aware of is a literal positivity that is always already perceived and posited by the soul. The literal from which to push off to the sphere of shared meaning and logical negativity has itself already its place within the soul and *is* by its grace. It is not *literally* outside, or the opposite, of soul. This can especially clearly be seen in language, where the physical sounds that it avails itself of—the linguistic equivalent of "the literal" and "positive-factual" in general—are not *natural* noise, but, *contra naturam*, sounds posited by language itself, sounds as language's own property, products of its own making, namely, *phonemes*, i.e., elements of a (logos-informed) system of distinctive oppositions.

The visual aid of a corpse is the inspiration because it invites the implicitly "existing" soul to *make* itself, to become explicit, by inciting the negation, the act of contradicting the corpse and, *in* the corpse, contradicting the realm of the positive-factual as such. The corpse is like a provocative bait that lures the soul out of its implicitness, its "hiding," and makes it come out into the open. The implicit soul simply cannot let the corpse as the manifest assertion of positivity stand uncontradicted, and so it has to come explicitly forward as what it is, as absolute logical negativity.

Before I said, "The soul is not an additional reality, not an Other, in addition to the corpse. For if we thought along such lines, we would be back to a mythological or metaphysical soul as a substance in its own right, back at the 'body plus soul' concept." And I stated that the soul is the negated or sublated corpse. But through the point made after those statements, I insisted that the corpse is conversely always already perceived by the soul and that the soul's making of itself takes place within its own sphere. This is vital. If we thought that the corpse was the ultimate reality and the soul only its determinate negation, we would, to be sure, have avoided hypostatizing the soul in the old mythological or metaphysical sense, but we would have done the simple opposite: we would instead have established a "materialistic" metaphysic by hypostatizing and taking literally the corpse and the sphere of positivity at large. But by realizing that even the corpse has its place in the sphere of logical negativity and is already apperceived by the (implicit) soul, we have left all hypostatizing behind. Neither reduction of the soul to some positivity, nor going off into a metaphysical beyond.

If we truly hold our place on this level of reflection, we are entitled to say that for the soul it is the corpse, the symbols, the cultural works that within themselves logically negate (sublate) *themselves* and symbolically point to their own inner absolute negativity. The soul is the dialectic process of producing works and symbols both as "corpses" and, at the same time, as self-negating ones. It is not we as empirical human beings who have to perform the negation. (If we performed it, it would merely be an acting out of the logical negation and not the real thing.) The birth, into the world, *of* soul and thus of negativity is itself a negative, self-contradictory birth. Soul phenomena are "in themselves different," exponents of the psychological difference. They open up within themselves their own inner mystery and inner infinity.

Jung, by the way, seems to have had *grosso modo* the same basic interest in leaving behind any metaphysical positivization and literalization of both extremes, material reality (in our case: the corpse) versus the immaterial, spiritual reality of soul or mind, (and together with this metaphysical positivization the possibility of reducing the one extreme to the other) and instead in viewing them both as *internal* moments of the sphere of soul. Speaking of physis versus spirit, matter versus mind, a naturalistic point of view versus one that sees the psychological legitimacy of the idea of God as the most real of beings, he says: "The modern psychologist[30] occupies neither the one position nor the other, but finds himself between the two ..." (*CW* 8 § 679). "If I shift my concept of reality on to the psyche—where alone it belongs—then the conflict between mind and matter, spirit and nature, as explanatory principles disappears. They become nothing but *designations of the [different] provenance of the psychic contents* that crowd into my consciousness" (*ibid.* § 681, transl. modif., Jung's italics). Although what Jung says is by no means the same as what I tried to suggest and although he is speaking about big philosophical concepts (mind and matter) rather than about "the corpse" and "the soul," one sees that he performs more or less the same logical move with respect to his topic, the move of interiorizing into the sphere of logical negativity what otherwise would be assumed to be positively given external realities.

In contrast to both the traditional medieval view of the soul as a kind of angel indwelling in bodily man and functioning as its pilot and the Cartesian view of the totally immaterialized soul as "thinking substance" (which cannot sufficiently answer the question how there could be a connection between this soul and physical man), our view, by starting out from the negation of the corpse, shows itself to be down to earth. The soul is nothing free-floating, totally otherworldly, but is anchored in concrete reality ("corpse" is a real phenomenon, after all, and so is the experience of the corpse as the negation of life). It comes about through a concrete performance of a logical act of negation. No mystification,

---

[30] "The modern psychologist" just as "modern psychology" are frequent ways of Jung's to refer to himself and to his own psychology.

no "angel." Our view shares this down-to-earth-ness and concreteness with the Aristotelian conception of the soul as a concrete living being's life principle. But by starting out from the corpse as the negation of life rather than from the living organism in its positivity, our view leaves the naturalism of the Aristotelian standpoint and comprehends the soul as absolute negativity, thereby regaining a sense of otherworldliness after all—however, a very concrete *this-worldly* otherworldliness far removed from any mystification. *Absolute* negativity negates both positivities, the one of metaphysical mystification and the one of naturalism.[31]

1.6 THE SPARK

Much like the literal corpses in prehistoric times *inspired* the notion of soul, so still today the cultural "corpses" are inspirations and allurements. The dead letter is, as it were, the appeal to read and make sense of it, to awaken the spirit; a dead music score is the appeal to play the piece of music and thereby breathe soul life into it; Greek temples are the call to us to appreciate their powerful depth and beauty.

The corpses, the dead letter, the formal institutions, the works as thing-like, lifeless shells are indispensable, just as indispensable as is the actual performance of the act of understanding and appreciation. Whereas natural life becomes present and fully embodies itself in each living being, each of which is *one* entity, the life of the soul only comes into being when *two* fundamentally separate things come together and interact, the sight of the corpse and the mourning person, the book and its reader, the dogma and its believer, the music score and the musician or audience, the sounds of a word and the mind that pushes off from them to its meaning.

---

[31] In the present text I derive the soul's autopoiesis from the experience of the corpse. There is another, very different type of the soul's autogenesis, which I described elsewhere as the *Selbsttertötung der Seele* (the soul's killing itself into being), namely through sacrificial killing, which I called the primordial soul-making. W.G., "Killings," in: *idem, Soul-Violence*, vol. 3 of Collected English Papers, New Orleans, LA (Spring Journal Books) 2008, pp. 189–265. Historically speaking, both modes are probably equiprimordial. The difference between them is that in ritual killing the *making*, the active doing and production by man, is emphasized and made explicit, man having to come forward and commit himself, whereas in the other case the *experiential* aspect is in the foreground and the making remains implicit: the soul's own making itself in the background.

The living soul is in the last analysis what is sparked off when a dead work and the right human subject touch.[32] The soul is the spark that is ignited. The spark itself is bodiless. It is a happening. Momentary, lasting only for as long as it lasts. It is neither in the work or letter per se, nor in the human person, be it in his brain or in the interiority of his mind. No, it *is* only as the between, as and in their contact, which corresponds to what on the interpersonal level is the sharedness of meanings. It is the encounter between something dead and the human mind. The dead letter is the steel and the human mind the flint that strike against each other; but at the same time, both are also the tinder that gets ignited. For the mind, the work comes alive, and the mind itself becomes aflame.

In the case of biological life we can imagine a single living organism all alone in the world that would nevertheless be fully alive. But as I showed, the soul cannot be present in isolation. Because its only embodiment is in "corpses" and dead letters, a society, a culture, is indispensable for soul. And conversely, for coming alive the dead letter and cultural works require a recipient, a subject; artists and thinkers need a receptive audience. The Mayan pyramids in the primal forests of Guatemala without a person seeing and appreciating them are just a heap of stones on the same level with natural rock. The same applies to a Greek temple, a Gothic cathedral, and a Roman aqueduct. A book without a reader, a painting without an art enthusiast are merely objects.

The fact that an event of soul is in truth the result of what happens when a dead letter and a human mind come together is why it is misleading to ground the soul in the imaginal or in archetypes, as if the notions and images fell down (or rose up) from an existing treasury of images into the human mind. Inevitably, 'the imaginal' and 'the archetypes' will be imagined in ontologized form. In them a trace of the metaphysical stance lives on,[33] no matter

---

[32] Of course, as Lichtenberg observed, the coming in contact with or crashing into each other of a book and a head can also result in a *hollow* sound (rather than in the event of inspiration, understanding, soul), in which case, he pointed out, it must not necessarily be the book's fault.

[33] Just as for Jung the archetypes-in-themselves, so also, although in very different ways, "the imaginal" and "the Gods" in Hillman's archetypal psychology are set up as fundamentally eternal and a priori givens. Hillman, the author who introduced the idea of "soul-making" into psychology, reserves soul-making exclusively for what happens on

how much one may subjectively renounce a metaphysical understanding of them as a misunderstanding. No, there was not originally a soul that had, as an inborn gift, the capacity to freely fantasize and entertain images. The soul *made* and still *makes* itself. It needs the corpse and a human mind's being struck by it to create that spark that we call soul. This spark, the event of the spark, is the "autonomous mind" that Jung spoke about. It is autonomous because it is unpredictable. We cannot arbitrarily produce it. The wind bloweth where it listeth. This is also why in ancient times a human poet like Homer did not feel that he was the true author of his work. He was only the place in which the autonomous mind happened. The true author was, mythologically speaking, the Muses, their singing, their dancing on Mount Helicon, that is to say, the personified event of the spark. The autonomous mind is the *encounter* between the dead letter (or the historical locus) and

the side of the human subject, in our dreaming, imagining, pathologizing, our behavior as well as in how we work with and react to our psychic experiences. But when it comes to the objective side, to the archetypal structures or "the Gods" there is no "making" any more. The gods are conceived as invariant dominants, supertemporal, absolutely independent of all the historical changes in the social organization of life and human culture. "The Gods," themselves immune, become *unidirectionally* effective in human life as the perspectives dominating our consciousness and behavior, but they are not conversely "produced" by the concrete historical situation of human societies, that is to say, they are not the self-articulation of the inner truth of the changing logical constitution of the particular societies' actual mode of being-in-the-world. In other words, the moment we turn to the objective side, soul-*making* comes to a stop in this scheme. The dialectic (or uroboric relation) of making and finding/experiencing, of producing and being ruled, of *a posteriori* and *a priori* is dissolved. From a structural point of view this means that such a thinking displays the logic of externality: something keeps out of the movement of the soul, reserves itself vis-à-vis it. Epistemologically it means that something is systematically kept in the dark, opaque, unconscious. It is saved from being seen through, becoming transparent. It is reified. True, in this theory "the Gods" and "the imaginal" influence or even determine the soul's life and in this sense "enter" it, but only *from* outside as themselves unaffected static factors, which, be it intentionally or unintentionally and notwithstanding the claim of the merely *metaphorical* use of the term "Gods," de facto gives them the status of frozen, quasi metaphysical hypostases behind the scene. Logically they are not integrated in the dynamic flow of the psychological process as fully internal to it, as mere internal moments of it. If they were, they would have been conceived as only to the exact same degree being dominants of human being-in-the-world that they are also, and at the same time, the product and reflection of human being-in-the-world. For a true psychology, the soul's logical life has everything relevant to it within itself. Nothing external to it must be allowed in the theory of it. Psychology has to account for whatever determines the soul's life exclusively in terms of this same life; it has to account for the dominants in terms of what is dominated by them.

the human mind that provides an occasion or opportunity for the autonomous mind to spark itself off, to give itself a real presence in and as the spark.

And this is still today visible in the fact that the soul or spirit lives only by means of the dead letter, the meaningless acoustic sounds of words, the formalized rituals and thing-like cultural works. The dead letter is not a fault, a degeneration. It is indispensable for the emergence of soul. The soul comes alive only in and by means of its dead productions. The spirit exists *only* through the letter, the soul's interiority *only* through its utterances, its externalizations, in the dead shells it produced—in written texts, in the physical sounds of language, in formal rituals, in works of art, in music scores, in dogmas, in social (usually sterile) institutions. It is the nature of the soul that because it is essentially self-expression it is the whole *dialectic* of interiority and outwardization, the dialectic of life and death, of positivity and negativity, of spark and dead work. It is both at once, their contradiction. (Biological life, by contrast, is one-sided. It holds life itself and death apart, pushing death [its own negativity] off into the future as its literal end. Biological life *is* the dissociation of the unity [of life and death] that is its ground.)

We must not identify the soul with its one half only: the spark. It *is* the tension and opposition of the spark and its other, the "corpse." Only if we understand the soul to *be* their *contradiction* and nothing else, do we not literalize, positivize, and substantiate the soul (or the spark) after all. The soul has no being (*Sein*), is not anything ontological, but a logical event. It is the contradiction that *makes* soul.

Usually we imagine the soul's interiority, which is its most essential characteristic, in analogy to rather taciturn, introverted people who have, we suppose, a rich inner life enclosed within them and who only under special conditions come out of their shell. Still waters run deep. Here interiority and external expression are neatly divided. But the soul is not a still water that runs deep. We already know that it does not exist. Without its outwardization, there is no soul at all and also no interiority and no depth. The soul only comes into being through its self-externalization. We may think here of Heraclitus (fr. 45 DK) who sends us on a journey out into the world even to its utmost borders in order to become aware of the inner depth of the soul's logos.[34] This is not really a discovery, but a production, *poiêsis* of the soul's logos. Logically, the outwardization comes first within the dialectical simultaneity of interiority and outwardization. The dead shell of the *ergon*, the work, is logically, although not temporally, prior to its *energeia*.

The soul does not exist. It is only product, result (product of its own autopoiesis). And, here I come to the epitome of my rehabilitation of "the corpse" in its significance for the soul, it is only by producing "corpses" and "dead letters," only by externalizing and positivizing itself in the in themselves lifeless works of culture, that the soul establishes itself as absolute negativity. Prior to its productions there was no soul. The deadness and positivity of the works is needed for the soul to come into its own in the first place, to make itself. In the positivity of its literal products, and only in them and by means of them, does the soul have its absolute negativity. After all, it is the sublated corpse and no more than that. The soul, we could therefore say, produces itself in the first place in the "corpses" produced by it. The soul's self-alienation that Schiller pointed out is precisely indispensable for its coming into being. "The moment the soul *speaks*, it is, alas!, no longer the *soul* that is speaking." How else could "absolute negativity" realize itself? Negativity involves negation. The soul *has to* refuse to be immediately present in its speaking, in the cultural works it produces. It *has to* produce them as spiritless and soulless, as dead letters and "corpses," because only thereby does it achieve its absolute negativity and thus give itself reality *as* this negativity. As negativity it has to be *not*. If it allowed itself to be alive in its productions, the way biological life is actually present in living organisms, then it would have lost itself. It would itself have become a positivity parallel to all other ordinary positivities. By losing itself it finds itself, comes home to itself. So Schiller is wrong after all. The ground for the disappointment Schiller felt concerning the soul is not the sign of something that ought not be, of a flaw in the order of the world. It belongs. There has to be a sense of missing

---

[34] Cf. Wolfgang Giegerich, "Is the Soul 'Deep'?—Entering and Following the Logical Movement of Heraclitus 'Fragment 45,'" in: *Spring 64*, Fall and Winter 1998, pp. 1–32. Now in: *idem, The Soul Always Thinks*. Collected English Papers, vol.4, New Orleans, LA (Spring Journal Books) 2010, pp. 131–163.

or loss or failure.[35] Precisely because it is no longer the soul that is speaking *is* its speaking the soul's speaking. The corpse precisely *as* corpse *is* the presence of soul, the only presence there can possibly be. In the case of soul it has to be negative (negated) presence, logical, not ontological presence: absolute negativity—mythologically speaking: departedness, ghosts, the underworld, the dead ancestors, Mnemosyne.

1.7 RETROACTIVE FETISHIZATION OF THE CORPSE

Earlier I had raised the question whether one can really consider our dream diaries, the magnificent Greek temples, all the splendid works of art and poetry, the sacred books, the myths and symbols and so on as nothing but "corpses"? Are they not much rather in fact authentic embodiments of soul? From what has been discussed afterwards we can see in retrospect that and why this question amounts to a *petitio principii*. Those phenomena are usually already apperceived from the standpoint reached by the operation of pushing off from them. We learned that "The dead letter is the steel and the human mind the flint that strike against each other; but at the same time, both are also the tinder that gets ignited. For the mind, the work comes alive, and the mind itself becomes aflame." Because the spark ignites not only consciousness, but also the dead works, the latter come indeed alive, and this is why they seem to *be* "documents of the soul," fully alive with soul depth and soul dignity. The secondary result of the soul's work upon them, of our appreciation, is retroactively projected into the dead works as their primary character. And so they are exclusively perceived as what the process *made* of them, in the light of the animation and glorification they receive from it. What they are in themselves is forgotten, obliterated. The "spark" that was ignited by the touching of the lifeless work and the receptive mind is smuggled into the dead work, so that the

---

[35] How failure can be the way how psychological success—success in the absolute negativity of the soul—can come about is especially clearly shown in the *The Princess on the Glass Mountain* fairy tale. See the discussion in my "The Climb Up the Slippery Slope" in: Wolfgang Giegerich, David L. Miller, Greg Mogenson, *Dialectics & Analytical Psychology. The El Capitan Canyon Seminar*, New Orleans, LA (Spring Journal Books) 2004, pp. 9–24.

latter thereby receives an aura and even appears to have all along been the causing agent of the mind's animation.

There is a helpful example of this viewing the "dead letter" from the standpoint of the finished result produced by its interaction with a mind and thus of seeing it already fully illumined and ensouled in the warm shine that falls from the soul's spark upon it, so that this illuminatedness is attributed to the "dead letter" itself as *its* a priori character. This example is Hillman's response to my thesis, with which I follow Hegel's insight, that we think, *if* we think, in names, in the words of language, not in images, and that the very point of the use of words is that words are contingent, arbitrary sound clusters with no meaning of their own and no intrinsic relation (likeness) to the looks of the things that they "mean"—sound clusters freely *produced* by the thinking mind itself.[36] Hillman says: "I'd say just the contrary. Words are themselves images"[37]—which they undoubtedly are *if* one stuffs the result produced by them in the mind retroactively back into them as *their* intrinsic nature and as the origin of the mind's illumination. I discussed this particular controversy in my paper, "Psychology—The Study of the Soul's Logical Life."[38]

If one follows the direction taken by Hillman's argument in this case, the full three-partite relation—a constellation and interaction of two opposites which between them produces a result (the spark) as a third—is reduced to a simple bipartite cause-and-effect relation: the allegedly *a priori* fully imaginal, soulful word or cultural work instills its meaning and archetypal depth into the human mind. But this is so because, as we can say following Schelling, "in the ordinary [mental] acting the acting itself is forgotten for the object of the acting."[39] The product is so impressive that the production disappears. We take the image that was produced for granted. This unconscious *fetishization*, as we might call it, of what actually is a "corpse"—in the case of words, the combination of in themselves utterly meaningless phonemes—is apparently the most natural thing, not only with respect to words,

---

[36] As I said: phonemes, not natural noise.

[37] James Hillman, "Divergences. *A propos* of a Brazilian Seminar on Giegerich/ Hillman – Organized by Marcus Quintaes," open letter 2008.

[38] In: W.G., *The Soul Always Thinks*. Collected English Papers, vol. 4, New Orleans, LA (Spring Journal Books) 2010, pp. 325–349.

[39] Friedrich Wilhelm Joseph Schelling, *System des transzendentalen Idealismus* (1800), Einleitung § 2. My translation.

but also to all cultural works. We normally see those works, at least those of our own culture (if not the things in the world and the world as such), always already *ex post facto* transfigured, one way or another, in the shine that falls on them by the soul's spark; we hear the words immediately, from the outset, as the meanings or images that are actually merely evoked by them and *produced* in the mind, so that the corpse or dead-letter character of the sound clusters, the sacred books, of great paintings and great poetry, of ritual ceremonies and so on are for us always already obliterated. It requires special conscious reflection after the fact to make us aware of the production process and what triggers it—the "corpse." But to make us aware of what invisibly happens in the soul behind the back of the I and what therefore is unconscious is of course psychology's job.

As part of ordinary life and ordinary mental action in Schelling's sense, this fetishization or transfiguration is psychologically fully justified, more than that: necessary, a condition of the possibility of human existence *as human*, intelligible existence. It is itself an act of soul-making, of "enchanting" or ensouling the world. An act, especially also, of establishing the realm of shared meanings *as* our horizon, *as* our primary reality, as the real home of our being (*extra corpus!*). Without it, without the words of language a priori *coming* as meanings or images within the realm of "shared meaning" we could not speak. We live always already *in* the world of language, *in* the magical circle that it draws around us. This transfiguration is the condition of the possibility of symbols in the true sense, of sacraments, and of a sympathetic world-relation at large. How else could gods, spirits, and daimones have been actually seen *in* real trees, rivers, mountains, *in* the sun and the moon? Coming back here to our immediate topic, *the cultural works*, we can say that *ordinarily* (in Schelling's sense) they themselves are indeed alive. This is our real experience and the sign that soul has manifested itself. A great literary work makes it indeed easy for the appropriate reader to create within himself an understanding or depth of feeling that he could never have reached without it, and if this happens the great poetic work does indeed have its lofty meaning within itself, or, conversely, the mind has indeed *its own* animation out there *in* the work that *ipso facto* is no longer dead; the great poem *is* itself the embodied presence of soul. A great painting may "give" us an aesthetic pleasure that would have been impossible without it, and again we can then say that then it *is* the concrete and sensible presence of its uplifting soul meaning. Because we experience "the spark" by means of them, we experience it directly *in* the great works and the image-sense *in* the words, so that they themselves *become* to us its locus, the actual source of light itself.

The fetishization is absolutely necessary because human culture is, as we have seen, a building of castles in the air. But the castle in the air has to become the *solid ground* of human existence, of the soul's life. What is a result of the soul's production has to appear as primordial, absolutely self-evident, and irreducible origin. The presence of soul experience in the works of culture has to be experienced as being *their* true nature. Speaking is only possible if the words we use in fact mean what they mean. *What* their precise meaning in each particular occurrence of them may be can be disputable and may be left open. But *that* they mean whatever their meaning may be must be absolutely reliable and unquestionable. This is why the production of linguistic meaning and its producedness has to be obliterated and forgotten. The moment our speaking were aware of the producedness and thus artificiality of the meaning of our words (as clusters of meaningless phonemes), it would find itself completely adrift up in the air without anything to rely on and thus experience probably much the same as what Hugo von Hofmannsthal described in his 1902 (fictitious) *Letter of Lord Chandos* to Francis Bacon in 1603 as the terrible crisis of language that he suddenly experienced:

> I felt an inexplicable unease to merely utter the words "spirit," "soul," or "body." The abstract words that our tongue naturally has to avail itself of ... disintegrated in my mouth like decaying mushrooms. My mind forced me to see all things that came up in a conversation in an uncanny closeness ... Everything fell apart into pieces, and the pieces again into pieces ... The individual words floated around me (my transl.).

Words became, for Hofmannsthal's Lord Chandos, whirls that led into a void. They had become nothing but "corpses." But his Lord Chandos also still remembered his previous condition, when he was an ingenious poet, and characterized it as one in which "in a kind of permanent intoxication, existence as a whole appeared to me as one great unity."

It is essential to see that such an effect as the one described by Hofmannsthal-Lord Chandos comes only about if it is a crisis of language itself; if it is our *speaking*, the words themselves, that so to speak become aware of their artificial production and thus lose their absolute certainty and conviction. By contrast, if merely *we*, if the *I*, reflect(s) on and see(s) through the product to the production that brought it forth, this danger does not exist because this awareness is a secondary act of reflection outside and after the particular use of language that the reflection is about. Conversely, even while thinking and speaking of the artificial production of meaning, this critical thinking and speaking themselves, in order to be possible, have to make use of the unconsciously *produced* meaning of words and to firmly rely on the innocent presupposition of the certainty of the words and concepts it avails itself of. The very reflection that sees through the production of the product and destroys the innocent belief in the irreducibility of the products is inevitably only possible through its unquestionable relying on the unreflected and *unseen-through* products.

Whereas ordinary life is dependent on the fetishization described, psychology must not take it at face value. Psychology must not be blind living, unconscious acting out, innocent believing. It is committed to awareness, reflection, seeing through: committed to the gift of the animus. Therefore it must not take the images simply for granted. It must not, "in the kind of permanent intoxication" that is the ordinary state of unpsychological man, take the image character of words literally. It must not see the imaginal as literal origin (as "*Ur-*," "arche-," as expression of "the Gods"). Even origins and gods are produced, are results (although their production is systematically—and necessarily so—"forgotten," having happened behind our backs and being, again necessarily, the production *of* something precisely *as* unproduced, *as* irreducibly originary). Taking the imaginal for granted would be, figuratively speaking, psychology's falling for the seduction of the anima as Maya, "the 'Spinning Woman,' the illusion-producing dancer" (*CW* 9ii § 20, transl. modif.), the anima who is responsible for the fact that "We are in truth so wrapped about by psychic images that we cannot penetrate at all to the essence of things external to ourselves" (*CW* 8 § 680, transl. modif.). The anima represents only the one side of the syzygial couple, anima and animus, who only together, in their contradictory dialectical interplay, give us the full reality of the soul.[40] Psychology must, it is true, appreciate the images in their own right and work with them, and even in *innocence* (albeit of course in a methodological, reflected, i.e., artificially produced innocence, not a naive one!). This is "the anima's" due. But it must also see through them as a projection after the fact, as the *product* of an (unconscious) soul-*making*: to give "the animus" its due.

Often, in the case of certain objects that are not magnificent in themselves, there is a fetishization in the literal sense that is even downright phony, such as when the pen or eye-glasses of a great man or a dress of a film diva are auctioned off for immense sums or in museums are piously gazed at in wonder by culture tourists, not because these relics themselves have the power to inspire the soul spark (in themselves they are trivial), but merely because, on the one hand, the people are filled with their own *longing* to come into presence of some tangible object to venerate and to project their longed-for admiration and veneration onto, in other words, to reify this subjective need and, on the other hand, because these objects benefit from the reputation of the owner, from the aura of the great name.[41] Of course, even this superstitious fetishization is an event of soul, too, although an empty and inauthentic one, because, on the first count, the relics' fetish quality stems from the admirers' subjective lack of and desire for an actual presence of soul and because, on the second count, it is metonymic, a substitute.

---

[40] Wolfgang Giegerich, *Animus-Psychologie*, Frankfurt/Main et al. (Peter Lang) 1994.

[41] Strictly speaking, the fetishized relic is thrice removed from "the real thing." The writer's pen receives the aura of greatness because it used to be the pen of a great writer. The writer, who is in truth just a normal human being, receives the aura of greatness because an auratic work came into existence through him. And the work or achievement is venerated as great because its "dead letter" character is obliterated and it is immediately identified with the "soul spark" facilitated by it. Of course, it may in fact be great, but this greatness requires a receptive soul, whereas for the philistine the greatest works of literature are just words, words, words, the greatest music pleasant or unpleasant noise, the greatest paintings colorful canvases. This shows that the works have their own greatness not within themselves as the printed texts or bodily objects that they are. They have it only in and through the contact with a responsive mind.—Having used the word relic I want to add that the relics used by the Church are not phony as long as they are apperceived by people on a primitive, magical level of consciousness.

1.8 WHY IS IT THE CORPSE THAT IGNITES THE SPARK?

To become actualized, the soul needs to *make* itself, and the mode of this making is its pushing off from biological life. The soul is, I insisted earlier, a dance to the power of two: the dance not upon the lifeless, but on biological life. But why, then, did it historically start out from the literal corpse? Why did and does it push off from what is in itself precisely the *negation* of life rather than from life itself, from the contact with living fellow human beings or from sexual desire? Why are the *dead* body, the *dead* letter absolutely essential for the sphere of shared meanings to come alive, in other words, their very opposite? If in biological life, life immediately inhabits and animates a lifeless body, why does the reality of the soul divide itself, indeed, tear itself apart, into two fundamentally separated extremes, the dead letter here and the spirit over there, the corpse and the soul, the fossilized organizational structures (Churches) and the living faith, the thing-like cultural work and the performative act of understanding and appreciation? This is a crucial question.

The answer is because mortality is inherent in (natural) life. Life is the unity of itself and death. Biological life is the dissociation of this unity or it is this unity in dissociated form: the *deferral* of its own origin, death. Life is the (metastable) always already having overcome "death," death here in the sense of lifeless matter. Life is not, as Heidegger said about human *Dasein*, a "forerunning to death," but rather the constant (but temporally limited, and therefore "metastable") triumph over death. Life has death behind itself, under itself, as *sublated* moment within itself. Life lives because it does not mind its own mortality. It lives in spite of it, never wasting a thought on or fearing it.[42]

If under these circumstances the soul would try to push off from *abstract* life—a life that has death outside of itself, life as the opposite of death, the life as it is visible in living beings—then it would not push off from *the sphere of life in its entirety* at all. Only with literal death—with the corpse—as the *absolute* negation of natural life have the borders, the *fines*, the definition, of life been reached and *ipso facto* logically exceeded. And only if they have been exceeded is one no longer

---

[42] Living beings may fear death. But life itself does not.

contained within it, but does one have it, as it were, logically in front of and vis-à-vis oneself. And only then can one really push off from it.

Whatever one would do while still staying contained within the sphere of natural life would inevitably be itself an expression of biological life (part of the dance upon the lifeless) and not radically transcend it.[43] Only with actual death has life as such, has the *dimension* and the real *concept* of life as a whole, been grasped rather than merely a particular life-internal and natural manifestation of life, and only then can the soul's pushing off be a veritable pushing off *from natural life* and *ipso facto* conquer for itself an altogether new and different, previously unheard-of dimension, the dimension of logos, the sphere of shared meanings, the autonomous spirit, the ghostly life of the soul. The corpse is the gateway to the *extra-corpus* realm.

For the soul the corpse is a symbol (in the strict sense) of soul itself, because in it, it has a physical analogue to its own true nature, which is logical negativity, absolute negativity: the having-been-ness of life, the ghostliness of spirit, thought, logical life. For this reason it is precisely the corpse that is the stepping stone for the autonomous mind to come explicitly home to itself. It is not like an *a priori* lifeless object such as a stone, but the visible absence of life, the experience of the departedness of person, the physical image of absolute negativity. As such it is subjective-objective. And the fact that another subject as a recipient is needed makes the reality of soul subjective-subjective-objective.

For biological life mortality is both its ground (from which it within itself has always already pushed off) and its ultimate boundary. The soul has overcome or sublated life precisely by making what used to be a boundary, namely death, its very center and explicit essence, the medium in which it thrives. It has *contra naturam* transcended beyond natural life.

Whereas biological life, in order to *be*, needs to push its ground—death—off into the future and constantly hold it there, the soul's life is the life of this death itself. In the soul, death has come home to itself. And this is why it does not materialize in soulful beings.

---

[43] This is why "the contact with living fellow human beings or sexual desire" would never have sufficed to produce soul and humanize the human animal as a being that is not merely one of the natural *animalia*.

It *is* ghostliness, presence of death, *logical* life: it *is* only as the *contradiction* of corpse and spark and not as a (however subtle, vaporous) substance or entity.

Soul, in contrast to life, does not need to *defer* death. It not only is *able to* hold its place in view of the veritable sight of death, the corpse. It also itself produces "corpses" because it finds itself in them, only in them. It has its presence, which is the presence of absolute negativity, in them. By the same token, the soul can find the physical universe and the things in it enchanting and feel at home in the world, because it beholds itself in them.

To overcome something you must already have overcome it, be beyond it. For unto every one that hath shall be given, and only unto him. You have to already be where you want to go in order to get there. You have to begin with the loss or end of the natural, with its failure. This is why the corpse is indispensable. But the insight into one's already having to be beyond something to truly get beyond it applies to the loss itself. For early man, the sight of the corpse was the awareness of a beyond of life. And a being with this awareness is in the state of "having" so that unto him could also be given. Early man's having been able to have this awareness in the sight of a corpse is the sign that he was already viewing the corpse from the standpoint of soul, as transfigured by its absolute negativity (i.e., as "fetishized"). An animal can only lose in a natural, positive-factual way. For it the dead body of another individual of the same species is only the simple negation of life, its natural end. The corpse remains a dead object. It is for the animal not subjective-objective. The latter is therefore not capable of apperceiving, in the corpse, logical negativity and the completion and supersession of the whole dimension or concept of natural life, in the sense of its beyond. And this is why the animal does not get into the land of soul, because it has not been there to begin with. It remains confined within the sphere of natural life as such. The physical environment around it does not become a "world" and "enchanted" for it. It cannot find itself in it.

The same as to the corpse applies to the act of pushing off. If it wants to be the pushing off into the dimension of the soul's *logical* life it already has to be *logical* pushing off from the outset, not a literal pushing off, not just a factual leaving the corpse behind. Any natural (empirical, behavioral) pushing off does not transcend the natural.

We are capable of describing the autopoiesis of the soul, its self-production, the process of the soul's making itself. But *why* human beings a priori "have" (in the sense of the Biblical quote) so that they can be given, *why* they implicitly already are where they explicitly need to get, *why*, furthermore, there is such a possibility in the first place of penetrating beyond life into the dimension of soul, *why* there can be such a thing as logical negativity and an autonomous mind and why through the encounter of dead letter and human mind a spark can be ignited and make itself present in reality—all this cannot be explained. It has to be accepted as a fact, as the inalienable presupposition as which we exist and that constitutes human nature, just as we have to acknowledge as facts that there *is* something rather than nothing, that there are gravitation and light in the universe and that there is biological life in our earthly world. In much the same way we also can see, and have to note, that there is in this our real world the sphere of logos and a wind that bloweth where it listeth. The autonomous mind is part of the real phenomenology of this world, an ingredient of its makeup. There cannot be any doubt that there are moments when a spark is ignited, that there are events of meaning and deep understanding, that words and texts can be made sense of, that at times soul happens. We can establish the "that" and "how," but not why.

1.9 THE HISTORICAL CONTINUITY OF THE SOUL'S LIFE. SOUL AS HISTORICITY

On one level the life of soul, owing to the soul's fleetingness and its performative or "spark" character, the soul's "mortality" is much more frequent than, but also not as definitive as, that of biological life. Potentially, the spark can strike us repeatedly and unexpectedly. But of course, most of the time we live on the level of the dead letter, stale routines, conventional phrases without that explicit spark that would amount to a moment of soul. I put "mortality" in quotation marks not only because it is a figurative expression, but above all since our normally living on the level of the dead letter must by no means be misunderstood as a living beneath or outside the soul. It does not mean a literal end of soul. Inasmuch as the dead letter exists only by grace of the soul, our not seeing beyond it still takes place within its sphere, albeit only within it as merely implicit, emaciated, alienated from itself. It seems that for us humans the only real exit from the realm of soul is biological death. But even this has been disputed. Former ages at least believed, as we know, that biological death was precisely the true gateway to the land of soul, the life of the ancestors, the blessedness of eternal life in heaven.

Concerning the fleetingness of the moments of soul, it must be remembered that through some techniques, through willful concentration, through the whims of memory, the lifespan of soul events may be extended for a longer time than it would last of its own accord. The melody of a piece of music, the mood or particular images of a dream may accompany one throughout the day. In addition, one may bring the same idea, and thus the soul invested in it, back to life numerous times by seriously devoting oneself to it anew. Some powerful ideas can even stay alive throughout a person's lifetime, such as a religious creed, a sense of honor, values, attitudes, and styles that have become part of a person's character and habitual attitude. They may then not exactly have the form of a spark, but nevertheless be a living spirit, at any rate more than a dead letter.

If on the first level the soul is much more short-lived than the life of living organisms, on a second level, however, the life of the soul can receive a much more long-lasting stability than the metastable dance of biological life. The latter is inevitably tied to individual living beings and their lifetime, precisely on account of the intimate unity of life principle and lifeless matter (body). But the life of the soul is especially also cultural life, the cultural life of peoples, not only of individuals. As such it can maintain itself in a curious way over generations, centuries, and millennia through what we call tradition. Tradition is that process through which each new generation tunes into, and at the same time instills new life into, the manifestations of soul of the previous generations. This process avails itself of initiations and/or schooling and study on the individual level and at a collective historical level realizes itself through periodic renewal rituals, reform movements, revivals. The age-old duration of traditions and customs is made possible precisely through the radical separateness in the dialectic of the soul of dead letter and living spirit: the dead letter survives the lifetimes of individual persons as well as generations. And the necessity of initiations and reforms is due to the fact that the fire kindled by one generation is always endangered of going out, the life of the soul of becoming frozen, traditions of turning into empty formalities and fossilized contents (dead letter). Initiations and reforms are equivalents to putting some more coal on a fire. It is even possible to reawaken disrupted traditions or even dig up cultural productions from bygone ages and strike new sparks from them.

In addition to a constant or periodic rekindling of ossified traditions there is also in the soul a potential of historical progression. I already mentioned that "sharing" or "division" in the realm of "shared meanings" does not mean partition, but is much rather augmentative, and that there is a cultural evolution because later generations can build on what earlier generations created. This potential of a cultural advance through a pushing off from the status quo exists only because the soul, other than life, exists only *unembodied* as logical life, merely as the *contradiction* of "corpse" and "spark." By contrast, life, by holding death at bay, gives itself an immediate presence in the body of living beings. But as immediate and literal *presence*, life must be all at once what it is, both aspects exclusively within itself, and this means *in* the living beings, *intra corpus*. The obverse of this is that when a living being succumbed to its mortality, its life is all gone, it completely and literally disappeared, without leaving a trace of itself. But the soul, inasmuch as it is expression ("speaking") and thus self-externalization (*Entäußerung*) rather than condensation or introversion (protecting its selfhood) by concentrating and enclosing its entire reality in ONE focal point (a being), and inasmuch as it produces itself precisely merely in the form of works as "dead letters" and "corpses" and not a living soul—the soul, I say, leaves the works as positivities that it produced behind (*thereby*, however, producing *itself* as absolute negativity in the first place). And these works, the expression of a former "spark," can be the inspiration for a new "spark" in persons of a new generation. "New" in "new spark" does here not merely mean a new occurrence or event (i.e., repetition) of the same spark that once produced the work, but truly new, different: a new meaning.[44] So it is precisely the non-existence of the soul, its being only as a result and as absolute negativity, that is the condition of the possibility of its life as evolution and advance. Biological evolution is said to be, due to its embodiment, dependent on accidents ("mutations"). In other words, evolution *happens to* biological life, it is external to it, contingent. Not so in the case of the soul's logical life. Its evolution is intrinsic to it, and it is its, the soul's, very own doing.

The fact that the soul is *to hayto kinoyn*, that which moves itself (Plato), that it is essentially actuosity, logical *life*, also means that the soul is fundamentally historical, historical process (both in the sense of the history of culture at large—this is the soul's *opus magnum*— and on the smaller scale of individual, personal experience, the level of the *opus parvum*). The soul *is* historicity.

The evolution and thus the historical continuity of the soul's life proceeds, however, precisely via repeated moments of discontinuity, ruptures, which demarcate and constitute distinct stages in the continuous development: the negation and sublation of each respective previous stage of consciousness (or previous historical locus) and the soul's *pushing off* from it to a new stage. Each consecutive stage *is* the negation of the former and as such it is of a higher complexity. Of course, when I speak of "pushing off" we have to be careful not to understand this in terms of a pictorial thinking as occurring in the externality space and in the object world. The soul's movement is not as if it walked up a staircase, with each move "pushing off" from the present step to the next higher step. The soul's movement is one within its own interiority. The "previous historical locus or stage of consciousness" from which it pushes off is *its own idea or concept* of the previous stage, so that it pushes off only from its own conception or interpretation, its own view. Its movement has the character of its own transformation, redefinition. Imaginally speaking we could say it

---

[44] This relation has been expounded in Gadamer's hermeneutic as the historicity of understanding. The texts or art works are to be interpreted in their own contexts and meaning. But the construction of their own contexts and meaning happens already within a "hermeneutic horizon" which is on principle formed by the hermeneutic presuppositions of one's own time. This is why interpretation must not primarily be viewed in terms of the work, but rather from the reception ("reception aesthetics"). Interpretation is inevitably *productive*. Hans-Georg Gadamer, *Wahrheit und Methode*, Tübingen (J.C.B. Mohr [Paul Siebeck]), 4th edition, 1975.

happens to and within the radically self-enclosed soul, in the soul confined in the *vas Hermeticum*, the alchemical vessel sealed with the sign of Hermes, so as once and for all to prevent both its escape and the intrusion of anything from outside. Being locked into itself, its movement has to be one into its own inner depth and complexity, its own interiority, alchemically speaking, its sublimation, distillation, vaporization.

1.10 Psychology's "*NOT* NOT." From the most general concept of soul to psychology's specific concept of soul

What I have expounded so far, the notion of soul in its most general sense as the status of shared meanings, makes the soul nearly all-inclusive. One could again feel reminded of Heraclitus (fr. 45 DK) who said, "You would not find out the boundaries of soul, even by traveling along every path: so deep a logos does it have." If soul in this sense is the generation and entertaining of meanings, of the words of language, of values, ideas, fantasies, laws, institutions, works of poetry, music, art, and so on, it comprises consciousness as such as well as the world as a whole. Nature, the cosmos, all things and objects, everything we see and touch, even the body are first of all psychic experiences, notions, and images and thus contents of our consciousness. As humans we live *primarily* in a linguistic cosmos, not in the body. We see what is and happens not directly, not as things-in-themselves, but only in terms of the words and concepts that we have of them. Jung thus rightly insisted:

> Without a doubt it [psychic life] is our only immediate experience. All that I experience is psychic. Even physical pain is a psychic image which I experience; my sense-impressions— for all that they force upon me a world of impenetrable objects occupying space—are psychic images, and these alone constitute my immediate experience, for they alone are the immediate objects of my consciousness. ... We are in truth so wrapped about by psychic images that we cannot penetrate at all to the essence of things external to ourselves. Everything we can possibly know consists of psychic stuff [*we* could say: of shared meanings]. The psyche is the most real entity [*Wesen*] of all, because it is the sole immediate there is (*CW* 8 § 680, transl. modif.).

The only problems with this statement are that Jung speaks of "psyche" instead of *extra-corpus* soul or communal cultural mind, says that psychic life is our only immediate experience, and posits an "essence of things external to ourselves." What he calls psychic images in *this* quote (in contradistinction to the completely different notion of psychic images as they occur in dreams, visions, myths, literature, etc.) are the *forms* of all possible experience that unconsciously predetermine our every experience. We are unwittingly enwrapped in them, but they are not at all themselves immediate experiences. In fact, they are only accessible to an "artificial" reflection coming late after the fact.

But otherwise it is true: it is unreasonable to assert "that something or other is 'only' psychic, as though there were anything that is *not* psychic. ... The presence of objects is entirely dependent on our powers of representation, and 'representation' is a psychic act. ... Nobody seems to have noticed that without a reflecting psyche the world might as well not exist, and that, in consequence, consciousness is a second world-creator..." (*Letters 2*, p. 487, to Tanner, 12 Feb 1959). Everything we can possibly know and experience consists of soul stuff, has been filtered through language and images.[45] We touch an oak tree and think that we touch the real thing, but what we touch is "oak tree," which is a human concept and image. We see a cow, a mountain, the moon, a fog, my mother, but all these perceptions are linguistic and mental concepts. Even the idea of something incomprehensible and the idea Jung toyed with in that quote of an extra-linguistic reality as an absolutely unknowable X ("the essence of things external to ourselves") *is a linguistic concept.* There is for us no exit from the soul, the soul in this general sense, and soul is here synonymous with consciousness. It is indeed, as Jung insisted, unreasonable to assert "that something or other is 'only' psychic, as though there were anything that is *not* psychic." Soul or consciousness is the All, and everything real, just as much as everything imaginable, has its place in soul and consciousness. Even our body, *even our physical pain*, as Jung pointed

---

[45] Strictly speaking, "filtered" should not be used. Phenomenologically, it is already a metaphysical prejudgment in the sense of the ordinarily prevailing subject-object opposition. This word presupposes that first and independently of our experience there is an objective reality which is only secondarily processed by the mind and apperceived through language and images.

out. We think that we live *in* the body, *in* the universe, and *on* the earth, but these are themselves ideas in the mind. We live in language and in soul, in consciousness, in ideas and images.

Of course, "consciousness" in this context is not to be understood as one of the innerworldly phenomena or elements of the world as a whole. If it were a particular function, realm, or organ that humans *have*, then we would already be dealing with the world *as a content of consciousness* and talk about how this content can be dissected into its various components. But here "consciousness" means the whole logical status and dimension of existence as such and not a special content of itself. It means the fact that being as such is inevitably and inescapably conscious-being, being absolutely wrapped about by language, concepts, and images: existence *as* consciousness, *as* mind or mindedness.

I can here recall the fact that Aristotle already saw that *hê psychê ta onta pôs estin panta*, "in a sense the soul is reality as a whole [is everything, all existing things]," *De anima* III, viii, 431 b 21, because for him the soul has the capacity to perceive and think everything that is contained in the cosmos. (Of course I do not thereby suggest that his concept of soul and of the identity [in some ways] of soul and All is exactly the same as the one established in the previous paragraph. Still, there is this sense of all-inclusiveness.)

That there is such a thing as the soul or an autonomous mind and therefore a good reason for insisting on a "psychology with *soul*" may have become plausible. But why do we need a "*psychology* with soul"? If everything is soul, and the soul is everything, the world at large, if there is nothing that is not soul, not concept, not image, not linguistic, is it then not that all the sciences—the humanities, linguistics and the various philologies, religious studies, intellectual history, philosophy, the history of ideas and mentalities, the studies of the arts and literature, ethnology, etc.—are the actual and true study of the soul? Do they not, all of them together, represent *the* legitimate and competent psychology? Is soul, and soul in its full extent and with all its details, not fully taken care of by them? In view of all these already existing fields, which clearly cover the whole range of phenomena and of human experience, what use or function could an explicit psychology have? What else could possibly remain to be done? What is the justification for an additional field, the justification for a psychology with soul (in contrast, of course, to an anthropological psychology that merely investigates what goes on inside people)? What is the special and specific viewpoint that it introduces beyond these sciences?

Psychology is not only a psychology *with* soul but also *of* soul. This means that its focus is on the soul itself. The humanities are interested in this poem here in its own right, they study ideas *as* ideas, as what they mean and say. For theology and religion the gods are part of its doctrines, belief systems. Religious studies devote themselves to the gods, angels, demons, etc., as historical topics, as elements of the faith and religious practice of former ages, exotic peoples, or present-day specific social groups. Philosophy talks about its topics with a view to establishing theoretical knowledge about them. *Psychology* has an entirely different and additional angle. It views all those phenomena *as expressions of soul and insofar as they are expressions of soul*—as "the soul's" self-representation, self-display, as the unfolding of its logic and of all the different moments of its truth. Psychology is not interested in what we can know, in the first principles of being and the world, in the laws of nature, in what is morally right, in whether in reality God exists or if there are many gods or only one or perhaps none at all. It is of no interest to psychology if a particular remembered childhood event was a fact or is a mere fantasy. It is not interested in the causes of psychic illnesses, nor in the techniques of curing. Psychology is concerned with the question what the existing ideas, views, values, symbols, tales, rituals, pathologies, wounds, memories say about the soul, what *in* them the soul says about *itself.*

Concerning the one topic of gods, Hillman pointed out the difference between the traditional field competent for God and gods, theology, on the one hand, and psychology, on the other hand, by saying: "Theology takes Gods literally and we do not. ... Gods are *believed* in and approached with religious methods. In archetypal psychology Gods are *imagined*. ... They are formulated ambiguously, as metaphors for modes of experience and as numinous borderline persons."[46] For me this is only a first attempt at distinguishing psychology from theology, but it does not adequately describe the

---

[46] James Hillman, *Re-Visioning Psychology*, New York (Harper & Row) 1975, p. 169.

difference. While I can accept what is said about theology, the special character of psychology is in my view not captured in this description. No, psychology does not imagine the gods. The difference between believing and imagining is not all that great: imagining is merely *suspended* believing, it negates the semantics of believing but does by no means leave the syntax or logic of believing as such altogether behind, as comes also out in this other part of Hillman's description when he speaks of the gods "as numinous borderline persons." Imagining is inevitably personifying. Archetypal psychology and "imagining" share the same substantiated form of the gods with the theological mode. *Psychologically* it makes little difference if you hold on to substantiation and personification in the literal form of believing or in the diluted and "ambiguous" form of metaphor. What counts is that in either case the gods are taken as persons, entities. The difference between believing in them and taking them as images boils down to a difference between two types of *secondary ego reactions* to the one real psychic fact of holding up the idea of gods. Whether literal or metaphorical, the ontologizing stays the same.

The specific difference of the psychological approach is not to be stated in terms of imagining, ambiguity (ambiguous formulation), and metaphor. Psychology must not be ambiguous. It must be precise and know what it is doing. It cannot leave things in suspension. It must commit itself.

And psychology's mode is not a "seeing through to the gods" but rather a seeing through to the soul. By this—"seeing through to the soul"—I mean that what the other disciplines, in this case the humanities, take as what and how it is meant—e.g., gods as supreme beings and as objects of faith and devotion, ideas as statements about the world or particular realities and as part of their theorizing and knowing, personal or collective memories as mental records of actual events, dreams and fantasies as archetypal revelations—all this psychology takes as the self-portrayal of the soul and its logical life. For psychology, in the gods, to take up this example, the soul is precisely not speaking about gods, but about *itself*, about aspects and moments of its logical life, namely, about its highest, deepest, most precious value(s) and its indispensable need of upward-looking, its logical status of dependence (its reality as a self-relation which, however, in this status of the soul is not experienced by it *as* its self-relation, but appears as [as if it were] a dependence on others, gods). Likewise, in the motif of the phallus, of sexual union, and of incest the soul is, for the psychological point of view, not speaking of the male organ, of sex and incest as objects and behavior in social reality, but it is speaking about itself, displaying some of its interests or needs, such as its own potency and its need of self-penetration, self-impregnation, self-unification, and self-transcendence. In the ideas of good and evil the soul is for psychology not speaking about ethics and morality (as ethical philosophy, theology, and law would assume), but about itself, its own radical self-division, self-purification, its effort to rise above itself. In the image of the virgin it is not discussing virginity as a body condition or social status, but its own purity, untouchedness, and self-enclosedness. In the motifs of birth and death, of mother and father, of male and female, fire and water the soul is, from the standpoint of psychology, not concerned with those literal subjects, but only with qualities or moments of itself. If in a dream the analyst appears, the soul is, for a *psychological* approach, not interested in the literal analyst and the transference, not in object-relations, but in itself. If we were to take the image of the analyst to refer to the therapeutic relationship, we would already have left the precincts of soul and be in the world of "the ego," in outer reality, in therapy as a technique of treating people.

But if the soul is not speaking about the gods, about particular ideas and meanings and concepts, not about sex, and not either about the analyst or the patient-analyst relationship, but only about itself, it seems that we are at point zero again and have to wonder afresh what this "itself" is, in other words, start all over again to raise and answer the question what soul is, a question that, after all, we believed to have answered already in the previous discussion. Our whole previous examination and its result, the soul as language, ideas, concepts, images, consciousness, meanings, works of art, etc., according to what I have just stated, does precisely not give us *psychology's* specific concept of soul. All the ideas, meanings, and values that the soul has come up with in the course of human cultural history (regardless of the difference between letter and spirit or spark) are precisely not what the soul in the sense of psychology is about. They are *not* soul.

"Soul" has now on this new level of reflection become for us just a word without determinations. All we can say at this point is that soul *is not* what is *not* soul, namely, *not* the idea of gods, of good and evil, of birth and death, incest, mother and father, virgin, etc. These are all not soul inasmuch as the soul is not speaking about them but only about itself. And we must retain, and hold our place in, the emptiness and negativity of this abstract formula ("is not what is not") and not desert it by trying in advance to fill it with any concrete content, meaning, quality, image as its definition.

On the other hand, "soul" as the root concept of psychology has become a specific concept distinct from the "soul in the most general sense" as consciousness as such, as communal cultural mind. It is no longer everything, but a particular reality or experience within the All.

A tree is not a lion, not a car, not a star. But when I said the soul is not what is not soul, this is fundamentally different from when we try to summarize the gist of the previous sentence by saying a tree is not what is not tree. The notion of the tree is unrelated to the notions of lion, car, star; all these concepts are totally other to each other, alien. None of them is to be defined by what it is not, but only by what it is. A tree can exist independently from whether there are lions or cars. Also, tree, lion, car, man, sun belong ontologically all to the same order of ontic, existing entities. But in the case of the soul the "not being what it is not" is not merely a formal-logical truism. It has a specific meaning. The soul is not only *different* from other realities. It *is* in itself—and intrinsically so—the negation of what it is not. This means two things: First of all, instead of being wholly other, absolute stranger to what it is not (the way a tree is to a lion), it is the latter's *own* other. Secondly, it is the essential, intrinsic *negation* of something positive. It is not itself something positive, something ontic. It is logically negative. It is to be *defined as* the "psychological difference"—rather than merely being "different from" something (the way everything is different from anything else). It is the soul's very nature to be in itself difference, to be different from itself.

The ghost of Hamlet's father is *not* the real, the living father. The shades in the underworld are *not* the persons in real life whose shades they are. My personal soul is *not* me as a physical being. The *anima mundi* is *not* the universe. These are four phenomenological examples of an intrinsic negation. Nevertheless, these examples, although in each case referring to the same, still contain a trace of otherness (the ghost and the living father are in some way two different entities). What we need, however, in our effort to determine psychology's concept of soul is examples for something that is different truly in itself, that as one and the same is at the same time posited and negated. More to the point are therefore the following theoretical examples taken from alchemical thinking. "Our gold" (*aurum nostrum*) is *not* the people's gold, gold in the ordinary sense (*aurum vulgi*). *Lithos oy lithos*: the (philosophers') stone which is *not* a stone.[47]

Above I pointed out that soul phenomena are "in themselves different," exponents of the psychological difference. In the same sense, the alchemical stone is in itself different from itself. It is in itself the negation of itself. It appears that the soul that is the root metaphor of psychology, psychology's topic and object, its criterion and its particular constitutive perspective, is nothing else but this very "not." It is negativity itself. It is by no means nothing, emptiness, zero, in other words, not simple and total negation. Rather, as *absolute* negativity it is a dialectical negation, the unity of position and negation. It is the negation of what the soul itself posited, what it itself produced.

The sciences and the humanities take, respectively, the concepts of natural objects and the ideas, images, works of art, and the meanings produced by the soul at face value and for real, as how they are meant. The humanities focus on what the ideas etc. are about, on their message, on what information they want to convey or what reality they refer to. They "fall" for the soul's "projections," take them literally, as Hillman had said. Psychology must not take

---

[47] Following a comment of Greg Mogenson's we may also think here of the alchemical idea of Mercurius as "fugitive stag." As Mogenson points out, "... the fugitive stag is not first an existing stag that merely happens to be fugitive (though, doubtless, the idea comes from the way one sees a stag one minute and then it is gone). No, it is only as fugitive, as departed, as negated that it is the fugitive stag and Mercurius in the first place. The fugitive stag is not a stag that in addition happens not to be there, i.e., to be fugitive. It *is* only *as* not there, *as* departed, absent, fugitive that it is at all." However, the stag's self-negation is different from that of the alchemical gold or stone in that *what* it negates is only its presence and not its very nature (*what* it is: stag). The full negation would result if we shifted to the statement that the fugitive stag is *not* a stag (because in truth it is the Mercurius, who, however, is also by no means a positively existing spirit inasmuch as it is, after all, a fugitive stag, for example).

them literally. But, as I pointed out, it must not take them imaginally or metaphorically either because this would not change the logic of them. Rather, it must take them as *not* what they seem to be about, as *not* what they explicitly state and intend; however, as we have already learned, not as something else either, in other words, not by coming up with another designation, an allegedly "corrected" or "better" expression. For chemistry, gold is simply gold, the real metal of this name with the chemical symbol *Au* and the atomic number 79 (*aurum vulgi*). For psychology it is of course not iron, lead, or silver, and also not imaginal gold or metaphorical gold. Rather, psychology's gold does not refer to metal (be it real or imaginal) at all,[48] and it does not refer to, or mean, anything else either. No, it is exclusively and strictly the negation of gold, gold *in its negatedness* or as negated. For it is, after all, *gold* that is not gold. The soul in a psychological sense *is* the negated *position*.

But what does this mean?

Our "not" cuts off the intentionality as such of the ideas. It excises their "about," their meaning *something*, pointing to *something* (to a referent). Thus it forces their inherent forward movement (what they intend to express) back into itself. The movement becomes uroboric instead. All judgments of the type "S is P" (or "S is not P") in ordinary parlance refer away from themselves to something outside of themselves (outside of the judgments). When we say, "The rose is red," we do not speak about the grammatical sentence subject "rose," but about a flower in reality. Even sentences about imaginary things or beings that do not exist in reality, like a vampire, dragon, griffin, or unicorn, nevertheless refer to something outside of themselves. In other words, it makes no difference whether the external referent in fact *exists* or not: the logical *reference structure* remains. Soul statements, by contrast, do not point away from themselves to something outside. They only mean themselves, inasmuch as they are the soul's self-portrayal. In them the soul presents itself, shows itself in one moment of its logical life and in one aspect of itself, much the same way as for our ordinary world-experience things (stars, mountains, trees, animals) or persons are not "about" some referent, but merely *present* themselves in reality.

---

[48] In a *psychological* sense both real gold and imaginal gold are literal!

In its statements and images, such as when I dream about a particular friend or a big house or a mandala, the soul is speaking about itself.[49] The ideas in soul statements are reflected into themselves, interiorized into themselves.

As long as the ideas or images had to mean something or refer to something they were tied to a kind of "program" (of communicating something in a "life" and, ultimately, "survival" context), and thus they were used for a purpose, were instrumentalized. Now that they have logically become inwardized into themselves they are released into their freedom: into their truth, their self. They just *are*. They have become absolute ("absolved" from their former functionality, their intentionality). The meanings they have did not disappear altogether, but by having lost their intentional[50] forward direction and functional purpose, they begin to vibrate and resonate within themselves; they become poetic or musical, a singing, or like an abstract painting of color compositions; they begin to dance. Here, in the context of the specifically psychological sense of soul, the metaphor of the dance appears for us a third time, on a third level.

Life embodies itself in living beings; the *soul in the sense of the previous section* about "the corpse and the soul," despite its fundamental fleetingness, still congealed into and crystallized out as "dead letters" and cultural works, and produced lasting traditions. The emergence of the specifically *psychological sense of soul,* by contrast, does not embody itself at all. There is nothing sensible or ontic. This is what makes the psychological standpoint so difficult for ordinary consciousness. The cutting off of the ideas' intentionality happens *only* as a doing in the recipient and for the duration of this doing. The psychological sense of soul is only a methodological one, a way of looking at things brought to bear on given phenomena or material. It is not in any way an ontological one. Like music, it needs to be made.

---

[49] This is why Jung's early ideas of an object-level and of a subject-level interpretation of dreams are psychologically insufficient. In the case of the object-level this is most obvious (here we clearly operate with the notion of an external referent), but it is also true about the subject-level interpretation. The latter does by no means leave the "about" or "referent" structure behind. It merely exchanges the extra-personal reference (e.g., my real father) for an intra-personal one (e.g., my father imago or a masculine personality component with father quality in my psyche).

[50] The word to be understood in the sense of Husserl's phenomenology (consciousness's inevitable directedness to ...).

It *is* only in the process or performance of truly psychological interpretation (interpretation of *meanings*, not of letters). But other than music it happens only in the apperceiving subjective mind, not objectively. It does not become audible or visible, it does not objectify itself and is therefore not transmittable. It remains enclosed in the subject, a fact that shows the departedness of soul.

A while ago I had to say that concerning the question what soul is we had at long last arrived at point zero again. Now we have to realize that "the point zero," rather than confronting us with a new question, is itself the answer! If the soul is not speaking about gods, about sex, about the philosophical tree, about the unicorn, about the transference relationship, about facts of one's childhood life, etc., but only about itself, this "itself" is of course not *an existing soul* behind the scene, now returned through the back door. It is nothing else but that negativity itself as which the "autonomous mind" (as Jung had put it) in its absoluteness exists. It is *nothing*—nothing other than self-*manifestation*. This is a self-manifestation that has nothing behind itself *of which* it would be the self-portrayal. It only *is*. Appearance. Display. Show. For example, the display and "dance show" of the stone that is *not* the stone, the phallus that does *not* mean the penis, gods that are *not* gods in the literal sense. Or that of a dream, the internal dance of the dream's images and meanings, its reflecting itself within itself.

For a psychological view, in a myth, a religious doctrine, a philosophy, a ritual, a dream, or a sandplay picture, the soul displays *itself* each time in one particular moment and aspect of its logical life. Or we could also say, it displays its own internal logic by *posing as* concrete figures, things, situations, events as so many costumes of itself and starting a game between them according to rules of the game (rules *ad hoc* designed for, and within, this particular game or dance) by making distinctions and differences, dissociating itself into opposites, establishing relationships between what is different or trying to unite again what is opposite, setting tasks, creating obstacles, inventing solutions, and so on. As Jung had said, "In myths and fairytales, as in dreams, the soul speaks about itself, and the archetypes reveal themselves in their natural interplay, as 'formation, transformation / the eternal Mind's eternal recreation'" (*CW* 9i § 400, transl. modif.). A mere interplay between what has been freely invented solely within and for this self-contained play or dance, with no external reference or message, without asserting anything or establishing a doctrine and theory. For the same reason Jung said about dreams (but he could have said the same about all psychological phenomena): "The dream is its own interpretation" (*CW* 11 § 41, *Letters 2*, p. 294, to Jacobi, 13 March 1956). It presents itself, and, other than natural phenomena, presents itself as a speaking, as meanings; but at the same time, it also uroborically and self-sufficiently returns into itself. It comes as in itself reflected.

This may be a bit difficult to understand. But who said that psychology should be easy? Psychology requires, as Jung pointed out, "a considerable degree of *subtler* intelligence" or "higher intelligence,"[51] subtler and higher than the "average intelligence" of the general public and also than the intelligence of "scientifically minded" and scientifically trained people. Another time we hear from Jung, "Of course I am pleading the cause of the thinking man, and, inasmuch as most people do not think, of a small minority" (*CW* 18 § 1616). After having listed "the demands I put to a pupil," very high demands indeed, Jung once wrote in a letter: "Naturally there are only a few people who can fulfil them, but I have long ago given up producing manufactured articles [*Fabrikware*[52]: mass-produced articles]" (*Letters 1*, p. 188, to Körner, 22 March 1935).

In the previous section the soul was for us "the spark" that is ignited between "the corpse" and a receptive human consciousness. As spark it is not dead letter, empty routine, but truly living soul. In this sense, the religious ardor of a pious person, the enthusiasm of a philosopher about some insight, the powerful feeling of people in love, the deep inspiration that a poem grants, the mystical bliss experienced by a visionary may all be examples of the spark and thus of true events of soul. But at this point the difference between the general and the specific concept of soul comes in. All these *events of soul*, as authentic as they are, are not psychological. They are emotional, experiential, psychic. Psychology transcends and has to see through them. They are at most a possible "prime matter" for psychology, a material for

---

[51] *Letters 2*, p. 410, to L. King, 14 January 1958 (my emphasis).
[52] In choosing the word *Fabrikware*, Jung as the avid Schopenhauer-reader that he was may have had a passage from Schopenhauer's *Die Welt als Wille und Vorstellung* (I § 36) in the back of his mind where he speaks of ordinary man as *Fabrikwaare der Natur*. (Schopenhauer's spelling of *Fabrikwaare* differs from the presently valid spelling *Fabrikware*.)

psychological study, a matter to be put into the "alchemical retort" to be subjected to the psychological *opus* of absolute-negative inwardization. Psychology's notion of soul is that of the negated, sublated spark, the soul come home to itself, to the land of soul, the land of logical negativity and departedness. It is therefore also *not*, just like that, identical with anything like "the numinous."

The dance of the meanings (such as that of the stone that is not a stone or, to use another example, of the ritual of the Mass) remains self-enclosed, self-sufficient; objective, cold; logical, not experiential; it is primarily not for us, but for itself alone, absolutely self-referential and fundamentally *departed*: in other words, *psychological*.[53] The negativity of the soul has therewith become interiorized into the concept of soul itself, and through this interiorization the general concept of soul discussed in the previous section has turned into the truly psychological one. It is this "ghostliness" (as which the total lack of a referent will naturally strike us) that sets the psychological point of view apart from religion, literature, philosophy, etc. and from the points of view of these disciplines towards their topics. They all are in possession of a real external referent, even if, as in the case of the history of religions and ethnology, it may be no more than something as insubstantial and irrational as the beliefs and superstitions of former ages and peoples.

This concludes my exposition of the *concept* of soul. Next I want to turn to the phenomenology of the soul. In what follows I do not aim at anticipating that which can only be the final result of all psychological research nor at providing a condensed summary of all the major manifestations of soul in concrete reality, as far as they are already known. In accordance with the topic of this essay, "What is soul?," the purpose of the following discussions will much rather be to work out *concrete criteria* that help us discern what kind of phenomena in our life experience deserve to be considered as soul phenomena and which not. Of all the countless phenomena in human

---

[53] It is of course possible that the event of a successful truly psychological interpretation creates in the person having performed it a feeling of being deeply moved or an emotion of joy and thus a "spark." But this is precisely not itself psychological. Rather, it is a psychic event *in view of* and *occasioned by* an actual happening of psychology, which *itself*, however, remains averted, averted even from the subject doing psychology.

experience, which ones are specifically such that we can say that they are manifestations of soul? Criteria are of course still only formal. My aim is to help us get our concepts straight, to acquire appropriate categories, distinctions, differentiations; it is not to deliver a listing and description of the soul phenomena themselves, an account of how soul empirically manifests in all its richness. We could therefore say that this essay is work on the differentiation, cultivation, and training of the psychological mind rather than doing psychology itself—or that it is doing psychology, but only to the extent, and in the same sense, that any psychological work is in itself work on the psychological mind.

My discussion is divided into three major parts according to three different ways how soul shows itself. I could also say: according to three areas and types of experience that exemplify what is meant by the natural language term "soul."

There are, first, certain events (like dreams, neurotic symptoms, visions) that in contradistinction to other events we experience as manifestations of soul.

Secondly, certain forms of people's *reactions* to events or things and ways to deal with them appear to us as soulful in contrast to others that we may perhaps feel as being downright soulless. We also have the notion, introduced into psychology by James Hillman, of soul-making, and for Jung, the alchemist's *opus* in his laboratory was a major model for describing and comprehending soul processes.

Third, there is the question of what the soul wants, what it needs, in what directions it is heading.

Therefore the titles for the three parts of the following discussion are: I. The *experienced* or *occurring* soul: verticality and incursion. II. The soul as *subject*, style, and work (soul-*making*). III. The *two opposite purposes* (directions, teleologies) of the soul.

One important aspect that does not appear in a separate part is that soul can also be recognized as a dynamic: as an innate will or drive forward to new forms or levels of itself and thus as a process. The reason is that the topic of the soul as "burrowing spirit," as historical *opus magnum*, as dynamic movement, as progression via different stages has already been touched upon in the foregoing chapter on the concept of soul and will reappear at various points in several of the following parts.

CHAPTER 2

The Phenomenology of the Soul (1): The Experienced or Occurring Soul. Verticality, Incursion

2.1 THE OPPOSITION BETWEEN *EVENTS* OF SOUL AND ORDINARY HUMAN EXISTENCE

2.1.1 A preliminary touchstone: "Intrusion." "The exceptional"

When we approach the concrete phenomenology of life in the world with our empty formal definition of the soul as "that which is not what is not soul," this empty form gets quickly particularized and filled with material qualifications. We know what is *not* soul: everything that is positive-factual, conventional, routine, matter-of-course, natural, human, all-too-human, the normal and familiar. If soul is what is *not* not soul, it is, within the *experiential* sphere, in the most general sense what is felt to *intrude* into normal life. It is the fundamentally exceptional, that which *disturbs* the customary order of things: the extra-ordinary. It is what *disrupts* or breaks through the normal routine of life and is contrary to our natural expectations. It is the unheard-of and the incomprehensible, that which cannot be explained in terms of our previous experience and knowledge.

Thus it is in particular the eerie, uncanny, the numinous as the
mysterium tremendum et fascinosum, often also the holy *in contrast to*
the profane, at least as long as the holy has not already become
conventional.[54] The experienced soul is by no means always "soulful"
in the sweet, romantic, beneficial, or harmless sense. Rather, it can
even be downright inhuman. At times the soul is a brutal reality. It
may ruthlessly pass over our human concerns, our survival and self-
protection interests, our needs for stability, comfort, and consolation.
It frequently forces *its* interests upon us, regardless of what *we* want.
It drags us away from what would be natural, ordinary, decent,
or reasonable and seduces us or compels us—whether we will or no
(cf. *"vocatus atque non vocatus ..."*)—to do something *contra naturam*,
be it exceptionally great or perverse.

Our whole *natural world* with all the things in it is soul in the
most general sense of the word. But this soul is in itself
fundamentally *contra naturam*. It comes into being by always
already having pushed off from biological life, just as the latter
within itself pushed off from the lifeless. Life is also *contra naturam*.
And so we have to realize that what "nature," as that from which
to push off, means is each time something different. For life
"nature" means the lifeless, the world of physics and chemistry. For
the soul in the most general sense "the natural" is biological life.
And for the soul as the particular concept of psychology the natural
from which to distinguish itself and to push off is the natural world
as a whole, both in the sense of the cosmos and of what is socially
considered "natural" or "normal."

In soul events, a counter-will makes itself felt. The soul has a will
of its own. It *is* will. And as counter-will it is non-ego, non-I. It often
directly *crosses our will*, as Jung liked to put it. Something that is not
our human will insists, obsesses us, wrecks our plans, forces our
attention. And that which crosses our will, as Jung also said, wants to
mitleben, to be acknowledged as our own, to become an integral part
of our life, our consciousness and attitudes.

---

[54] The contrast is essential. It contains the negation. We are concerned here with
the numinous to the extent that it disrupts, violates ordinary experience. But that
"numinous" that has been taken for granted and is viewed as one of the many possible
phenomena of ordinary experience is positivized and was rightly rejected at the end of
the previous chapter as a possible indication (and concept) of soul.

Clearly, the type of manifestation of soul that we are here talking about shows the soul in the form of otherness. This form is, as a matter of course, psychologically authentic in the archaic, the ancient, and still in all the later pre-modern situations, where the soul generally was objectified as gods, demons, angels, fairies, little people. In the modern world, which is characterized by the fact that in it the soul has reached the logical form of itself as self (self-relation, self-awareness), the form of otherness is in the main inauthentic. As this inauthentic form it appears in individuals above all as neurotic symptom, as the result of a consciousness that systematically and stubbornly insists on its untruth and thereby—artificially—forces its already real and implicitly known truth into the form of radical otherness (the neurotically dissociated "non-ego"). There is, however, also one authentic possibility of the form of otherness in modernity, and the sign of its authenticity is that it is essentially only temporary. This occurs when there is a need for advancing from the present to a new logical status of consciousness, a new stage of one's development, from the customary to a new soul truth. We usually do not gradually "grow" in a natural way into a new form of consciousness. There is no simple transition. Rather, the new constitution of consciousness is sprung on us, on, and right into, the old constitution of consciousness. Within the old form of consciousness the new one all of a sudden appears, and it appears initially merely as an isolated disturbing, sometimes even pathological (symptomatic), factor and precisely not yet as what it actually is or is meant to be, consciousness's new constitution. Just think of puberty and the intrusion of the awareness of sexuality. By being this thorn in the flesh of the old form of consciousness it slowly decomposes and corrodes the latter and thereby becomes the new form of consciousness—unless, of course, the soul at this point chooses to go the way of neurosis, of absolutely refusing and denying this its new truth and celebrating its untruth as its truth.

Soul events are intrusive and disturbing. By contrast, all events or phenomena will be experienced and have to be seen as what is not soul if they conform with our expectations, social customs, and personal habits, are immediately understandable and can be explained in terms of our knowledge about the laws of nature, of cause and effect, and of all everyday life experience, if they strike us as familiar, ordinary, conventional, natural (also in the sense of "as a matter of course"). Above all everything that falls for us into the sphere of the "human, all-too-human" is in radical contrast to what we mean by events of soul. The world in general, to the extent that it is, on the one hand, in practical regards domesticated, civilized, humanized, regulated, or, on the other hand, in theoretical regards made familiar and subjected to scientific knowledge, belongs to this side of our opposition.

2.1.2 The *soul* sense of "exceptional"

But things are not as simple as they appear from the description I have given so far. The description needs at least two qualifications to do justice to our question what soul is.

The first qualification concerns the determination of what is meant by "the extra-ordinary," "the exceptional," "the incomprehensible," "the *fascinosum*." Not everything exceptional and unexpected, not everything that is awful or fascinating is as such necessarily expressive of soul. The huge, the outsized, the sensational and uncommonly impressive are not *ipso facto* events of soul. We need to introduce an additional distinction.

The battle of Stalingrad in World War II and the bombing of Dresden at the end of World War II were certainly something extra-ordinary and gigantic, happenings of exceptional emotional and physical impact. But from a *psychological* point of view they were nevertheless ordinary empirical-factual disasters; for the people involved they were events of ordinary human misery, and not manifestations of soul. All the catastrophes of the type that frequently become the topic of disaster films are likewise enormous occurrences that intrude into and disrupt the customary order of things, but they nevertheless have no soul dignity. They excite our human, all-too-human emotions, incite our survival instincts, and call for our efforts to cope, to rescue what can be rescued, but do not speak to the soul. In other words, they belong to and remain within the world of positivity, factuality. We know that the possibility cannot be excluded that some day a huge meteor might hit the earth with the most terrible consequences for all life on our planet. If that happened, it would certainly be something truly exceptional and spectacular, and yet it would be without psychological relevance, just as was the comparatively minor event of the destruction by terrorists of the New York Twin Towers. The soul has no stake in such phenomena, they may be as monstrous and unheard-of as they may be. They are phenomena that address only the ego, its emotions and its desire to survive.

What then are extra-ordinary phenomena that in fact possess soul significance? How are they different from the just-mentioned ones? What distinction do we need to introduce to get criteria to distinguish soul events from the merely positive-factually extraordinary? Whereas we can call the psychologically trivial occurrences, even if they are spectacular and huge, merely-objective, events of soul are in themselves objective-subjective. They are not merely flat physical facts vis-à-vis the subject. Although they, too, are objective facts, soul events nevertheless also have subjectivity within themselves. They objectively come to the experiencing subject as a kind of thou. They have a meaning, or rather, they *are* events of meaning. They have *logos*-character and "the quality of consciousness" (*CW* 8 § 658). They are in themselves linguistic. They *speak*. They are intriguing and contain a "mystery."

This means that the subject, when hit by a soul event, is not only confronted with an objective fact, some occurrence that is totally an other. Subject and object do here not have their place each on opposite banks of a dividing river. No, although a soul event is happening to the subject as something other and unexpected, maybe even as utterly disturbing, and although as such it is undoubtedly something objective and factual, the subject nevertheless wittingly or unwittingly encounters *itself*, or some aspect of itself, in this object. It senses that in what is out there it, the subject, is already in some way contained and involved. *Tua res agitur*. Involved or implicated not in that external sense how we may realize that certain events are the effect or outcome of our own earlier decisions, actions, or omissions. Such an effect does not immediately speak to us; only through an external reflection or insight do we relate it to ourselves via the memory of our earlier behavior. Cause and effect remain fundamentally separated by time as two different events. A soul event, by contrast, does not refer to any other event outside itself. It has the subject-quality or consciousness-quality immediately within itself, within its objectivity. This is why it is experienced as significant and meaningful for *ourselves* (ourselves as persons, as humans, not merely important for us as animals the way, for example, medical results or natural catastrophes are important for us).

So soul phenomena cannot be thought of except in terms of a self-relation.

However, keeping in mind the essentially intrusive character of soul events, we must not understand this self-relation as *our* relation to *ourselves* via the objective event, nor as our relation to our own other, but conversely as an alien self-relation that we find ourselves drawn into. It is the soul's relation to itself, its speaking to itself about itself (the *logos psychês pros haytên*[55] already referred to), a speaking that is fundamentally self-sufficient, has its own purposes, finds its own fulfillment within itself, but for which it is nevertheless essential that it both manifests in something objective and reaches the human subject. It is a speaking that makes both the objective reality in which it manifests and the human subject who feels addressed by it *sublated moments* within itself. The human subject is, as it were, merely the antenna or the receiver which, however, makes this self-relation not only audible but also possible in the first place. Because other than with radio programs, the soul's dialogue with itself has no radio station broadcasting its programs somewhere "out there" regardless of whether anybody turns his radio on or not. The soul is, as we learned, not an existing substance or entity. In the case of psychological reality it is much rather the receptivity of the human subject that dialectically is the condition *a priori* of the soul's speaking to itself, a speaking to which the human subject is exposed or which disturbingly intrudes into the human subject's own concerns. The human subject is merely a moment in the soul's self-relation and yet also its precondition. But conversely, the human subject is only turned into the antenna for the soul's speaking to itself through this very speaking, which in man creates its own antenna, and thus its own precondition, within itself. This whole complex and self-contradictory relation is what we call soul.

Soul, understood this way, sounds very mysterious, and it *is* of course also mysterious in a certain sense, but it is nothing that belongs to a metaphysical backworld behind this world. It is a very real part of our human experience. Let me illustrate this by an example. It is

---

[55] Cf. Plato *Theaitetos* 189e and *Sophistes* 263e.

an obvious fact that there is such a thing as poetry. Poetry is part of our human world here on earth. Our conventional idea is that it is the poet as author or subject who *makes* the poems as objects, as works (*erga*). But Goethe for one once said in passing, "... just as with poems, I did not make them, they made me."[56] The poems, in other words, are the true acting subject, they create themselves and merely utilize a human subject to realize themselves.[57] It is they that turn the human being into a poet in the first place. In the process of the emergence of poetry the so-called human author is in reality not the true author at all, but merely a sublated moment in this whole process. What makes a poet a true poet is precisely his capacity to allow himself to become sublated as a being in his own right and to become instead an integral moment of the self-production of his poem. At the very beginning of our Western poetic tradition Homer likewise denied his authorship. The *Iliad* was the result of the singing of a goddess, the muse. And in modernity, on May 13, 1870, another poet, Rimbaud, wrote similarly in a letter (to Izambard): "It is wrong to say: I think. One would have to say: it thinks me... I is an other." This otherness of I experienced by Rimbaud is exactly the I's *sublatedness* as I in the conventional sense of *author* and self-sufficient *subject*.

This is one aspect. The other is that poems are of course not independently free-floating all around us the way the radio-waves from our broadcasting stations are. The latter could be received by several individuals. That poets are sublated moments in the creation of poetry does not mean that they are merely technical antennas, passive mouthpieces or recorders (and thus in some way external to the poems, namely merely instruments). Rather, their poems are *also* uniquely *theirs*. Nobody else could have come up with Goethe's poems. He as the individual that he is has become integrated into his poems. It is this particular, singular human being Goethe, just as it is this other particular, singular human being Rimbaud, who is necessary not only for their poems to come into existence, but who is also indispensable as the precondition of the poems' capacity to turn Goethe or Rimbaud into their (the poems') sublated moments and thus making them poets

---

[56] Joh. W. von Goethe, *Kampagne in Frankreich*, Aug. 30, 1792, my transl.

[57] Cf. *Magnaque pars mendax operum est et ficta meorum: / plus sibi permisit compositore suo* (a large part of my works is freely made-up and invented: *they* have taken more liberties than their author), Ovid, *Tristia* 2, 355f.

in the first place. Neither poet nor poem comes first. Both are each other's precondition. Both are equiprimordial. It is a uroboric relationship. But they are equiprimordial preconditions of each other only within *the event of poetry*. The event occurs out of the blue—or it does not occur.

The event of poetry is one example of an event of soul. Events of soul are phenomenal, empirically real, and yet they are mysterious in the sense that they cannot be understood in the simple conventional logic of the relationships of cause and effect, condition and result, author and product. The inexplicable, fundamentally unpredictable event-character of soul events points to the fact that soul is an extraordinary phenomenon that is not part of the natural course of events and the natural order of things, but intruding into it.

2.1.3   The relativity of what is exceptional

This was my first qualification of my earlier description of the difference between soul and what is not soul. The second qualification can hark back to the insight that soul events are objective-subjective. When they happen, they always already contain the subject within themselves. I pointed out that Goethe has—logically—become integrated into his poems, poems that he did not make, but that rather made him. One cannot subtract the experiencing subject from the soul event that happens to it. This has consequences. The distinction between soul events and what is not soul, as it has emerged here, must not be viewed as an ontological one. It cannot be operationalized; we cannot make a list of events and objects of reality that intrinsically and always belong to the side of the soul and another list of those that do not. The difference is itself psychological. It is essentially relative to the experiencing consciousness (especially to the logical status it has reached) and to the specific situation. One cannot *a priori* and abstractly decide to which side a given event belongs. The "same" event may under different conditions appear on either side. There are also poems that were indeed made by the human author rather than "making him." Writing poems can also be a craft. The extraordinary must not be thought of as something spectacular, and something spectacular can despite its extraordinariness be flat. For example, on the stage of mythological consciousness the sun is usually seen as divine and thus as being "out of this world," a god or goddess. As such it belongs to soul. For us moderns, by contrast, it, the "same" sun, is primarily a very ordinary celestial body to be studied by physics and astronomy.[58] But this does not necessarily preclude that in a special situation, unlikely as it is, the experience of the sun could even for a modern person take on a truly numinous quality. For archaic consciousness an earthquake or the eclipse of the sun was a soul event, whereas for us the earthquake is a natural disaster (if it is serious enough) and the solar eclipse maybe an interesting curiosity, a "touristic" attraction. In Europe, prior to the Enlightenment, i.e., way into the 18th century, flashes of lightning and thunder were still numinous, still moments of shared fear. Typically, all the occupants of a house would gather together in one room and remain there kneeling and praying throughout the thunderstorm. There were special hymns to be sung at the beginning of a thunderstorm and other ones when it was over. Abbé Poncelet in his book about *La Nature dans la formation du Tonnere et la reproduction des Êtres vivant* (Paris 1769), mentioned the vehement agitation that thunderstorms caused in people during daytime and the mortal perturbation it induced when they came at night.[59] Fifty years later, thunderstorms had generally completely lost this frightening quality. It is important to realize that the fear was not caused by terrible experiences of damage done by lightning. Already Lichtenberg pointed out that in Göttingen within a few days twice as many people died of a dysentery epidemic than during more than the previous fifty years of lightning. The terror was "caused" by the soul, it was a soul event, just as conversely the dying in masses from an epidemic or, today, from car accidents, is experienced as part of ordinary life.

In some archaic cultures, the sun is divine (and thus soulful) only at the moment of its rising above the horizon. Here we see that what is undoubtedly an everyday event can nevertheless be experienced as something not worldly, something that breaks into our ordinary world. Rituals that are regularly performed, such as the Catholic Mass or the Communion, can on account of their ritual character be holy moments,

---

[58] As Jung, speaking to a chief of the Pueblo Indians put it in a still rather pre-modern religious, but nevertheless Western way: "a fiery ball shaped by an invisible god," *MDR* p. 250.

[59] See Gaston Bachelard, *La formation de l'esprit scientifique* (1938).

but on account of their regular repetition they can under altered psychological circumstances just as well be experienced as empty "routine" events. It all depends on the actually prevailing standpoint. This is the tension between "corpse" and soul, letter and "spark" discussed above. All sorts of complications can arise from the fact that the distinction is psychological and not ontological. We could, for example, imagine a priest for whom the obligation to perform the Mass every day has become a dead convention, but who because of his priesthood vows is afraid to admit this even to himself, so that subjectively he may still be convinced, try to be convinced, that the Mass is holy for him.

The border between soul and what is not soul is dynamic, alive. Each time, with each phenomenon in each situation (in each "now"), what belongs to the one and what to the other side has to be determined anew. The decision in the case of a particular phenomenon cannot be a mechanical one; it cannot be operationalized (as if a computer could make it by going through a checklist routine). It requires our intelligence, sensitivity, and flexibility—and our coming forward and risking ourselves with our personal judgment,[60] our subjectivity. *Oportet me adesse* (it is indispensable that I am present), Luther had said (although in a very different context). I have to enter the situation and show my true colors, which is why earlier civilizations had initiations. How do I have to enter, how can I enter? The answer to this question lies in its dialectical opposite: by allowing the event to turn *me* into a sublated moment of *itself.*

This is, of course, absolutely contrary to the general trend of our time, which aims at the self-abdication of the subject as personally responsible judging intelligence. Questions of quality are supposed to be reductively translated into ones of quantity, measurements. To mention only one single example, scientists are ranked by the number of their publications in top journals ("bibliometrics"), the frequency with which their publications were cited ("impact factor"), and the amount of third-party funds they were able to raise, rather than by the importance and intrinsic worth of what they produced. Mindless,

---

[60] This is a judgment that above all requires a well-developed "feeling-function" in Jung's sense (as a *rational* function and as an *orientation* function, i.e., as "objective" feeling: an appraisal of the worth or value of something objectively real).

mechanical counting is supposed to be more "objective" than the judgment of an informed mind who actually reads and understands those published texts. But *psychology* cannot do without, simply cannot come about without, the presence of the subject.

2.1.4 The difference between "the psychic" and "the psychological"

Jung had a very clear idea that the human, all-too-human belongs to what is not soul. This is shown, for example, when he introduces a startling distinction going right into or through the very center of therapeutic psychology. He insisted, contrary to the thinking prevailing in most quarters of psychotherapy, that "It is the smallest part of the psyche, and in particular of the unconscious, that presents itself in the medical consulting room."[61] Most of what the therapist in the consulting room is confronted with belongs, to be sure, to the *psyche,* including the "personal unconscious," but the *soul*—here, in Jung's language, referred to as the larger, excluded part of what he called the "unconscious"—is a rare guest. The work in the consulting room, our attending to our dreams, our striving for wholeness are basically ego work. Psychological theory (I am speaking here exclusively within the sphere of depth-psychology) is commonly supposed to be based on what empirical experience learns through the treatment of patients in the consulting room. If so, then it is precisely the "smallest part" that is turned into the basis and the measure of the whole and believed to be the real thing. Jung says to this with brutal clarity: "the false [or pseudo] picture of the human soul becomes the theory of psychic suffering" (*CW* 10 § 368, transl. modif.). What is not soul (because it is merely human, all-too-human) is implicitly given the status and rank of soul.

This also applies to all more recent research (and therapy) based on empirical baby observation, on attachment theory, and studies of human mother-child bonding and the development of empathy, together with research on the serious consequences that it has for human individuals when things go wrong in these areas during the first few years of their life. The insights gained in these fields are no

---

[61] *Letters 2*, p. 307, 17 June 1956, to Nelson. When Jung speaks of "the unconscious" we can frequently substitute our term "the soul."

doubt very important, just as the field of biology at large is important. However, they are not of psychological significance. They explore human biology, the biology (ethology) of the human *animal*, not psychology, the logos of the soul. In this context, whether one studies human babies or, like Konrad Lorenz, greylag geese makes no difference. The founder of modern attachment theory, John Bowlby, was even directly influenced by Konrad Lorenz's work. In other words, what he at bottom did was to extend the biologist's ethological field of research to now include also the human animals: the human beings insofar as they are animals with instinctive needs and reactions characteristic of the species. He did not enrich *psychological* theory.[62] In all the different animal species (of fish, reptiles, birds, mammals, humans) the relations between mothers and their offspring is very different (baby fish frequently grow up without any relation to their mothers, while human babies at the other end of the spectrum have a very deep and enormously differentiated one), but each form of relation (or non-relation) is one possible variation of the same biological theme. And even though something radically new, a *relating* and thus a logical quality, appears on the scene with the emergence of what Konrad Lorenz called "imprinting" and of the phenomenon of attachment, it nonetheless still remains on the level of biology. Much of the older psychoanalytical theory of object relations and the work in therapy on the level of interpersonal relationships and of transference-countertransference belongs to the same category, human biology, at least to the extent that they are true phenomena (in the sense of what shows itself of its own accord)

---

[62] The question must here be left open whether in the therapy of adults who as infants had been deprived of the possibility to develop an adequate attachment these defects must be treated on the "same" biological (human animal) level on which they arose, the level of emotions and body sensations, or whether the treatment of people with such problems must not also already be a *psychological* one. One must certainly keep two things in mind, first, that the present-day notions, in the therapeutic discourse, of body and body sensations are modern abstractions ("the body" is intellectually dissociated from the intellect and the soul; the real I or me as *homo totus* is already departmentalized); and, secondly, that adults even with such defects are generally irrevocably beyond the infant stage, now having a conscious awareness of themselves and of their environment and therefore probably also a need to learn to deal with their defects via a conscious relation to them through understanding and feeling ("feeling" in contrast to "emotions" and "sensations") rather than through the (alleged) immediacy of emotional experiences. Can an early-childhood defect in the area of attachment be repaired, or does it not, on the entirely new level of adult maturity, need to be constructively integrated into consciousness?

and not artifacts, results artificially generated through the psychoanalytic technique itself.[63]

Furthermore, as already the word suggests, all work in neurobiology, important as it is within the community of sciences, is also of biological, not of psychological relevance.

There is in all such cases either no awareness of soul in the strict sense at all, soul as a dimension in its own right—the concept of soul has not even been sighted, the category of soul has simply dropped away—or, as above all in certain Jungian quarters, the *name* soul is retained and maybe even profligately used, to be sure, but by means of a systematic, intentional projection, the soul dimension is reductively stuffed into ordinary personal lives of common people, whose ordinary lives are therefore sometimes said to be a reenactment of this or that myth and in this way get glorified and inflated with extraordinary meaning.[64] In both cases the psychological difference between what is soul and what is not soul is ignored or even undone. In the former case, because the one side of the psychological difference simply drops away, there is exclusively the positivistic reality of psychic life as the "behavior of the organism, of the human animal," which, however, is as such nonetheless given out as the true object of psychology (whereas what is *truly* soul "is left to the poets," as Jung, *ibidem*, says derisively). In the latter case, the case of painting the ordinary with the colors of the extraordinary, both sides of the psychological difference are short-circuitingly collapsed into one, and, to be sure, on its banal[65] side.

From here it is easy to see that, with another wording, the psychological difference can be defined as the difference between

---

[63] To a large extent, psychotherapeutic techniques are methods for *producing* the "phenomena" that psychologists then interpret and build their theories on.

[64] In this connection we can also think of certain Jungian approaches that focus on the *literal* transference/countertransference emotions and reactions (in a completely personalistic, downright Freudian psychoanalytic sense), but give these so-understood processes out as instances of what Jung in his alchemical psychology worked out as the "psychology of transference." The behavior of the two organisms (therapist and patient) is directly *identified* with the background processes taking place between Rex and Regina, an identification merely by naming. The *psychological* level is missed. The soul is *reduced* to literal human emotions and relations. The more complex and logically negative is expressed in the terms of the much simpler level of positive facts, subjective felt experience or imagination.

[65] "Banal" of course only from the point of view of soul.

the *psychic* and the *psychological*.[66] The use of these terms in the
technical sense that I give them *in my work* is admittedly rather
artificial, but helpful and more than that: precise. They are nearly
synonymous and yet different. The near-synonymity is necessary to
express the fact that the difference we are talking about is not to be
understood in terms of the totally other, the altogether heterogeneous
(the way "tree" and "car" are different from each other). "Psychic" and
"psychological," by sharing the first part of the words, correspond to
the alchemical *lithos oy lithos* or the *aurum nostrum non est aurum vulgi*
patterns. "Psychological" is the negation of the psychic, it is "*oy*"
psychic, the *non est* psychic, and yet not an absolute stranger to the
latter, but rather its *determinate* negation. Whereas the psychic is what
can be positive-factually known, the psychological contains the word
"logical," which points to the *logos*, the mental, noetic, intelligible
reality of the psychological, and thus to the comparative "ghostliness"
of the psychological over against the psychic. The noun corresponding
to the adjective "psychic" is psyche, the human psyche (man's
intellectual and emotional faculties, his drives, desires, etc.), which is
an aspect of the life of the human organism and as such fundamentally
belongs to the larger sphere of biology and anthropology. The noun
corresponding to "psychological," by contrast, is *soul*. (The German
language makes this connection clearer: in this context where it does
not refer to a field of study but to a quality of phenomena or to
orientations, "psychological" is *seelisch*, "soul" is *Seele*.)

This terminological differentiation does of course not preclude that
in practical usage the term psyche can occasionally be applied where
soul is meant and vice versa. We don't need to be pedantic, word-
fetishists. The point is to comprehend the difference and always *think*
in terms of it, not to rigidly formalize it and mechanically apply a fixed
technical terminology. Why should one not, as long as it is clear from
the context what is *meant*, sometimes use the word psyche or "the
unconscious" for soul? Why insist that always the same word is used
for one particular meaning and that one particular word must always

---

[66] Other keywords for expressing the psychological difference are: soul vs. man
(the human animal or organism; the human, all-too-human; the anthropological point
of view); *contra naturam* vs. the natural; interpretation (event of meaning, what has in
itself the quality of consciousness, is subjective-objective) vs. fact; reflected vs. immediate;
"our gold" vs. the popular sense of gold (*aurum vulgi*).

have the same meaning? It would be a lack of urbanity. But this lack comes of course out in the frequent tendency nowadays to relieve us of the burden of ourselves having to actively perform the distinctions in our mind by letting external, objective structures, institutions, or terminologies or politically correct forms of expressions *mechanically* carry this burden for us (which would be another example for the above-mentioned self-abdication of the subject as thinking and understanding subject).

Very clearly the psychological difference comes out in Jung's writings when he, for example, writes that "Heaven and hell are fates meted out to the soul and not to civil man, who in his nakedness and dullness would have no idea of what to do with himself in a heavenly Jerusalem" (*CW* 9i § 56, transl. modif.). The soul *and not* civil man! Soul is the negation of the human being, not merely another part of or something "in" the human being. We also know that for Jung the word "man" can simply stand for the ego or the ego-personality and thus in contrast to soul ("the ego—that is, the empirical man—", *MDR* p. 346, cf. "man—that is, his ego," *MDR* p. 337, "the ego, i.e., the empirical, ordinary man as he has been up to now," *CW* 11 § 233, transl. modif.). And for civil man a "heavenly Jerusalem" would be an absolutely meaningless combination of words. But, within the Western tradition, the soul immediately knows what it is and knows it as one image for its highest value.

What all this means cannot better be illustrated than by Jung's exposition and differentiation of two types of literary products. I refer to *CW* 15 §§ 136–143. Jung astonishingly asserts that the "psychological novel" is not very useful or interesting for the psychologist! "In general, it is the non-psychological novel that offers the richest opportunities for psychological elucidation." Even before we go into a more detailed description of what Jung means, we see clearly that this is a case of the psychological difference in action, merely by looking at the formal structure of the sentences with their affirmation of the negative term and their negation of the positive term. Jung's statement follows the logic contained in "the soul is not what is not soul" or *lithos oy lithos, aurum nostrum non est aurum vulgi*. "The psychological" (which in the terminology of this quote corresponds to what I above termed "the psychic") is psychologically (that is, for the interest in the soul) rather irrelevant, while "the non-psychological" (in the sense of what in my terminology is the not-psychic) is the real gift for the psychologist.

2.1.5 Difficulties concerning the psychological difference

It is wonderful that Jung did not try to avoid the ambiguity of the word psychological by simply using different terms. This is not at all confusing, as the editors of the *CW* seemed to think, who felt obliged to add a footnote on Jung's confusing use of "psychological" (*ibid.* § 139, note 2). No, this use of the same word "psychological" in two clearly distinct senses precisely makes things very clear— provided you go thinkingly along with, and focus on, Jung's *thought* and on the *reality* he is discussing, rather than treating *words* (the terms) as the actual objects talked about. The terms are merely the means for talking about something real.[67] This ambiguous use of the word 'psychological' brings out the ambiguity or "difference" (and thus complication) inherent in the nature of psychology itself. Psychology only comes into being through its self-negation, through its own pushing off from itself as immediate psychology, where "immediate psychology" is the interest in what Jung here called the psychological, in other words, what I term "the psychic." We are not simply dealing with two *separate* compartments lying side by side, the psychic here and the psychological there. To begin with, there is only the psychological in the sense of the psychic, and the psychological in the

---

[67] For the problem of this word fixation, compare Jung's statement in a letter (*Letters 2*, p. 468f., 22 Dec 1958, to von der Heydt): "Your question evidently emanates from an atmosphere in which many words are buzzing about. The real situation cannot, however, be clarified by mere concepts but only by the inner experience that corresponds to them. ... That is why things that previously seemed all confused suddenly become clear when one lets experience speak. [...] From such discussions we see what awaits me once I have become posthumous. Then everything that was once fire and wind will be bottled in spirit and reduced to dead nostrums." Instead of "experience" we could insert "thought to be expressed" into Jung's sentence. The point is not "experience" but simply *what* one is talking about, *die Sache.* "When one lets experience speak" = when one *thinks* the idea the sentence is supposed to convey. Experience does not speak, unless *we* think it. It needs our fire and wind.—To this we may add Jung's advice to another correspondent: "May I give you some advice? Don't get caught by words, only by facts" (*ibid*, p. 475, 27 Dec 1958, to A. Tjoa and R.H.C. Janssen) and his critical comment to yet another correspondent: "Thus you chiefly deal with words and names instead of giving substance. ... I try to describe facts of which you merely mention the names" (*ibid.*, p. 185, to Calvin S. Hall, 6 Oct 1954).

strict sense only brings itself about *within* this psychic through its *logically* pushing off from the latter. Not away from it, but deeper into it. The moment you dissociate the two, literalize them, conceiving them as two separate alternatives, you have, to be sure, greatly simplified matters by relieving yourself of the necessity to in fact do the work of logically "pushing off," but you also have foregone the possibility to arrive at the true notion of psychology.

The reason why this is so is that the construal of the "psychic" and the "psychological" as simple alternatives is reductive. Reduction is the "horizontalizing" of a "vertical" difference, comparable to a geometric projection of a three-dimensional body upon a two-dimensional plane. What is in truth the difference between two *orders* or *levels* or *dimensions* is expressed as a content difference on one and the same level. In our case, the difference between the psychic and the psychological, which can also be comprehended as the difference *between* the semantic *and* the syntactical, is itself described as a semantic difference (different species). The difference is not denied or obfuscated, but it has now become the flat difference of different descriptive qualities or features on the same structural plane. The syntax of a sentence is not a peer to semantics (i.e., to the contents or meanings of the words of a sentence). You can reach the level of syntax only by negating the whole level of contents, systematically "forgetting" it, and rising above it (or descending beneath it) to the level of formal structural relations. But the level of syntax is not either, like another floor of a building, something separate literally above or below the level of meanings. One and the same sentence contains both levels at once. Despite belonging to a radically different dimension, the syntax inheres the words (the semantic elements) of the sentence and can only exist in them, never independently.[68]

This is why you can only get to it through the logical act of the sentence's self-negation. There is no existing passageway, bridge, ladder, or staircase via which you could simply "walk" out of the sphere of the semantic and in its stead walk or climb into that of syntax. A passageway or ladder would imply that the other dimension is a mere

---

[68] And it truly inheres them as their own logical relation; it is not superimposed on them like an adhesive label (the way psychologists often superimpose mythic patterns on completely ordinary human biographies).

annex or extension, or the addition of a second story. The idea of a
second story seems to do justice to the requirement of verticality, but
this verticality is only literal, spatial, sensibly imagined. And as the
two stories are independent of each other, the very verticality of the
difference between the semantic and the syntactical is itself construed
as a merely semantic and *in this sense* horizontal difference, inasmuch
as the "upper" one and the "lower" one, although semantically, and
for the imagination, clearly in vertical opposition, are logically just as
horizontal, just as much juxtaposed alternatives, as the left and the
right or the front and the back one. Constitutive for psychology is the
logical, syntactical, or psychological verticality, which requires
psychology's self-negation or self-sublation.

There is no denying that Jung unfortunately himself stayed pretty
much stuck on the semantic level, firstly in his theoretical description
of the opposition between consciousness and the archetypal images
of the collective unconscious, secondly in his tying the psychological
process to the literal human individual, and thirdly in his idea about
what the solution of the problem of our time was, for example, that
what was needed was "to *dream* the *myth* onwards." Jung refused to
acknowledge psychology's need to enter the level of logical form, of
strict thought, of syntax.[69] He regressively tried to get away with
tackling on the level of contents (images) psychological problems that
we can see through as unambiguously syntactical ones. Even the text
of his on literature, that we will look at more closely in the following,
with its distinction of two types of literary products as well as two
types of artistic creation, could suggest a thinking in terms of horizontal
alternatives or opposites.

---

[69] Jung's refusal to let himself in for the dimension of syntactical form may even be
reflected on the physical level, namely in his vehement aversion, during his student years,
to physiology and his complementary fascination with comparative anatomy and its
"morphological point of view in the broadest sense" (*MDR* p. 100f.). Of course, Jung
explains that what was revolting for him in physiology was the practice of vivisection
merely for purposes of demonstration, something I can easily sympathize with. I also
agree that he probably "had imagination enough to picture the demonstrated procedures
from a mere description of them." Nevertheless, given his stake in *morphê, Gestalt,* figure,
even his rejection of vivisection itself may have had to do with his wish to protect the
morphê as such, now, however, the intact *Gestalt* or image of the animal as a *living*
creature. Physiology is not only an attack on the living animal itself, but even more
fundamentally so on a consciousness committed to the morphological point of view.
Compared with anatomy and its emphasis on thing-like components of the organism,
physiology studies the abstract functional relationships within the organism, its "syntax"
or "logical life," as it were.

But first of all, whereas the two classes of literary works can indeed be horizontally juxtaposed, according to Jung's exposition the different notions of psychology required by and at work in them cannot and are not two opposites side by side: his idea that the non-psychological is what is psychologically significant clearly demands an interpretation in terms of a vertical relation. And secondly, underneath the explicit logical form of his thinking and writing, Jung had a clear intuitive knowledge of the sublatedness of psychology. And there are time and again places in Jung's works where his intuition of the necessity of a logical negation forces an expression. But while a logical sublation is absolutely nonviolent, the idea of it, when squeezed into the form of an on principle semantic, imaginal thinking, necessarily takes on the form of an image of violent liberation. Perhaps the best example is: "... analytical psychology has burst the chains which till then has tied it to the consulting-room of the doctor. It transcends itself ..." (*CW* 16 § 174, transl. modif.). The image is that of a tied prisoner who bursts open his fetters. But after this self-liberation psychology does not simply walk out of its prison. If it needs to transcend *itself* in order to come into *its* own, then this means that it *exists as* its own self-sublation. Its sublation does not lead out and away, but deeper into itself.[70]

If Jung had been ready to move to the logical level and thus truly *think* "sublation," the consulting room would not have been a prison, there would not have been any fetters, and there would not have been any violent affect and no need of a forceful liberation. There would only have been a very calm overcoming of the logic of the consulting room (or rather: an already *having* overcome it). The prison and the explosiveness occurring in this fantasy are the symptom of the inadequacy of the level on which the idea to be expressed is perceived. The real prison and chains painfully sensed by consciousness are the latter's own semantic-imaginal style of thinking. It is a prison because it is absolutely inappropriate for the type of reality (the reality of true psychology) that emerges and wants to be expressed within it: a three-dimensional body is, as it were, squeezed down into

---

[70] Despite my general appreciation of Hillman's emphasis on the concept of "The Yellowing of the Work," I had to critique for this reason his *on systematic grounds* leaving the consulting room. See my *The Soul's Logical Life*, Frankfurt/Main et al. (Peter Lang) 1998, pp. 191ff.

a two-dimensional frame.[71] This semantic style of thinking is by
definition incapable of self-reflection, of reflecting such a thing as a
logical level (or dimension or consciousness). For it, the only things
conceivable are *contents* of consciousness (images or ideas that *appear*
on this logical level). This is why, when it is reached by the idea of
true psychology as Jung indeed was, it has to displace the prison-
character from *itself* (from its form) to one of its contents. And this is
how the consulting room suddenly has to bear the brunt of the
prison feeling that in truth is caused by the confining mental
framework, which in turn is the reason why even the most explosive
liberation does not really free consciousness, because the bursting
of the chains is itself only a semantic event and thus psychologically
only confirms the real prison. The problem here, in other words, is
that of an "acting out," not in the sphere of behavior, but on the level
of theory, whereas what would be needed is "*Er-Innerung*," an absolute-
negative inwardization, here of "the consulting room," into itself. The
latter is something that for sure needs to be transcended, but we have
to realize that it would transcend and sublate itself all by itself provided
that one would allow it to be experienced *thinkingly*.

2.1.6 Human emotions versus the soul's archetypal truths

After these preliminary clarifications of the formal issues raised by
Jung's discussion of two different types of literary products, let us look
at his semantic descriptions of them.

The first type, not only represented by the "psychological novel,"
but also by "all the novels dealing with love, the family milieu, crime
and society, together with didactic poetry, the greater number of lyrics,
and drama both tragic and comic" (§ 140), is what "the layman gets
his 'psychology' from" (§ 137). It takes its themes from "the lot of
humankind, repeated millions of times down to the hideous monotony
of court rooms and the penal code. Nothing remains mysterious, for
everything convincingly explains itself in its own terms" (§ 139, transl.
modif.). The experiences described "have nothing strange about them;

---

[71] Cf. Jung's discernment of an analogous problem in Freud of a fundamentally
inadequate frame of mind for what was actually supposed to be expressed by him:
"Basically [Freud] wanted to teach [...] that, regarded from within, sexuality included
spirituality and had an intrinsic meaning. But his concretistic terminology was too narrow
to express this idea." *MDR* p. 152.

on the contrary, it is what is always already known [*das Urbekannte*]: passion and its fated outcome, human destiny and its sufferings, eternal nature and its beauty and horror" (§ 140, transl. modif.), behavior clearly motivated by subjective emotions, fears, desires and informed by subjective mindsets and personality traits. It is "the realm of clearly understandable psychology" (§ 140), i.e., the psychic over against the psychological in my terminology.

The second type, which with works like Goethe's *Faust II,* Dante's *Divine Commedia, Poimandres,* and *Shepherd of Hermas* in mind, Jung calls, rightly or not, "visionary" in contrast to "psychological" [§ 139], is separated from the first by "a gulf." The themes of this type are precisely characterized by the fact that what they describe is "nothing familiar; it has a strange character, an enigmatic nature, [...]. Its value and impact result from the uncanniness[72] of the experience, which, alien and cold or pregnant with meaning and sublime, arises from timeless depths." When it appears as alien and cold, "it bursts asunder our human values and the beauty of our aesthetic forms" and amounts to a "*crimen laesae majestatis humanae,* to use Nietzsche's phrase." When it is pregnant with meaning and sublime, it "can be a revelation whose heights and depths are beyond our fathoming [...]" (§ 141, transl. modif.).

The psychological difference that Jung discerns in literature is, however, not restricted to literature. Literature is for us merely a handy illustration and example of something of general importance. On the one side of Jung's description of this difference we clearly find the human, all-too-human, the ordinary passions, problems, and suffering that have existed as long as there are human beings, all the things that are the daily topics discussed in the consulting rooms of all psychotherapists. Because they are self-explanatory and belong to the realm of "clearly understandable psychology," they are not any concern for psychology proper.[73] Psychology proper begins where something truly alien, not human-all-too-human,

---

[72] *Ungeheuerlichkeit* usually means "enormity, monstrosity." But the adjective *ungeheuer* can also mean "uncanny as if haunted, eery, absolutely out of the ordinary" and I think that this latter sense is rather implied in Jung's context ("alien, cold, enigmatic," etc.) than that of monstrosity.

[73] The other side of Jung's dictum that "It is the *smallest* part *of the psyche,* and in particular of the unconscious, that presents itself in the medical consulting room," is that the greatest part of what presents itself in the consulting room is not of truly *psychological* interest. Rather, it is "what the layman gets his 'psychology' from."

fundamentally not familiar intrudes from out of nowhere into our human sphere.

An example from Jung's own life may make this difference clearer. In *MDR* (p. 314f., transl. modif.) he relates what happened when he was on the way back from his mother's funeral.

> I went home immediately, and while I rode in the night train I had a feeling of great grief, but in my heart of hearts I could not be mournful, and this for a strange reason: during the entire journey I continually heard dance music, laughter, and jollity, as though a wedding were being celebrated. This contrasted violently with the devastating impression the dream [that he had had immediately prior to his mother's death] had made on me. Here was gay dance music, cheerful laughter, and it was impossible to yield entirely to my sorrow. ... I was thrown back and forth between these contrasting emotions.
>
> This paradox can be explained if we suppose that at one moment death was being represented from the point of view of the ego, and at the next from that of the soul. In the first case it appears as a catastrophe ...
>
> From another point of view, however, death appears as a joyful event. In the light of eternity, it is a wedding, a *mysterium coniunctionis*. The soul attains, as it were, its missing half, it achieves wholeness. On Greek sarcophagi the joyous element was represented by dancing girls, on Etruscan tombs by banquets. ... To this day it is the custom in many regions to hold a picnic on the graves on All Souls' Day. Such customs express the feeling that death is a festive occasion.

The grief Jung felt belongs to the "clearly understandable psychology" and is *ipso facto* psychologically insignificant. It is a natural effect in a human being of the situation at hand and as such merely a *psychic* event, not a *psychological* one. The soul in the strict sense is not involved. As Jung explains, it is the moment of death *from the point of view of the ego*. It is only human emotions. Mourning is not the archetypal reaction to death. The fact, however, that in this same situation Jung heard dance music, laughter, and jollity is no longer clearly understandable. In fact it is absolutely alien, even disturbing, shocking, which is why Jung needs to go into his psychological explanations for the uninformed reader to be able to make some sense of it. And the jollity is not *his* emotion at all (as it might have been for somebody who hated his mother and who through her long hoped-for death finally received a rich inheritance), not the emotion of the "civil man" Jung. It is an objective jollity, the "emotion"—if we still want to use this inappropriate word at all—of the soul, the experience of death from the other, non-human side, "in the light of eternity." Subjectively Jung had been very close to his mother and more than that, in a deep underground relation with her, so that his mournful feelings were natural and were *his* exclusive feelings. The jollity intrudes from a non-human[74] sphere into the human sphere and violently contrasts with Jung's own emotion as a human being. This experience of death as a kind of wedding festivity clearly has an archetypal depth.

Because of the simultaneity (or, to be correct, incessant quick alternation) of both feelings in Jung, this experience is a marvelous representation of the psychological difference itself, its representation *as* (i.e., in the medium of) a *psychic* experience. *What* is experienced is both, the psychic emotion and the psychological "emotion," the subjective human feeling and the feeling of the non-human objective soul. But *both* sides of the psychological difference have become here empirical experiences and in this sense psychic. An archetypal experience is the experience *of* something psychological (of a soul event, a soul *truth*), but the *experience* of it is of course something psychic, indeed an ego event. The soul truth is projected from the soul into the ego and converted into the ego's currency: felt experience.

Let me add here that this little example can also be helpful for in general distinguishing between manifestations of *ordinary human emotions* versus *archetypal* experiences. It provides us with a clear criterion. It above all helps us see that the event per se, here the event of death or burial, does not relieve us of the necessity to determine on our own account whether it is human, all-too-human OR archetypal, psychic OR psychological. One and the same type of event can come as an experience either "from the point of view of the ego" OR "from the point of view of the soul, in the light of eternity" (and in such a rare case as Jung's even as both at once). Even such momentous events

---

[74] Of course, this "non-human" sphere is also human. All that is meant is that it is non-ego, non-"civil man," not "human, all-too-human."

as death, birth, baptism, marriage, illness are not *per se* archetypal. They can just as well, and usually are for us, ordinary events of human life, with ordinary and clearly understandable feeling reactions and a just as ordinary meaning. The opposite is of course also true. An everyday event can, in a particular situation for a particular human being, amount to an archetypal revolution, an incursion of the soul.

In therapy confronted, for example, with a patient's suffering from feelings of loneliness, the question that needs to be decided is whether it is a *social* loneliness or a *psychological* one. Feeling alone, having no friends, no intimate relationship, as a social loneliness only leads to simple sadness, simple suffering, where "simple" means psychologically uncomplicated. It is just like being poor and having little to eat. This is certainly uncomfortable, maybe very painful, but not a psychological problem. The solution to such problems has to be pragmatic. First, one has to learn to accept this situation as one's truth, and secondly one has to try to make the best of it and possibly see what can be done to better the situation. It is all very straightforward. Psychology does not have to come onto the scene. If, however, the loneliness felt manifests in the form of symptoms, of a neurotic depression for example, then the soul is involved. The problem of loneliness may then be the form in which an (ultimately neurotic) contradiction manifests, the contradiction between one's *knowing* that one has fallen out of one's *a priori* containment in the fold of some community, family, or meaning and *ipso facto* is now *logically* alone (not merely socially), on the one hand, and one's simultaneous *absolute demand* that this must not be.

Just as we must not attribute an archetypal mystery to our ordinary emotions, love, hate, anger, desire, mourning, etc., we must, conversely, not see in mythical images something that immediately refers to aspects of human life. Speaking only of one single example, the child motif in mythology, Karl Kerényi says: "The divine children's childhood and fate of being orphaned do not have their origin in the stuff of human life, but in the substance of the world's life. What in mythology seems to be biographical is, as it were, an anecdote in which the world tells its own biography [...]."[75] Myth is not speaking about us humans,

---

[75] Karl Kerényi, "Das Urkind," in: *idem, Humanistische Seelenforschung*, München, Wien (Albert Langen, Georg Müller: 1966), pp. 68–115, here p. 93, my transl.

about the empirical, positive-factual aspects of our life. For Kerényi, it is precisely the other way around, inasmuch as according to him the special character of myth is such that for it even the literal events of life are allegories of the mythical truths. Again concerning the motif of the primordial child he says that the rising sun and a newborn child, both as literal natural phenomena, are themselves allegories of the primordial child. "In both ways—in the way of the rising sun and the human newborn and in the way of the mythological child—the *world itself* speaks about origin, birth and childhood. It speaks a language of symbols: one symbol is the sun, another one the human child ('Everything transitory is only a simile') and again another symbol is the primordial child."[76] What Kerényi here calls "the world itself" is what we call the soul and its logical life.

2.1.7 Excursus on "*staged* spontaneous event" and "systematically employed cryptomnesia"

I return to the example of the feelings and inner experience that Jung had when he was on his journey home from his mother's funeral. It served us as a striking illustration of the difference between subjective, human-all-too-human emotions and the experience of a soul truth or archetypal images. I used this example *despite the fact that* in itself the event described by Jung is psychologically not very convincing and must not be taken at face value. There are above all two problems that tend to discredit the psychological validity of the "archetypal" part of it.

The first problem is that the way Jung tells this story, the impression is created as if this hearing of dance music and jollity was a completely spontaneous intrusion and took Jung totally by surprise. Now I do not doubt Jung's veracity about this: I do assume that as he described it, he was *subjectively*—as ego personality—in fact taken by surprise. However, it is most unlikely that objectively, i.e., psychologically, it was an absolutely surprising experience for him. His mother died in 1923. By this time, Jung had widely and thoroughly steeped himself in the symbolism of the soul as it appears in mythology, folklore, ethnology, and religions. We can hardly imagine that in his extensive and passionate studies of the available literature

---

[76] *Ibid.*

on the mythologies of the world, ethnology, folklore, religion, etc., Jung had not come across, and had not long been thoroughly familiar with, the archetypal idea of death as a joyful wedding event prior to his personal experience of the laughter and jollity. The sound of dance music, therefore, in all likelihood emerged in and came to a scholarly informed consciousness and not to an innocent, unsuspecting consciousness. The explanation that Jung adds to his *narrative* of the event *historically* antecedes his experience. He knew.

If so, how is this to be understood?

I will attempt an answer. Jung was a committed psychologist, and psychology meant for him above all the psychology of the "collective" (as he termed it) or archetypal unconscious. He knew beforehand from his studies what death means to the soul and "in the light of eternity." In a situation of a death that directly concerned him, would his being a true depth psychologist not, so to speak, require of him to also actually experience what he *knew* was the archetypal soul meaning of death, rather than that he only dwelled in his egoic feelings of personal grief, like any ordinary layman?

In his early book *Versuch einer Darstellung der psychoanalytischen Theorie* (1913), translated as "The Theory of the Unconscious," Jung discusses the case of a woman who suffered from acute hysteria after she had had a frightful experience with cabhorses. After his detailed analysis of the psychological background and the uncovering of a gruesome experience during her childhood, Jung states,

> The theoretical gain from this story is the clear recognition that an unconscious "intention" or tendency stage-managed the fright with the horses... ... the nocturnal scene with the horses— the starting point of the illness—seems to be only the keystone of a planned edifice. The fright and the apparently traumatic effect of the childhood experience are merely staged, but staged in the peculiar way characteristic of hysteria, so that the *mise en scène* appears almost exactly like a reality (*CW* 4 § 364).

We learn from this example the general insight that what for the subject concerned is an utterly overwhelming, unforeseen, and unwanted emotion, may nevertheless be unconsciously stage-managed by the same subject. Following this line of thought we can say that the intrusion of the noise of dance music, laughter, and jollity into Jung's feeling of great grief seems to be staged in a similar way, similar also in its appearing "almost exactly like a reality," as an intrusive surprise event. There was an unconscious "intention" or tendency that stage-managed this experience, but staged it precisely as a totally spontaneous and unintentional, even disturbing phenomenon. Consciously it was definitely unintentional and surprising, truly intrusive. But unconsciously the event itself, together with its spontaneous and surprising character, was the product of a *mise en scène*. However, in Jung's case a *mise en scène* certainly not for hysterical but for *theoretical* reasons. Jung owed it to his status as inventor of the psychology of the collective unconscious (a) to personally prove himself a true psychologist capable of immediate depth experience and (b) to objectively show that archetypes in fact spontaneously emerge in the psyche in real life. The staging had to be unconscious, it had to be obliterated, in order to "work" as an (apparently) convincing archetypal experience. (Of course, that it was this way, had to be this way is only due to Jung's empiricist stance, his need to semanticize and thus positivize the soul's speculative truths as "facts." If, by contrast, he had opened himself to a thinking in terms of the syntax of the soul it would by no means have been necessary.)

The second problem that supports this thesis of stagedness is the question of the authentic form of a manifestation of the soul truth of death as a *mysterium coniunctionis*. The examples Jung himself gives are in great contrast to his own experience. The representation of dancing girls on Greek sarcophagi, the banquets depicted on Etruscan tombs show that there was a traditional and an, as it were, official, canonical art form of how death was to be presented in those cultures. The custom of a picnic on graves on All Souls' Day was a ritual celebrated by each family of the whole community and visible to all. It was done the same way each year on the same day. No surprise, no spontaneous emergence. In former times, the "wakes," for example in Ireland, and the actual solemn, mournful funeral ceremonies also in certain rural parts of Germany were traditionally ended in a kind of party precisely characterized by frolic and merriment with clearly erotic overtones. Also, in Jung's own city of Zürich, the novelist, Gottfried Keller, had in his to a large extent autobiographical novel *Der Grüne Heinrich* described, about 70 years before the event related by Jung, the old custom of particular dances after a funeral, including hints of the concomitant ancient "wedding" motif.[77] In all these cases, the idea of death as a joyous festivity was part of public life, public knowledge, public customs, and established traditions. It was institutionalized. The laughter and jollity happened "out there" in actual life. The dance music at the funeral party was in fact played and audible to everyone. The Irish wakes often ended with the young people leaving the house of the deceased united as couples. Such marriages were accepted as valid and were thought to be especially happy ones: actual unions, real marriages!

But what Jung describes as his own experience was an absolutely private jollity enclosed within his own mind, an utterly subjective experience by the solitary individual Jung, cut off from the generality. No other passenger in the night train could hear the dance music and the laughter. And even Jung's own "personality No. 1," we might say, could not hear it because "No. 1" was filled with the opposite emotions. The quick alternation between his two contrasting emotions shows that "No. 1" was successfully screened from what "No. 2" experienced.

It is to be assumed that none of the Greeks or Etruscans or any of the peoples who had the described funeral or All Souls' Day customs ever personally heard dance music and laughter in connection with a funeral *in the privacy and silence of their minds*. The authentic form and native home of soul truths is their public, communal, and institutionalized celebration, enactment, or representation. Soul truths are essentially cultural, literally *shared* truths. They exist, in real life, precisely as *ta drômena* and *ta legomena* out in the open: as what is done (enacted) and what is told (and what as such is the official knowledge of the whole community, "the general faith" [*MDR* p. 56] or "the faith of the world" [Hegel]: or, as Jung liked to quote, as *quod semper et ubique et ab omnibus creditur*). "I am inclined to think that things were generally done first and that only a long time afterwards somebody asked a question about them, and then eventually discovered why they were done. ... Faust aptly says: 'Im Anfang war die Tat' (in the beginning was the deed)" (*CW* 18 § 540 and 553). In the

---

[77] Vol. II, chapter 3 (in the revised version of 1880 it is chapter II, 4, where it is significantly entitled "Totentanz," although in a fundamentally different sense from the one that we traditionally connect with this word, the medieval dance of death).

archaic situation people perform the *drômena* the way "they had always done it," "but do not know what they are doing and never have known" (*CW* 8 § 411). Soul truths do not come from and have never been *inside*. They are precisely not born in private individuals ("in their unconscious") and are not distinctly spontaneous. Their authentic home is traditions, what *always already* has been said, believed, and done in the realm of "sharedness." Even "spontaneous" *dreams* and *visions* of individual persons, such as in initiations, followed long-established cultural patterns and merely activated them for the individual.

And to the extent that soul truths appear as gods, those gods also do not reside in the human breast, as William Blake thought. Michael Vannoy Adams insists, in the same vein as Blake, that, "The 'gods' continue to 'exist,' as they always have, in the psyche."[78] As they always have? No. Not always. Never! This is a modern psychologistic superstition. Adams also cites an example taken from Ginette Paris about a young woman who felt induced to buy certain sexy looking sandals on impulse, which elicits from Paris the comment, "Here comes Aphrodite," which in turn is seconded by Adams's assessment that Paris "demonstrates just how mighty Aphrodite still is." I will discuss these ideas later in section 2.3.10 in more detail. But for the moment it must suffice to say that this alleged goddess, Aphrodite, did neither reside in the human breast (be it of the young woman or of Ginette Paris or Adams himself), nor in the phenomenon (the real event itself), but exclusively in the reporting psychologists' *rhetoric about* it, the same way that "the taste of freedom" cannot be tasted in the Marlboro cigarettes and is possibly also not experienced in the psyche, but exclusively "exists" in the Marlboro advertizing rhetoric. As long as gods existed, they resided partly in the inner sanctum of temples built by the community, partly in the sky, in trees and rivers, and other natural phenomena in the real world (which is a fundamentally common world, the world *the way* it is experienced by a traditional perception), and partly in pious devotional practices and rituals performed by the

---

[78] Michael Vannoy Adams, "Does Myth (Still) Have A Function In Jungian Studies? Modernity, Metaphor, and Psycho-Mythology," paper presented at the "Psyche and Imagination" conference of the International Association for Jungian Studies at the University of Greenwich, London, July 7, 2006 (in: http://www.jungnewyork.com/ myth_function.shtml, accessed in Nov. 2009).

community or in sudden epiphanies experienced by individuals or groups, but at any rate "out there" in the real world. "Gods" were the cognitive apperception of the specific aspects of the logic, syntax, or inner truth, of man's actual mode of being-in-the-world as it was constituted at the various stages of cultural development. They were intellectual intuitions, which is why they *appeared* in imaginal form despite the fact that in truth they are concepts.

So what we witness in Jung's description of his after-funeral experience is what we could call *systematic cultural cryptomnesia*, in other words, a cryptomnesia not in the sense of a personal inadvertent "plagiarism" (the subjective conviction that one is oneself the one who generated an idea, whereas in reality it happens to be a copy of something one read long ago, but is not at all aware of), but rather in the sense of the intentional, albeit unconsciously performed translation of cultural public patterns into a private person's subjective inner experience.[79] The subjective experience seems absolutely spontaneously to pop into Jung's consciousness from out of the unconscious, a fact, however, which for us is precisely what makes it ring unconvincing. It seems to be, as Jung liked to see it, an *Urerfahrung*, a primordial, archetypal experience or, as he also termed it, an "*immediate* experience," whereas in reality it is mediated partly by (often subliminal) cultural reminiscences and partly, as above all in Jung's own case here reported, by scholarly learning. It is the—unconscious— staging *as* a vivid, numinous (perhaps even overwhelming) inner event *of* what used to be a public practice or knowledge (and as such an objective soul truth), but has culturally long become obsolete. Inner experience is a subjective substitute for and simulation of former objective soul truths, at a time when these soul truths that were relative to the cultural stage of hunting and agricultural societies have long been superseded because mankind has entered an entirely new mode and logic of being-in-the-world.

A staging precisely for the purpose of retroactively establishing the private "inner" and "the unconscious" or subjective so-called

---

[79] Jung's *Red Book* is the paradigmatic large-scale example of this type of programmatic cryptomnesia: the vast mythological knowledge amassed by Jung through his reading is translated into "spontaneously" emerging (but methodically induced) fantasy experiences. See my "*Liber Novus*, that is, The New Bible. A First Analysis of C.G. Jung's *Red Book*," in: *Spring Vol. 83* (Minding the Animal Psyche), Spring 2010, pp. 361–411.

"archetypal experiences" as the primordial source even of those cultural customs and ideas which in truth are the origin of what now has become internalized and psychologized. At the same time, this staging has the purpose of establishing as "immediate" personal experience and thus as empirical fact the theory of the absolute autonomy of the archetypes as quasi-metaphysical otherworldly entities or powers totally vis-à-vis and independent of a people's cultural behavior and "conscious" life. The archetypes are seen as the true subjects and agents ("factors" in the literal sense) whereas people are merely exposed to them as their objects. It was the intrinsic intent of Jung's archetypal theory to dissolve the uroboric relationship of active *and* passive, conscious *and* unconscious, a posteriori *and* a priori, human production *and* experience, made *and* found, in favor of a dissociation, an undialectical opposition and unambiguous distribution—so as to arrive at a modern substitute for and psychic simulation of a bygone world situation in which human life here was officially experienced as being ruled by almighty gods up there.

I speak of cryptomnesia because the cultural memory—what is known to have once been public knowledge and public cult practice—has now theoretically (and perhaps also experientially) been assigned to and entombed in the *crypt* of "the unconscious," of course by no means for the purpose of getting rid of it there, but for illegitimately and secretly[80] preserving it beyond its time, indeed for mummifying (and thereby "eternalizing") it.

Cryptomnesia in the usual sense is a mishap. What I here call cryptomnesia, by contrast, is a method, a logical (although certainly unconscious and unacknowledged) strategy, we could also say a ritual *on the level of theorizing*. It has to be unconscious and unacknowledged, because if it and the "'intention' or tendency" (so Jung in the above quote) behind it were conscious, it would not work. Such experiences as the one related here by Jung must be considered "keystone[s] of a planned edifice," the edifice of the theory of "*the* unconscious" as the mother of human culture and the archetypes as absolutely independent "factors."

---

[80] I am not suggesting a subjective practice of secrecy, but an objective logical secrecy: the soul truths are logically set up as once and for all radically removed and dissociated from public conscious life by being "crypted," if I may say so, and thereby also insulated, immunized.

But as already Jean Gebser succinctly put it, "there is not a so-called unconscious. There are only different kinds (or intensities) of consciousness ...."[81] The soul is consciousness. It is subjectivity. But consciousness is in itself the unity of itself and its other. Only consciousness can be unconscious. A stone is not unconscious (and does of course not have an unconscious). Even if there is not "THE unconscious," substantiated as a separate region of the mind and an agent (author) or as a reservoir of archaic impulses (Freud) or, in the form of the idea of the collective unconscious, of archetypal images (Jung), there is unconscious*ness* (and plenty of it!); there is the possibility that consciousness is unconscious to a lesser or greater degree. Jung once spoke directly of "consciousness's becoming unconscious" (*CW* 12 § 563, transl. modif.). We should use "unconscious" only as an adjective, describing states or degrees of consciousness, and never as a noun, which would turn it into a substance. And this adjective can be used to describe (a) the state of consciousness or (b) a quality of objects and facts (whether and to what degree they are conscious to, known by, a consciousness and present in the mind or not).

2.1.8 The soul's coldness

It is noteworthy that in his description of the two types of literary works quoted above, Jung stressed the enigmatic, uncanny, and cold character of the experiences that belong to the true sphere of the psychological. The criterion is not the *degree* of emotion caused by a happening; the crucial difference is not the quantitative differences between a minor mishap that one might get over relatively easily, on the one hand, and a true disaster, on the other, i.e., between petty misfortunes and truly tragic misery. Both such possibilities belong to the same realm of "clearly understandable psychology" and therefore fall outside the sphere of true psychology, because even veritable disasters belong to "eternal nature and its beauty and horror" and thus to what is "always-already known." The question is also not whether an event is *subjectively* absolutely unexpected, unheard of, and singular *for* a particular individual who so far has lived in undisturbed harmony, but whether what happens is objectively alien, objectively bursting

---

[81] Jean Gebser, *Ursprung und Gegenwart*, dtv edition, vol. 1, 1973, p. 290, my transl.

asunder our (or an individual's) human values and aesthetic forms as such: the logic of our (or his) world. In other words, the difference is not one of our personal feelings and emotions; it is a logical one. This is what makes it a *"crimen laesae majestatis humanae."* Emotions are heated, hot. But as Jung points out, what arises "from timeless depths" is *cold.*[82] What hurts our feelings, disturbs our peace, destroys our hopes and wishes and as such is perhaps a narcissistic blow to us is one thing. The *"crimen laesae majestatis humanae"* is a totally different thing. The former befalls the ego personality or the psyche (in the terminological sense), the latter befalls the soul, where "soul" means the organ in us humans that is open to the "cold" logic of our being-in-the-world, and this is why it is called uncanny. What is uncanny, eery, mysterious seems to come from a logically or ontologically other world (Jung thus says figuratively, e.g.: "from the abyss of prehuman ages or from a superhuman world" § 141); as such it threatens the entire logical constitution of consciousness or the very syntax or truth of our world itself, our belief-system, whereas a terrible fate merely destroys things, beings, or empirical conditions *in* this world; "only" our empirical existence, well-being, happiness or our hopes and plans *within* this world. Only the former threats are truly terrible for us because they threaten us in our soul, whereas we are wont to take the latter ones in our stride. As already the Stoic Epictetus put it, "What really upsets people is not the factual events, but the fixed notions [*dogmata*] about the factual events" (*Encheiridion* 5[83]).

The "coldness" of the soul in the sense of emotionlessness also shows in those actions that clearly are in the service of soul: rituals. Thomas Hardy once noted,

> A traditional pastime is to be distinguished from a mere revival
> in no more striking feature than in this, that while in the revival

---

[82] "Cold" refers back to the etymology of the Greek word *psychê*, which is related to *psychros*, "cold, chill, frigid, frosty" and points to the ghostliness of the *psychê* as "cool breath" (cf. *CW* 9i § 55). The *CW*, by translating Jung's "kalt" in our present passage with "chilling the blood," destroy his very point. Whereas Jung describes the objective quality of what arises from timeless depths, *its* chilliness and thus ghostliness, bloodlessness, "chilling the blood" focuses on the human subject and its (despite the chilled blood!) always *heated, excited* emotion, as if with the experience of soul we were in a horror movie. In terms of the quote from Hardy that I give in the next paragraph, we could say the *CW* translation aims for "excitement and fervour," whereas Jung's statement is characterized by "a stolidity and absence of stir" that shows that the soul's coldness is *logical* coldness.

[83] Ταράσσει τοὺς ἀνθρώπους οὐ τὰ πράγματα, / Ἀλλὰ τὰ περὶ τῶν πραγμάτων δόγματα.

all is excitement and fervour, the survival is carried on with a stolidity and absence of stir which sets one wondering why a thing that is done so perfunctorily should be kept up at all. Like Balaam and other unwilling prophets, the agents seem moved by an inner compulsion to say and do their allotted parts whether they will or no. This unweeting manner of performance is the true ring by which, in this refurbishing age, a fossilized survival may be known from a spurious reproduction.[84]

The same perfunctory mode of performance applies to rituals. They don't appeal to the ego and its emotional satisfaction. They aim for the objective fulfillment of the soul, for the representation in concrete reality of the soul's (otherwise hidden, irrepresentable) logic, for its becoming *true*, apparent (*offenbar, a-lêtheia*: unconcealedness). Rituals are the soul's concrete performance and celebration in real life of (specific aspects of) its own truth. An "event of truth," on the one hand, and a "happening" in our modern sense as an emotional event, on the other, exclude each other. No doubt, the soul, being absolute-negative, needs people to perform the ritual for it, but beyond their being needed and used as a means for in fact *going through the motions* of the ritual,[85] empirical or "civil" man or the ego drops away altogether. Subjective emotions and the personal experience of "meaning" or "the numinous" are what the modern ego (who is fundamentally a "tourist") longs for, but do not count in the performance of rituals. Subjective emotion is the modern substitute for the *logical motion* or *motive logic* that finds its objective representation and sensible enactment (going through the motion) in rituals. The performance of rituals is not about the persons and what they feel or think and what it means to them, which is why Jung introduced the concept of the *objective* psyche, i.e., the soul.

To this we can add what Cesáreo Bandera, an ethnologist who for years studied how rituals were performed in India, once stated in a discussion: "But even the question of believing or disbelieving is not of fundamental importance. The only important thing is to do the

---

[84] Thomas Hardy, *The Return of the Native*, Harmondsworth (Penguin Books) 1978, p. 178.

[85] *Oportet me adesse* (it is indispensable that I am present)!

rituals in the prescribed manner."[86] Similarly Jung noted concerning the Communion ceremony he participated in as a boy, "I had the impression that here something was performed and executed in the traditionally correct manner. My father [the minister], too, seemed to go to great pains to execute it above all according to rule [...]" (*MDR* p. 54, transl. modif.). What counts is solely the correct representation in visible reality of the objective logic of the matter.

2.1.9 The twofoldness of what we call soul

The jollity connected with death the way it showed itself to Jung is an event of soul because it expresses the truth about death, in contrast to our subjective, human-all-too-human feelings about death. The coldness of the soul comes from soul having the character of truth. Our theory must not place truth in the "collective unconscious." It is not something collective, but communal, or rather: something that has the status of a logical universal (the objective character of sharedness). And as truth it is in itself conscious, intelligible, illumined: disclosedness (*alêtheia*), something that has always given rise to the light metaphor. It is not, as is the case with archetypes, unconscious fact as mere subsisting pattern and dominant of consciousness.[87] Truth in its most general sense means life's having opened up into the internal *clearance* (*Lichtung* in Heidegger's sense) of the psychological difference, a clearance which was mythologically expressed, for example, in the wide-spread images of a world tree or culture hero (Atlas) holding heaven and earth apart and in the stories of a primordial bloody disruption of the eternal embrace (*gamos*) of Father Heaven and Mother Earth, which in turn were ritually enacted

---

[86] *Violent Origins*, ed. by Robert G. Hamerton-Kelly, Stanford (Stanford Univ. Press: 1987), p. 187.

[87] However, we must not overlook the fact that late Jung also tried to give expression to basically the same idea of an internal dialectic of psychological truth by comprehending the *unconscious* (his term for soul) as a multiple *consciousness* and as luminosity, as *scintillae*, "sparks" (*CW* 8 §§ 388 ff.). "[N]uminosity entails luminosity" (§ 388). But of course, due to his dogmatic "empiricism" and by way of disownment, he had to cloak this *his* late conception of the soul in the "objective," but in itself obscure (not-luminous), form of quasi "mythological" images *found* above all in alchemy. He felt that he was not allowed to speak of such matters on his own responsibility. And he presented his view as a kind of distant ultimate vision, without feeling impelled to turn it, a late result of his thinking, into the basis and starting point of his theory about the soul, that is to say, to revise his scheme of the unconscious accordingly.

in corresponding sacrificial acts. More specifically, truth here means the actual logic of being-in-the-world, the actual logic of existence, of lived life. Because the logic of being-in-the-world is complex, it has many aspects which amount to diverse *moments* of truth in the plural. Soul events show truths. And soul consists of truths.

But this is only the one half of soul. The other half is the soul as *organ* of truth: the receptive organ for the soul truths. The soul is the unity and difference of its own truths and its own potential to apperceive and appreciate those truths and enact them. In this sense the soul, which we know is not an entity, in its totality is a *relation*, the same relation of correspondence as the one that exists between the sun and the eye. Plotinus (*Enneads* I, 6, 9): "Never would the eye have seen the sun if it were not itself sun-like...." And Goethe seconded: "If the eye were not sun-like, / How could we behold the light? / If God's own potency did not live in us, / How could what is divine delight us?"[88]

If the soul is truth, it *is* a knowing, it *is* consciousness. Forget the unconscious. The truth is only truth if it knows itself. Only like can know like. That which is known is the soul in the objective sense, and that which knows is the same soul as the apperceiving and enacting soul. The soul is self-relation. This was in olden times depicted in the symbol of the uroboros, about which we hear from the alchemists that it is "the tail-eater, which is said to beget, kill, and devour itself" (*CW* 16 § 454). Production and reception are contradictorily united.

Although in the objective sense the truths produced by the soul *implicitly* are already in themselves truths and thus a knowing, they nevertheless also need to be explicitly known by the soul. The soul wants and needs to know itself. The logic of being-in-the-world wants to come to light. It wants to become explicit. Soul truths need to be *made true*. This is what soul-making is about. It is not enough for truth to be in itself true, in itself luminous. It in addition has to become true in the world, be released into its actually being true (ἀλήθεια, *Unverborgenheit*, unconcealment). This means it needs to be acknowledged and objectively represented, indeed celebrated. Rituals, mythic narratives, hymns, religious dogmas, the

---

[88] "Wär' nicht das Auge sonnenhaft / Wie könnten wir das Licht erblicken? / Lebt' nicht in uns des Gottes eigne Kraft, / Wie könnt' uns Göttliches entzücken?" From *Zur Farbenlehre. Didaktischer Teil. Einleitung* (1810).

"non-psychological works of literature" in Jung's sense, art and metaphysics are the major forms in which the soul's truths find objective expression. Truths, in addition to being true by origin, also want to be explicitly released into their truth. They need to become what they have been all along.

But if there is an "eye" that is able to see the "sun," if "soul" means the twofoldness of *logos eôn* (subsisting logic, Heraclitus) or soul truth AND the public celebration of those truths, their thereby being *made* true (soul-making), does this not contradict the thesis of the soul's fundamental avertedness (that I will discuss more closely in the next sections)? It would be a mistake to think so. The "eye" that sees the "sun" must not be confused with people's eyes. The public celebration of the soul's truth such as in openly enacted rituals is the soul's celebrating its own truth by releasing it into its being true, the soul's self-relation and self-correspondence, not people's personal celebration, despite the fact that they of course are the ones who are needed to perform the rituals. If the human persons enacting the rituals (or whatever other forms of celebration) tried to be the actual subject of this celebration and perform it on their own authority, it would precisely have lost its truth. The soul makes *itself*, it becomes true to itself—even if only through humans. We may here be reminded of the theological view that a prayer is only a true prayer if it is already God who through one's human praying is speaking the prayer to God, in other words, *not* the human person per se—not the ego.

2.1.10 Practical gain versus blessedness

About that fundamental historical change to be observed at, and even prior to, his time and briefly sketched out above in my discussion of the demise of the concept of soul, Hegel wrote in the Preface to the First Edition of his *Science of Logic*,

> Theology, which in former times was the guardian of the speculative mysteries and of metaphysics (although this was subordinate to it) had given up this science in exchange for feelings, for what was popularly matter-of-fact, and for historical erudition. In keeping with this change, there vanished from the world those solitary souls which were sacrificed by their people and exiled from the world to the end that the eternal should be

contemplated and served by lives devoted solely thereto—not
for any practical gain but for the sake of blessedness [...]."[89]

Nicht um eines Nutzens, sondern um des Segens willen! The difference
here is that between utilitarian purposes and the purpose of
blessedness. It is not simply two different motivations, but there is a
diametrical opposition between them, as Hegel's description makes
clear: "vanished from the world," "solitary souls sacrificed by their
people," "exiled from the world."

When as Jungians hearing of the purpose that the eternal should
be contemplated, we are of course reminded of utterances of Jung's
like the following presenting a similar contrast:

> You see, man is in need of a symbolic life—badly in need. We
> only live banal, ordinary, rational, or irrational things—which
> are naturally also within the scope of rationalism, otherwise
> you would not call them irrational. But we have no symbolic
> life. (*CW* 18 § 625)

And when Hegel speaks of lives devoted solely to the contemplation
of the eternal, that other passage of Jung's comes to mind about the
"fact that the primitive Australians sacrifice to it [the symbolic life]
two-thirds of their available time—of their lifetime in which they are
conscious" (*CW* 18 § 649). In our context, where we try to acquire a
concept of "soul," we are exclusively interested in the two contrasted
categories. What I called "the psychic" comprises, with respect to
the sphere of motivations or purposes, all pragmatic, useful, goal-
directed intentions and strivings. We need food, we need shelter,
we need consolation, we want comfort, pleasure, love,
entertainment, we choose what we think is to our advantage and
benefit, we long for companionship and partnership, some of us
strive for knowledge and insight, we may want to become famous or
rich, we try to stay or get healthy, we plan to secure our future and
that of our children. And even where we shortsightedly or stupidly
choose a momentary benefit and through it incur a long-lasting painful
disadvantage, we nevertheless are motivated by the purpose of a practical
gain. Of course, all the concerns and conflicts within the "social arena,"

---

[89] *Hegel's Science of Logic*, translated by A.V. Miller, Atlantic Highlands, NJ
(Humanities Paperback Library: 1989), pp. 25f.

the whole complications of "object-relations" and the "family romance" in Freud's sense, are governed by ego desires and fears—and thus by practical considerations.

The opposite case is human behavior motivated by the needs, intentions, and telos of the soul. To build huge pyramids and to bury treasures of immense monetary as well as cultural value in them is clearly not practically useful. The entire cult of the dead, rationalistically considered, does not make sense. Human and animal sacrifices, especially the Aztecs' sacrificially killing hundreds or thousands of humans at one time, does not serve any practical gain or benefit. To stand on a pillar in the desert as a stylite has no conceivable pragmatic purpose. To die a heroic death to gain fame or to commit *harakiri* to protect one's honor is not exactly in the interest of life. According to Jung, Pueblo Indians performed rituals every day to enable the sun, their Father, to go across the sky. Also not very useful, inasmuch as the sun goes across the sky anyway and all by itself. All these things are clearly done "for the sake of blessedness," that is, for the soul.

Of course, nowadays we witness certain people trying to construe some sort of "evolutionary advantage" even of the cult of the dead, of sacrifices, etc. But these totally unconvincing attempts require a rather twisted mind and amount to a leveling of a category difference. It is the reductive desire to take even the very category of blessedness prisoner for the category of practical usefulness and to establish the latter as the exclusive one. (Another matter, however, is that once certain social customs and values have been established, it becomes possible that a person abuses for practical ego purposes an activity that *in itself* is for the sake of blessedness, for example, a hypocrite; one can practice charity to enhance one's reputation, perform some feat that goes along with enormous hardships to get into the *Guinness Book of World Records*. But this does not explain why those in themselves not useful activities received such high esteem and were instituted in the first place.)

For the Romans, a person's birthday was the holiday of his *genius* and not his own. For us it is the special day of the person as ego-personality ("Happy birthday *to you...*"). This contrast allows us once more to see the reversal of focus and direction that is the essence of the psychological difference. In the one case I revolve around myself;

I celebrate myself. In the other case I revolve around "him," the *genius*; I celebrate the other, the soul. Hegel's distinction between practical gain and blessedness can also be understood in terms of this fundamentally different directionality, just as can Hardy's distinction between the stolidity with which traditional pastimes used to be performed and the excitement and fervor of modern revivals or modern festivities. True rituals are for the sake of the respective "soul content" or "soul truth." *It* is what is celebrated. *Its* gratification is what rituals are about, and this is what "blessedness" means: that the soul finds *its* fulfillment. *Ipso facto* true rituals imply a negation of the ego personality, a decided disregard for the gratification of the ego, for the emotions, concerns, and desires that "we" have.

What I mentioned concerning the *genius*/human person relation in Roman antiquity calls of course to mind a pertinent passage by Jung about Socrates' *daimonion*. After some critical comments in a very late letter about Socrates, Jung continued: "But at least he has shown us the one precious thing: 'To hell with the Ego-world! Listen to the voice of your *daimonion*. It has a say now, not you'" (*Letters 2*, p. 532, 9 Jan 1960, to Charteris). Jung makes the negation of the human person explicit: "not you." On the other hand, Jung's emotion-laden and aggressive diction ("To hell with...!") shows clearly that he is himself a child of the modern world and is speaking from the standpoint of the very Ego-world that he wants to send to hell. Otherwise, his rebellious language and the conscious effort implied by the imperative he uses (which is naturally directed at the ego-personality, at whom else?) would not be necessary. For the Romans to celebrate the *genius* rather than the person who had a birthday had been a matter of course, the complying not only with an established tradition, but also, which is much more important, with an objective, self-evident truth, a truth that simply prevailed without any human effort (much like Heraclitus's *logos eôn* [subsisting logos]). For Jung, it is no longer a truth. It is something he *wants* to be, something he fights for, a "psycho-political" program, if I may say so, to be carried out ("acted out") by us, in other words, as an ego effort (which is counter-productive). "But at least," so we might apply Jung's words to himself, "he has shown us the one precious thing," namely, the logical structure of the psychological difference: it, not you.[90]

The psychological difference found also static expression in pairs of "geographical" symbols or metaphorical *topoi* vis-à-vis each other. Mythology, fairytales, and theology are full of such motifs. The *village* in fairytales or the *city* (*polis*) are the realm of civilization, of cultivated fields and socially regulated life: of the fenced-in "garden" of ordinary human existence. The *woods* in fairytales, but also the land on the other side of a river, mountain range, or border, by contrast, stand for the sphere of the soul, of the uncanny and mysterious, if not the underworld. They are intramundane images for the beyond, the otherworldly; a horizontal or semantic expression for the vertical dimension. Likewise, the hermit's *desert* or the lama's *mountain* world are contrasts to the ordinary human-all-too-human life sphere. The *world* in the sense of the worldly, the *saeculum*, empirical *reality*, and the *vale of tears* belong to the I or the ego, whereas Paradise, the Kingdom of God, the underworld, Elysium and hell, the City of God, and the heavenly Jerusalem are images for the home of the soul. In a temporal (mytho-historical) sense the Iron Age and the Kali Yuga contrast with the Golden Age. In addition, we have of course the more abstract opposition of the sacred and the profane.

2.2 A HISTORICAL COMPLICATION

Rituals, myths, symbols (and the soul's truth in general) are not only *not* for the sake of people and their benefit. They are for the sake of blessedness. The converse of this is that strictly practical-minded people also have no use for and no understanding of them. It is inherent in the very nature of the ego or (modern) empirical man that he stands with his back turned to the soul. It is an illusion that there could possibly be a *Relation between the Ego and the Unconscious*,[91] if we take "the unconscious" as Jung's covert term for the soul and not merely for the ego's own repressed or ignored contents. It is more than folly. It is a sowing of a terrible confusion, a leveling of the psychological difference. The moment there would indeed be such a relation, the

---

[90] Just as in his later years he had discovered that "the unconscious" (as he called it) was itself a multiple consciousness, itself luminosity.

[91] Title of one essay in Jung's *CW* 7.

ego would have ceased being ego. But usually, in wide-spread Jungian pop psychology "in this refurbishing age" with its "spurious reproductions" or, better, *simulations*, there is not a real relation between the two. There is only the pretense that the ego's indulging itself in particular ones of its own ego contents—namely fascinating images of a "mythic" quality and experiences of something allegedly "sacred" or "numinous" (that are given out as soul)—is such a relation. If the soul is non-ego, as we know from Jung, the negation here is not an indifferent one simply meaning "something else than," as in the statement that a bed is not a door and not a dog. It is the active negation of on principle or by definition refusing a relation and thus: impossibility of a connection.

2.2.1 Avertedness of the I versus blindness of the modern ego

Let us here come back to what we heard from Jung above about the fundamental difference of soul and empirical man or ego (illustrated by one particular example he gave). "Heaven and hell are fates meted out to the soul and not to civil man, who in his nakedness and dullness would have no idea of what to do with himself in a heavenly Jerusalem" (*CW* 9i § 56, transl. modif.). We could even go a step further than Jung and say that a heavenly Jerusalem (or a hell, for that matter) simply would not exist at all for the ego. The ego could not even be bored by it. It is the very job of the ego to be blind to the soul. But whereas the real blind could stumble over an object and in this way become aware of it, the ego cannot even stumble over manifestations of the soul, because its blindness is logical or ontological, not just empirical. When the ego stumbles over something, even if it should in fact be the soul, it only finds more "ego," but not soul.

We have to distinguish between the I, which is part of our being human, and the ego as a particular historical, namely modern, constitution of consciousness or self-definition of man (Jung's empirical or civil man). Even long before there was what we call the ego, there was already a fundamental *avertedness of the I from the soul*. The counterpart to the irrevocable avertedness of the I from the soul is the fundamental *departedness of the soul for the I*. Both the avertedness and the departedness are two sides of the same coin and describe the primordial and authentic relation between I and soul, the psychological difference, and the *contra naturam* quality of soul, its (logical) coldness, ghostliness. Thinking back of formulations in the quote above from Hegel about the decisive difference between "practical gain" and "blessedness," we can say that soul comes precisely into being only by being cast out, "exiled from the world," severed from the ordinary life of people, averted from "us." There has to be a "sacrifice." For soul to *be*, the I has to let go of it and give the psychological difference, the negation, its due. That the soul is not for the benefit and enjoyment of the human beings as "civil persons" can clearly be seen from the fact that, e.g., the ancient Egyptians buried their greatest works of art in pyramids and royal graves where they were never supposed to be seen by humans. Similarly, in European medieval cathedrals sculptures and paintings were often put up at places so high and dark that nobody could see and appreciate them. Human seeing was not the point. This shows that the soul's life is not only in fact self-serving, an end in itself, but that it also has to be explicitly allowed and acknowledged to be intrinsically self-serving, if there is to be soul at all. It is not about us and for our sake.[92]

The departedness of the soul also shows in the fact that the soul historically first came into being through the cult of the dead, through the sight of the corpse of literally departed ones, and that often offerings to the dead were given to them by the sacrificer with an averted face or body. What on this archaic level of consciousness was in this way played out concretistically is the visible display of the logical nature of soul. There is a picture by Jakob Böhme, repeatedly referred to by Jung (e.g., *CW* 9i p. 297, Fig. 1), of two half-circles back to back within a larger circle. If we interpret the two half-circles as a representation of the human being and the soul, we must say that this image depicts the authentic, not, as Jung saw it, a false, pathological way of how I and soul stand "vis-à-vis" each other. It is not the depiction of a neurotic dissociation. The avertedness of the I from the soul is one thing; the systematic blindness to, and neurotic dissociatedness of the modern positivistic ego from, the soul is wholly another.

---

[92] This again shows that our modern striving in psychology for our self-development, self-actualization, and "individuation" as well as our longing for "meaning" belong to the sphere of "practical gain" and revolve around the ego. They have nothing (or at best only little) to do with soul. The wish for meaning is a wish for self-gratification.

Nevertheless this depiction has its shortcomings. It presents the ego and the soul as realities on the same level. In this way the fundamentally different dimensions to which they belong get lost. I therefore prefer our earlier distinction between horizontality (the world of everyday pragmatic consciousness, today particularly the positivistic world of the modern ego) and verticality (the reality of the soul). The sphere of soul is, as it were, at right angles to the world of the ego. This is why if soul makes itself felt in reality, it experientially comes as a veritable intrusion, incursion, and crosses our will, as Jung often put it.

As I already pointed out in the section above on the *soul* sense of "exceptional," the notion of intrusion, incursion, needs some differentiations. Let us take, for example, an eruption of a volcano or an earthquake that destroys a village. On the phenomenological level, this is certainly an intrusion into the normal world. It may even turn out to be a truly catastrophic intrusion. But nevertheless it is—for adults with some experience in the world—a natural event, an empirical fact, a positivity. It may be totally unexpected, but as a natural event it still belongs to our familiar world, being known to be one of the manifestations of nature that can possibly occur. The experience of this event thus falls into the realm of the human, all-too-human. As part of an intra-worldly process, it happens on one and the same plane of all other natural happenings and can in this sense be called horizontal. True, the eruption comes from the depth of the earth, but *this* depth, *this* verticality as empirical-factual one is itself "horizontal," because it does not interfere with the normal logic of the world. Those experiences, by contrast, that are the proper subject of psychology proper *logically* penetrate the plane of the positive-factual nexus of events, confronting us with something fundamentally alien and mysterious. It is the logical intrusion, or the intrusion of something threatening the very logic of our consciousness, that is meant by "verticality."

My example of the eruption of a volcano also helps us to see one other thing. In mythological ages, such things as the eruption of a volcano, earthquakes, the eclipse of the sun, and clefts in the earth were precisely experienced as phenomena in which "verticality" in our sense became accessible. Whereas we, with our natural-scientific understanding of nature, see in them "horizontal" events or positive facts to be explained by science, for the archaic mind something numinous, something divine, manifested itself. The mythic or imaginal mode of experiencing therefore sees such phenomena as "symbols," that is to say as special empirical objects or events within the horizontal world in which, however, the presence of the vertical became true.

2.2.2 The fundamental deficiency of the imaginal mode outweighed by premodern man's unbornness

This is a point where the problem mentioned above of the inadequacy of the frame of mind or style of thinking for what is to be expressed becomes visible once more. It is the *fundamental* inadequacy of the imaginal or semantic mode (pictorial thinking mode) for the psychological. Undoubtedly, on the level of the consciousness of those times, it was truly the logical verticality that was experienced in the eruption of a volcano. But this logical verticality is only what is *meant*. It is not actually and truly *expressed* in this eruption because this eruption is clearly only a horizontal verticality. A cleft in the earth, imaginally experienced as an entrance into the underworld, was certainly felt to be this entrance that it was supposed to be, but even for those people it was clear that it was not literally an entrance to the underworld, but an ordinary crack twenty or a few hundred meters deep. The crack is merely *supposed to* or *claimed* to express the logical truth of "underworld," but it does not in fact and objectively *express* it by itself. As appropriate as it was for an archaic or medieval form of consciousness, in itself the imaginal or mythological is a fundamentally deficient mode for expressing what is actually supposed to be expressed. "It must generally be noted," said Hegel, "that *in images* [...] a deeply speculative content cannot be represented in its peculiar, truthful way and therefore essentially not without contradiction."[93] In our example it is the contradiction between the alleged infinity (an opening to the underworld) and the thoroughly finite reality of the cleft in the earth.

---

[93] G.W.F. Hegel, *Vorlesungen über die Philosophie der Religion. Die vollendete Religion*, ed. by W. Jaeschke, Hamburg (Meiner, Philosophische Bibliothek no. 461) 1995, p. 42. My translation. Hegel does not say that a deeply speculative content *cannot be represented* in images at all; he only states that such a representation cannot really do justice to it in its essence. Such a representation will inevitably fall short of what it is supposed to represent. Images, as images, are *structurally* deficient modes of expression for speculative, that is, soul contents.

All soul truths are "deeply speculative contents."[94] Images qua images, that is, as inevitably belonging to the realm of sensibility, even if it is sublimated and sublated sensibility (poetic imagination), merely *suggest, intimate* what is actually meant by them, namely the soul truths, but they do not manage to really make these soul truths actually explicit in their "truthful way." Images (the same applies of course to ritual enactments and symbolic objects) are, as it were, merely "visual aids."

The symbol therefore works only for a consciousness that manages successfully to completely ignore what is empirically seen and to fundamentally downgrade to total insignificance what is already known. An archaic and even a medieval consciousness has no difficulty with this. In fact, it comes natural to it. Such a consciousness is still given over to, and thus easily impressed and seduced by, what the images *suggest*, the "suggestive power of primordial images" (*CW* 7 § 269).[95] The power of the soul truths is so great, they are still so close and so immediately, so *overwhelmingly* evident to a consciousness contained in and absorbed into the soul, that it needs only some little thing or event in empirical reality that, on account of its representing a slight sensual analogy to a soul truth, offers itself as a "sensory aid" and trigger for symbolic or mythic experience—and whoosh! this soul truth has made itself actually (although merely implicitly) present in

---

[94] There are two other deficiencies of the imaginal images. First, the image gives to the respective content the *form* of independent existence vis-à-vis the experiencing consciousness, the form of an other. It objectifies, personifies, substantiates, reifies that which is actually the soul's own property, a moment of its own logical life, its thinking. The image is not capable of giving the content the form of subjectivity, the form of self. Imaginal thinking is always a (soft) kind of literalism. Secondly, precisely because of having been given the form of independent existence, the image is free-floating (it has no specific time, no locality; it appears to be good for any time and any place). It is incapable of actually comprehending (*begreifen*, grasping, penetrating, overreaching) the Real that it is about. It can only be a "model" *in the light of which* you may try to see the Real. It remains aloof, "ideal." It belongs to the sphere of the virginal anima. There once was a book entitled, *Images of the Untouched* (edited by Joanne Stroud and Gail Thomas, Dallas, Spring Publications, 1982). I am not commenting on this book, but only on this title phrase. This phrase has to be applied to itself: whatever the image is an image of is *ipso facto* untouched by the image *qua* image, just as conversely the image itself is immune to what it is an image of.

[95] I think this formulation by Jung needs some reworking. With his term "primordial images" (more correctly translated it would be "unconscious images"), he means what is actually the truths of the soul. These soul truths, however, are not really "suggestive." They are simply true and as such attractive and *seductive for* a consciousness still enwrapped in soul. Rather, it is the visual, imaginal, representational aspect of symbols, pictures, gestures, and ritual performances that have this suggestive power, and *what* they suggest is the actual presence of those truths.

this real event or thing with full force. In this status of consciousness the soul truths fundamentally outshine, eclipse, and overlay the positive-factual aspects of real-life events (which in our scientifically trained view seem so evident and absolutely dominant).

In this spirit, Jung, talking about certain particular Christian dogmas, pointed out that while "for us the object of belief is no longer inherently convincing" and, furthermore, while for us "[t]he dogma of the trinity, the divine nature of the Redeemer, the Incarnation through the Holy Ghost, Christ's miraculous deeds and resurrection, are more conducive to doubt than to belief," "[t]his was not so in earlier centuries, with their very limited knowledge of nature.[96] It needed no *sacrificium intellectus* to believe in miracles, and the report of the birth, life, death, and resurrection of the Redeemer could still pass as biography" (*Letters 2*, p. 485, to Tanner, 12 Feb 1959).[97] Archaic consciousness is still unborn, still contained in the soul as if in a womb; it thus is in all *essential* regards (concerning the speculative truths) for the most part the exponent and executive agent of the soul, which under those circumstances is the true subject in man.[98] The soul truths are immediately and truly *convincing* for it, indeed captivating.

This also means that for premodern man the soul's truths were not at all what Jung described as the distinctive mark of veritable soul phenomena, namely that they are "nothing familiar," have a "strange character," and threaten to "burst[-] asunder our human values and the beauty of our aesthetic forms" (see section 2.1.6 above). In a certain sense they were much rather precisely completely familiar, even "*das Urbekannte* [what is always already known]" (which was one of the

---

[96] Jung, I think, suggests here a wrong causality. It is not our gaining more extensive and reliable knowledge of nature that removed us from, and blocks for us the way to, the soul truths. It is man's having been born out of the soul in a long historical process and thus his inevitably having lost consciousness's intimate and immediate proximity to the soul truths which made it possible in the first place to gain that kind of scientific knowledge of nature that we have.

[97] For the same reason, but in the very different *secular* area of Greek and Roman historical writings, the long verbatim speeches allegedly given by historical personages in certain important situations, speeches *invented* by the respective historians and placed into the mouths of these personages, could pass as history, as their actually spoken words: fictional story and positive-factual historical reality were simply not yet seen as mutually exclusive opposites. The truth character lay in the power and rhetoric of the text, rather than in any factual evidence (e.g., proof through authentic documentation).

[98] This is not to say that archaic man could not perceive and decide rationally and pragmatically in the sphere of life *not* concerned with speculative truths, i.e., in the sphere of the human, all-too-human.

terms with which Jung had described the very opposite of the soul truths, the events in the sphere of the human, all-too-human). The strangeness and unconvincingness for consciousness of the objects of religious belief, of miracles, visionary experiences, and, to go back to our example from section 2.1.6, of the experience, "in the light of eternity," of death as a joyous wedding festivity with laughter, jollity, and dancing results from the fact that for modern, born man the soul truths have inevitably receded into the *privacy* and silence of the individual's mind. They are no longer, cannot be any longer, *shared* truths, publicly enacted, celebrated, part of "the general faith" or "the faith of the world."

Because in the premodern situation it is really the soul that is experiencing its own truths *through* the human being, the event of a soul mystery can be experienced quite calmly and soberly. It is a deeply fulfilling *truth*, something intelligible, logical. It is nothing mind-blowing for consciousness, but *a priori* deeply familiar. No need for excitement and a big stir. No "numinosity" as an emotional experience. This unbornness of man is the *sine qua non* for myths and symbols.

The consciousness of modern man has been born out of this containment in the soul, out of the realm of *shared* speculative truths.[99] Modern consciousness experiences on its own account and *ipso facto* apperceives soul truths in the fundamental privacy of the individual mind, as personal experiences. This is why modern man can generally no longer experience real life events as a manifestation of the presence of gods or other soul truths and why it now would need a *sacrificium intellectus* to do so as well as to believe in miracles and accept the birth of Christ from a virgin at face value. Verticality has no chance; modern consciousness starts out from the unquestionable presupposition that everything has an explanation in terms of horizontality (either in terms of empirical causality or of having to be understood as merely symbolic, allegorical, or imaginal[100]). Only in certain niches, in special reserves within the dominant modern consciousness, or as certain erratic

---

[99] It is not that the realm of sharedness has been left altogether. The world of facts, our scientific knowledge, but also much of subjective (egoic) opinions, beliefs, ideologies, and emotions have their place in the sphere of sharedness. It is only the speculative truths that have irrevocably left the status of shared truths.

[100] Which, as we know from Jung, means that the symbol is dead (*CW* 6 § 816). "No sooner do you know that this thing is symbolic than you say, 'Oh, well, it presumably means something else.' Doubt has killed it, has devoured it" (*CW* 18 § 632). The distinction, dissociation, between the literal and the imaginal or metaphoric *is* the death (negation, sublation) of the symbol.

remnants of bygone modes, can modern man have some weak analogue to mythic and symbolic experience. The main example for the first possibility (the one of the niche) would be poetry, or the sphere of art in general (painting, music, just think of Bach or Mozart); an example for the second possibility (the erratic remnant case) is superstitions.[101] Both poetry and superstition know themselves to be special and marginal cases, to be not the general and valid truth of modern consciousness, and thus they are fundamentally different from mythic or symbolic experience as publicly true, despite the great abstract-formal similarity that exists between them. The mythic form of experience had not been a special island within the ocean of a generally prevailing positivistic, scientific consciousness. It did not have to compete. It had been the other way around: the perception of naked factualness of the natural world did not come naturally; it was rather something special; a scientific and critical understanding of reality required special psychological efforts (logical negations). One just has to remember the struggles of the philosophical and scientific mind during the Middle Ages (and later) to free itself from the theology of the Church and from ancient symbolic and metaphysical presuppositions.

2.2.3 Born man's inevitable blindness to the soul

The situation of modern man comes out most clearly, indeed paradigmatically, in Jung's description of his Communion experience as a boy.[102] With greatest hopes he had looked forward to going to his first participation in the ceremony, but having experienced it, he felt desperately disappointed because "nothing at all had happened." "I had not noticed any sign of a 'communio,' nothing of a union, or becoming one with ...," "this ceremony contained no trace of God" but had "all amounted to no more than words" (*MDR* p. 54f., transl. modified). Instead, he complained about the flat taste of the bread

---

[101] Although superstitions are factually an individual's private beliefs and not publically shared, they nevertheless, qua superstitions, are in the *status* of sharedness. *Mutatis mutandis* the same applies to the experience of art as a modern equivalent to mythic or symbolic experience. It is inevitably private, subjective, personal, and yet its logical status is that of sharedness—a not-shared sharedness.

[102] I discussed this topic at greater length in my paper "The Rejection of the *Hic*. Reflections on C.G. Jung's Communion Fiasco," forthcoming in vol. 5 of my Collected English Papers, New Orleans, LA, Spring Journal Books.

and the sour taste of the wine. For earlier centuries the bread and wine of the Communion, no matter whether flat and sour or not, would have objectively been the true presence of Christ and would have brought about, as well as in fact confirmed, the "communio" both with the Lord and that of all the participants into the true community of the faithful. Many years later Jung spoke about a similar theme, the Roman-Catholic Mass. He said, "I cannot experience the miracle of the Mass; [...]. It is no more true to me [...]" (CW 18 § 632).

This incapability of Jung's to experience the Communion is not *his* fault. It is not really due to his knowing "too much about it" (the Mass) either, as *he* suggested by way of explanation (*ibid.*). Because there is no conflict between knowing much (academic and conceptual knowledge, one's being an intellectual, having deeper insights into theological matters) and being able to participate in the Communion or the Mass as the true event of "communio" and/or "transubstantiation." St. Augustine, Thomas Aquinas, Luther, and many other highly learned theologians knew very much about these things, but did not have any problem with these ceremonies. It is a typical modern fallacy to think that it is knowledge and the intellect that destroy the connection to soul. If this indeed were so, one should think that all people who do not know anything, let alone too much, about the Mass would still be able to experience its miracle, which is obviously not the case.

No, Jung's problem was that as a modern, he had *logically* been fully born out of the soul, expelled from the soul, emancipated from it. He was irrevocably *extra ecclesiam*, and that means *extra animam*. His fundamental blindness to the soul truth of the Communion was of an entirely different order compared to the—at all times prevailing—intrinsic avertedness of the I from the soul. His consciousness had already become constituted as the modern ego and thus had lost its access to truth. And so naturally he also went to Communion (and decidedly so) already as the modern positivistic ego, as that very "civil man" whom Jung rightly set absolutely apart from the soul. The Communion *is* only for the soul. There *is* no such thing as a Communion for "civil man." If the latter, as Jung stated, would have no idea at all of what to do with himself in a heavenly Jerusalem, why should he know how to appreciate the bread and wine of the

Communion? For the positivistic ego, the bread is by definition *theologically* or *psychologically* flat, even if it were positive-factually the best-tasting bread in the world, because, as we said earlier, the imaginal and the sensible (like the bread and the wine) are not by themselves and objectively capable of representing what they are claimed to represent. The *empirical flat and sour taste* therefore come in handy, because they allow the boy Jung, who in this case is identified with the ego, to use these positivistic features as corroboration of the *logical flatness* that the soulless ego projects upon, and therefore indeed sees in, the object, although it is actually the flatness of its, the ego's, own logical constitution of consciousness, the consciousness of born man. It is only *for* a premodern consciousness that the bread and wine in fact and without any *sacrificium intellectus* fulfill the claim of in truth representing the mystery of Christ's body and blood, only for a consciousness still *objectively* enveloped in the soul and thus *objectively* susceptible to the "suggestive power" of the sensible object, its immediately and convincingly suggesting the soul's corresponding truths and letting these truths be present for it. Jung's experience clearly demonstrates the objective structural deficiency of the sensible and imaginal. If the bread as sensible object were capable *of its own accord* (and thus *objectively*) to truly represent and express what it is supposed to be in the Communion, Jung would not have been frustrated.

Jung obviously had unconsciously hoped for and insisted on a kind of literal miracle, something spectacular, maybe bread that had literally fallen from heaven like manna rather than ordinary human bread coming from the local baker, and a ceremony that produced a "happening," an intensive "high" like a drug experience does, a peak experience, and an overwhelming emotional sense of becoming one with the whole world, as is nowadays maybe experienced at a rock festival or an exciting mass sports event accompanied by lots of alcohol, or by (especially violent) mass demonstrations by anti-globalization or peace movement activists. He had given a thoroughly *superstitious* interpretation to a *religious* ceremony, to the alleged effects of the ritual of communion as positive-factual *psychic* effects, whereas for unborn man they had been very real, but of course *psychological* effects, effects for the soul, not for the ego. The spectacular (as a quality of what objectively happens) and emotions

(what is stirred up in the subject by it)—clearly something psychic—
are the only way that the ego in terms of its own positivistic categories
can imagine what the experience of *soul truths* must be like, soul truths
which are absolutely foreign to it and therefore are envisioned as
something "exotic." A clear category mistake.

The confirmand Jung had not been ready for either one of the two
honest reactions to the modern situation; he had neither been willing,
as a modern person, to give up altogether any hope for any effect of
the ritual and turn his back on religion as such, *nor* to view (and
appreciate) the Communion in a truly psychological way, where
"psychological way" means the full integration into its stance of the
wholehearted and irrevocable renouncement of any such wishes—in
other words, the acceptance of the soul's absolute departedness, its
having become historical, not a present reality and immediate presence,
but a historical truth present to us only in Mnemosyne. From the
outset Jung was barking up the wrong tree. He wanted something from
the Communion ceremony that on principle grounds it cannot and
is not meant to provide. The soul is not a positivity, not psychic but
psychological; it is not competent for ego excitement and for peak
experiences, but only—very soberly and quietly—for its own truth.

When Jung later said that the Mass "is no more true to me" (what
he means is: "true for me"), he is right in a superficial, colloquial sense,
the sense of a statement of fact. But the truth of the matter is that
being constituted as a modern ego, he had *a priori* become blind to
such a thing as truth and soul. As "civil man," he had "no idea of what
to do with" truth, no use and need for it, no access to it. It simply did
not exist for him. Because of the fact that as born man he could no
longer want—psychologically—*truth* from the Communion, but—
psychically or rather psychologistically—wanted ego excitement and
ego fulfillment, a ceremony that does not aim for such things as a
matter of course had to be for him no more than "a wretched memorial
service with the flat bread and the sour wine" (*MDR* p. 55).

2.2.4 Psychology as *ersatz* for soul

This is why Jung became a psychologist. Psychology is *Ersatz* for
the soul which—for born man—is once and for all lost, because to be
modern means precisely to have become *emancipated* from the soul.

Jung actually understood this. "It required an unparalleled impoverishment of symbolism to bring about the rediscovery of the gods as psychic factors, that is, as archetypes of the unconscious. [...] This is why we have a psychology today, and why we speak of the unconscious. All this would be quite superfluous in an age or culture that possessed symbols" (*CW* 9i § 50, transl. modif.). In other words, the fundamental loss of soul is the very condition of the possibility of psychology as a discipline. If there were still soul, that is, if modern man were still contained in soul, perceived the world and life from the standpoint of soul, i.e., if he were still unborn, psychology would be superfluous (and impossible). The danger of psychology, one that it all too often succumbs to, is that it pretends to actually *be* or *bring* the real thing, the reality of soul, of which it is, after all, only the surrogate, the late simulation—unless of course it comprehends itself as a *historical* discipline that has the leave-taking from the soul behind itself as its logical ground.

It is fair to assume that—*objectively* (though certainly not subjectively)—the soul in confirmand Jung was from the outset aiming not for the fulfillment of his high expectations, but for his and their (the expectations') utter disappointment—and precisely thereby for his initiation into the modern truth of the soul. The negative, destructive experience was the purpose behind his building up all the emotion-laden fantasies of what would have to happen through the Communion, and they had the purpose of making the disappointment absolutely thorough and final. The frustration of his hopes was needed, wanted, and those hopes themselves were not innocent, naive hopes (spontaneous natural events), but simulated hopes, because deep down it had from the start already been the modern ego in the boy Jung that approached this whole topic and event. But as modern ego it was a priori known to him that bread and wine are "nothing but" ordinary bread and wine. The innocence of his hope that through the Communion it would all of a sudden be something heavenly was a mock-innocence.

Although he of course "knew" ahead of time that the outcome could only be what it was, Jung needed to act out and go literally through this hugely disappointing experience with its clear-cut "nihilistic" or at least positivistic result, because what for other people would have been a simple and convincing insight into a truth, he generally needed to enact and stage as a drama in the way of a literal *experience* (dream, vision, synchronistic experience, etc.). He had to push his own thoughts and insights (or rather, what *could* have been his insights, if he would have accepted them as binding) into the form of otherness, of experiences *happening* to him as events, in order to give them the appearance of objective fact and himself the appearance of innocent observer.

He needed this particular disappointing experience as a solid base to push off from, to push *himself* off, not of course into true psychology, but into what was to become his "psychology of the unconscious" (where "the unconscious" is the compromise formation or deceptive package of a new promise that at one and the same time is kept alive and yet by definition kept out of reach and is *ipso facto* fundamentally immunized against any possible disproof and disappointment).

As psychotherapy, psychology in Jung's sense aims for *Urerfahrung*, for the direct encounter with, and the felt experience of, the archetypal images in the unconscious, and for the *Relations between the Ego and the Unconscious*. This means that instead of the fundamental avertedness of the I from the soul we have the direct opposite: a fundamental orientation towards "the unconscious" ("the soul"). And instead of the I's fundamental openness to the "suggestive power of the primordial images" as in former times, we have the unbridgeable (because *logical*) gap or fence between consciousness or the ego and "the unconscious." It is a complicated situation. To be sure, the ego is capable of having dreams and visions, but they are now construed as the event of archetypal images of the collective *unconscious*. Unconscious means: logically inaccessible, by definition cut off from consciousness, from the responsibly thinking wake mind.

The ego can only *peep* across the logical fence and *imagine* what is on its other side. It perceives these images the way a visitor of a zoo watches the wild beasts behind the bars of the cage that separate him from them; or the way a visitor to a museum sees precious objects behind the glass of a display case that remain fundamentally out of reach. The archetypal images can be emotionally impressive as well as intellectually understandable. But both the emotional impression and the understanding occur on this, the ego's, side of the fence, whereas the archetypal images themselves remain yonder, behind the fence, the cage, or display case. Dream events are windows, display cases. It is not that by having a dream, unconscious contents leave the unconscious and enter consciousness, just as by visiting a museum the displayed objects do not wander from the display case into my pocket. They remain behind glass and in the museum and I had merely the opportunity of seeing and being impressed by them.

We have to be very clear about this: what Jung means by "primordial experience"[103] is an ego event, an event solely on the ego side, and not the direct encounter with the archetypes. It is not an event of truth, of soul. However, it is, so much is certain, the *simulation* of a soul truth, a truth translated from the language of the soul into the language of the positivistic ego, we could also say: converted into the currency of the positivistic ego. As such, the ego manages to take possession of the abstract contents—the memory images—of the former truths for itself, while ipso facto giving up their *truth* character.

Truths are *known* (and/or possibly ritually enacted/acted out, *displayed*), but not experienced.[104] Truths are notional and objective. If they require something from the subject, then it is at most insight (awareness) and the act of simple affirmation, explicit confirmation: "yes, this is most certainly true"[105] (whereby this affirmation must be more than a verbal statement; it must be the lived affirmation of a person as *homo totus*). They open and free the mind to what *is*. The mode of *experiencing (Erleben)* is just as unsuited and incompetent for truths as a telescope is to receive television images. The point of felt experience is to produce a subjective state in a person. It is competent for sensations and impressions (one's being impressed).

Furthermore, Jung also leaves no doubt that the content of primordial experiences, the *archetypes*, are not even considered truths— indeed, *must* not be considered truths under any circumstances. Because if they were, psychology would have transgressed its limits and become metaphysical, prophetic, a religion. Archetypes and archetypal images can at most be "psychologically true," in other

---

[103] A wholly different problem of "primordial experience" is its alleged, but fictitious primordiality and directness (immediacy). I will come to that aspect below.

[104] Nor, of course, imagined.

[105] "Dies ist gewißlich wahr" (the formula with which Martin Luther ends each of his explanations of the different articles of the Apostles' Creed in his *Small Catechism*).

words, true in a fundamentally reduced, fenced-in sense of which one knows that it does not mean really true, unreservedly true: not simply *true*. "Psychologically true" means true only for an experiencing ego in its private interiority, not—like, e.g., scientific truths—officially and publically true for everybody, for society at large. This means: what is "psychologically true," the archetypes, is, by penalty of inflation or insanity, not allowed to cross the border and become part of ordinary consciousness, ordinary binding knowledge. The phrase "to make conscious" does precisely not mean to fully integrate into consciousness, i.e., to unreservedly give something its place within the range of accepted truths. It merely means having gone to an exhibition and having seen what was on display.

Above I used Jung's report of his experience after the return from his mother's funeral as an illustration of the psychological difference on the experiential or behavioral level. There were his psychic (human, all-too-human) emotions of sadness, on the one hand, and in absolute contrast the psychological "emotions," on the other hand, that were not really his own (in an ego sense), but an ongoing, objective jollity merely perceived by him and representing the soul's archetypal view of death. Now, after what we just had to realize, I have to add that even this archetypal assessment of death was *only* what in Jung's language was a *Urerfahrung* of his, a primordial *experience*, and this means an experience in his private inner, but *not* a soul *truth*. A truth can come out into the open. But even for Jung himself, it was clear that it was only an inner experience, not a general truth, not binding for consciousness, for our general knowing. It had its place exclusively in the collective unconscious and not in public discourse. As belonging to the unconscious, it was *logically* (not necessarily empirically) excluded from consciousness and real life, and thus on principle deprived of the status of a truth. The content of this experience had already become historical, psychologically obsolete, a mere curiosity for Jung's consciousness. He knew that it had once been a soul truth, but precisely *had* been. It needed his research, his learned explanation (and thus the opposite of an avertedness of the I), to make sense of it. The experienced phenomenon was of course fascinating and thus attractive for Jung. In his explanation Jung spoke as the modern rational scientist of the soul, which means that in effect he looked at this experience of his like a biologist looks at a dead specimen of a butterfly species in his showcase.

This, his particular so-called *Urerfahrung*, was also not really all that *Ur-*, all that primordial, immediate, or direct. I discussed this above (ch. 2.1.7). As I already suggested, we can be sure that prior to this experience, Jung, in his many years of studying myths, local legends, rituals, and beliefs of former and exotic peoples, had fully familiarized himself with this ancient notion of death as a wedding festival. The content of his experience was thus for him not only a piece of sunken cultural history in general, it was also personally, in his inner experience, a piece of sunken knowledge that reemerged in him as a seemingly spontaneous event. Jung needed his psyche to let it "spring *his own prior* knowledge on him" *as* a surprise experience "from out of the unconscious" (much as years earlier an inner "unconscious" figure like his Philemon had "taught" him the idea of the reality of the psyche—as if it had been a new revelation for him, although it had been an idea that had been his own [at least dim] conscious conviction long before[106]). This is Jung's specialty: his own thoughts and insights were not allowed to become fully conscious *as* his own thoughts, thoughts *thought by him*. They had to be sunken into what he termed the unconscious only to unexpectedly emerge from there in his consciousness, because Jung needed his insights to have the form of quasi-natural facts, spontaneous events. In our example, the death of his mother offered itself as an opportunity for the *unconscious* production of a spontaneous, subjectively unwanted experience of the archetypal view of death. We need to stress that the enactment was unconscious. It was not a conscious, and thus dishonest, stage production.

Be that as it may, it is clear that the archetypal jollity did not arrive as a truth for Jung, but as an emotional event, a subjective *experience* and that means an ego-experience, which is inevitably an experience, *on* this side of a fence, *of a content on* the other side of the fence. The experience is a Now, but what is experienced is something historical. "Psychological experience" means that a fence fundamentally separates

---

[106] See on this my "Psychology as Anti-Philosophy: C. G. Jung," in: *Spring 77 (Philosophy and Psychology)*, June 2007, pp. 11–51, which will also be a chapter in the forthcoming volume 5 of my Collected English Papers.

the *experience*-by-the-ego from the *contents* of the ego's experience.[107] In fact the very term archetype or "the archetypal" openly demonstrates that even a psychology of the collective unconscious is dealing only with *former* soul truths, with sunken history, with fundamentally fenced-in or canned contents—"canned" because they are encapsulated in our inner. If the experienced archetypal contents had the character of truths for us, we would not speak of archetypes: we would speak of them the same way we speak of all truths (2 x 2 = 4; the continental drift, the Jupiter moons, etc.). The label "archetype" screens consciousness from the contents referred to and protects it from having to integrate them into its general official knowledge.

So we landed ourselves with a strange contradiction. On the one hand there can be no doubt that in the two opposite feelings that Jung experienced at that time we have a clear manifestation of the psychological difference between the psychic and the psychological or between the human, all-too-human and the archetypal. On the other hand it now turns out that *this* psychological difference as a whole (i.e., including the archetypal aspect) is itself only psychic. It is an ego-experience, an ego event. The study of our psychological experiences, even of our numinous, archetypal experiences, is the study only of the *opus parvum*, the "little work," the work on personal and subjective stuff. It has lost the character of being a logical universal.

2.2.5 The psychological difference absorbed into the one side of itself

The psychological difference has itself disappeared in the one (the psychic) side of itself. The whole difference has become a sublated moment within the psychic, the human, all-too-human. To be sure, on (or within) the level of the *opus parvum*, archetypal experiences are truly psychological, truly not merely psychic. *On* this level we can rightly distinguish between soul, on the one hand, and human psyche, on the other. But this whole level itself is psychic and human-all-too-human in a wider sense, and therefore archetypal experiences, too, are in this sense ego-experiences. The psychic (*that* psychic which has swallowed the whole former psychological difference) is now unrivaled, without its counterpart, without the psychological in the true, not

---

[107] Just as an image in the sense of imaginal psychology is fundamentally separated from what it is the image of.

merely historical, sense, because on the level of the *opus parvum* everything is experience, and we know that everything experienced is *ipso facto* merely psychic. This is the fundamental flaw of "psychology," as it historically developed, even if it is a psychology of the collective unconscious. It is fundamentally difference-less. At best it knows of the "little" difference, the logically a priori depotentiated, literally "done-in" difference, that is to say, the *semanticized* difference. Especially Jung's psychology of the collective unconscious contributes to the soul's self-immurement in the Platonic cave because it expressly "takes care of" the whole difference, semanticizing and diminutizing it in the inner.[108] Freud's psychology, being openly positivistic, reductive, psychologistic, is a much more harmless version of this immurement in that it simply excludes the psychological (the soul truths with their "speculative" character, the "spiritual," archetypal) and devotes itself more or less solely to the psychic (the desires, anxieties, and defense mechanisms inside people).

In the context of the statement quoted above, "... analytical psychology has burst the chains which till then has tied it to the consulting-room of the doctor. It transcends itself ..." (*CW* 16 § 174, transl. modif.), Jung also said, "[...] Therefore this psychology lays claim to becoming *Allgemeingut* [common knowledge or part of the culture as a whole]—even more so than the previous stages [in history] which, each in its own right, are bearers of a general truth."[109] We must categorically reject this claim. Analytical psychology can on principle not become a truth, let alone a general truth, something logically universal, because it is committed to the notions of the unconscious and the inner. It is on principle dealing only with private (even if possibly archetypal) *experiences* and thus not with truths at all, and with experiences whose privacy is absolutely necessary and

---

[108] Cf. my "The Occidental Soul's Self-Immurement in Plato's Cave," Chapter Nine in my *Technology and the Soul*, vol. 2 of my Collected English Papers, New Orleans, LA (Spring Journal Books) 2007, pp. 213–279.

[109] Jung's term "Allgemeingut" is difficult to translate, but what the *CW* made of this part of the sentence ("can claim to serve the common weal") completely misses Jung's point. As the rest of Jung's sentence shows he is here thinking in terms of truth and generality, not public usefulness or charity. The translator seems to have read into the last component of this word (*-gut*) the meaning of *"das Gute, das Wohl."* In connection with *Allgemeingut* we may also remember how important notions like *sensus communis, communis opinio, consensus gentium* or *omnium* were for Jung. They show that deep down he was worried about the truth question concerning the archetypal experiences.

irrevocable, not merely contingent. Because if analytical psychology in earnest claimed that the inner experiences are general truths, it would have overstepped its limits and become a metaphysic or religion. This is also why it could not and cannot *really* transcend itself and burst the chains which tie it to the medical consulting room: with its notions of the unconscious and the inner it carries, and constantly reproduces, those very chains within its own theoretical structure. The consulting room is, after all, nothing else but the externally objectified and literally acted-out "inner." And so it is no surprise that we see analytical psychology today more than ever in the hands of the practitioners in the blinders of their clinical outlook and personalistic technical focus; institutionally, the intellectual home of analytical psychology is accordingly the training institutes for Jungian analysts.

This is not exclusively the fault of the practitioners. It is also the structural fault of a psychological theory that systematically encapsulates what it is dealing with in "the inner" and "the unconscious."[110]

These reflections lead us to an important general insight: there is no objective semantic quality of an image that unquestionably would establish its mythical or archetypal nature. A dream motif may clearly have a mythological or archetypal content and yet itself, as a whole, be only an ego content and ego-experience, part of the *opus parvum*. In fact, this is the normal state of affairs in modernity. What Jung termed the individuation process as part of modern psychology belongs to the sphere of the ego and its internal complications. The sphere that once upon a time was myth is unreachable for *born* man. The semantically mythic that is experienced in dreams is already-psychologized historical props from the psychic's property room. It all has already been subjugated to the ego.

The sublation of the whole former psychological difference and its demotion to an internal moment within one side only of itself is the result of the birth of man (his having been born out of soul, having emancipated himself from soul). As long as man had his place inside the soul, inside "nature," he existed as the tension and clearance

---

[110] The only place where Jung's theory really transcended "the inner" in a certain way was with his theory of synchronicity. But the dear price for *this* transcendence was that his theory left the soul behind by going into cahoots with physics and dealing with irrational factual events, thereby actively affirming "consciousness's becoming unconscious" (this phrase comes from Jung himself, *CW* 12 § 563, transl. modif.).

between Heaven and Earth (to express it in mythological terms), as the twofoldness of "sun" and "eye," of soul as objective truths and soul as the organ for perceiving and enacting those truths. He was Atlas, both holding Heaven (Mercurial meaning or soul) and Earth (positive fact or the human, all-too-human) apart *and* at the same time being the living *copula, ligamentum,* or *vinculum* between the opposites.

For born man, neither Heaven nor Earth, neither "sun" nor "eye" (in Plotinus's or Goethe's sense) exist. The whole natural world is over. Heaven has, as Jung repeatedly pointed out, itself become positivized into the universe of the physicists, and Earth has become intellectualized; it dissolved into ideas, constructs, computer models, mathematical formulae. The whole opposition between Heaven (as veritable Heaven) and Earth can thus today only exist either in intellectual form as a historical memory and scholarly knowledge or in an emotional, touristic, subjective-event form as inner experience, both of which are psychic. And both are a "Looking Backward" from the position of born man.

The psychic pole of the psychological difference, now being unrivaled, has become orphaned or widowed—at least *for* a perception guided by what once upon a time had been its frame of reference. But the psychic's other within the psychological difference, the psychological, cannot truly be totally missing on the utterly new level of born man. The seemingly orphaned psychic does have its counterpart, too. It is not *really* orphaned. The psychological difference is inescapable.

2.2.6 The new psychological difference

Its other side, "the psychological" on this new level, the level of the *opus magnum,* must of course again be something that is characterized by the fact that the I is truly *averted* from it, that mankind really turns its back to it, and conversely, that it represents "the soul" as a truly *departed* one: alien, not perceivable, cold, abstract, sober, matter-of-fact—not an experience, not an image, not a semantic content, but simply a truth. And this is the logic or syntax that quietly, invisibly governs and animates our modern world. It is the logical form of our collectively lived life, its spirit Mercurius. The psychic gets enormous attention in our days and attracts people's personal interest (just look at the overflowing self-help sections in bookstores, on the one hand, and at the likewise overflowing mythology-and-meaning and esoterics sections, on the other hand), showing to what extent the ego is oriented towards it. By contrast, the logic of our life and world in psychology goes by unnoticed and disparaged, precisely because it is not spectacular, not emotional, but cold and abstract, and, on top of it, hard to see. In Jungian psychology the ego indulges in the semantics of "the unconscious" and "the imaginal." The unconscious and the imaginal are by no means *in via ejectus* and experienced as *exilis* (uncomely, worthless) the way alchemy's *lapis* was. They are "in." Popular (at least in certain circles of society).

Why? Because "the unconscious" and "the imaginal" have the logical form of "ego," although they of course pretend to be "non-ego" (and, semantically viewed, are indeed non-ego). They speak immediately to the ego, presenting it with easily accessible positive contents and evoking emotions of mystery, bewilderment, thrill, fear, guilt, shame, exaltation, higher meaning, deeper significance. They appeal to the ego's desire for what can be sensibly imagined. This is even true in those cases where imaginal psychology penetrates precisely to the very opposite of visibility, to alchemy's "Black Sun," to the ideas of the Unassimilable and Unspeakable, the Void. Those are all merely the *semantic* and in itself *imaginal* negation of the visible and the sensibly imaginable, not the syntactical negation, and as such they celebrate the semantic orientation even while seemingly transcending or destroying it. They are well suited to satisfy the ego's mystical longings, as Mogenson insightfully pointed out.[111]

The *soul* of and in the Real, the *Mercurius* "imprisoned in the matter" of our reality, the *logical form* animating our real world, are logically or syntactically negative (the negation of the semantic as such). They can only be thought. They are not immediately accessible. And even if comprehended, they remain cold, aloof, distant—much like mathematical or scientific truths (which, however, are of course not direct evidence of soul) remain distant. The coldness of logos, of conceptual thought, is the mark of the departedness of the soul and thus of soul.

---

[111] Greg Mogenson, "Marlan's Bardo Thödol," in: *San Francisco Jung Library Journal,* 2005, Vol. 24, no. 4, pp. 6–16, here p. 15.

Now that we have arrived in our discussion at the soul's *magnum opus* and regained the soul side of the *new* psychological difference and thus the psychological difference as a whole, we can see that the psychological difference has not changed at all. It is not really new. It is what it has always been. Whether in the times of myth or today in modern technological civilization—the soul is and has always been the soul of the Real, the *logos eôn* of Heraclitus. This is constant. The fact that once upon a time mythology was the authentic form of the soul's expression and that today this form is no longer possible, merely points to a form change, not a substantial change, of the psychological difference. Mythology was the expression of the innermost logic or truth of actually lived life at the time of a *nature-based* life. What in the transition to modernity has changed is the medium or element in which the soul of the Real is immersed. In former times, the medium was Nature. Life was fully governed by and integrated into the natural sequence of day and night and the seasons, of birth, life and death, fully dependent on the natural conditions of the land; human views and knowledge were determined by what could be seen with the naked eye and touched with one's hands and therefore led to an imagination that, even where it was inventive or miraculous, nevertheless worked with thing-like shapes, personified or animal-like figures, and processes modeled after familiar events in sensible reality; human production and manufacturing relied on what nature had provided. Therefore the psychological difference could under those conditions legitimately express itself in semantic form; the soul side of the difference could take the imaginal form of myth, symbols, ritual, or, later, the already more abstract, but still imagination-based form of classical metaphysics with its notions of substance, first cause, principle, ground, etc.

Now that the soul has been born out of nature, that it has—logically, psychologically—left nature, substance, and content fundamentally behind itself, now that man has been able to go to the moon and, via satellites, essentially looks down upon the Earth from outer space, now that he manipulates the innermost constitution and workings of nature itself (nuclear power plants, nanotechnology, genetic engineering) and lives and thinks on a very abstract level of functions, logical relationships, structural forms, now mythic imagination has fundamentally become incapable of expressing the soul. Our equivalent to what Jung called the "symbolic life" of former ages is precisely not a *symbolic* life, precisely because it is still the same life of the soul as at all times: namely the life expressing the innermost truth of the Real. To be true to the soul, you have to go along with the alchemical changes that the "matter" undergoes in the *opus magnum*, changes that determine the *form* of the at all times "departed" (irrepresentable, nonperceivable, alien, cold) soul of the really lived life and the world.[112]

Here it is important to add a quote from Heraclitus to help us counteract a possible wrong impression that might have arisen from my emphasis on "*the* departed" and *our* "avertedness." In fragment 72 (DK) Heraclitus says, "They divorce themselves from that, the logos, with which most of all they are in continuous contact, and what they daily come across, that appears to them as alien." The word "divorce" takes up the meaning of our "avertedness" just as "alien" is parallel to "departed." This stance of divorcing themselves from the logos is, according to Heraclitus, people's fault or shortcoming. Conversely, the logos of which Heraclitus speaks is precisely what people are intimately in contact with and what they come daily across. In other words, what I tried to emphasize seems to be completely contradicted by this statement. But that is only the first impression.

On second sight we become aware that both views confirm each other. We have to think them together. The departedness of the logos or soul is *logical* departedness, not physical, spatial, literal departedness, and the avertedness is likewise logical avertedness. The logos is not altogether and literally transcendent, otherworldly, yonder, a second and exotic reality in some distant region or dimension. It is right here, in real life. In other words, it is departed *while* being an everyday reality. The reason for this is of course that it is the soul of and in the Real. Thus, *as* the *logos* (or soul, or syntax) it is "departed," invisible, but *as* the logos, or soul, or syntax *of and in the Real* it is nevertheless everywhere, a daily reality. The logos or the soul thus is, in Goethe's words, an *offenbares Geheimnis* (a manifest [or disclosed, unconcealed] mystery). We might also remember here Hegel's insistence upon the parousia of the Absolute, its being "with us, in

---

[112] The soul of the world in the sense of the soul of the Real or of actually lived life must of course not be confused with the *anima mundi*, which is a cozy, romantic ego concept.

and for itself, all along, and of its own volition."[113] And while in fact being intently oriented towards all the things and events in ordinary life, while concentrating on the semantics of reality, people are at the same time "averted" from and blind to the soul *in* those very things and events, the syntax animating ordinary life. While they are in constant contact with what contains the logos as its *spiritus rector*, this logos is absolutely "alien," even as if nonexistent, to them.

What by comparison with the former ages is missing in our modern situation is the explicit and communal celebration, the open acknowledgment. The *logos eôn*, the soul's truth, is not released into its being true. The "sun" is there, but the "eye" is lacking. The soul's twofoldness has not become established again under the new conditions. The modern blindness to and dissociation from the soul is the prevailing state of affairs, but it is wrong. Why? Because the soul's emancipation from itself, modern man's bornness, are its emancipation and his bornness only from the soul in its former natural form, not from the soul as such. By having emancipated itself from itself, the soul has not totally left itself. Its emancipation from itself happens only *within* itself.

2.3 ORDINARY HUMAN EXISTENCE SURROUNDED BY THE SOUL

Before, I spoke of a simple opposition between soul and ordinary human experience. Opposites can be imagined in terms of being positioned left and right, above and below, or vis-à-vis each other. But now we have to advance to the insight that the soul as the one side of the opposition is all around the ordinary human world as the other side. The civilized world of man is, as it were, an island surrounded by the wilderness of the soul, an oasis in the desert of the soul.

"But to have soul is the whole venture of life, for soul is a life-giving daemon who plays his elfin game above and below human existence, for which reason—in the realm of dogma—he is threatened and propitiated with superhuman punishments and blessings that go far by the possible deserts of human beings" (*CW* 9i § 56). Jung's idea and language here is clearly informed by the mythological imagination of old, as if we were still in the nature status of soul. The soul is

---

[113] G.W.F. Hegel, *Phenomenology of Spirit*, transl. by A.V. Miller, Introduction, Oxford *et al.* (Oxford University Press) 1977, p. 47.

personified and thus hypostatized, it is perceived as a daemon, the latter is said to play an elfin game. It is his identification with the mystifying, befogging anima that made Jung describe, and probably also experience, the soul this way. For our purposes let us treat all this as if it were a merely poetic-rhetorical embellishing form of expression (although it probably was more to Jung) and leave it aside. For then we can sift out the one precious insight this statement contains, namely the idea that the soul is *above* and *below* (and also above *and* below) human existence, and also, we could add, to the left and to the right of human existence, in other words, all around but not *in* the sphere of the specifically human.

The sphere of the human, all-too-human is free from soul (in the specific sense). It is as if it were an island or a walled garden, a safe place of civilized life to be led under familiar conditions. It is the middle between two extremes. As this middle ground, it can be, but does not have to be, mediocre. But at any rate, it is without mythic overdetermination. It is the sphere of the ordinary, commonplace, conventional. Also, it is the realm of (relative) human freedom and arbitration, of where man can make his own pragmatic decisions guided by what is felt to be truly his own human advantage, unburdened by the restraints and heavy load of Meaning imposed on life by the soul. In the modern Western world, most of our daily life takes place in this sphere of relative irrelevancy and liberalism, the sphere of emancipation from soul.

This safe island or garden is "threatened" on both sides ("above" and "below") by the incursion or manifestation of the soul, the "inhuman" soul.

With this conception or observation, we get a threefold scheme, whereas before we only had, as I pointed out, a duality and strict opposition of the human realm and the realm of the soul. Now it appears that the latter realm, that of the soul, is divided into two different regions with the realm of our human interests in between.

What Jung had in mind with "above" and "below" was, as the context shows, primarily to be understood in terms of the situation of mythological or metaphysical man; his next sentence begins with "Heaven and hell..." He obviously links his "above" with the upper, noble, ethically "good" forces of light, whereas "below" refers to the demonic, possibly destructive forces of darkness. Heaven and hell belong to a bygone time. For us, living after the rise of psychology and the emergence of "psychological man," "above" and "below" take on a different meaning.

2.3.1 "From below"

"From below" the ordinary human realm, it is, in our modern psychological age, above all individual and collective psychopathology in which "the soul" makes itself felt. "The soul" disturbs our peace of mind by plaguing us with neurotic, irrational anxieties, obsessions, compulsions, psychosomatic disorders, hysterical symptoms, phobias, irrational impulses, depressions, and so on. In all these symptoms or conditions, the soul as the psychic Other, the "non-ego," stirs within us and demands attention. People can, for example, be possessed by jealousy to the point where they kill, kill either their rival or the person loved who rejects them.

It is also a well known phenomenon that all sorts of feeling-toned complexes can get the better of us and drive us to irrational, often unwanted behavior or maybe even to a behavior that is absolutely incompatible with our conscious attitudes, our values, belief systems, and habits. We also know this phenomenon from the collective level. In a crowd that turns into a mob, people can all of a sudden be induced to commit actions that they would never have dreamed of doing if they had been alone or in the company of only a few acquaintances and actions that afterwards they feel deeply ashamed of, acts of violence and destruction, rioting, vandalism, lynch law. On a political level, whole nations can go mad and systematically commit terrible atrocities, just think of Nazi Germany and Rwanda a few decades ago.

The soul can of course also present itself in psychotic symptoms, hallucinations, delusions.

Historically, the "from below" gave rise to the early psychological ideas of the subconscious and the unconscious (which was also usually located "beneath" consciousness, at least in the early days of psychology).

But concerning those phenomena that come from below, I now must express a warning. Things here are a bit complicated. Not everything that comes from below is *ipso facto* produced by the soul and a manifestation of it. We have to be very careful when there is a kind of "explosion" of an emotion or a complex. What erupts from below can be a manifestation of soul, but it must not always be. Even if we ignore here cases of pathological behavior due to organic brain damage and the already mentioned *psychic* disorders, we must state that not every psychopathology is psychologically relevant. Many instances of pathological behavior (and I count emotional outbursts under psychopathological symptoms, even if they may be isolated and of minor importance) are psychic events, belong merely to the human, all-too-human, rather than to the soul and are expressions of the psyche, i.e., human biology. There are several distinct possibilities, both on the personal and collective level. We need to keep them theoretically and in therapeutic practice clearly apart, because if we ascribed soul dignity to what does not have any (or vice versa), we would be committing serious blunders. But we also have to know that it is not always perfectly clear whether a complex reaction is a moment of soul or of psyche.

What is clearly not a case of soul manifesting itself are those outbursts of emotions that are simply due to a lack of civilization, education, and adaptation. Children often go into temper tantrums because they have not learned to control their emotions in an appropriate way. Many adults unfortunately stay children in this regard, and often certain types of psychotherapy even foster in their patients the free expression of their emotions, confusing civilized self-control with repression and opting for an uninhibited display of what is going on in oneself. Jung was very clear about emotional outbursts. "And you always have emotions where you are not adapted. If you are adapted you need no emotion; an emotion is only an instinctive explosion which denotes that you have not been up to your task. When you don't know how to deal with a situation or with people, you get emotional. Since you were not adapted, you had a wrong idea of the situation ... ... to be emotional is already on the way to a pathological condition."[114] "Affects always occur where there is a failure of adaptation" (*CW* 6 § 808). Very true. With an outburst of emotions, affects, and impulses, the human animal, the beast inside a person, is released. This is obviously something that has no soul dignity. What Jung here called "instinctive" explosions are events of (human) "nature."

---

[114] C.G. Jung, *Nietzsche's Zarathustra. Notes of the Seminar Given in 1934–1939*, ed. by James L. Jarrett, vol. 2, Princeton University Press 1988, pp. 1497f.

But in addition to such phenomena which display simply a lack of civilization and education, there is another possibility of emotional outbursts: outbursts (as well as other pathological behavior) as a reaction of a feeling-toned *complex*. Complexes are of a different order from "instinctive" emotions. Complexes are not components of human "nature." They have a history. They originate in a person's life from experiences as the soul's response to those experiences.

Now Jung's view was that ultimately complexes had an archetypal nucleus. This would mean that they possessed some veritable soul dignity and a truly mythic dimension. I think this is a mistake. I find it essential to understand complexes and complex reactions as purely subjective and belonging to personal, private psychology, to the personal unconscious, which is *the ego's* unconscious, whereas with Jung's idea complexes would have one foot or root in Jung's collective unconscious and in the sphere of mythic meaning. The autonomy of complexes results, and can be sufficiently explained, from the fact that unresolved conflicts, resentments, narcissistic offences, and disappointments through the factual refutation by life of one's highest aspirations, values, and beliefs have been split off from consciousness and repressed. They are bundles of psychic energy which in each case are attached to a specific content that are not integrated into the personality and are, as it were, automatically triggered by appropriate stimuli. In other words, they are a case of systematic maladaptation in the psychological sense of the word, namely the soul's maladaptation to itself (rather than to external reality [which would *psychologically* be irrelevant]). Dissociation. An already in fact experienced truth is, against the soul's better knowledge, denied by the soul. Or, the other way around, something that has already been experienced to be a illusion is stubbornly maintained as a soul truth. Feeling-toned complexes (i.e., complex reactions[115]) are either so to speak "local" neuroses, neuroses *en miniature*, or individual components of a fully developed neurosis.

Because this alleged soul *truth* in complexes is in truth an untruth, (implicitly) *known* to be an untruth, you get explosive reactions or powerful, obstinate, irrational behavior the moment a life situation

---

[115] A complex is not a subsisting thing, but exists only, indeed comes into being only, in its manifestations, in complex reactions such as emotional outbursts or stubborn irrational behavior.

touches on the topic that is at the core of this complex. The untruth has to make an excessive fuss, a powerful show of itself, to compensate for its lack of real truth and in order to pretend to be an absolute truth.

(Of course, most of what in adult life may appear as an "instinctive explosion" is also based on complexes. In that case, it is not simply, as discussed before, a lack of civilization, but truly the manifestation of an uncontrollable force. Jung therefore spoke of the autonomy of complexes. I disregard here the correct assessment that even in the case of complex reactions one can speak of a lack of civilization after all, namely if one understands that it is the task of a civilized person to free himself of complexes. The difference to the former case of a lack of self-control remains nevertheless. Complexes cannot, and also need not, be controlled because it is part of their nature that they are autonomous powers, split off. They can only, and ought to, be *dissolved* through being made conscious and seen through as being an obstinate defense of an untruth, so that the dissociation of consciousness is ended. Simple emotions and desires, by contrast, can be kept in check. This is what education, and self-education, is about.)

It is crucial to see that in neurotic symptoms and complexes, although they belong to subjective, personal psychology and to the modern ego-personality, nevertheless *the soul* expresses itself. It is the *soul* that makes neurotic. But the soul that makes neurotic is a sick soul. In speaking about a sick soul what is meant is not that the *person* with a neurosis or with feeling-toned complexes is sick (or only indirectly so). Nor is meant that through the neurosis the soul becomes sick. No, it is really the soul that is sick and for this reason produces neurosis as its way of self-manifestation in a human being. And this is why psychotherapy must not be conceived as our curing the neurotic person, the human being,[116] but as a work that allows the neurotic

---

[116] With this I contradict Jung's view: "Its [medical psychology's] business is not with neuroses but with human beings—that, in fact, is the grand privilege of medical psychology: to treat the whole man and not an artificially segregated function" (*CW* 10 § 354). While I agree that we should not be concerned with artificially segregated functions and while in very different contexts the *psychological* notion of "the whole man," the *homo totus*, has a prominent place in my thinking, I nevertheless think that the focus of psychotherapy is the soul, which in the present context means neurosis and neurotic complexes, and *not* the human being (which is an extra-psychological concept!). Not only for reasons following from the logic of the discipline of psychology, but also for ethical reasons the human person should be taboo. The human being must not be made an object of treatment. No trespassing into the sphere of the patient's absolute freedom!

soul to cure itself. Neurosis has no redeeming value, despite the fact that it is produced by the soul. It is truly sick and nothing else. This essay about what soul is is of course not the appropriate place for a discussion in detail of the particular theme of neurosis; this will have to be the task of a separate study. But the unfamiliar notion of a sick soul needs some comment.

2.3.2 Excursion on "the sick soul"

The ruling idea in Jungian psychology is that the soul is healthy and that, if for whatever reason a psychological disorder happened to have come into being, it aims for the restitution of health. Jung explicitly conceived of the soul as a system of self-regulation (e.g., *CW* 7 § 92), and he integrated neurosis into the idea of self-regulation. This means that for him neurosis, far from being a real *noxa*, is much rather the compensating correction of a one-sidedness of consciousness, an attempt on the part of the soul to supply a person with what is missing or has been repressed, but essentially belongs. Maybe it is even the harbinger of a new personality that wants to emerge in the individual concerned. The neurosis is precisely the first manifestation of "the values which the individual lacks" (§ 93), and this is why Jung can say, "In the neurosis is hidden one's own best enemy or friend" (*CW* 10 § 359, transl. modif.). "We should even learn to be thankful to it.... *Not it is what is cured, rather it cures us*. A human being is ill, but the illness is nature's attempt to heal him" (§ 361, transl. modif., Jung's italics). Ultimately, neurosis thus becomes for Jung a *morbus sacer* (*CW* 11 § 521).

This standard Jungian view of neurosis distinguishes clearly cases of neurotic behavior from cases of emotional outbursts due to a simple lack of adaption and civilization. Neurosis is by Jung rightly not interpreted in terms of a lack or breakdown, nor as caused by mishaps (traumatic circumstances) in the sense of a causal-reductive approach, but on the contrary as being creatively productive and purposive. We can even say that neurosis is decidedly a project. Jung's "final-constructive" or "synthetic" interpretation is indispensable and accords with the real character of neurosis, as also with the finality intrinsic to the more isolated feeling-toned complexes.

However, where I differ from Jung is that I claim that having the nature of a project must not *ipso facto* mean that it is a good and healthy one, and having a telos can under certain circumstances just as well be an obsessive getting on a dead end track as it can, under other circumstances, mean the way into an open future.

The idea that a new personality (or personality aspect) that wants to emerge in a person frequently, indeed usually, shows itself in its first immediacy in the form of a pathology, in disturbing symptoms, is a precious insight and a valuable heuristic premise of psychotherapy that I completely concur with. It helps to open one's eyes to the true nature of certain real phenomena in psychic life that otherwise might be seriously misunderstood. Here the *morbus sacer* idea, although far too high-faluting, is in place. But only here. However, this refers to entirely different phenomena from cases of neurosis proper. We must not confound the two types of phenomena.

Neurosis properly understood is precisely not a case of the soul's self-regulation and of an attempt on the part of the psyche to heal itself by completing the personality through bringing in "the values which the individual lacks." It is not in itself therapeutic, not one's *best* enemy or friend in Jung's sense of "best," although it is certainly *the neurotic's* (or rather *the neurotic soul's*) best *friend*—inasmuch as he (it) clings to it at all cost, loving it more than his well-being and sometimes even more than his life (just think, e.g., of *anorexia nervosa*, which in its most severe cases entails the only too real possibility of a lethal end). Neurosis (*if* it is truly a neurosis[117]) is simply sick, a terrible aberration, and a dead end. In contrast to certain other phenomena of psychopathology, in the case of which Jung's ideas are very much in place, it certainly does not cure us. It has, as I said, no redeeming value.

Furthermore, neurosis does not have an archetypal or mythic depth. It does not come about through the intrusion and powerful influence of archetypal images. It is not a mode of the survival of the mythic gods, the way Jung's dictum about "phobias, obsessions, and so forth: in a word, neurotic symptoms" suggests, namely that "The gods have become diseases; Zeus no longer rules Olympus but rather

---

[117] Not every psychopathological condition that is not psychotic, psychopathic, etc. is neurotic. There are also merely *psychic* disorders. But neurosis is a *psychological* disorder. See the following paragraph.

the solar plexus..." (*CW* 13 § 54). A terrible mystification. The term "numinosity," which has its legitimate use in the area of religious experience in the widest sense, must not be brought in if one wants to discuss neurosis. The psychologist needs a well developed feeling-function in order to be able to resist confusing hysterical emotionality with genuine numinous experiences and manifestations of archetypes or gods. There is nothing epiphanic in neurosis proper. *Neurosis has no soul dignity*, despite the fact that it is the work of the soul.

But this was not possible for Jung to accept. Just as he felt in general that neurosis was, so to say, a sacred illness because he ascribed an archetypal depth to it, so he also was seduced into interpreting a socio-political mass movement, the Nazi movement, as an expression of an archaic Germanic god, Wotan ("They are all drunk with a wild god" *CW* 18 § 639). In my opinion, preposterous. Again we have to apply Occam's razor. There is no need, in fact it would be utterly wrong, to introduce the category of archetypes or gods for comprehending the Nazi movement. The latter can be adequately explained as resulting from a mixture of deep resentments due to undigested disappointments and not accepted losses, of unresolved conflicts, inferiority complexes compensated by a hysterical demonstration of grandiosity, of severe social and economic problems, genuine political fears, the use of ideology-formation and simulation as an ennobling cover, ingenious propaganda, much bluff, etc. etc.— at any rate in terms of nothing but human, all-too-human factors. No Wotan, no god. Nothing numinous or archetypal. Quite banal. Very worldly and superficial. As far as the semblance of numinosity is concerned, we find in the Nazi movement merely impressive theatrics, a great skill at staging bombastic shows and inciting emotions in masses. As I said: simulation. It is akin to what in art and religion is kitsch.

The influence of so-called archetypal powers or gods (such as Wotan) would mean that the Nazi movement had at its core a true substance, a real soul value. But in reality it was fundamentally empty, nihilistic. Not to see through to its real nihilistic hollowness and instead to view it as a sign of the alleged fact that the god Wotan had stirred in the German soul means falling for the hysterical theatrics and pompous ideological phrases. And in Jung's case it was probably also due to his enthusiastic belief in his own theory of archetypes and in the survival of gods in what he called "the unconscious," a belief that was enthusiastic because it was backed up by a deep-seated personal desire or need for the continued presence of God or gods in our godless age and thus made him see the numinous everywhere, if only the least sign of a heightened emotionality offered itself as a peg to hang it on. Jung's own refusal to face modernity and his compensating enthusiasm about the compensating idea of "the collective unconscious" made him see a wild god even *into* such a phenomenon as the Nazi movement in which nothing of the sort can really be discovered.

Quite apart from the fact that the one word *furor* is far too poor and abstract a notion to do justice to the rich, complex nature and depth of a mythic god, an essential point is that from Adam of Bremen's brief definition, *Wotan id est furor*, one certainly cannot conclude that the reverse is also true, in other words, that also every *furor*, in our modern times, *est Wotan*. It is regrettable that the inventor of the notion of the feeling function did not show enough of a sophisticated psychological feeling function to be able to keep the heightened emotionality of a modernistic fanatic-ideological movement and the (rather rare) numinosity of manifestations of the divine apart. Regrettable, too, is his failure to set the quantitative impressiveness of emotions on "the horizontal plane" apart from the qualitative impressiveness of soul experiences belonging to "the vertical dimension." In this case Jung short-circuited the two levels or dimensions that in truth (and, as we have seen, often also for him) are objectively kept apart by the psychological difference, thereby inflating the banal (banal deludedness and hysterics, banal complex-riddenness) with a soul mystery and soul dignity merely on the basis of its inflatedness and enormousness.

Whereas in mythic experiences there is a fundamental "innocence of being," modernity is characterized by cunningness, scheming, tricky contrivance. This distinction is not identical with that between the unconscious and consciousness. Modern ideology, simulation, and kitsch may be a product of very conscious deliberation. But in many cases, and so also in the Nazi movement, it happens to a large degree unconsciously. The fact that it may come from unconscious motivations must not be confused with innocent "primordial" experience. In modernity, unconscious impulses can be a manifestation of an unconsciously occurring contrivance that is far removed from any soul dignity. The difference—"unconscious origin" and "conscious origin"—is not psychological, not decisive. It is only a psychic difference. It is not, just like that, identical with the psychological difference between archetypal (mythic, imaginal [in Corbin's and Hillman's sense]) and egoic (or ordinary human). This particular identification of course suggests itself the moment that "the unconscious" is substantiated as a subsisting separate realm radically dissociated from "consciousness," as is the case in Jung. Then it is likely that the vertical difference between two psychological dimensions is positivized and the one dimension is projected upon the construct of "the unconscious." The reified (and in this sense, ontologized) "unconscious" obviously invites its being identified with the realm of the archetypes, the imaginal, "the gods" that belong to a completely different *order* of categories. In psychic reality, on the empirical, horizontal level, the conscious/unconscious *split* normally does not exist. Most behavior, most human experience and producing, is both conscious and unconscious at the same time. Unconscious and conscious are descriptive adjectives for conditions of human consciousness. And they are an inseparable pair of polar opposites, so that normally every psychic phenomenon is (a) more the one and less the other one, but always both, and that in addition (b) it may also be the case that certain facets of a psychic phenomenon are conscious while others are unconscious.

Now I seem of course to have maneuvered myself into a contradiction: on the one hand, I claim that neurosis is a manifestation of soul; on the other hand, I say it has no soul dignity. This impression of contradiction also comes across from what I said earlier about complexes, which, after all, I view as "small-scale neuroses," namely, that they belong to and can satisfactorily be understood in terms of the ego's personal unconscious, an idea which likewise seems incompatible with the interpretation of neurosis as an expression and work of the soul. The resolution of this seeming contradiction is that it is not a contradiction in my theory, my contradicting myself, but the objective contradiction of the soul (soul in the traditional sense) the moment it makes its appearance in modernity. My seeming self-contradiction is a reflection of the fact that neurosis *is* the existing contradiction. The phenomenon of neurosis forces upon us the paradoxical concept of *a soul without soul dignity.*

Once upon a time—during the ages of myth and metaphysics—the soul used to be the organ of truth. As such, it was both the reflex in the human world of speculative (mythic or metaphysical) truths and provided man's access to those truths. It had veritable substantial contents, above all gods or, later, God. But in modernity it was ousted from within itself, alienated from its primordial unity with itself, exteriorized, and thus came under the sphere of jurisdiction of the ego. It is the soul on the *level*, or in the logical *status* of externality, the soul in the element of modernity and this means the ego. As such, it is a truthless soul, only the placeholder of the soul, an empty soul, the soul as sublated, in the status of negation and absence of self-fulfillment. (This absence and emptiness we can, however, understand as the first immediacy of the fact that the soul's fundamental quality of absolute negativity has now at long last come home to the soul, become syntactical and explicit).

As long as it holds its place in this emptiness and thus remains totally inconspicuous, no more than the "fair memory of things that once were" (*CW* 9i § 50), everything is fine. But the moment the soul, under the conditions of modernity, nevertheless wants to become a present reality in life and to revive its former status of being in possession of substantial truth, it can only do so by way of simulation and thus turns into the sick soul. "Sick" because what its simulation achieves is by no means a new present reality of mythic, archetypal, or metaphysical truths, but only their imitation and thus the former truths *as* untruths.

But it is not really the former truths in the plural that make themselves felt in their simulation. More specifically, it is only the naked abstract concept of "The Absolute" in the singular, into which former metaphysics *as a whole* has been contracted or reduced, metaphysic's zero stage so to speak (much like, two and a half millennia earlier, in the transition from *mythos* to *logos*, the whole imaginal wealth of the mythic world was sublated and contracted into the one philosophical concept of Being and the manifold of the sensuous polytheistic pantheon was sublated into the One God of monotheism). The sick soul's thoroughly modern "The Absolute" (not to be confused with the same-named term in classical metaphysics) is only an idle claim to absoluteness per se, sheer power, or claim to power, totally contentless. This contentlessness is, however, the reason why in concrete neuroses "The Absolute" attaches itself to, and decorates itself with, whatever happens to be their respective particular topic (what happens to have been chosen to be *absolutely* feared, to be considered *absolutely* intolerable, *absolutely* to be defended, avoided, or insisted upon, etc.), so that empirically (on the phenomenological level) the impression is created of a plurality of (simulated) archetypal truths ("the imaginal") as the core of the diverse types of neurosis. Only the naked abstraction of "The Absolute" is substantial. All particular contents are merely its indifferent dressing. If psychology "falls for" this impression, it becomes easy for it to understand itself as "polytheistic psychology."

Neurosis comprehended as a project means: the soul wants something, it wants to establish "The Absolute" as an unshakeable powerful truth and principle and thus as a token of verticality (metaphysics). It wants this principle to become real in lived life: a present reality, an obliging, committing truth, a fact. It celebrates "The Absolute" in whatever it chooses as its own particular highest values, its soul needs and purposes—values and purposes that, of course (as we have seen), have already been experienced as being untenable, untruths. And, reckless of our human interests and well-being, the soul forces these neurotic values on a person. As we know from Jung's thesis, neurosis is not, negatively, a mishap, something having gone wrong, the effect of a trauma or traumatizing circumstances. Nor is it the result of a *person's (ego's)* defense against, resistance to the soul. Rather, it is, positively, a program, intentional, in fact a devious plot, the neurotic soul's establishment of and insistence on its *untruth* as a truth. The person or ego-personality is in the grip of the sick soul, just as conversely the sick soul is a soul on the logical level of the modern ego. But usually people like to see neurosis exactly the other way around, as caused by traumatizing events and by the ego's defense mechanisms against or its repressions of indigestible or overtaxing aspects of one's reality—which, however, is itself the *neurotic* interpretation of neurosis.

Neurosis is the soul's having become stubbornly set on cocooning itself (and together with itself also the person suffering from it) in a scheme of which it precisely knows that it is its own untruth. If it were otherwise, it would not be *neurotic*. In neurosis the soul unyieldingly pursues this scheme. It is the soul's free decision to refuse its real truth, a truth which in the case of the modern soul is its emptiness or absence, i.e., its negativity, and instead to insist on "The Absolute" as an artificial substitute for the lost metaphysics of two to three hundred years ago. Neurosis is not, as many people think, a natural reaction to, or caused by, events or circumstances, but rather fabricated. It is a creative design, a "planned edifice," as Jung had put it. As such, it is *contra naturam* (a negation of, and pushing off from, what is given, a logos work of freedom), which is the distinguishing mark which unmistakably shows that what produces a neurosis is the *soul* rather than the ego personality (which only has to dearly pay the price for the soul's indulging in a neurosis). But the neurosis is also sick, because it is the modern exteriorized soul's deliberate decision *against* its own truth (against what it already experienced, and knows, to have become its new truth) and its spiteful (and powerful) *mise en scène* of a *counter-*"truth."

The soul's general freedom to turn against its own truth is the condition of the soul's possibility to become a sick soul. Historically, this possibility has come into the world with the soul's entrance into modernity. Since the soul is essentially not a piece of nature, it has a choice. It can choose to go along with its own movement and fully adapt to and integrate the changes in its self-constitution that are imposed upon it either by the soul's own work upon itself or by altered external conditions. *Or* it can spitefully refuse to let itself be transformed by those changes, in which case it chooses to become sick. In addition to *psychic* disorders, which are caused by biological[118] or external conditions, we have to take note of and distinguish between two kinds of *psychological* psychopathologies, those in which new or excluded soul aspects make themselves felt and try to force their way into consciousness, on the one hand, and neuroses, on the other hand. The former are expressions of the so to speak innocent self-movement, self-unfolding of the soul's life, whereas the latter are a devious, insidious plot on the part of the soul, with which it precisely disrupts and, once and for all, puts a stop to its own self-movement (and thus also to its "self-regulation" in Jung's sense).

---

[118] Biological conditions are actually also external to the soul.

These few basic comments on the issue of the special case of a "sick soul" must suffice in our context. There remains of course a pressing question, namely, why the soul would choose spitefully to refuse to go along with its own movement, in other words, why it would want to turn into the sick soul. I will propose a very brief answer to this question below in the last chapter (4).

* * *

After this excursion we can return to the topic of the manifestation of the soul "from below."

So far, I have concentrated on pathology and neurosis. But the experiences or phenomena in which the soul manifests literally "from below" must by no means always be pathological, unpleasant, detrimental ones. Its manifestations can also be extraordinary in a very different, positive sense. "From below" generally means emerging from within the individual, as private experience. In this sense, the soul can come to us "from below" also in spontaneous personal experiences of meaning, general inner experiences of dreams and symbols in the context of what Jung called the "individuation process," spontaneous fantasy images in the course of other transformation processes and the like. They all belong to the group of phenomena in which the soul comes "from below." In some cases, mystic visions, auditory experiences, and experiences of illumination (like the Zen *satori* experience) may also fall under this heading.

The distinguishing *qualitative* characteristics of such illumining experiences inasmuch as they come from below (in contrast to "from above") is that what emerges here is the raw, crude, often incomplete (fragmentary), unrefined, unprocessed, uncivilized, sometimes downright barbaric. It has to be the raw in contrast to the cooked because it comes directly from the private individual mind and is a spontaneous or even eruptive manifestation of soul: "immediate" (of course only *at first glance* immediate! For a deeper view there is nothing truly immediate, because what seems to be immediate has also its own historical background through which it is mediated). A very good example of this is the wild, crude imagery and language of alchemy.

What comes "from below" ipso facto always belongs to the sphere of the *opus parvum* and is fundamentally private. It inevitably falls short of the ordinary standards and of the cultural level of consciousness already reached. It may at times even be "sub-human" (where, however, one always has to keep in mind that only humans can be "sub-human"). It can also act subversively, undermining the established order of consciousness, for example when it is a manifestation of what Jung called the shadow. (But precisely as the shadow in Jung's sense, it may also be the germinal beginning of something new, the herald of a new emerging personality, as mentioned before. A while ago I already referred to that possible type of psychopathology, different from neurosis, in which new or repressed soul aspects try to force their way into consciousness because, as Jung said, they want to *mitleben*,[119] i.e., to become an integral part of our actually lived life and self-definition. "That thing in you which should live is alone; nobody touches it, nobody knows it, you yourself don't know it; but it keeps stirring, it disturbs you, it makes you restless, and it gives you no peace" [*CW* 18 § 632]. This is an essential aspect of what Jung calls the individuation process. It is characterized by the fact that it is the private individual person which is (a) the vessel and container of this process and (b) that it is what the process is aiming at in the sense of what it wants to transform.)

2.3.3 No "immediate experience." *Mediated* immediacy!

The imagery of alchemy is an example of the raw, but it also helps us to see that I was right to put the attribute "immediate" in quotation mark, when I called the spontaneous or eruptive manifestation of soul immediate. As always, the spontaneity of what the alchemists experienced, too, must not be taken at face value and believed in. Immediacy and spontaneity are certainly part of the surface phenomenology of those experiences. *Psychically* they are no doubt usually immediate and spontaneous, i.e., *for* the experiencing I. But these on the face of it immediate experiences are in themselves essentially embedded in and in keeping with the long tradition of alchemical imagery and conceptions, in other words, they are always already shaped by it. Psychologically, i.e., for the soul, they are therefore by no means "immediate," but precisely mediated and unconsciously

---

[119] *Erinnerungen, Träume, Gedanken von C.G. Jung*, ed. by Aniela Jaffé, Zürich and Stuttgart (Rascher) 1967, p. 331 (the translation in *MDR* p. 329 is inadequate). *Mitleben*: to live as an acknowledged part of oneself, to have a real share in one's living life.

or subterraneously formed by the tradition in which the alchemists lived. Soul is (actively) *made, produced*, not merely (passively) *experienced* in the strict sense of being "simply found" or of "out of the blue happening *to* consciousness."

I assume that the same applies to the visionary experiences of the initiands in archaic initiation rituals. On the face of it spontaneous, they were nevertheless preformed by all the mythological images and conceptions prevailing in the initiands' respective culture. And the minds of the initiands had even, on an at least implicitly conscious level, been actually prepared for their initiation experiences through all the tales they had heard and rituals they had witnessed during childhood and youth. Especially fairy tales, as tales of the *exemplary* enactment of initiation processes (Heino Gehrts), presented the young uninitiated mind with numerous models for the proper way of how to go through initiatory experiences that they later would themselves have to go through in one way or another. Their experiences, thus, were by no means an eruption from, an immediate manifestation of, "the unconscious" as pure, unadulterated nature, the way Jung liked to think of "Urerfahrung." Rather, what subjectively was "spontaneously" experienced had already gone through the conscious cultural knowledge of the tribe, had been preprocessed by it, and was only unconsciously *re*produced and re*produced* by the individual soul as its own private experience and with its limited, crude means. We already discussed the exactly analogous process as it *mutatis mutandis* showed itself in Jung himself (ch. 2.1.7; also 2.2.4). Here again we have to emphasize that the soul is *made*, and a *making* of what it then (possibly) thrusts upon itself as a seemingly virginal surprise experience: the soul is uroboric, innocently experiencing only what it itself artfully produced.

The sunkenness of the conscious cultural inheritance into the "night-like mine or pit in which is stored a world of infinitely many images and representations, yet without being in consciousness" (Hegel, *Encyclopedia*, § 453, William Wallace translation), on the one hand, and the limitations (lack of genius) of ordinary individuals, on the other hand, is what necessarily makes its contingent reappearance from this unconscious night-like pit in the consciousness of private individuals to be raw and fragmentary, far inferior to the great cultural products.

In addition to alchemy and archaic initiation experiences, we must even say about modern dreaming (such as in analysis) that it is not "immediate" in the sense of directly coming from out of "*the* unconscious" as unadulterated nature, the way Jung saw it: "The dream is a natural occurrence, ... a natural product" (*CW* 11 § 41). "The archetype is pure, unvitiated nature ..." (*CW* 8 § 412). "The unconscious is a pure natural process ..." (*CW* 7 § 386, transl. modif.). The dream is "a spontaneous product of the unconscious," dreams are "direct productions of the unconscious" (*Kindertraumseminar* p. 19 f., my transl.). It is not as simple as that. On the basis of his own experience, Jung himself had to admit that "[a]s soon as certain patients come to me for treatment, the type of dream changes." And in response to this experience he comes up with the general conclusion that, "In the deepest sense we all dream not *out of ourselves* but out of what lies *between us and the other*" (*Letters 1*, p. 172, to James Kirsch, 29 Sep 1934). This (rather isolated) statement of Jung's points to a very different reality. Not pure nature, not direct production from "the unconscious."

A propos the last-cited view of Jung's, I remember that soon after I started training as a Jungian psychotherapist I got into a conversation with an older auditor of some of our courses, who had over a period of time undergone analysis in different cities with several different analysts from different schools. He told me to my surprise that when he had switched to a particular Jungian analyst (one who had just written a book on dreams as a source of religious experience), he all of a sudden started to have numerous mandala dreams that he never had had before, nor after his analytical work with this analyst. This is a drastic example of what Jung had stated: "the type of dream changes." Those dreams of his did not come "out of himself but out of what lay between him and his analyst."

In this particular case, it can even be questioned whether those mandala dreams that this man had were in fact dreamed "out of what lay *between* him and the other." For it is not altogether inconceivable that they were not really his own dreams at all. Maybe what he dreamed was actually only "the Other's," the analyst's, "dreams." Many patients are extremely receptive and impressionable. Themselves *psychologically* relatively nondescript and vacuous, their psyche longs or needs to attach itself to strong convictions that it senses in others, where the content of the convictions and whether they are true or not is more or less irrelevant. What alone counts is the felt *strength* of the person's conviction and the aura or charisma of the other *personality* (especially if the other person is their analyst, or, in other cases, their guru). Jung said (*ibid.*), "The feminine mind is the earth waiting for the seed," waiting to be spiritually fecundated. Here it would be a severe mistake if *we* understood "feminine mind" (Jung said "*weibliche Geist*") the way Jung might possibly have meant it, namely as the Geist *of women*, in this case of the female patient analyzed by his correspondent; the "feminine mind" as an in itself vacuous one waiting for the seed must be understood as a *psychological* (rather than biological or, as they now say, "gender") concept. As such it can of course occur in persons of either sex.

But, another caution in the same vein, what is longed for by the "feminine mind" waiting for the seed, is also not so much a seed. A seed would imply having to go pregnant with it for a long gestation period and finally giving birth to something new. Only great thinkers, poets, artists, only persons primarily deeply, *existentially*, concerned with and focusing on the *truth* of the age (or of aspects of life), have such a feminine mind that is capable of conceiving (then *substantial*) impulses as seeds from others *and carrying them to term* within themselves as *homines toti* (i.e., with *inclusion* of their conscious artistic and thinking powers), with the result that they produce a great *work*. The phenomenon that we are concerned with in the case of analysands dreaming not their own, but their analysts' dreams, is very different. It is the phenomenon of a longing to merely become the mirror of the analyst's or guru's inner conviction and to do the bidding of the other's soul. The psyche of such patients unconsciously produces—seemingly as the "hard facts" of *their* true nature, as *their* "self-experience" and part of *their* "self-actualization"!—the confirmation of what they, also unconsciously, intuit to be the somewhat charismatic analyst's psychological theory, his pet beliefs. Participation mystique.[120]

Truth and the deep inner conscious-unconscious wrestling with ideas, as in the case of the great minds, is here not an issue. Those patients' own consciousness, their own veritable participation is

---

[120] This topic plays a decisive role in Greg Mogenson's study, *The Dove in the Consulting Room. Hysteria and the Anima in Bollas and Jung*, Hove and New York (Brunner-Routledge) 2003.

excluded, probably because there *is* nothing in vacuous minds that could actively and productively participate. Therefore any psychological theory will do. Shamdasani was right to speak, on the very general level of 20ᵗʰ century culture, of "the malleability of [here I would add: *modern*] individuals, who have been willing to adopt psychological concepts to view their lives,"[121] all sorts of concepts. He was right to conceive of "psychologies as social formations"[122] (in contrast to: scientific knowledge) and of "psychic reality" as "the fabricated real," in extension of William James' observation that "the most remarkable 'property'" of the trance state "was its capacity to present itself according to whatever theory one held about it."[123] But be that as it may, the fact that the type of dreams can change depending on whom one is working with, or (outside therapy) whom one is relating to, shows that at least in such cases one's dreaming is decidedly mediated.

As an aside, we may in this context also wonder whether those of Jung's favorite analysands whose visions, dreams, or paintings "from the unconscious" he incorporated into and discussed in his seminars and published works as documentation of what allegedly came directly "from the unconscious" were not in truth *their* "dreaming" *Jung's* dreams, having Jung's "visions," painting Jung's thoughts, rather than dreaming their *own* as part of *their* individuation process. "The feminine mind is the earth waiting for the seed"! Elsewhere we hear, "There are women who are not meant to bear physical children, but they are those that give rebirth to a man, which is a highly important function" (*Letters 2*, p. 455, to Carol Jeffrey, 18 June 1958). This statement also does not have to be restricted to literal women (although there are enough historical examples of this phenomenon with women), but should rather be taken as a psychological statement about the *weibliche Geist* in the psyche, i.e., in either sex. Maybe what some of Jung's analysands were doing was "giving rebirth" to "Jung"—where this name should, however, not so much stand for Jung the man or personality

[121] Sonu Shamdasani, *Jung and the Making of Modern Psychology. The Dream of a Science*, Cambridge (Cambridge University Press) 2003, p. 11.
[122] *Ibid.*, p. 9.
[123] *Ibid.*, p. 11. In this context one might also be put in mind of Jung's description of the "miraculous" cure through hypnosis by him of a woman with a paralyzed leg (*MDR* p. 118f.).

as for the author of his psychology, for what Jung intellectually stood for ("rebirth in a *spiritual* sense").[124]

What is experienced in analysis is at any rate not *evidence* of images in "*the* unconscious" as unadulterated nature. And now that Jung's *Red Book* has become publically available, we can even see that all those seminal dreams and visions Jung himself had during the essential years after his separation from Freud were not spontaneous products of "the unconscious" appearing in him as pure observer or recipient, but rather (unconscious and thus "raw") reproductions (regurgitations) of material stemming from his vast reading and learning about myths and symbols—reproductions, of course, that were adapted to, selected, and required by, the personal *speculative needs* Jung had as *homo totus*.

The rawness of these personal experiences results from the fact that they are devoid of any real participation of consciousness and its cultivating, artistic, refining processing. As Jung said, in doing active imagination you have to "switch off" consciousness[125]! What you then produce (not *from* "the unconscious" but) unconscious*ly* has naturally the primitive form of a careless, sloppy scribble, contingent, fragmentary products.

When Jung, however, stated about himself that "My problem is to wrestle with the big monster of the historical past, the great snake of the centuries, the burden of the human mind, the problem of Christianity. ... Other people are not worried by such problems, they do not care about the historical burden Christianity has heaped upon us. But there are people who are concerned with the great battle between the present and the past or the future" (*CW* 18 § 279), he revealed two things for us. First, that he was one of the great minds whose distinction I described earlier, and secondly that contrary to his usual self-representation, his productions did really not directly come from "*the* unconscious" as pure nature, but were fundamentally mediated by the historical past and his being "worried by such problems," that is, in the depth of his psyche being reached and fundamentally challenged by them. His productions are the results of his *wrestling* with the great snake of the centuries rather than being what nature, or God, or the unconscious sent him as their revelations.

---

[124] See Greg Mogenson, *The Dove in the Consulting Room, op. cit.*, especially Chapter 10.

[125] *Letters 1*, p. 83, to Keyserling, 23 April 1931.

It is not true that, as Jung claimed with respect to the material recorded in his Red Book, "All my works, all my creative activity, has come from those initial fantasies and dreams ...." (*MDR* p. 192), but precisely the other way around: even those initial fantasies and dreams were results of his being "worried by such problems." They are part of his (the whole man's) response to his historical locus.[126]

2.3.4 Modern versus premodern experience

I suspect that Jung's insightful statement, "In the deepest sense we all dream not *out of ourselves* but out of what lies *between us and the other*" is expressive of, and applies more or less exclusively to, the modern situation. As his context shows, "the other" clearly refers to the other person. For premodern times, by contrast, I think we could, to be sure, still retain Jung's wording ("between us and the other"), but "the other" would here precisely not have to be understood in terms of personal relations. The *prevailing essential* relation of people (individuals) during those ages was, rather than between each other, the relation to the "metaphysical" or "religious" substance, to the truth of the whole culture or people of whom they were members. In that situation, this substance and truth, together with all the cultural heritage mentioned before, was "the other," so that the dreams individuals had would come from what lies between the individual person and *this* Other (just as for Jung himself, as *mutatis mutandis* for all great men, his initial fantasies and dreams came from what lay between him and the burden of the human mind). Personal relations (psychologistic psychology's "object relations") are "horizontal"; the relation to the metaphysical treasures around which the deepest life of a people revolves is "vertical." Personal relations are the sign of modernity. The other *person*, as a positivity on the empirical plane, has become all-important and now has to be the source of fulfillment, be it mother or father, or, later, one's partner in an intimate relationship, one's analyst in a therapeutic relationship, and so on, as well as on the collective level certain idolized movie actors, singers,

---

[126] One must not succumb to the fallacy of confusing the fact that Jung's early fantasies and dreams were unconscious productions (in the case of the dreams) and semi-conscious productions (in the case of his active imaginations) with the idea that they were products *of* or *by* "the unconscious." They were, of course, products of the thinking *mind* as which the person, the whole man, C.G. Jung existed.

political leaders, etc. *In a truthless age* "personal relationship" or, in psychotherapy, personalistic "transference" had to become so important, so loaded: the sphere of the personal was the only "truth"-substitute left.

In former ages, however, personal, distinctly subjective relationships in our modern sense were rare. By way of only one example let me point to the phenomenon of marriage. A marriage was primarily an objective social and legal institution with clearly-defined roles, duties, and areas of competence and with an objective (both natural and societal) purpose: the begetting of children; in addition it was, in Christian Europe, also an objective religious or metaphysical reality, in Roman Catholicism even a sacrament, that transcended (and often completely ignored) the personal level of the individuals concerned (that is, whether they liked each other or were perhaps incompatible). Personal feelings and the spouses' "speaking with each other about themselves and their feelings," nowadays the most important aspect of a relationship in addition to sex, were of decidedly secondary importance and frequently occurred, if at all, only to a minimal extent, but were probably also not expected and not missed—because one simply did not have yet a concept of a relationship based on speaking about one's feelings. Indeed, one did not *have*, and could not have, any such *feelings* (in more than a rudimentary form) that one could have talked about. It is the other way around: our modern "speaking with each other about ourselves and our feelings" is the (ritual) way how such relationship feelings, and the realm of such feelings, are *generated* (fabricated) for the first time.

In former times, relationship feelings (including the feelings of love) had their authentic place in the objective, not the subjective psyche: in poetry, literature, and ritualized enactments *and not in the actual personal relationships of real human beings themselves.* These feelings, far from being inherent in human *nature*, were first invented, created, and practiced as cultural acquisitions in the public and objective sphere of literature. And only much later, in modernity, did they sink down into the private sphere of intimate personal contacts, where, as sedimented cultural acquisitions, they were imitated by individual persons. I want to illustrate this briefly with one striking example, the weddings in royal houses during the Baroque age. Reigning princes and kings traditionally kept court poets and court musicians. Most frequently marriages at such courts came about between two people who had hardly had an opportunity to get to know each other before their marriage, if they ever had met or seen each other before at all. Whether they liked each other, let alone loved each other, was irrelevant. As everyone knew, the unions had been dictated by political and dynastic interests and necessities. As everyone also knew, princes and kings generally, and often quite officially, had mistresses and favorites, and their wives also sometimes had lovers. The real function of such a marriage was the possibility of the production of a legitimate heir to the throne, not human happiness through personal relationships.

However, at the luxurious wedding festivities, the court poets had the task of extensively celebrating the union of this couple as one of heavenly love and to praise this love and the undisturbed harmony of husband and wife literally to the skies, for example, by comparing it, with much rhetorical elaboration, to the infinite and unending love of divine lovers of mythology. In poetry as well as in theatrical performances, the union was represented as if the two persons had been predestined by Heaven for each other (in what *later* would be the romantic sense of love) and had now finally found each other.

The discrepancy between the frequently rather dreary empirical reality of royal marriages and the poetic idealization of it in highest mythological images is striking. And yet it did not seem to bother anyone at the time. It was not felt as a false show, an illicit glossing over of a drab reality, as cheating or hypocrisy. This drab reality was by no means seen as an objection to the idealized presentation of it, as its refutation, its exposure as fake. This strange discrepancy asks for an explanation.

The people of that time lived within the psychological difference. The empirical aspect of reality, the way "civil man" experienced marriage, simply did not enter the picture; as the ordinary and human-all-too-human reality, it was negligible. Nothing higher or absolute was expected of it. *It* was not the place where the soul's truths had to show themselves. Conversely, the *real event* of a royal marriage[127] was

---

[127] Something similar on a lower level is true for ordinary marriages. Even today. When a freshly married couple comes out of the church, people happening to pass by at this moment will automatically feel drawn to look at the bride in her white wedding-gown, not because she is necessarily superhumanly beautiful, but because they are subliminally motivated by the soul's reminiscence that the bride (only) on this one day of her wedding once upon a time objectively used to be the manifestation—the actual presence—of the Goddess.

an *opportunity* for, and an *occasion that called for*, society's honoring and celebrating *the soul's* truth of marriage, the heavenly mysterium coniunctionis, by publicly articulating it in poetry and ceremonially displaying it with some pomp as a substantial reality in its own right and as a higher reality than ordinary reality. Truth, here the truth of marriage, resided in "the show": in the poetic eulogy, in pertinent theater or opera performances, and in the ritualized or theatrical *representation* of this truth by the royal couple on the day or days of their wedding festivities. The bride and the bridegroom had to publicly represent for society as a whole the truth of the union of the divine couple. They were actors who had to *serve* the soul's truth by making *it* visibly present for the community *on that day*. It was absolutely evident and doubtlessly convincing. This wedding ceremony here today, between these two royal persons, was the *event* of truth, its actual presence in the human world, one instant of Heaven's having come down to and entered the earth, and it could not in any way be impaired and spoiled by the general conscious awareness of how the daily reality of human marriages, especially in royal houses, usually is. Why not? Because it was independent of that reality. *Much like the shining sun,* it had its authenticity and conviction, its evidence, within itself rather than, if at all, deriving it from empirical facts through a correspondence with them.[128] Soul truths have everything they need within themselves, even their substantiation. Nothing in the way of expectations or demands followed from it for people's marriages, the daily reality of married life in the sphere of the human all-too-human. In former ages people were not so naive as not to understand the radical difference between Heaven and Earth, the truth of the soul and empirical reality, as two fundamentally different realms with their own separate rules. Render unto Caesar the things which are Caesar's, and unto God the things that are God's. Only our deep modern utopian conviction demands that Caesar, just like that, realize Heaven on Earth.

But this celebrated archetypal truth of marriage was the soul's truth, not people's ("civil man's") own truth. And in the premodern mode of being-in-the-world, the soul's truth was prioritized whereas

---

[128] For the same reason "the report of the birth, life, death, and resurrection of the Redeemer could still pass as biography," as Jung had said, and the speeches that in Antiquity Greek or Roman historians placed into the mouths of historical personages passed for their actual historical speeches. See section 2.2.2 above.

everyday reality (with all its misery) was taken for granted as a fundamentally deficient one. It would be a total misunderstanding if we wanted to play the reality of people off against the celebration of the mythic or archetypal truth. The level of myth and religion or metaphysics was the sphere in which people sought their deepest fulfillment (ultimately even in the afterlife). Heaven—the sphere of absolute negativity—was the level on which people lived their *real* life; their real life was not this life on earth, and the real locus of their real life was not the sphere of positivity. Modernity is characterized by the fact that the whole dimension of "heaven" has dropped out from our scheme altogether, so that absolute fulfillment is sought as positive fact ("immediate experience").

2.3.5 The historicity of soulful feelings

When the Song of Songs, Ovid, the medieval Minnesingers, Petrarch, Shakespeare, and so on express feelings of love, we must not retrojectively read their poems as their self-expression, *their* personal feelings "coming from their inner," as if they had already been modern individuals. Their poems—and the love feelings articulated in them— are essentially *literature*. The articulation of those feelings occurred as literary events.[129] They were revolutionary inventions and productions, discoveries at the very forefront of cultural development. Anticipations. The feelings were born "above" and "outside of" the poets as literal persons; they first appeared in and as those literary *texts*, in and as *words*, in and as the poetic rhetorical phrases, images, and metaphors they found, not in the person or psyche (let alone "the unconscious") of their authors. The possibility to articulate these feelings as poets did not at all mean that they as human beings, as "civil men (or women)," would already have been capable of actually having such feelings as subjective emotions. The place of where "the real action was," of where the true life of people was lived, was up there, in what was above the heads, above people's practical reality. We remember: man is (or at least was) an "*arbor inversa*," a tree that has its roots in the sky and its treetops in the earth (*CW* 13 § 410 ff.).

---

[129] In my *The Soul Always Thinks*, New Orleans, LA (Spring Journal Books) 2010, p. 383, I referred to and discussed Niklas Luhmann's thesis that love needs a linguistic code.

The general insight to be gained from these reflections is that feelings are not anthropological constants, part of the psychic inventory of *homo sapiens*, nor that they are caused by eternal archetypes, but that they are historical cultural acquisitions, creations, inventions. They are not discovered, the way certain continents, the Jupiter moons, or pathogens are discovered, but the result of a *making*, "soul-making."

An excellent example of how entirely new feelings and perceptions came into the world at a certain point in history, feelings that previously had been simply unimaginable, is the idea and phenomenon of the *soror mystica* that we find in alchemy. For all antiquity and even much of later times it can be said that a spiritual relationship to a woman, a relationship for the purpose of a meeting of souls and a spiritual transformation of the mind, would have been absolutely unthinkable. In classical antiquity, a man would normally see his wife only in the bedroom. Woman was seen in that society by men as the mother of their legitimate heirs and as the means to continue their lineage. It is not uninteresting that the Greek word for woman, *gynê*, has the meaning, "she who gives birth." A man spent his waking time exclusively with men. Normally there would also not be any common family meals. The husband would eat with his (male) friends in a club-like situation. Therefore, it is quite natural that *soul or spiritual needs* had to be fulfilled in relationships with other males and that when Eros was seen by Plato as having an educational purpose and as being an important motor for the soul's ascent to the contemplation of the divine, it could only be conceived as a love between male partners, a man and a boy, in accordance with the general strong institution of pederasty in antiquity, which, e.g., in Sparta, seems to have been a regular part of a boy's initiation period, in other words, which also there had a "higher" spiritual purpose, even though in the case of Sparta one that was still on a more archaic *ritualistic* (rather than, in a more narrow sense of the word, *pedagogic*) level. In Plato, the spiritual dimension becomes explicitly spiritual. "A man's falling in love with a beautiful boy is 'the best and noblest of all the forms that possession by a god can take,'" we read in *Phaedrus* (249). For Plato, the beautiful bodies of boys started off, beyond immediate sexual desires, the deeper longing for the spiritual Idea of the Beautiful and the Good. Metaphorically, the mythological model of spiritual love was the love of Zeus for Ganymede (*Phaedrus* 255 c 1).

The possibility of the revolutionary idea of a *soror mystica* in medieval times was based on the fact that over the centuries, through the influence of Christianity and its inwardness, through mysticism practiced by monks as well as by nuns, in particular and above all through the mystic devotion of the pious to the Virgin Mary, and, in a more secular sense, through the almost cultic devotion of the Minnesingers to an idealized woman, slowly the feminine had acquired a totally new soul aspect unknown before. This was a truly new *conquest*, an extension of the range of feelings beyond what previously had been possible: an *invention*. Just as in prehistoric times the non-existing soul was primordially made through the counter-natural cult of the dead and through the equally counter-natural institution of sacrificial slaughtering, and just as in classical antiquity the counter-natural pederastic love as philosophical eros creatively established the non-existing realm of the spirit in the sense of philosophy,[130] so the repurposing (as we might say) of the (already repurposed and counter-natural) philosophical eros, by directing it all of a sudden to "the feminine," invented and established the inwardness and depth of *feeling* as a totally new addition to the inventory of psychological possibilities and regions of experience, making mystical as well as romantic soul love possible. Always new non-existing continents,[131] or, on a smaller scale, new tracts of land, new peninsulas, are in this way added to the non-existing soul.

The fact that in one case, at the earliest prehistoric times, cultural development or the making of soul proceeded via the dead and the act of killing, in the other, in classical Greece, via the masculine (male-male erotic relation), in the third even later case via the feminine[132] must not be misunderstood in biological or social terms, not literally. What was at stake was not the dead, the men, the women (or the masculine and the feminine). Rather, they are merely the empirically existing vehicles or the stuff by and in which the soul conquers and

---

[130] Jung saw the educational function of masculine homosexuality in ancient Greece, but interpreted it more naturalistically as social glue necessary to tie the polis together.

[131] Castles in the air!

[132] In each of the three cases mentioned it was the soul that made itself. But in each case the soul made itself of course as something different. The result of its making itself through the cult of the dead and sacrificial slaughter is very different indeed from that soul that is made, to mention only this, via the feminine (through Virgin Mary mysticism, through an alchemical *soror mystica*, or in Minnesang).

works out for itself its own non-existing regions (the region of the mind as such, the sphere of philosophical thought and Platonic Ideas, and the potential to feel deep mystical feelings of soulful love), much like in sandplay therapy sand and toy figures are the very real material medium for the creation of non-existing soul images. Ritual and cultural institutions, social roles and practices must psychologically be understood as sandplay-like processes, if I may say so. As far as, for example, the relation between the sexes was organized in a premodern society and the whole issue of matriarchal and patriarchal forms of organization is concerned, there is of course nothing to stop us from viewing them in terms of power struggle and suppression, but this is then not a psychological assessment but a socio-political one. For a psychological understanding, the factually existing men and women were the "toy figures" in a play in which the soul worked out for itself certain of *its own* concerns and celebrated them as its truths. As such "toy figures," they had been allotted their determinate roles that they had to play. They were dressed in what we could call a "mythical garment." Rather than aiming for their personal self-actualization, they had to represent and enact what the soul, at the respective historical and cultural locus, needed to give a visible cultural presence to. The fact that it was the soul and not people who dictated those roles and the further fact that premodern man had not been born out of the soul is what gave to the allotted roles, even in the eyes of those who had the burden of playing them out, the form of a truth of nature and thus their unquestioned and unquestionable conviction. They could not be seen and felt as *roles* that had been unduly imposed on them. The roles were self-evident, a matter of course, so to speak ego-syntonic.

That the individual persons were not totally identical with their roles, that they also had their own ego-personalities (as we retrojectively can say), allows for the fact that within the soul's social, cultural "sandplay" there is also room for personal or group power games and subjective nastinesses as well as for a degree of freedom concerning the specific form one gives to the enactment of one's role, just as for personal generosity in view of infringements of the rules by others.

Not only soulful feelings, even the very notion of the inner and "the unconscious" are historical acquisitions, rather than eternal givens. Surprisingly, there is one side of Jung that knows of the radical newness

182 WHAT IS SOUL?

of "the inner" and of the fact that soul truths for millennia used to be outside. After having discussed certain aspects of the "Seelenproblem des modernen Menschen," Jung warns,

> [...] everything I have observed lies *in the soul*; everything, so to speak, on the *side of the inner*. I must, however, add at once that this is something peculiar, inasmuch as the soul is not always and everywhere on the inside. There are peoples and epochs where it is outside, peoples and epochs that are unpsychological, as, for example, all ancient cultures, and among them especially Egypt with its magnificent objectivity and its just as magnificent, naïve, negative confession of sins. Behind the spirit of the Apis tombs of Saqqara and the Pyramids we cannot possibly imagine psychological issues, no more than behind the music of Bach.
>
> Whenever there exists externally a conceptual or ritual form in which all the yearnings and hopes of the soul are absorbed and expressed, that is, for example, a living religion, then the soul is outside and there is no soul problem, just as there is then no unconscious in our sense. It was therefore logical that the discovery of psychology took exclusively place during the last decades, although former centuries possessed enough introspection and intelligence to gain knowledge about psychological facts. [...] The reason for this is that there existed no compelling predicament. [...] It needed the spiritual predicament of our time to force us to discover psychology. (*CW* 10 §§ 158 f., transl. modif.)

"The inner" is a product of history, the history of the soul, the result of the interiorization of what used to be part of cultural institutions, customs, symbols, ideas into the individual person through a process of sublation and sedimentation.

2.3.6 The objectivity of the objective soul: works of culture and cultural institutions

Usually we think that the movement in the production of manifestations of the soul is one from inside out, that it begins deep down in ourselves, in our inner or "the unconscious," and that what is said, felt, or done, in other words, what becomes manifest and is displayed, is literally its "expression," "utterance," its fantasizing. All new ideas, and inventions have their true home inside, in the unconscious, in the psyche. Just as the old sensualist creed used to be that, "nothing is in the mind that has not before been in the senses" (*nihil est in intellectu quod non antea fuerit in sensu*), so the usual psychological creed is that nothing is in the personal or collective mind that had not been born from the individuals' unconscious as the generative matrix of all creativity. Although we entertain the notion of the objective soul, we nevertheless conceive it essentially subjectivistically.

But that everything comes from within is an illusion. We must reverse the direction of our usual psychological idea of cause and effect, origin or source (or true author) and resulting product and realize that what is (consciously or unconsciously) in individual consciousness must before have been in a cultural institution or work; in very early times predominantly in ritual enactments, but then also in proverbs, mythic tales, artistic productions, in which it existed "out there," as ritual deed (*opus operatum*) or enacted custom, cultural ideas, or as factual creative work. Consciousness makes its way ahead, as it were, *hangelnd*, hand over hand. It "de-pends" on or from the cultural products as its "extraterrestrial satellites" shot up into an orbit around the human "Earth." The works of culture are not *self-expressions*, not fantasizings in the sense of the unconscious's projection of images onto the screen of the conscious mind. Cultural works are their own origin, *they* produce themselves and come as a "surprise" to people. We already know: *It begins above people's heads*. Everything new comes from outside ("above") into consciousness. It first hovers "in the sky," as it were, and is marveled at and revered as something higher (often, however, only after initially having been experienced as something threatening by consciousness, which therefore violently rejected it as a scandalous attack upon the culture's established and familiar truth). And only slowly can it come down into people's consciousness as their inner possession (or part of the make-up of their personality), either through a "leap after the throw," i.e., a long process of integration of what had been "thrown" far ahead and up into the future, or through a gradual accustoming and sedimentation process that results in the new forms and ideas ending up as sunken cultural assets in people's inner.

One could, by way of objection, claim that, even if not for the general public, then at least in the poets themselves (or in other producers of cultural works), what they produce must certainly come from within them. Even if, as I suggested, they indeed "throw"

something entirely new into the future, it must nevertheless first have
been in them, for how else could they "throw" it, pro-duce it? But
this is a mistaken assumption. We remember Goethe's statement that
it was not he who made his poems, but that they made him. The
creative person, in his creating, is building castles in the air, and is
used *by them* for *their* need to become produced. They are
fundamentally beyond him as "civil man." He, too, essentially makes
his way "hand over hand" when producing his work. What we call
creativity is precisely the capacity to become used by works that want
to be produced. It is the capacity to build castles *in the air*. "By its
colorful tunes the lark blissfully climbs up into the air."[133] Creativity
means to trust the air, its absolute negativity, as the only *ground* upon
which, as well as the only *stuff* out of which, *great* cultural works can
be created. If the work of creative people were their self-expression, if
it would, as one says, come out of their "unconscious," it would
necessarily be only of ego significance and nothing great (just as our
modern patients' dreams and paintings "out of the unconscious").

There are instances where Jung thinks along similar lines, reversing
our customary explanatory pattern. In one case the idea of a reversal
becomes explicit. In *MDR* (p. 323 f.) he says after reporting his dream
of 1958 about two UFOs, one in the shape of a lens of the objective
of a telescope, one like a magic lantern, both of which were pointing
directly at him, "Still half in the dream, the thought passed through
my head: 'We always think that the UFOs are projections of ours. Now
it turns out that we are their projections...,'" and after reporting
another similar dream about a meditating yogi who had Jung's face,
he gives this résumé: "The aim of both these dreams is to effect a reversal
of the relationship between ego-consciousness and the unconscious
and to represent the unconscious as the generator of the empirical
personality." The trouble with this interpretation is that he translates
both the UFO and the yogi with his ideological construct of "the
unconscious." This is uncalled for. The dreams do not say anything
about an "unconscious." They show precise images, a UFO and a yogi
vis-à-vis and outside of the experiencing subject. What the dreams, if
one reads them as pointing to a reversal of our usual explanatory

---

[133] This line is the beginning of the poem "Liebesfeier" by Nikolaus Lenau (my
translation). I discussed it in Chapter Fifteen of my *The Soul Always Thinks*, New Orleans,
LA (Spring Journal Books) 2010.

direction, do show is that his own consciousness is not his innate and innermost property, but comes to him from outside. He, his consciousness, his personality, rather than being the result of his own self-unfolding, is the result of what is "projected" *upon* him, in the UFO case from outer space.

Another even more relevant passage than the preceding ones comes from a very different context. "... Consequently, man derives his human personhood [*Persönlichkeitscharakter*, his being constituted as a personality] so to speak only secondarily, as the myths state, from his descent from gods and heroes. That means in psychological terms, his consciousness of himself as a personality stems from the influence of person-like archetypes" (*CW* 5 § 388, transl. modif.). Leaving aside in this case the psychologically highly problematic concept of archetypes[134] and sticking to the phenomenology of the phenomenon referred to, we can say: what Jung suggests here is that man's existing as a personality is not part of his internal make-up that is given to him all along with his nature. It is not an anthropological constant. Rather, it is a historically and culturally acquired characteristic, something essentially secondary, an attribute that originally was not in or on him but, when it *first* emerged, existed only either *up there* as a characteristic of gods (who originally were the *only* owners of "personalities") or, alternatively, *way back* in the darkness of the past as an attribute of mythic culture heroes (of whom can be said the same as about the gods). The emergence of the notion of gods in the soul's history was the *invention* of the idea of personality.[135] This idea

---

[134] Jung usually conceives them naturalistically as primordial givens, entities, as existing ahistorical dominants and effective causes, which is a kind of metaphysical presupposition and incompatible with a true psychology. It is in this sense significant that in the *context* of this passage, Jung is more interested in the personality character of the archetypes than in the fact so important in my context (and referred to by Jung precisely only as an argument for the personality character of the archetypes) that man does not have his personality character as a natural possession of his, but derives it from archetypes. The theory of archetypes is ambivalent. With his one hand, Jung uses it to reverse the conventional order and to advance the idea that what appears in the human mind comes from above and outside, but with his other hand he substantiates the archetypes, thereby turning his view of them into a *fundamentalist* theory: instead of wholeheartedly trusting the thin air, he posits a solid ground, real entities, "factors."

[135] In our context where we are only concerned with the general idea of this necessary reversion of the conventional order of origin and product, we do not have to be sticklers for historical accuracy. It is to be assumed that long before the gods and culture heroes, (a) the cultically revered dead and (b) the big game hunted by prehistoric man were the first appearance of "personality."

therefore first appeared up there in the sky. Only in his gods (or in primordial culture heroes as his ancestors) did man indirectly, implicitly have the first immediacy of his own personality and not in himself, nor as his own property, let alone as his conscious self-understanding—just as only in their shaman, king, or Pharaoh all the ordinary people had (the first immediacy of) their self which only after a millennia-long historical development ended up in each modern individual as its private possession.

Most relevant and clearest concerning the reversal of the usual understanding as internal are (a) a fundamental theoretical statement of Jung's and (b) his insights about the poet, the artist.

(a) The fundamental theoretical dictum is concerned with what, "for immediate experience, is autonomous images." Jung states, "... we are compelled to reverse our rationalistic causal sequence, and instead of deriving these figures from our psychic predispositions, must derive our psychic predispositions from these figures" (*CW* 13 § 299, transl. modif.). Of course, for Jung the figures, images, which form people's psychic reality, are of archetypal nature. For us, by contrast, they are decidedly of cultural origin.

(b) Talking about art, the poet, Jung lets us know: "He is in the highest degree objective [*sachlich*], impersonal, and even inhuman—or superhuman—for as an artist he is his work and not a human being" (*CW* 15 § 156, transl. modif.). When he says, "For art is innate in him like a drive that seizes him and makes him its instrument," the words "innate" and the analogy to a "drive" could still tempt us into giving this a biological and subjectivist interpretation. But the very next sentence removes this possibility. "That which in the last analysis wills in him is not he, the human being as person, but the work of art." "It is quite plausible that the artist must be explained by his art and not by the insufficiencies of his nature and his personal conflicts..." (§ 158, transl. modif.). Just as Goethe had said that the poetic images made him, not he them, so Jung stated, possibly without knowing Goethe's own dictum, that "It is not Goethe that creates *Faust*, but *Faust* that creates Goethe" (§ 159). The objective work as literal *opus operatum* and as an in external reality existing "thing," which in temporal sequence is obviously secondary, namely, the final product, the end result of his creative process, is logically, psychologically the first beginning and initial "cause." This priority of the final product over the creation process is a case of the soul's *hysteron proteron*. "It is the great dream which has always spoken through the artist as a mouthpiece. All his love and passion (his 'values') flow towards the coming guest to proclaim his arrival" (*Letters 2*, p. 591, to Read, 2 Nov. 1960). Like Aristotle's prime mover, so the work moves the artist, and works in him as an effective cause, *hôs erômenon* (like an object loved, *Met.* 1072 b). The work as that "which in the last analysis wills in him" does not drive the artist from behind, but pulls him, attracts him from the future as "the coming guest."

The artist is "a bearer and form-giver of the unconsciously productive soul of mankind. That is his office ...." (§ 157, transl. modif.). "... at this level of experience it is no longer the individual that is the experiencing subject, but the nation (*Volk*)" (§ 162, my transl., omitted in *CW*), or rather than *Volk*, we could say, the historical locus as the soul in its respective actuality: "a poet or seer lends expression to the unspoken inner depth [or inner truth] of his time [*dem Unausgesprochenen der Zeitlage*]" (§ 153, transl. modif.), or, as we heard from Jung's letter to Read, to the "great dream." My view that the creative person makes his way ahead "hand over hand" is perhaps, at least indirectly, supported by Jung's statement that the artist "is in the deepest sense an instrument and for that reason *beneath* his work..." (§ 161, transl. modif., my italics).

In the whole text from which these quotations are taken Jung has for once left behind the entire logic of the inner, of the unconscious, and of personalistic psychology as such (although the term "the unconscious" still occurs in it occasionally[136]). The notion of "the *unspoken* inner depth or logic of his time" makes the concept of *the*

---

[136] What, however, is not entirely overcome in Jung's discussion of "psychology and literature" is the logic of Jung's concept of *Urvision* (primordial vision) and timeless "primordial image" (or archetype) in the sense of an image which "has been engraved in the unconscious since the dawn of history, where it lies dormant until it is awakened by the propitiousness or inauspiciousness of the time, ..." (§ 159, transl. modif.). Although this quote also mentions the historical moment, and this historical moment as the awakening factor at that, *what* is awakened is nevertheless the eternal archetypal image. The image is ahistorical, suprahistorical, and as such "everpresent," even if only in a dormant state. And the circumstances of a given time serve merely as the trigger that actualizes ("constellates") it. Does this not mean that the psyche is reduced precisely to the "executive organ of eternal ideas" after all, a concept that Jung (*CW* 6 § 78, I will come to this in the next chapter) tried to reject? This conception is not really compatible with the idea that the poet lends expression to the unspoken depth or logic of his time.

unconscious (including "the collective unconscious") superfluous. For a psychological view, the *Zeitlage*—the situation, the internal problematic, the logical configuration, and inner truth, of an age or epoch—is *concrete* in the sense of having everything it needs within itself. It does not, in the style of bad metaphysics, refer back to ageless and everpresent *primordial* images, i.e., to images stemming from outside of the time in question itself, and images belonging to the (logically independent) "collective unconscious" or, as later Jungians say, "the imaginal." The logic or inner truth of a historical locus is the historical locus's own inherent logic or truth, in much the same way that each biological organism carries its inner organization and laws, its potential and deficiencies—its logic—as its own internal property within itself.

All that the *Zeitlage* or the truth of the historical locus does indeed need as a human addition or contribution is that its fundamental unspokenness becomes expressed, is given articulate form, turned into a *work*, and is in this way celebrated, which is what we call soul-making. Truth as the *logos eôn* (the existing or prevailing logos) wants to be *made* true (disclosed, unconcealed), so as to become in the first place what it implicitly has been all along: *alêtheia*.

It is in the same spirit that Jung says, the "poet voices the truth of all [everyone]" (§ 159, transl. modif.), i.e., of the whole community or nation. It is the truth of the time *in which* all have their place, and as such it is the soul (not, in the quasi statistical sense of opinion polls, all the actual opinions shared by all individuals as their own opinions). Just as "... at this level of experience it is no longer the individual that is the experiencing subject, but the nation" as a whole, so it is also the truth of the nation as a whole, the *communal* truth.[137] The perspective of individuals with their own truths or opinions has here been left behind. "Nation" does not mean an aggregation of all the atomic individuals that empirically are contained by it. Noteworthy is here also that art is seen as the manifestation of *truth* and not as the artist's self-expression, not the representation of "a personal experience" (§ 146), not *his* feelings, opinions, imaginings, or dreams (and that for Jung, to mention this as an aside, the psychologist, too, is motivated by "love of knowledge, in search of truth" p. 85, transl. modif.). Just

---

[137] Not collective!

as "the life-style of an English gentleman or a Prussian officer, or a cardinal" cannot be reduced to personal factors because the gentleman, officer, and cardinal "represent objective, impersonal *officia* which have their own inherent objective psychology [*sachliche Psychologie*[138]]" (§ 157, transl. modif.), so also is the artist an office-bearer, and therefore our mode of explanation has to focus on "the psychology of the work of art" in contrast to "the personal psychology of the poet" (cf. § 147).

Since I already devoted some space to Jung's discussion of the psychology of the artist, I might as well include another aspect of importance that is to be found in that text of Jung's. It is significant for our question "What is soul?" in two respects. First, because it gives another example of the psychological difference, and an example from a new area, namely the reality of a human being. Secondly, it points to the Great, the exceptional in contradistinction to the ordinary.

Talking about the artist, Jung says, "His life is necessarily full of conflicts, for two forces are at war within him: the ordinary man with his claims to happiness, contentment, and security in life, on the one hand, and the ruthless creative passion, on the other hand, which may go as far as to override every personal desire" (§ 158, transl. modif.). "As a person he may have moods and a will and personal aims, but as an artist he is 'Man' in a higher sense," namely, as we already heard, "a bearer and form-giver of the unconsciously productive soul of mankind" (§ 157, transl. modif.). So the artist is two men in one, each of which has its own separate psychology. He is ordinary man just like most of us, namely as the human, all-too-human person that he is, and as such he has "the personal psychology of the poet," that we heard about. And in addition he is artist who *is* artist because, and to the extent that, "That which in the last analysis wills in him is not he, the human being as person, but the work of art," and whose psychology is therefore "the psychology of the work of art." This is obviously a manifestation of the psychological difference (the difference between psyche and soul, or human being and soul) as *objectively*

---

[138] "Sachlich" is more specific than "objective." It refers to *Sache*: matter, thing, also subject-matter, issue, in legal regards the case, and evokes the contrast to human person. The *officia* Jung speaks of are objective figurations with their own inherent logic which has a reality that antecedes and is independent of the contingent bearers of the offices. For a *sachliche Psychologie*, the soul's life is logical life.

existing in a real phenomenon (rather than as a methodological distinction that we make), namely in the artist, going through him. But it also delineates for us the difference *between* people, between those who are great artists, great philosophers, composers, or great in some other area of cultural production, those in whom, in addition to their ordinariness, *soul* happens, on the one hand, and those—that is, most of us—who are not "great," not seized by a cultural work or by the truth of the age, those who are *only* ordinary persons, *only* human, all-too-human, on the other hand. When Jung said, as quoted above, "My problem is to wrestle with the big monster of the historical past, the great snake of the centuries, the burden of the human mind, the problem of Christianity. ... Other people are not worried by such problems, they do not care about the historical burden Christianity has heaped upon us. But there are people who are concerned with the great battle between the present and the past or the future" (*CW* 18 § 279), he expressed the psychological difference as one whose sides are embodied by different individuals, one could almost say different types of persons, just as with the comment added to this statement: "Certain people make history and others build a little house in the suburbs." The former give voice to the soul, the others circle around themselves as private individuals with their "claims to happiness, contentment, and security in life."

2.3.7 Beyond imagining and fantasizing

Being serious about the notion of the objective soul requires that the imagination is dethroned as the topmost or inmost reality of the soul.

Earlier I said that in the history of the soul new non-existing continents, or, on a smaller scale, new tracts of land, new peninsulas, are always being added to the non-existing soul. This statement of mine blatantly contradicts the Kantian imagination of "the land of truth (enchanting name!), surrounded by a wide and stormy ocean, the native home of illusion, where many a fog-bank and many a swiftly melting iceberg give the deceptive appearance of new lands" (*Critique of Pure Reason* B 294 f.). Freud also made use of the metaphor of solid land and ocean, but in a very different context. He tried to imagine the development of culture in the (naturalistic, "positivistic") image of the reclamation of land from the Zuiderzee. Both land and sea in this metaphor are positivities, empirical realities, and both appear on the horizontal plane. For him culture is something that is, as it were, snatched from the wild force of nature, and cultural development is a mere shifting of the border between them.

Nietzsche, however, was in principle able to envision culture as happening in the air. At a time when airplanes and the possibility of real flying did not yet exist, he spoke of "*Wir Luftschiffahrer des Geistes*" ("We aeronauts of the spirit").

Culture and soul are freely invented, created. The soul, which as we know makes itself, is, in making itself, truly only building castles in thin air, ever new castles (or ever new extensions to and internal divisions/differentiations of the already built ones). It precisely invents its own lands, although not as Kantian illusions, but as realities and truths that it actually *fabricates* in the real world, giving what is and remains to be "castles in the air" a powerful existence in human life.

That Jung who made the oft-cited statement, "This autonomous activity of the psyche, which can be explained neither as a reflex action to sensory stimuli nor as the executive organ of eternal ideas, is, like every vital process, a continually creative act. The psyche creates reality every day. The only expression I can use for this activity is *fantasy*. Fantasy is just as much feeling as thinking; as much intuition as sensation" (*CW* 6 § 78), probably wanted to express a similar view. His conception, however, is hampered by the idea of fantasy. This conception is too psychologistic, subjectivistic, and ego-psychological, starting out from a psychic function or faculty ("fantasy") of human beings (it is in this regard noteworthy that Jung speaks of "psyche" and not "soul"!), and it ignores the absolutely essential *objective*, quasi "material" aspect of the production of cultural works and institutions by the soul, in which the building of actual "*castles*" in the air is reflected, through which soul regions are to some extent once and for all established or at least permanently made available.

Therefore the psyche also precisely does not have to create reality *every day*. If that were the case, it would be disastrous. We would not get anywhere. Creative acts, however, are rare. Just as the psyche does not have to create language every day anew, but can rely on the existing language,[139] so most aspects of the soul are generally available options that the psyche merely has to avail itself of in everyday life. And just as language is not a part of the individual human being, but a cultural and communal reality, *around* all the individuals of a culture, so also all the essential acquisitions of the soul in its history. And it is not really fantasy that creates, for example, new works of art. What fantasy produces is not creative, but is rather to be understood along the lines of what Kant referred to when he spoke of "giving the deceptive appearance of new lands" ("*neue Länder lügen*"!), where in reality there is nothing or merely a fog-bank. Fantasy means merely imagining things, which, psychologically, is neither here nor there.

When prehistoric man started to build dolmen and tumuli, when the ancient Egyptians erected pyramids, they did not fantasize, did not make claims about seeing land in the middle of the ocean of illusion. No, they very really constructed and established something here on the solid ground of the earth. When people started to sacrifice animals or humans to the gods, when other people began to practice head-hunting, they did not imagine things, but *made* soul in a very concrete, practical sense. When Jung's Elgonyi in Africa greeted the rising sun by spitting into their hands and raising their palms towards the sun, they did not fantasize. They followed an ancient custom, a real cultural institution. "'That has always been done,' they said. It was impossible to obtain any explanation, and I realized that they actually knew only *that* they did it, not *what* they were doing. They themselves saw no meaning in this action" (*MDR* p. 266, transl. modif.), in other words, they did not imagine anything; rather, it was an established cultural practice, a custom, a habit. When the year was divided into ordinary work days and into special sacred festival times or holidays, this was not caused by the necessities of physical or biological (instinctual) time, but also not due to "the imaginal." Rather it was the free invention and production of the time of the soul *as the real time* of human life. What, on a wholly different cultural level, Plato's *paidikos erôs* (see

---

[139] Psychically, the functions of habit and memory must be mentioned here, as Hegel showed in his *Encylopedia III* (1830 ed., § 409 and §§ 461-8). It was Hegel who broke with the old dominating Aristotelian tradition that operated with the idea that we think in images, a tradition that still informed Kant, Fichte, and Schelling. Hegel dethroned "productive imagination" as the ultimate ground of consciousness and realized the foundational role of (1. *retentive*, 2. *reproductive*, and 3. *mechanical!*) memory for the thoughts that we have.

Symposium 180 a ff.) produced was not fantasized ideas, nothing imagined, but the very *real* and *objective dimension* of ideals, Platonic Ideas, idealistic philosophy, and idealistic strivings by real people. What the love poetry of the Minnesingers, Petrarch, and their followers as well as the Christian mystics produced in the long run was the real objective possibility to feel deep soulful feelings of love. When around 600 B.C. the Lydians produced the first gold and silver coins, when in modern times paper money and much later credit cards took the place of gold and silver coins, this was not fantasizing, but different moments of only too real soul-making. All the things mentioned *seem* to happen on Kant's ocean of illusions extending around that island that for him was the land with the "enchanting name" of truth, but in reality they are precisely not on that ocean, but rather in our real world here on earth. And yet they are free inventions, true "castles built in thin air," moments in the continued making, unfolding, and further construction of the non-existing soul.

Soul starts out as a real doing (ritual enactments), real speaking, and as produced works, objectively created things and institutions. Ideas, fantasies, theories, and explanations about what has been done and about the works created only come later, when what was objective deed or product was sublated and distilled, interiorized into the mind. They are *people's* interpretations of what the *soul* produced. The deed comes first. And: ritual acts, as Jung told us, are "performed without thinking" (*gedankenlos vollzogen*)![140] About the Elgonyi's greeting-the-sun ceremony Jung said similarly, "They just do it, they never reflect on what they are doing, and are consequently unable to explain themselves. They are evidently just repeating what they have 'always' done at sunrise... It is most unlikely that these primitives ever, even in the remote past, knew any more about the meaning of their ceremony. On the contrary, their ancestors probably knew even less, because they were more profoundly unconscious and thought if possible even less about their doings" (*CW* 18 § 552). And he adds, "Faust aptly says: 'Im Anfang war die Tat' (in the beginning was the deed). Deeds were never invented, they were done. Thoughts, on the other hand, are a relatively late discovery; .... Yet unreflected life existed

---

[140] William McGuire and R.F.C. Hull (eds.), *C. G. Jung Speaking*, London (Picador ed., Pan Books) 1980, p. 332 (transl. modif.).

long before man; it was not invented, but in it man found himself as an afterthought. First he was moved to deeds by unconscious factors,[141] and only a long time afterwards did he begin to reflect about the causes that had moved him" (*CW* 18 § 553).[142] Likewise, real objects like a

---

[141] It would be more exact to say that the deeds produced themselves in and through him as their medium and place of appearance, without *his* consciousness of why, what for, with what meaning. There was not first an idea or image or desire and only then the deed as its execution. *In the beginning* the deed contained "everything it needs" within itself, even its motivation, purpose, and meaning. The separation of motive, theory, purpose, on the one hand, and deed, on the other hand, belongs to a later stage of cultural development. Whether Jung's Elgonyi indeed lived, as Jung suggests, at the "in the beginning" stage or not, is not our topic here. But in regard to the ritual mentioned, we must say that it was *only* a true ritual *if* the doing was its own origin and purpose and if the deed logically contained everything it needs within itself.

[142] In the paragraph from which the last quote was taken (*CW* 18 § 553), Jung says something with which he goes decidedly wrong, as should be clear from my discussion in Part I above: "We would laugh at the idea of a plant or an animal inventing itself, yet there are many people who believe that the psyche or the mind invented itself and thus brought itself into being. As a matter of fact, the mind has grown to its present state of consciousness as an acorn grows into an oak or as saurians developed into mammals." Apart from the confusion of two entirely different issues, the question of self-production of the mind or consciousness versus the question of the further unfolding ("growing") of an already existing consciousness from an early to the present state, the fatal mistake of this statement is that Jung ontologizes and biologizes the mind as if it were a subsisting entity like a plant or animal. Maybe one can say that saurians developed into mammals and that *homo sapiens* later on developed from other mammals. But whereas *homo sapiens* is a real biological being (or species of beings), the mind or soul is not. It is logically negative and nothing ontological (the Bible expressed this in the idea that man IS God's image and likeness). And while, as Aristotle said, *anthrôpos anthrôpon gennâ* ("a human being produces a human being"), the soul makes (produces) uroborically *itself*, just as does, on another level, life (which is not an entity either). Also, the mind does not develop like an acorn, which develops according to a fixed program coded in its genes. Jung could, of course, also see things very differently. Jung is not a monolithic theorist. Another time he said for example: "And just as life as such fills the whole earth with animal and plant forms, so the psyche creates an even vaster world, namely the *Bewußtheit* [the fact that there is a conscious awareness], or better: the *Ge-wußtheit* [the known-ness], of the universe" [i.e., the fact that there is a knowing about it] (*CW* 17 § 165, transl. modif.). There is, to be sure, something problematic about this statement, too, and this is that, in speaking of life and the psyche as producers, Jung uses a mythologizing manner of speaking straightforwardly, substantiating "life" and "psyche"; life, however, does not really produce anything, because it does not subsist as a subject or agent in the first place. Only living organisms subsist and produce living organisms. In the same way, the psyche does not create that "even vaster world," as if it were a subsisting agent behind the scene. What rhetorically by way of personification we call the psyche (or rather the soul) is in truth precisely nothing else but this *produced* "vaster world" itself, the universe's knownness, the world of the mind. But in our context, what is to be appreciated as an important contribution of Jung's statement is the insight that soul is not just another piece of the universe, one element in it; as the reflectedness of the universe as a whole (as its duplication or reflection in the sense of its being known and, by extension, of a more developed *theoria*), it is of a fundamentally different and logically higher order than the universe itself. It is the latter's truth, its soul.

statue of a god, the sword of a man *were* the real presence of their soul meaning, which resided in them and not in people's understanding.

We are concerned with the *objective* soul. Soul-making is the *real* construction of human reality and thus neither fantasy in the sense of "entertaining images in the mind" (or of the Kantian speculation about distant shores in the fog at the end of the surrounding ocean of illusion), nor, as a matter of course, a clinging to positive facts and being determined by natural necessities. It is the reversal of those two options, a veritable *inverted world*: the actual building of freely "invented"[143] castles in the air, but only *as* the land of truth, *as* the real reality of human life here on earth, a life *as* mind and soul.

With our reflections about the objectivity of the objective soul we have already prepared the ground for the counterpart to the manifestation of soul "from below": the phenomenology of the soul "from above."

2.3.8 "From above"

The soul manifests "from above" in the Great, the exceptional. In *works* of culture, in great art, literature, music, philosophy, in the myths and gods as well as highest values of a people, in temples, pyramids, castles, in the constitution and truly great representatives of states, in the great institutions and rituals of a society, but also in the great cultural revolutions and in the fundamental further developments of a people's economic life and technology. Obviously we are here always in the decidedly public sphere. This is the only authentic sphere of *the soul proper*. It was a serious mistake of 20th century psychology to see the private inner of the atomic individual as the true locus of soul, although it had been clear from the outset that the soul is essentially communal and "around" people, the realm of shared meanings and thus the element or medium *within which* they as individuals live their lives. In contrast to what we saw in all the manifestations of soul "from below," with the discussion of the soul "from above" we have finally entered the realm of the *opus magnum*. The vessel and container for the soul's process and the "matter" to be

---

[143] Or "posited," "fabricated." In contrast to "conditioned by biological drives or external necessities," or produced as the natural outcome of external factors.

worked on in the soul's *opus magnum* is the culture as a whole, the form of human consciousness at large, its logic or constitution.

The Great is also inevitably "the cooked," refined, cultured. It is something that has passed through the human mind, has been processed and worked, digested and elaborated, so that it is past that first immediacy in which something new tends to appear. It builds on traditions and deepens, intensifies them. It is the crowning and transfiguration of life.

In what comes "from above," the soul is not concerned with the pragmatics of life, but is partly the direct, explicit articulation or self-display and celebration, and partly the indirect reflection of the *truths* of a people's actually lived life. These truths are not themselves tangible entities or phenomena, not empirical "facts" that can be established, not the opinions held by people, etc.—in short nothing semantic. As the basically invisible (implicit) underlying inner logic or syntax of a people's actually lived life and as such the *logical form* structuring consciousness, consciousness is fundamentally unaware, unconscious of them. They are the inherent, but secret determinants of its perceptions and reactions, its beliefs and feelings. Here one sees once more how wrong it is to invent a literal subsisting "the unconscious," a special segregated "collective unconscious" vis-à-vis consciousness and to ontologize its contents as eternal archetypes. The dominants of consciousness that Jung mystified as timeless archetypes are for psychology the *inherent* logical form of consciousness, of which consciousness is inevitably unconscious because consciousness as such is in itself the awareness only of its contents—much as in speaking we concentrate only on the message we want to convey, the meaning of the words and sentences, whereas the syntax of language that our speaking inevitably has to avail itself of goes by unnoticed. This is what is called the *intentionality* of consciousness (Husserl).

Intentionality in this sense means, if I may use a remote comparison, that while watching a movie we cannot see the movie projector and when studying the projector we do not watch the movie. Niklas Luhmann from the point of view of system theory spoke of the "blind spot" inherent in the standpoint of the observer. 150 years earlier, Arthur Schopenhauer had already viewed the I as "the dark point in consciousness, just as precisely the point of entrance of the optic nerve in the retina is blind, just as the brain is completely insensitive, the body of the sun is dark, and the eye sees everything except itself."[144] And for Husserl the "transcendental ego" or "pure consciousness," in performing the *noêsis* (intentional acts), can only focus ahead, on the *noêma* (the intentional objects), but not simultaneously reflectively back on itself. In this scheme consciousness could of course nevertheless also turn its attention to the *noêsis* itself—however, only if this *noêsis* became an *object* of attention (i.e., itself a *noêma*) for a *new* intentional act, a second *noêsis* and thus was ipso facto the *noêsis* no longer. It could never happen at one and the same time. A *noêsis*, therefore, can never catch up with itself, or rather the other way around, become aware of itself. It inevitably flees, escapes itself. This relation, which resembles that between language and metalanguage, also applies to psychotherapy. There cannot be any veritable self-reflection, self-observation, or consciousness of self. The moment we practice, for example, introspection, the I observes itself not as I, but inevitably "itself" *as an Other, an alien*. This is the unbridgeable difference that prevails in modernity, in its "functional logic" without copula.[145]

The Great is great because it performs the miracle of making the invisible soul's hidden logic[146] visible for consciousness. The syntax or logical form of consciousness as it prevails at a specific historical locus becomes accessible in the great works of art, in myths and rituals, but visible and accessible precisely not on the level of a kind of "metalanguage", the way Husserl's first-level *noêsis* can itself be observed as a *noêma* in a second-level *noêsis*. It is not made present as a (logical) Other,[147] as some additional semantic item, empirical phenomenon, or positive fact on the same old flat horizontal plane

---

[144] Arthur Schopenhauer, *Die Welt als Wille und Vorstellung*, vol. 2, ch. 41.

[145] In numerous publications Claus-Artur Scheier has discussed these issues.

[146] "Hidden logic" and "invisible soul" are of course synonyms. My wording is therefore pleonastic. Or the genitive has to be taken as no more than a *genitivus explicativus*.

[147] We have to distinguish between the logical Other due to the unbridgeable difference and the experiential "wholly Other," for example, in Rudolf Otto's sense. In our context, what the Great makes present for a people is wholly Other in the sense of "otherwordly" or "mysterious," however precisely not logical Other, but self. (A totally different concept of Other is psychology's notion of "the soul's own other," the "other of itself." What previously may have *appeared* to consciousness or been emotionally *experienced* by it or *theoretically distinguished* as a literal other is now seen through as a part of a *soul-internal* otherness, the soul's self-unfolding, self-division into itself in the narrower sense and its opposite.)

as all the other contents of consciousness and ordinary objects of experience, but truly as self, as the truth and soul of the real, its syntactical form. It is in the status of absolute negativity and as the truth of consciousness it is all-encompassing. Consciousness is, as it were, "surrounded" by this truth on all sides as well as permeated and governed by it in all its acts. All human world experience takes place within the horizon of this truth. This is why what the Great and exceptional makes explicit for consciousness inevitably transcends consciousness. It is too "large" for it. It consequently tends to be experienced as mysterious and unfathomable, something "otherworldly," "transcendental," or "metaphysical" in the most general sense of the word. It is more divined than discursively known and is present above all in the depth of feeling and faith. In the Great it becomes for consciousness a *phainomenon*, that is to say—in contradistinction to positive-factual phenomena—the innerworldly radiance of the otherworldly, a Particular that nevertheless *is* the presence of the Universal and not *merely* (not nothing but) a Particular. What the Great makes accessible is numinous for consciousness, the sacred, the gods or God, or a fundamental mystery, like, e.g., the grail, or a high ideal or "symbol" in Jung's sense. At any rate, it is the object of human upward-looking, of veneration or adoration, and both experienced and acknowledged by consciousness as hovering high above consciousness.

This allows us a glimpse into the workings of the soul's historical progress. What at one stage of development was a *phainomenon* fundamentally transcendent for consciousness can become integrated into consciousness. Jung discussed this movement briefly under the heading of the "death of symbols" (*CW* 6 § 816). What used to be a mystery is then not a mystery any longer. It has become "secularized" and irrelevantized. It is no longer the appearance of the soul's truth, of the all-encompassing syntax of consciousness in phainomenal form, but now merely a well-circumscribed individual *empirical* phenomenon, a sunken, sedimented cultural asset, whose possibly still special value or high estimation relies solely on the culture's memory of what it once was, i.e., what the still surviving old *word* or *name* once referred to. In truth, however, it, i.e., now: not the name but the former phenomenon's substance,[148] has become absorbed into the ordinary, conventional middle space, the realm of human arbitration, pragmatic concerns, and free disposition. Naturally, this sinking of a former soul truth and soul value to a more or less everyday empirical idea or phenomenon within the sphere of the human, all-too-human necessarily goes hand in hand with a fundamental change of the prevailing logic. It has to go hand in hand with such a change because if the logic or syntax stayed the same, the great soul *phainomenon* would still be claimed by it and not be available for integration into consciousness. Only when a new logic makes itself felt, is the old phainomenon released from the hold the background had over it and ready to be reduced to a fossilized *former* value, and only if consciousness integrates what used to be transcendent to it, can the underlying logic of consciousness change. Both aspects are one and the same process. But if there is a new logical form ruling over consciousness, then there is also (in principle) the possibility of a *new* authentic *phainomenon* in which this logic or soul truth can be experienced.

Through these processes the island or garden of the human, all-too-human in the middle between the two realms of soul manifestation ("from below" and "from above") gets in the course of historical time tremendously enlarged. More and more of the former mysteries and what was the carrier of highest soul values and of strict taboos becomes irrelevantized and thus integrated into the sphere of the ordinary. It becomes simply commonplace, conventional, maybe an everyday routine, or something instrumental at people's free disposal according to their pragmatic purposes. But it can just as well be freely ignored or dismissed. The special soul dignity, the spell that it once held, has gone out of it. In contrast to soul manifestations "from below," what is in the safe middle space, as the *sublated* and *sunken* great, is also

---

[148] The historical progress with its integration of previous soul truths leads to a separation of name and *Sache* or substance. By way of one single example, that by the 19th century God had died refers to the psychological substance of the former soul phenomenon named God. But the word or name God survived as part of the language and in people's imagination, although it has lost "its soul," its living substance or truth. The surviving name is only the empty shell or cloak of the former full phenomenon. This discrepancy between surviving word and already long inwardized and *ipso facto* irrelevantized substance is a source of much misunderstanding, confusion, and delusion. The hollow name can, as in religious fundamentalism, pretend to be, and appear to consciousness, as a true substance. Much the same applies to "the Gods" in archetypal psychology.

"cooked" and not "raw," and also public and not private. But it is not *opus magnum*, indeed, not *opus* at all. It is just routines and psychologically irrelevant.

Of course, much of this is practiced by individuals, which may give rise to the illusion that it is truly their quite personal and private thinking, willing, acting, and feeling, while in reality it is a thoroughly *collective* way of thinking, willing, acting and feeling. Let us take as an example the phenomenon of falling in love, marrying, and living in a marriage relationship. Usually, this is subjectively *experienced* as completely personal and individual. But it is conventional. More or less the same process takes place in millions of people. Because falling in love happens within the individual and captivates consciousness, the individual thinks that it is personally his.[149] The individual does not realize that he or she is just an *example* or *instantiation* for something general. Jung in his paper on "Marriage as a psychological relationship" (*CW* 17) speaks of the "collective nature" of the usual marriage relationship in contrast to the rare development of it into a truly "individual relationship." In this sense the middle sphere can in a sense be private like what comes "from below," just as it can be cooked and public like what belongs to the sphere of the Great. But being culturally preconditioned and unwittingly following the patterns established in literature, folk tales, custom, traditional religious ideas, etc., it can never be totally raw.

The miracle that the Great performs lies in the fact that it makes explicitly appear before consciousness what lies in the back of consciousness, thereby forcing consciousness's otherwise *intentional*, and thus inevitably linear, relation to the Other, a relation which is forever diremted from itself, into a closed circle, into the soul's uroboric self-relation and self-reflection. This is true soul-making. And it is why the Great has true soul-dignity. Because through the Great the soul can return to itself, come home to itself, consciousness feels elated and liberated by it. The Great is what releases consciousness from its bondage to the other in the sense of intentionality (the

---

[149] This *illusory appearance* is only in part due to our animal nature (cf. *CW* 11 § 841), our existing as biological body. The body is obviously individual, separate from all other bodies. Mainly, however, it is the unique absolutely captivating and inflating power of the intensity of those feelings that creates a uniquely heightened sense of "me" and this is what seduces one into the belief that also the feelings themselves are absolutely singular and uniquely "mine."

directedness of consciousness at some object) and opens a realm of freedom. But the realm of freedom that it thereby opens up is a higher soul freedom than the ego freedom in the middle sphere (the freedom within the realm of irrelevancy, human arbitration, and pragmatics).

The fact that the character of what the Great displays remains "metaphysical" and thus an instance of absolute negativity prevents this content from being resorbed into the sphere of mere (semantic, positive-factual) contents of consciousness, contents that may, to be sure, be semantically "extraordinary" in the sense of being exotic, but are nevertheless logically quite ordinary. The soul truly comes home to *itself* and not to a fundamental Other. The mysterious otherness protects the self-character and prevents what is experienced in the Great from becoming reduced—two other dangers—either to something fundamentalist, an ideology, or to something emotional and sentimental, to kitsch. On the other hand, it also means that the self to which the soul returns does not explicitly have the *form* of self. It remains of course in the *form* of otherness (i.e., phainomenal), although certainly not the otherness prevailing in the sphere of the intentional unbridgeable difference.

We realize that what I described here does not only apply to specific instances of experience, to the perception of individual great works, but also to the whole logical large-scale constitution of consciousness prevailing during the ages of myth and, later, of metaphysics. Myth as well as metaphysics were themselves, each in their own particular way and at different historical stages, "the general faith," "the faith of the world" at large, as Jung and Hegel put it, the all-life-encompassing and permeating logic. This is why, on the level of mythic world experience, one's gaze into the world at concrete phenomena did not only show them, but together with and in them simultaneously revealed sympathetically the soul's own background in the form of divine epiphanies, as if the phenomena were mirrors or Rorschach blots. And it is why, shortly before the closure of the Western project of metaphysics, Schelling and Hegel explicitly saw the I or self-consciousness—in blatant contrast to post-metaphysical Schopenhauer's "the opaque spot in consciousness"—as "der lichte Punkt im ganzen System des Wissens" (the bright [clear, translucent] spot in the whole system of knowledge, Schelling) or "a *clarity* transparent to itself" (Hegel). The pre-modern *theoretical*[150] I was uroboric, illumining itself.

Why was the I uroboric, and why did mythic world experience allow for the perception of gods and mythic personages in the real phenomena of the natural world? Why could ("semantic") phenomena in themselves be translucent for the deeper general syntax of lived life, so that it could implicitly appear and be experienced through them? Because the soul had not yet been *born out of* itself, had not expelled itself from its containment within itself. This is why there was also no self-*observation* (in the strict sense) of the I and no *fundamental* otherness for it. One's seeing was naturally led along the orbits of the soul's uroboric self-reflection. The metaphysical I had its place in the center, so that, on the level of classical metaphysics, the soul was the *manifestation* of its uroboric identity, that is, the event of the *appearance* of both sides (what is at the back of consciousness and what is before it) at once. From the observer standpoint (modern intentionality), by contrast, one looks at everything inevitably from outside and *ipso facto* even at oneself (the I) as an other vis-à-vis oneself. The modern soul is a *born* soul. It has been catapulted out of itself, and therefore its seeing can no longer follow quite naturally the course of the soul's uroboric, circular self-relation. The intentional I is no longer self-consciousness, it is no longer reflected into itself, now having to direct its glance straightaway outward, away from itself to its objects. Thus it can of course still have a consciousness of itself, but precisely only *have* a consciousness *of* itself, only as a higher-level (so to speak metalanguage) I, a consciousness of the observed I, which is something totally different from a "clarity transparent to itself."

The uroboric identity that once upon a time used to be the general logical medium within which human life as a whole had its place is, under the conditions of modernity and the intentional I, reserved for special moments of experience and happens mainly only through particular great works of art or philosophy, but is no longer the prevailing general truth of life, the way the mythic world and

---

[150] "Theoretical I" is of course not intended to mean the I as a theoretical construct. The attribute refers to the nature of the I, to the fact that it is essentially one whose world relation is determined by *theoria* (Intuition, *Anschauung*). Its theoretical nature confirms its in-ness in soul, its not having been born out of it, and is in contrast to the modern I's observer stance.

metaphysics were at their own times. Events of soul in the sense of the manifestation of this uroboric logic in a true *phainomenon* have become isolated special cases within otherwise commonplace reality. Soul is no more than a fundamentally *sublated* moment in modern culture, and naturally so *for* a soul born out of itself. Before, when I briefly discussed the historical process of irrelevantification of former highest soul truths, I stated that if through the progress of the soul's history there happens to be a new logical form ruling over consciousness, then there is also in principle the possibility of a new authentic *phainomenon*. But this statement can of course no longer be true for the born soul, for the modern intentional I. For it the uroboric circle has been stretched out into a straight line holding I and experienced reality irrevocably apart.

2.3.9 The difference in modern psychological life between authentic and simulated soul phenomena

Under the heading of "The experienced or occurring soul" our main purpose has been to establish a clear criterion that would allow us to distinguish veritable events of soul from other phenomena of whom it would make no sense to claim them for soul. We have found it in the difference between the ordinary and the exceptional and illustrated it, for example, with Jung's distinction between the "psychological novel" and what he called the "non-psychological" or "visionary" type of artistic creation, or between death experienced as a moment of deep grief and death experienced as a joyful event, namely, a wedding, a *mysterium coniunctionis*, the former being the experience from the point of view of the ego or civil man, whereas the latter is the experience of the same event from the point of view of the soul. In all cases it is a material difference, a "semantic" difference, that is, one that can be observed in, demonstrated from, the particular character of the experience or phenomenon, and unambiguously described. The difference between grief and joy, between the psychological novel and a work like *Faust II*, the way Jung saw it, as well as between the personal and the social or cultural, is relatively obvious. But now we have to formally introduce another general distinction between phenomena of true soul dignity and others without such dignity, this time a formal or "syntactical" one. I have already made use of it or referred to it above when I critiqued Jung's interpretation of the Nazi movement for giving to it, with the god Wotan, an archetypal underpinning. This new distinction is to be made on the one side only of the former material pair of opposites, namely *within the exceptional*. It is the distinction between:

- that which comes into being of its own accord, by its own necessity, is the product and result of the soul's own stirrings; that which has psychologically the true ring of archetypal depth, of the dignity and weight of a soul manifestation; that which is expressive of Necessity (*anankê*) and the wind of history. The emotions, intentions, conceptions, pathological reactions coming from what Jung at times called the "host" (the "landlord") in us or, on the collective level, from "the historical locus" at which we happen to been placed.—And, on the other side,

- that which is in truth the product and result of *ego* intentions and machinations because it merely *imitates* or *simulates* the soul's opus and its mysteries. The phoney. What is fed by ideological needs, cravings for meaning, power interests, in other words, ego desires. What has the status of fads, kitsch. Or what results from petty ego fears and defenses; what is just talk and superficial alehouse-level opinions; momentary mass hysterics as well as theatrics in individual life.

It is immediately obvious that this additional distinction applies only to the situation of modernity, the situation of born man. A *simulation* of soul phenomena requires a logically highly sophisticated, devious, cunning soul that has lost its innocence. The conditions of its possibility came into being only after the birth of man from out of the soul. As long as man (and the soul itself) was still contained in the soul, and the more rooted the personality was in what one might call (in a *psychological* sense) "the natural instinctual life," i.e., in local customs and firm cultural traditions, there was an innocence of being that meant that the production of simulations as well as the wish and need for them was *a priori* out of the question. Neither would you find under these conditions mere ego opinions and empty words, slogans. For under those conditions, owing to its logical containment within itself, the soul lived from within the logically always-already prevailing gratification of its needs. And since this containment was one in the absolute negativity of the soul (or in the soul as absolute negativity), the notion of gratification did not have to be positivized, i.e., gratification did not have to be present as a positive-factual, emotional one (as a gratification of the ego rather than of the soul). It was a logical one.[151] Only once the soul has been ejected from its containment within itself, once it has taken on the shape of an ego-personality that is to a large extent *emancipated* from itself (the soul) so that a psychic "two-stories" situation results, only then does a fundamental craving (for meaning, for love, for soul fulfillment) arise, a craving that as craving attests to the prevailing unbridgeable difference and *ipso facto* to the impossibility of fulfillment. As a craving of the born soul expelled from its containment in absolute logical negativity, the craving had to be one for a "positivistic" gratification, which is a contradiction in terms. The *soul* can find its gratification only in absolute negativity, not in practical reality.

Being in modernity encumbered with this craving, the soul is in the situation of which we hear Mephistopheles in Goethe's *Faust* say, "For precisely when *concepts* are lacking, then mere words conveniently tend to take their place." And with words, Mephistopheles knew, one can wonderfully operate, develop complex arguments, and even construct entire systems. That is to say in our context, it is precisely the *lacking* meaning (the lacking containment in the absolute negativity of the soul) that tends (in Derrida's sense of the word) to *supplement* itself with surrogates, with simulated soul manifestations. The lack, as craving, actively invites supplementation through simulation.

There are conscious, deliberate simulations: persiflages, caricatures, satires, parodies, citations, etc. They are psychologically unproblematic and of no concern. They are not full-fledged simulations either, because they themselves openly display their simulating character. A true simulation is simulation only to the extent that it manages to conceal its simulation character and forcefully gives itself out as absolutely authentic. Its simulatedness must remain *unconscious*.

---

[151] Remember: The place of where the true life of people was lived, was up there, in what was above the practical reality of the persons. See 2.3.5 above.

Simulated soul events are, of course, of a much higher logical complexity than innocent ones.

In this connection I may be permitted to add in passing that we also have to distinguish between "the cooked" (the refined product, what has gone through the human mind), on the one hand, and conscious processing, on the other. The former refers merely to a process of elaboration and refinement, cultivation—an "alchemical cooking," as it were—*of a veritable soul substance* either by the "whole man" (soul and consciousness) or by the culture as a whole. The latter, by contrast, has its origin or source in *deliberate* acts of an individual consciousness performed upon what has already lost its true soul character.

In practice, it is clear that it is much more difficult to find a reliable criterion for determining what true soul phenomena are, in contradistinction to simulated ones, than to distinguish between the ordinary and the exceptional or the personal and the cultural. Since the difference is no longer "semantic" but "syntactical," we cannot rely on the external material characteristics of the phenomena. There is nothing tangible, obviously discernable and demonstrable, nor anything countable that would unambiguously relieve us of the burden of a decision. What belongs to the one side may *look just like* what is on the other, just as symbolic, mythic, archetypal. The change from the semantic to the syntactical means that also the locus of the decision is interiorized from "out there" (one's dwelling on the phenomenon itself) to the interiority of the soul, from the "external" sense to a finer inward sense: it is a move from seeing to feeling, to a feeling sensitivity. Using Jung's terminology we can say that we need here a highly developed, differentiated *feeling function*, an organ capable of discerning differences in the degree of such otherwise imperceptible qualities as depth, dignity, status, rank, and value. It is perhaps comparable to the capability to appreciate the nuances and different depths of different kinds of wines, although this skill also involves what Jung called the sensation function. We could even say that one has to be able to "taste" the flavor of soul in phenomena. In addition to a psychological giftedness this of course also needs a certain amount of experience, a long familiarity with all sorts of psychic phenomena and a knowledge as rich as possible about the whole history and phenomenology of the soul to develop the feeling function in this area and arrive at what one might call *connoisseurship* in analogy to the skill of a wine taster.

The difference that I am here speaking about or rather the assessment of this difference, inasmuch as it amounts to a feeling judgment, could be viewed as being merely subjective, a matter of personal preferences or moods or so: some people happen to feel one way about a certain phenomenon, others another way, some see a given phenomenon as an authentic manifestation of soul, others as phoney. But this would be a mistake. This assessment is not subjective. It is objective, just like with wine tasting. It is not without reason and justification that Jung called the "feeling function" in his sense a *rational* function, which is frequently not understood and not heeded. The feeling function discerns objective differences. Only if, while assessing a given phenomenon, the focus is on one's own personal likings or dislikes, on the needs, desires, interests, and emotions of the ego, rather than on the specific quality of the phenomenon itself, is the assessment subjective (which is of course the more frequent case. Most people have not learned to distinguish a rational assessment of the concrete feeling quality ["the feel"] of an objective reality from their own personal subjective feelings they get merely in view of, or triggered by, this objective reality). In the first case we are concerned with the phenomenon, while in the second case we merely register, and focus on, our own emotional states; we are thinking about ourselves, not about the object.

In therapeutic practice in the consulting room it is most important to be able to make this distinction, for dream interpretation, for the evaluation of a patient's symptoms and reactions, his fears, etc. It is, for example, particularly easy to be misled by the intensity of emotions and take them for a sign of soul importance, and to be misled by an abstract, formal similarity to archetypal or mythic patterns and take this for a sign of soul depth. The latter is what I call "mythic illusory appearance."

Outside the consulting room the feeling function is indispensable for evaluating social and historical phenomena, such as works of art (in contrast to patients' paintings), modern technological civilization, political events, the diverse topical problems, and social phenomena that come up. Here the naive criterion of archetypal "likenesses" inevitably leads astray. You need the depth of objective feeling to feel the depth, or lack of depth, of phenomena. This, rational feeling, is a fundamentally different criterion from "imaginal likeness,"[152] and much more sophisticated. The fact that in the latter case "criterion" refers more to the characteristic features to be compared while in the former case it means more a court of judgment underlines once more the move we had noted from an "external" to an "inward" sense, from the obvious to the subtle, from innocence to critical reflectedness.

A particularly important example for modern *simulated* soul phenomena in the social sphere are those in the area of religion and spirituality. Some people are very impressed by the fact that *within* the modern secularized world and *after* that modern experience which is best summarized by Nietzsche's "God is dead," there all of a sudden again seems to be new and increasing interest in religion, spirituality, and in the belief in some sort of transcendence. The point to be made in our context is that all this new interest, all these diverse new phenomena of religious faith or spiritual movements, of this new openness to the possibility of transcendence, are not psychological phenomena at all. They are not of soul significance because they are from the outset fundamentally *sublated* phenomena. They belong to the sphere of the ego, its emotional needs and cravings. They are psychic phenomena, phenomena that certainly can be the legitimate study of sociology, but not of psychology. The soul has no stake in them.

Why are they not veritable (psychological) phenomena? Why are they *sublated* phenomena? Because they are occurrences on the modern *market of meanings* where "anything goes." There you find people who practice, or are in their feeling and thinking committed to, Celtic druid wisdom, others who are devoted to witchcraft, to astrology, to Catholicism, to Buddhism, to Tantra sexuality, to angelology, to American Indian shamanism, to "the occult," and what have you. All these seeming "phenomena" in today's world exist side by side and compete with each other in this market of meanings, thereby showing that they themselves are not real *phenomena* at all (phenomena: revealing the soul's truth), but sublated phenomena, specific individual

---

[152] It goes without saying that impressive, intensive emotion ("numinosity") can be just as misleading a criterion as imaginal likeness.

exemplifications and components of "anything goes." The only true phenomenon here is the higher-level phenomenon of the "MARKET (of meanings)" itself on which anything goes and which has swallowed all seeming first-order phenomena. *It* is what today, within medial modernity, expresses the soul's truth. To still attribute soul validity to each of the individual *moments* of this "anything goes" would be a great psychological blunder. The time of phenomena in the plural is over. In modernity there is only one single phenomenon.[153] The soul has left that innocent level that once upon a time made concrete religions, belief systems, cults, archetypal and mystic experiences and the like be true soul phenomena, phenomena in which the soul expressed its truth at its respective historical locus. It has risen from this *semantic* level to a fundamentally higher (or fallen to a fundamentally deeper) level, the level of logical form or syntax. On this new, the modern level of the soul's life, psychological *phenomena* have themselves to be of a not-semantic, but "abstract," logical, syntactical nature. Not contents, not symbols, not gods and beliefs, but general form.[154]

This is the type of distinction that the feeling function has to make, the difference it has to discern.

It is especially difficult for some people to realize that even those age-old, traditional, and formerly certainly authentic phenomena of the past like the Catholic Church that survived into the age of

---

[153] This is a sign that monotheism has become completed and fulfilled. It is no longer a subjective religion, a personal faith, but has become inwardized into itself and thus objective, "autonomous," a general logical form, independent of, indeed, emancipated from what we as individuals believe. From here we see also quite clearly that a "polytheistic psychology" is regressive.

[154] Paradoxically, what is merely phenomenal is *ipso facto* no longer a true phenomenon. The MARKET (which is our true phenomenon) is precisely not phenomenal. Itself invisible, it appears only in the individual "phenomena" that are offered on it. (Here we can remember: life as such is not phenomenal. It appears only in all the living beings.) This invisibility of today's true phenomenon, on the one hand, and the thus unchallenged obtrusive presence of the now sublated former phenomena, on the other hand, is the reason why so many people become overly impressed by the empirical surface of modern reality and blind to what really counts. (By contrast, everybody celebrates famous conductors and not the individual members of the orchestras on which, as *sublated* players, he plays as on his "instrument," because in this case the higher-level phenomenon [the conductor] has a literal and visible presence and makes the sublatedness of the first-level players obvious.) A second reason is of course that consciousness usually sees things from the standpoint of *people*, what *they* as individuals believe, feel, say, and do, rather than from the standpoint of soul. Because the subjective impressiveness for oneself of one's own opinions and emotions is taken *theoretically*, one immediately credits people's beliefs and experiences in general as full-fledged realities, if not even as exclusively decisive in this area of "religion" and "spirituality."

modernity are no longer veritable phenomena, but sublated phenomena. The floor on which they once stood and which allowed them to be authentic soul phenomena has imperceptibly been pulled out from under them so that what remains is only the simulation of their former reality.[155] On account of their venerable past and their rich substantiality they of course seem to possess a higher dignity than those spurious modern (and ultimately nihilistic[156]) involvements in abstract "spirituality," in abstruse attempts at revivals of archaic, or import of exotic, cults and religious beliefs. But their greater internal dignity and substance could not prevent that the soul's logical life has today irreverently reduced them to mere competitors on the modern market of meanings and thus logically put them on the same level.

2.3.10 Excursus on two fundamentally different concepts of "amplification"

In chapter 2.1.7 we learned from Kerényi that *in myth* even the literal, ordinary events of life appear as allegories of mythical truths. The psychological method of amplification devised by Jung (in contrast to Freudian free association) seems to be the way to draw the practical consequences of this insight. On the other hand, if we have to observe the radical difference between human complexes and archetypal truths, as well as between phenomena of soul dignity and others without soul relevance, we have to guard against a misuse of amplification that tends to obliterate this difference.

---

[155] Simulation does here not mean imitation of alien forms and contents. In the Catholic Church, the traditional rituals and dogmas—the semantic forms and contents—have precisely been retained more or less unaltered. The simulation lies here paradoxically in this very preservation of the revered old tradition, a preservation that defies the fundamental psychological change that has occurred. The simulation lies in the fact that the modern mind that has inevitably advanced *from* the semantic *to* the syntactical level in Catholic piety simply continues what it has always done and thereby keeps clinging to the semantic level, giving this, i.e., the old practices and beliefs, out as the still authentic expression of the soul's truth. Jung had intuited this problem, but expressed it too personally. Speaking about the central ritual of the Catholic Church he said, "I know it is the truth, but it is the truth in a form in which I cannot accept it any more" (*CW* 18 § 632). The second "I" should be seen as the "I" of truly modern man as such, or as the modern soul. The problem, Jung rightly realized, was a problem of *form*. That this form problem was the one of the obsolescence of the semantic level Jung was, however, not able to realize. The whole issue of the syntactical level of the soul, the level *of* form, remained closed to him. *His* word "form" is by him itself reductively still understood on the semantic level.

[156] "Nihilistic": as favorite pastimes of the Last Man (Nietzsche).

Jung had introduced the method of amplification into psychology as a *hermeneutic* method explicitly taken over from *philology*, and he accordingly described it by means of the following example. "For instance, in the case of a very rare word which you have never come across before, you try to find parallel text passages, parallel applications perhaps, where that word also occurs, and then you try to put the formula you have established from the knowledge of other texts into the new text. If you make the new text a readable whole, you say, 'Now we can read it.' That is how we learned to read hieroglyphics and cuneiform inscriptions and that is how we can read dreams" (*CW* 18 § 173, cf. 179). "... I follow the well-known method of comparative anatomy or of comparative history of religions or that of deciphering difficult ancient texts..." (*Letters 2*, p. 186, to Hall, 6 Oct. 1954). A "dream is too slender a hint to be understood until it is ... amplified to the point of intelligibility" (*CW* 12 § 403).

Two points are essential: first, the method of amplification is applied to "contents which are difficult to understand, such as dream-images, manic ideas, and the like" (*CW* 17 § 162), "images that can only be described as 'archaic'" (*CW* 16 § 246), "irrational data of the material, that is, of the fairytale, myth, or dream" (*CW* 9i § 436), and, second, its purpose is nothing else but the "elucidation of the meaning" (*Sinndeutung*, *GW* 10 § 771), "so that it (*viz.* its symbolic language) may yield itself more easily to our understanding" (*CW* 11 § 788), or, as the earlier quotes had it, so that it makes the text "readable," the dream motifs "intelligible."

In many quarters of professional Jungianism as well as with people involved in so-called "myth studies" something very different from what it meant for Jung has nowadays become of "amplification." Although they believe and claim to be employing Jung's method, they nevertheless use amplification in an altered sense and, above all, for a different purpose. We can be grateful to Michael Vannoy Adams for time and again in all innocence displaying this wrong interpretation and use, which is wrong because it is given out as Jung's method of amplification.

For example, Adams calls a certain journalist, Maureen Dowd of the *New York Times*, "a 'Jungian' journalist" because, when she "practices newspaper mythology, she compares modern politicians to ancient heroes in order to identify similarities between them. (She also contrasts them in order to identify differences ....)"[157] This is in keeping with Adams' explanation of amplification: "Amplification is a comparative method. It compares images from the modern psyche to images from other sources—among them, ancient myths—in an effort to identify significant similarities, or parallels."[158] We see immediately that the two main characteristics of Jung's version of amplification are lost. One can of course compare anything with anything else and determine their similarities or differences, and so also modern politicians with mythological heroes. Perhaps a nice pastime, perhaps also a way to bring out certain striking features of the politicians in bold relief, but psychologically pointless. Adams himself tries to see Barrack Obama in terms of the myth of Icarus. His exploration of this theme makes him wish to establish a new diagnostic concept, that of an "Icarian Personality Disorder," as an addition to the "Narcissistic Personality Disorder," which he claims is a "mythological diagnosis," and the only mythological one in the *DSM-IV.* In many circles, modern individuals try to find their "personal myth."

The first mistake—at least by the standard of Jung's idea of amplification—that becomes visible in the examples given is the abstractness of this procedure. Modern events, people, or phenomena are by means of some *tertium comparationis* linked to, or rather as special cases conceptually subsumed under, mythic names which were, in turn, previously and unwittingly reduced to abstract generic concepts. One is reminded of the use of the name "Ajax" for a household detergent or "Apollo" for a spacecraft. In the latter two examples the *tertium comparationis* may be pretty meager or even far-fetched, but the same principle prevailing in them applies also to the other ones in which there might certainly be a higher degree of similarity.

---

[157] Michael Vannoy Adams, "Obama and Icarus: Political Heroism, 'Newspaper Mythology,' and the Economic Crisis of 2008," in: *Spring. A Journal of Archetype and Culture,* vol. 81, Spring 2009, pp. 291–318, here p. 293. (In the following quoted as: Adams, "Obama.") By the way, the phrase "newspaper mythology," which occurs both in the title of the cited paper and in the passage just quoted, is expressly taken from Jung, who, however, meant it in a derogatory if not devastating sense, whereas by Adams it is understood and used as if it was a positive, affirmative expression.
[158] Michael Vannoy Adams, "Does Myth (Still) Have A Function In Jungian Studies? Modernity, Metaphor, and Psycho-Mythology," paper presented at the "Psyche and Imagination" conference of the International Association for Jungian Studies at the University of Greenwich, London, July 7, 2006 (accessed in: http://www.jungnewyork.com/myth_function.shtml in Nov. 2009). Hereafter quoted as Adams, "Function."

"Ajax" as a trade name is not a sign of a mythological perception of the strength of that household cleaner. By the same token, a narcissistic personality disorder is not at all a *mythological* diagnosis, but a *modern medical* designation of a modern phenomenon that merely avails itself of a mythological name remembered from our cultural heritage which is stuck onto this phenomenon as no more than a label. A certain superficial similarity exists, of course, but is extremely thin and, on top of it, based on a fundamental misunderstanding of the Narcissus myth. This diagnosis has nothing do with mythology proper.

Adams uses another example in support of his view of amplification. He says, "'The latest incarnation of Oedipus,' Joseph Campbell notes, is standing 'this afternoon on the corner of Forty-second Street and Fifth Avenue, waiting for the traffic light to change.'"[159] This is ridiculous.[160] For two reasons.

(1) Do mythic heroes "incarnate" in other persons at all, let alone modern men? Is "incarnation" not a concept totally incompatible with the myth of heroes? Gods, we know, take at times the shape of humans. But this is by no means their *incarnation in them* but a form of their epiphany *for others*. Certain special human beings that are the institutionalized representation of the Self for a whole people, like the Pharaoh or the Dalai Lama or Sai Baba, are seen as an incarnation of a particular god. But Jason, Achilles, Icarus, Narcissus, Hercules, Oedipus, Medea, and other not-divine figures exist *only* in mythology, only as literary imaginings, and do not even there manifest themselves in the shape of others, the way some gods do. True, when Alexander the Great had the feet of the valiant defender of Gaza pierced and tied his living body to his chariot in order to pull him around before his

---

[159] Adams, "Function."

[160] The fact, pointed to by Adams ("Function"), that Jung himself stated that "Oedipus is still alive for us" (*CW* 5 § 1) is not a counterargument. First of all, this was early Jung, Jung speaking in 1911, while still very much under the influence of Freud. Secondly, Jung is here not talking about amplification at all. It is of course well known that he thought that the archetypes are ageless and everpresent, that "The gods have become diseases" (*CW* 13 § 54), that Wotan manifested in Nietzsche's idea of Dionysos as well as in the Nazi movement, and so on. This is a *thesis*, a *tenet* of Jung's, that as such has to be clearly distinguished from amplification, which is a *method* to be applied to all sorts of relevant phenomena. Methods imply a certain formal *procedere*, but not a particular thesis or conviction. Thirdly, Jung is not above criticism. This particular thesis of his just mentioned about the presence of the gods in our neurotic symptoms and, for example, in Nietzsche and the Nazi movement, etc. happens to be not tenable.

sneering soldiers, then, as Nietzsche said, this was a disgusting and exaggerated caricature of Achilles maltreating Hector's corpse. But it is by no means an incarnation of Achilles. Merely a caricature and imitation, a "citation *in actu*": *simulation*. We can say: it is incompatible with the notion of mythic figures to think that they incarnate in real ordinary human people.

(2) What has the man standing this afternoon on the corner of Forty-second Street and Fifth Avenue, waiting for the traffic light to change, to do with the mythic Oedipus—*even if* he suffers from what Freud happened to call an "Oedipus complex"? The myth of Oedipus and the modern Oedipus complex are incommensurable. Admittedly, there is, as in the case of narcissism and Narcissus, a superficial similarity, an abstract-formalistic *tertium comparationis*, that establishes a seeming likeness. But the very thing that is at stake here, the whole dimension of the mythic, is missing in the modern neurotic and his banal screwed-up "object relations," while, conversely, the personalistic aspect of "object relations" and hidden inner feelings in the Oedipus complex is absent in the myth.

Let us take another example. Ginette Paris, Adams tells us,[161]

> more eloquently than any other Jungian, reclaims Aphrodite for modern life experience and, like Woody Allen, demonstrates just how mighty Aphrodite still is. Paris is not naïve. She, too, notes how the moralistic distortion and commercial appropriation and exploitation of the beautiful, erotic, or sexual in the modern situation abuse Aphrodite, but when Paris practices mythological amplification, she does not abuse Aphrodite. She describes how Aphrodite is alive and well in the modern psyche and is still relevant to the modern situation .... For example, she recounts an anecdote in which Aphrodite manifests to a modern young woman. On a spring day, the young woman sees a pair of sexy sandals in a store window, and, although the sandals are extremely expensive, she impulsively buys them. The young woman calls the impulse "spring fever." What impels her, she remarks, is "the season for love." Paris says that if the young woman had been a Jungian, "she would probably have said: 'Here comes Aphrodite.'" The young woman, Paris notes, "didn't know Greek mythology and didn't identify Aphrodite by her

---

[161] *Ibid.*

Greek name." As Paris says, the young woman did not call her "Aphrodite" but called her, equivalently, "the season for love."

According to Adams this is not naïve. Maybe not. Maybe it is calculated. But it is certainly frivolous: a demonstration of a fundamental lack of respect for the dignity of the ancient gods and thus for the soul. The second of the biblical Ten Commandments tells us: "Thou shalt not take the name of the LORD thy God in vain." *Mutatis mutandis*, the same applies to all gods, not only to Yahveh, and even when they have become historical for us these historical figurations of the highest cultural and soul values of our forefathers or of foreign traditions still deserve respect. Here, however, the name of Aphrodite is used vainly. It functions as nothing but an empty label on the same level with ordinary down-to-earth designations such as "spring fever." "Spring fever" is perfectly sufficient to label the described event. That a young woman may find sexy sandals attractive, especially in springtime, and lets herself be tempted to buy them, belongs, with Jung's words, to "clearly understandable psychology." It is part of human biology. Even on the level of animal life we find that March hares go mad from sex impulses. In other words, it is something psychic and thus *psychologically* of no interest at all. Psychologically it is a triviality, completely self-explanatory, and thus not in need of any further explanation, especially not from a psychologist—because it has nothing to do with "soul."

To interpret the fact that—of course; who would doubt it?—there are still today erotic desires, sexual impulses, and flirtatious behavior as proof of "how mighty *Aphrodite* still is" is reducing Aphrodite to nothing but a label and sticking it on everyday phenomena.

There is, of course, nothing wrong with having several names for one phenomenon. Flowers and illnesses have scientific names in addition to popular ones, and people often have nicknames or pen names in addition to their official names. Therefore—if we leave aside the serious problem mentioned of the vain use of the name of the goddess (which means that she, and along with her the divine at large, is reductively cheapened, her name having become an inflated, depreciated currency)—one could of course also use the word Aphrodite as a label *as long as* nothing more was intended as is with calling a household cleanser "Ajax" and a spacecraft "Apollo."

But the fact is that much more *is* intended. The intimation is that the event described is indeed the manifestation of a goddess, that it has a mythic or sacred depth. After all, it is supposed to show "just how mighty Aphrodite still is." Adams and Paris refer to her as "she," a person, an agent. While "Aphrodite" is *in fact* nothing but a label duplicating "spring fever," it is nevertheless used for the purpose of creating the impression that there is something more, something higher (mythic or divine) *behind* (or in) the ordinary and self-evident phenomenon. The petty and human-all-too-human receives a divine halo. The natural event is fraudulently mystified, glorified. I say "fraudulently" because this alleged added value does not come from, and has not been demonstrated to be inherent in, the phenomenon itself as *its* self-manifestation, but is literally added (stuck) on by an ego on the basis of its hidden agenda. There is a dogmatic interest behind this move: the desire is to dress up the ordinary in mythic garments as an external embellishment of it. Exactly as in the modern advertizing industry: the mythic name, here Aphrodite, is supposed to create a cloud of diffuse feelings of higher importance, excitement, meaning.

Paris' logic apparently follows that of the protagonist of Molière's *Le bourgeois gentilhomme*. Having learned that what he speaks is in rhetoric called "prose," newly-rich, uneducated, and simple-minded but vanity-ridden Monsieur Jourdain started to stride around proudly telling everybody that he was speaking "prose," as if simply through the new scholarly name "prose" his ordinary, everyday utterances, too, had just like that been elevated to a fundamentally higher scholarly level. But just as it was not Monsieur Jourdain's speech that had suddenly become more noble and scholarly, but merely the naming of it, the vocabulary used, and just as a sparrow does not in any way become a more noble animal if you call it by its scientific name: *passer domesticus*, so the (fictional) "Jungian's" commentary to the young woman's experience, "Here comes Aphrodite," would also not really turn the simple and natural event into an epiphany of the goddess. It, too, is only a name or label change.

Availing ourselves again of alchemical terms, we can say that the function or aimed-at effect of this boastful renaming (and of the corresponding view of "amplification" in general) is that the *aurum vulgi* is given out AS the *aurum nostrum*. The psychological difference is obliterated. The negation, the inexorable NOT that separates the latter from the former and allows it to push off from the former, is gotten rid of. The ordinary IS, just like that, the extraordinary, the exceptional. What—in a *psychological* sense—is the banalities of everyday life (and what is more petty than the sphere of politics and our modern politicians?) IS mythic. "The election of Barack Obama," Adams claims, "was, in the experience of all Americans, an event of mythological proportions," and, so Adams quoting Maureen Dowd, "Barack 'Jason' Obama['s]" seeking the Oval Office was "tantamount to seeking the golden fleece."[162] The golden fleece! Ridiculous. Outrageous. How can one do that to a mythic image! What an act of violence toward an innocent, helpless image that cannot defend itself against a modern cynical intellect! Or: "(T)he mythic nature of [election] campaigns"[163]: the phenomenon of a lot of hot air, of an immature population carried away by emotions and inflated with silly, illusionary hopes is confounded with something of mythological proportions. What a depraved notion of the mythic! It is, I assume, "the mythic" as imagined by a generation that grew up with television, talk shows, and the institution of advertizing and made *their* logic their own.

I mentioned the fraudulent aspect of this mystification through which an ordinary event of human life is supposed to get imbued with a divine or mythic aura and through which at the same time the idea of gods, of a "psychology with gods," a "polytheistic psychology," is supposed to be substantiated. But now I have to mention a second fraud, one, however, that is equiprimordial with the first. Here I can again turn to Adams who states in response to the familiar thesis that the gods are dead, "I would say, the literal is dead, but the metaphorical is alive and well. As Hillman says, 'Nothing is literal; all is metaphor' .... The 'gods' continue to 'exist,' as they always have, in the psyche. In this respect, to be psychological is to be

---

[162] Adams, "Obama, " pp. 293 and 294. I would say that if this were indeed what the Americans felt about Obama's election, it would have been pretty hysterical. It is depressing to see the degree of incompetence of the "feeling function," which obviously is not capable of distinguishing between the dignity of manifestations of the objective soul (here, the mythic) and the pettiness of subjective emotions.

[163] Ibid. p. 294.

metaphorical. It is to realize, once and for all, that the 'gods' are metaphors—personifications (or deifications) in the psyche."[164] The talking of the gods, so it all of a sudden turns out, is not really meant seriously. Just metaphors, gods only in quotations marks, bracketed, immunized. Gods, yes—but by no means religion or theology. You cannot nail Adams or Paris down to their talk about Aphrodite and the gods.

The specific fraudulence of this cheap excuse lies in the fact that it is only a verbal statement that is contradicted by the actual use made of the words *gods* and *polytheism*. The talk of gods or of "mythological proportions" in Adams', Paris', and, generally, "polytheistic psychology's" parlance is by no means meant to be a mere rhetorical trope or poetic device *used by the psychologist* for his own purposes, only a *façon de parler*, tongue-in-cheek, the way the figures from ancient myth were used for centuries before our time by our (deeply Christian!) poets and artists, after the time of those figures had long been over and nobody seriously believed in them anymore. Of course not. How else could Adams have spoken of "just how mighty Aphrodite still is"? The might of Aphrodite is considered *literally* real and along with her Aphrodite "herself," too. The divine aura and the higher dignity that polytheistic psychology's "Aphrodite" rhetoric in particular (in contrast to "spring fever"), or that of "gods" in general, is supposed to bestow on ordinary experiences is meant quite literally. The mind-lifting and deification *effect* that the operation is supposed to have is meant absolutely seriously and precisely not merely metaphorically. It is, after all, the whole point of the operation. Why else the talk about gods at all?

However, this (allegedly) real and mighty Aphrodite, just as all of the gods in polytheistic psychology, is now construed as being *in* "*herself*" a metaphor, i.e., as having the character of a really existing metaphor as an active power. *Not the psychologist's use of "Aphrodite" is metaphorical, but she herself:* "the 'gods' ARE metaphors," they "come as" metaphors. The metaphorical resides in the events themselves that factually happen. This means: the very meaning of the concept of metaphor is reversed. "Metaphor" has ceased being a poetic or rhetorical trope, an element of human speaking, and is now instead ontologized:

---

[164] Adams, "Function."

an existing personification *in the psyche* rather than a creative use of language by the *human mind*. Metaphor has become naturalistic.[165]

We see this also through another reflection. Superficially viewed, "Nothing is literal; all is metaphor" could sound much like Goethe's "Everything transitory is only a simile," referred to by Kerényi as mentioned above. But if the former statement is understood as meaning, "the literal is dead, but the metaphorical is alive and well," it becomes clear that the psychological difference referred to in Goethe's dictum is obliterated altogether and empirical events are instead supposed to be *directly* and *just like that* the metaphorical. Metaphor has become a positivity. For myth as well as for Goethe's poetic world perception, the transitory is and remains the *transitory* and only as such, only as the literal, can it *represent* something higher or deeper.

Comparing the two senses of metaphor, we can say that the metaphor "spring fever" *as* metaphor in the usual sense (or, if you wish, that a merely rhetorically or poetically used metaphor "Aphrodite") is not mighty. *It*, the metaphor, IS not a "she," a person, a subject. It may merely metaphorically be *referred to* as a "she" in *our sentences* about events. Genuine metaphors do not do anything. As metaphors they are just a way of evoking certain poetic meanings *in the thinking or understanding mind* (not in the existing "psyche").

Now looking at what, in the example given, was *really mighty* we can say that it was the psychic (not psychological) *desire* of a *real* (not-metaphorical) human being down here on earth, the very ordinary and natural (and of course also egoic) desire to look sexy and pretty.

And conversely, the sole purpose of the polytheistic psychologist's withdrawal from the religious-theological sense of "gods" to the idea of "metaphor" is to immunize the claim of this artificial "deification," that is to say, to render it absolutely *inconsequential* for the human persons concerned. It is the purpose to free the mind making this claim of having to take any intellectual (let alone moral) responsibility for it. No price is supposed to have to be paid for it. Neither does one, on

---

[165] Of course, in defense the polytheistic psychologist can again say that the "is" or "exists" is metaphorical (rather than ontological) and that just as the word "gods" Adams also put the word "exist" in quotation marks ("the 'gods' continue to 'exist,' as they always have, in the psyche"). But that is merely the same problem once more and does not get us any further.

the level of theorizing, have to convincingly *show* that the actual phenomenon in fact amounts to a divine or mythic epiphany, that the claimed experience of the god or goddess has any truth, that the impulse to buy sexy sandals has indeed in itself the surplus dimension and added value of something *divine*; nor does the talk of "the god in the event" commit one, on the level of ethical behavior, for the future to obedience, service, worship, and *religio* (in the sense of being bound, committed).

In other words, as far as the aspect of the intended effect is concerned, this whole talk of the gods follows the logic of the drug culture, with the only difference to the literal drug culture that the chemical drug is replaced by bombastic rhetoric, pompous vocabulary. Literal drugs are also based on this kind of double fraud: you try to get your "high" without having *deserved* it (deserved be it through *who* you *are*, or through hard work and initiation trials), and your "high" experience does not commit you to a different life. It is just a self-contained bubble, subjective self-indulgence, self-gratification. But whereas the use of drugs is a costly habit and also has very real and terrible consequences, the talk of "gods" comes free of charge. Enjoy!

"Gods as metaphors" is a contradiction in terms. The moment gods are seen through as metaphors, they are no longer gods. You cannot have it both ways. But the polytheistic psychologists precisely want it both ways.

Jung pointed to the problem of what he called "the right means in the hand of the wrong man" (*CW* 13 § 55, cf. § 4). It is not enough that the means one uses are the right ones. The right means would only be the *abstract* idea of what is right. What Jung suggests is that it is also necessary that the man who uses the means is the right one for this means, especially so in psychology and psychotherapy (and education). To these two aspects we would have to add a third qualification, and I can do so by quoting a *bon mot* of Lichtenberg: "S. rarely did anything wrong, but what he did he generally did at the wrong time." All three have to be right: the means, the person, and the moment (situation); the object, the subject, and the time. Only together do they make up the *concrete* idea of a right action. That method of amplification which is criticized here fails on all three counts. I already showed that the rhetoric of gods is emptied out, phony, and thus the wrong means. Now I ask: is today the right time for interpreting modern life events in terms of the gods? And, furthermore: are *we* the right persons for the use of "the gods" as categories? *Are* we such that we can feel entitled to make use of the word god? What right do we moderns have to speak, in our own name, of gods (i.e., "gods" outside of strictly historical contexts, as memory contents concerning psychic realities of former times, as "quotations")? Do we deserve the use of the term gods or God? Is this jargon of gods and myths in any way backed up and authenticated by our real being, our real psychological constitution, modern man's actual being-in-the-world? Or—do we not much rather have to agree with Jung that with this use of vocabulary[166] we are "feigning to be in possession of something to which we are not the legitimate heirs at all" (*CW* 9i § 28, transl. modif.)? Jung knew well enough: "we cannot go back to the symbolism that is gone." And about a particular former symbolism, he said, "it does not express my psychological condition" (*CW* 18 § 632).

Earlier I qualified the psychological use of the term god as frivolous, whereby I mainly had in mind the objective aspect that it was not backed up by the phenomena to which it was applied, not shown to be the phenomena's own epiphanic self-display, their own self-transcendence beyond their empirical-factual reality, but merely a stuck-on label which thus at the same time depreciated the notion of god. Now, focusing on the subjective aspect, I add that this use of "god" is also shameless. It is shameless because it is a case of confidence trickery, pretense. The psychologist as imposter, posing (not as Jung, in his own context, suggested as "Indian potentate" [*CW* 9i § 28] but) as a psychologist "with gods"—of course in such a tricky, devious way that, as we have seen, what *psychologically* is in fact his pose is *psychically* concealed behind his disclaimer that the talk of gods is "only metaphorical, not literal."

After this moral disqualification of the mythological jargon, I will add a few more methodological reflections.

To say, metaphorically, about the young woman's experience that it was a sign of "spring fever" is perfectly sufficient. Whatsoever is more

---

[166] "This use of vocabulary": in the passage referred to Jung was not critiquing the phony use of the term god and of mythological vocabulary, but nevertheless some very similar abuse.

than this cometh of evil. With "Aphrodite" in addition to "spring fever" we get a *chôrismos* in the sense of an empty duplication (the way Aristotle viewed the Platonic Ideas). We get once more exactly the same, however not *as* the same, but now rather as a goddess. Structurally, a *Hinterwelt* (a kind of metaphysical backworld behind this world) is established behind the ordinary empirical phenomenon. The given phenomenon is presented as having mythic or divine persons behind itself that make their presence felt in it. Jung might have said about the introduction of Aphrodite that this is clearly an instance where Occam's razor[167] needs to be applied: principles or categories are not to be multiplied without compelling necessity. Since the interpretation from ordinary human desires is perfectly adequate, the assumption of a mythological or divine personage behind it and the introduction of the fundamentally "higher" category of "gods" are on methodological grounds out of the question. Mystification.

Comparing the Jungian concept of the method of amplification with what was done to it by certain later Jungians like Adams and Paris, we can say that they are two incompatible concepts. In linguistics and other fields, there is the distinction between synchronic and diachronic perspectives. Analogously, we could here introduce the difference between a *syncategorial* and a *diacategorial* perspective. Jung's amplification belongs to the syncategorial type because in it only like can be compared with like, that is to say, only motifs that both belong to the category of the mythic, symbolic, or archetypal. Both have to have their home in the imagination. To use Jung's words, (unknown, hard-to-understand, puzzling) "hieroglyphics" are compared with (already readable) "hieroglyphics"; fragmentary dream symbols that give us "too slender a hint" are compared with other more complete occurrences of the same type of symbols, "archaic" or "irrational" material with other archaic or irrational material, the exceptional with the exceptional. It must already be clear from the outset that the motif in question that gives rise to the application of amplification is not a self-explanatory phenomenon of the human-all-too-human sphere, not anything belonging to "clearly understandable

---

[167] Occam's razor is the epistemological equivalent to the political subsidiarity principle according to which superordinate units are supposed to take on only such tasks that subordinate units cannot perform.

psychology." It must be "extraordinary," a symbol in the strict sense—"archetypal," as Jung would say. The fundamental distinction between the ordinary and the exceptional, between the everyday empirical world and mythic or archetypal reality, between what belongs to the mental horizon of Jung's "civil man" and what belongs to the sphere of symbols like "heavenly Jerusalem" is on principle presupposed and respected.

By contrast, in Adams' form of amplification, what is compared is a perfectly ordinary event, factual behavior, or empirical phenomenon of daily life in the sphere of positivity, on the one hand, and mythological figures belonging to the sphere of the imaginal, on the other. A present-day New Yorker's neurotic problems with Mom or Dad, a man's striving for the Oval Office, a young woman's buying a pair of sexy-looking sandals—these are neither particularly "manic ideas," nor "images that can only be described as 'archaic,'" nor "irrational data of the material, that is, of the fairytale, myth, or dream." They are part of "clearly understandable psychology" and not in need of psychological interpretation, indeed irrelevant for a psychology with soul. The decidedly modern is, as regards its psychological dignity, identified with the archaic and mythic, the "scientifically" or commonsensically understandable with "the irrational."

This is the diacategorial type of "amplification," because with systematic intent it in each instance crosses the border between the empirically real (or positive-factual) and the images of myth, always comparing an item belonging to the one category with another item having its home in the category of mythic imagination. The petty and banal is likened to mythological patterns or interpreted in terms of "the gods." We could call this border crossing vertical because, expressing it in mythological language, it compares and identifies facts here on Earth with gods up in Heaven and views the former as instantiations, if not incarnations, of the latter. The syncategorial amplification, by contrast, moves horizontally within the one sphere of "Heaven" (archetypal meanings).

This diacategorial type of amplification has a particular purpose. In order to see what it is we first have to recall what Jung's interest in employing the method of amplification was. His interest had simply been the "philological" or hermeneutic[168] one of trying to make hard-to-understand archaic images more intelligible and readable, to elucidate the meaning of difficult symbols by mirroring them in their peers. Amplification was fired by a strictly intellectual or theoretical interest. Otherwise, the amassing of parallels would have appeared to Jung pointless as well as methodologically unjustified. Conversely, only through this theoretical interest in fully understanding the specific meaning[169] of a motif was the mythological "surplus value" or soul dimension of the motif made concretely explicit and was it at the same time authenticated.

The motivating interest behind the other kind of (so-called) amplification, by contrast, is altogether different. Intelligibility is here of no concern. Primarily there is no wish to *know* better and *comprehend* more fully. "Aphrodite" does not add anything to our *understanding* of "spring fever" or of a woman's being attracted by sexy-looking sandals. All that the label Aphrodite does (at least is supposed to do) is to heighten, to inflate, the *importance* and *valuation* of an ordinary event by, here I use Adams' concepts, "personifying" and "deifying" it. The sole purpose is, more generally speaking, to rhetorically blow up ordinary phenomena of daily life in the modern world to "mythological proportions." It is to provide a divine underpinning to (or, to be more correct, a "divine" superstructure [in Marx's sense of the word] for) what in itself is human-all-too-human and perfectly self-explanatory, and what is also inadvertently *admitted* to be without soul meaning. For why else would one have to stick the label "Aphrodite" on it? Only a consciousness which at bottom clearly, although unadmittedly, sees the world and life in a thoroughly modern, ultimately "nihilistic" light needs this kind of embellishing "amplification," by way of compensation and consolation.

---

[168] It hardly needs mentioning that Jung's hermeneutics is fundamentally different from what, for example, Gadamer has in mind when speaking of hermeneutics. Jung does not mean *interpretation* of *texts*. His paradigms are the deciphering of hieroglyphs and, interestingly enough, comparative anatomy! He is focusing on morphological equivalents. Another difference is that Jung, as depth psychologist, operates with the theoretical notion of the objective psyche and with timeless archetypes, which is incompatible with a strictly hermeneutic approach in Gadamer's sense.

[169] Again, "meaning" not in the sense of modern hermeneutic understanding, but of the functional significance of the "type."

"As they [some people in the modern situation] experience myth, it is a projection of the psyche," Adams states.[170] I have never come across anyone who "experienced myth," so I am not in a position to know what their experience might be. But what is for sure is that the inflating of ordinary events with mythic importance advocated by Adams is clearly not "a projection of the psyche." It is the doing of the subjective mind, a deliberate procedure by modern psychologists on their own responsibility and out of their own interests, that is, by the ego-personality. It is not the objective psyche that does this personifying and deifying today, as we clearly see even from the example of our sandals lady in which the phenomenon in question did not display any personification and deification of its own accord, but spontaneously presented itself as "spring fever," that is, as the woman's own subjective psychic condition. And as such it excludes the notion of a god or goddess. Only by inventing and injecting some imaginary Jungian (but what a phony sort of a Jungian!) did Paris manage to rechristen the event in (poly)theistic terms: "Here comes Aphrodite."

This is a point at which I can more closely illustrate the fundamental difference between a modern psychological (i.e., already psychologized) experience and the ancient mythic experience of what in both cases was seemingly "the same" empirical event, and also make clear the mutual exclusiveness of the two types of experience. I will do this by means of the famous example from the *Iliad* (I, 194 ff.) of infuriated Achilles' self-control that stopped him from acting out his original impulse to use his sword against Agamemnon. What for us, for modern consciousness, is Achilles' self-control, for archaic consciousness[171]

---

[170] Adams, "Function."

[171] Although this example is very helpful for us to *illustrate* the archaic situation, the consciousness that displays itself in the composition of the *Iliad* is precisely not itself really such a truly archaic one. The explanation of Achilles' self-control through the intervention of Athena is *not* evidence of "mythic experience"! The scenes with gods in that work are already beyond myth proper and part of "literature," literature written for the entertainment and amusement of an upper class of nobility that took at least *those* gods no longer seriously (Walter Bröcker, *Theologie der Ilias*, Frankfurt/M. [Klostermann] 1975, p. 23). Also, in our very passage, a taking the Athena part of the scene naively at face value is already discredited by the immediately preceding lines (188 ff.) that show that the consciousness underlying the *Iliad* has already advanced to a "psychological" comprehension of what happens as an internal mental process in Achilles. But this is precisely what makes the subsequent Athena scene so helpful for us because it records an already obsolete mythic view with greatest clarity. As always, something can be best articulated when it is already over for consciousness, having just recently lost its immediate power over it, but when this consciousness is still very close to the formerly enthralling experience.

was precisely not *his* self-control, *his* restraining himself on the basis of a reflection about the disastrous consequences that his unrestraint acting out of his fury would have had. Rather, in this early status of consciousness, "his" exercising self-control was precisely experienced as not his, but as a necessity miraculously emerging *for* him and urged *upon* him from outside, by the goddess Athena. As the goddess of prudence concerned about his uncontrolled temper, she approached him from behind and, pulling his hair and becoming visible exclusively to him, cooled his wild anger.

Because this "his" self-command was not experienced as part of his own self-relation and as the result of his own doing, but as something that suddenly *happened to* him as a fundamentally superior epiphanic insight, the idea that a goddess has unexpectedly entered the scene is in this case, and only in this and analogous cases, perfectly natural and psychologically fully appropriate.

The moment, however, that one's exercising self-control in a situation of rage is *in fact* understood to be a person's own doing, part of his or her (internal, be it conscious or unconscious) self-relation and no longer as an *encounter between* self and a divine Other (an alien intrusion "from outside"), the notion of a god or goddess (in this connection) has become impossible, obsolete. But it is precisely this new kind of apperception that is inherent in the modern experience of the impulse of buying sexy-looking sandals. Consciousness is here in such a status that it *in fact* experiences this as an intra-psychic, completely subjective and completely natural event, the woman's own impulse, her own emotional state and desire. It is already, and exclusively so, part of the human psyche and *ipso facto* nothing divine, nothing that involves the manifestation of any deity, its intrusion into the empirical world. As a kind of "fever," "spring fever" is apperceived as a subjective, intra-personal emotional condition and thus as part of what Jung called "clearly understandable psychology."

In the modern situation, so we can say more generally, there is already a subject that *is* subject because it has logically integrated into itself what once upon a time might have been, for archaic, psychologically unborn man, something that logically truly happened to him from out of the vertical dimension. In archaic times, mental illness was usually seen as one's being possessed by some spirit; being ill with the plague might have been experienced as man's having been hit by an arrow of Apollo. For modern man, AIDS (to take this more current health problem) is the *patient's own* having infected *himself*[172] with a virus (on the horizontal, empirical-factual level) and *his own* immune system's not being able to overcome it (within the system of his own body). "Acquired Immune Deficiency Syndrome" says it all: acquired = no divine influx, and immune deficiency = the organism's internal problem. Likewise, neurosis is always "my" own being screwed up in my psyche as a no longer self-regulating, but malfunctioning system.

Speaking of "the psyche," I become of course at once reminded of the fact that Adams precisely insists that "The 'gods' continue to 'exist,' as they always have, in the psyche." But this is obvious nonsense. Gods never existed in the psyche. They always were (and, in order to *be* gods in the first place, *have to be*) external to the psyche, external to self: as epiphanies, visitations, happenings, occurrences, or as cosmic forces, and thus in any case essentially alien Others to whom man felt exposed and objects of worship to whom he was *objectively* upward looking like a child to his parents, regardless of whether he was subjectively willing or not to revere them. Gods originally existed in the cosmos and later, after the emergence of religion and metaphysics, in "transcendence." And the moment they, i.e., what they once represented, has been fully integrated into and appropriated by the (only *thereby generated concept* of) psyche as *its* internal moments or states, they have ipso facto ceased to exist and *objectively* turned into psychic properties of the human being, which in turn thereby turned into a *subject* in the "early-modern" sense. For the objective psyche the gods have been superseded; they have become sublated. It is the objective psyche that irrevocably experiences what happens in terms of "intrapsychic processes" and of "empirical events and causes."

The soul has on a cultural level objectively advanced to the status of subject, which is characterized by the fact that it objectively *knows* (a) our emotions, ideas, impulses, decisions, conflicts, and reactions to be its own and thus our own internal processes, and *knows* (b) even

---

[172] Which is also true if it happens, e.g., through a blood transfusion. The question here is not *behavioral* activity versus being a victim, not being caused by others versus personal responsibility. The point is that logically it is in any case the biological *organism's* own infection.

everything that happens in the world outside to be part of positive-
factual reality, that is, of a reality long comprised, and in this sense
sublated, by consciousness-as-such. For the soul in this new status of
subject, reality is one that is constituted as an uninterruptedly
continuous and systematic whole within which each single
phenomenon or fact without exception is fully determined by its
position within this integral whole and is known to be in principle,
even if not always in practice, capable of being explained by
consciousness's own science in terms of this whole.[173] Once the soul
has attained this status, it cannot go back (just as on a personal level
one cannot go back beyond puberty). Only subjectively, as a kind of
private pastime and on the surface (i.e., in the realm of ego feelings
and opinions), is it *perhaps* still possible today for people to mimic
(simulate) for themselves a "mythic experience" of sorts, and is it *indeed*
possible to *ideologically* keep "the gods alive," as exemplified by
"polytheistic psychology" using its un-Jungian understanding of
amplification, or, in very different ways, by creationist movements.

It is also inherent in the orientation of the psychology devoted to
diacategorial amplification that Everyman is supposed to be made to
believe that he could or should discover in his own biography his
"personal myth." Naturally also, for this kind of thinking, a child's
experience of its human mother is of course, just like that, its experience
of the mother *archetype*; shoplifting is a manifestation of Hermes the
thief; in every psychopathology there is a god, and so on ...[174]

By aiming, through its comparative *reconstruction* work, to fully
produce before our inner eyes the respective mythic or archetypal

---

[173] Only because this is so could Jung feel the need to develop his theory of
synchronicity.
    [174] I make in this discussion about amplification a sharp contrast between Jung
and certain of his followers who gave to Jung's concept of amplification a, let me say,
simplistic interpretation. This contrast is justified, but, I admit, only partially so. There
are also numerous passages that indicate that the here criticized type of amplification,
and the corresponding thinking behind it, occurs at times also in Jung himself. My
onesidedly identifying Jung with only one (even if a major one) of his tendencies is to be
explained and justified by my purpose of working out a true psychology rather than
wanting to write a historical essay about Jung. If my aim here were "Jung studies," I
would of course have to try to give the full and a balanced picture of Jung's ideas on our
topic. But I do not try to examine Jung, nor do I use Jung as my authority, but I cite Jung
where what he says is in fact an instance of true psychological thinking. Not Jung how
he really was, but *where Jung is at his best* is what counts. Following Mogenson we could
call this "the Jungian difference."

substance so that it can speak for itself, Jung's amplification allows us, as reflecting mind, to see for ourselves what makes it indeed mythic or divine, what gives it its extraordinary soul dimension, its higher dignity, and its transcendent shine (similarly perhaps to how, when listening to Bach's *St. Matthew's Passion* or to a Mass by Haydn, we get experientially in immediate contact with their religious truth and depth, regardless of what our own religious or areligious convictions may be). Jungian amplification, we could say, *celebrates* the soul truths themselves, it "amplifies" (in the sense of "intensifies") the illumining shine of the mythical or symbolic *meanings*.

The diacategorial amplification, by contrast, merely wants, as Adams declares, "to identify significant similarities" between life events and myths, that is to say, to establish, quite abstractly, no more than the claim *that* a correspondence (a merely *formal* correspondence) *exists*, just as Adams also praised Maureen Dowd because "she compares modern politicians to ancient heroes in order to identify similarities between them." The interest is in identification, in the similarity, not in the mythic substance, its meaning, and the radiance of its verity. Not having a genuine theoretical interest in *understanding* more deeply, and therefore not aiming for the respective content's particular *meaning substance*, it cannot—and possibly does not want to—make the mythic dimension itself in its substantial truth truly present and alive for the experiencing mind. It contents itself formalistically with similarities.

Jung criticized and rejected the common misunderstanding and misuse of his doctrine of "psychological types" that consisted in treating it as if it had the purpose "to stick labels on people at first sight" or as if it were a physiognomy or anthropological system (*CW* 6, p. xiv f.). Our topic of amplification belongs, of course, to a completely different area of psychology than Jung's typology. But structurally, the attempt to identify similarities between modern phenomena and mythic images is at bottom also nothing but the mindless activity of sticking labels on people and events, a kind of identification and classification (with the only difference that it uses mythological images and "the gods" as *typological categories*, whereas the misuse of Jung's typology uses the categories of "extraversion" and "introversion" in combination with the four "orientation functions").

We now have to ask: what makes it so important for some people to find parallels between modern politicians or other ordinary life events and mythology? What is the function of demonstrating these similarities? Our answer to this question as given so far had been the following. The purpose is to establish, so to speak, the *gentility* of the modern phenomena, to establish the alleged fact that they are something "higher," phenomena of "mythological proportion." The driving interest in amplifying is here to borrow the numinous aura or halo from the mythic images and from "the gods" in order to adorn petty modern reality with it. Enhancement, ennoblement, transfiguration, indeed, as Adams put it, *deification*. In other words, an *ideological* interest has taken the place of Jung's intellectual or hermeneutic interest.

This means that what we really get instead of Jungian *amplification* is mythological *inflation* in the double sense of (a) puffing up the specific ordinary reality in question and (b) thereby *ipso facto* depreciating—banalizing—the mythic and "the gods," using their names vainly, disrespectfully, irresponsibly, reducing them to abstract labels: the Oval Office as the golden fleece; the impulse to buy sexy-looking sandals as Aphrodite ...

But what is the *general ideological* purpose of this kind of procedure, beyond the purpose of embellishing this or that specific everyday phenomenon? In the last analysis, the function of the diacategorial type of amplification is to make it appear as if the gods still existed "as they always have." Amplification is now repurposed for nothing else but to time and again *prop up* a dogmatic general tenet, namely the claim, which we unfortunately also find in Jung, that there are gods in the neurotic diseases as well as in the (not necessarily neurotic) behavior of ordinary people or politicians in everyday life. Its function is to *prove* an ideological presupposition (whereas Jung's amplification had the purpose of deciphering something not understood), prove it at least emotionally: it is to create and confirm, as a matter of principle, the (diffuse and in practice totally inconsequential) impression of an actual *presence* of the gods and myths in modern life—*as if* nothing had happened in the history of the soul, *as if* the soul had not come of age, had not long integrated the former gods into itself. Thus, the other way around, the purpose is a denial of history, of the divide between the time of gods and the time of modernity, as well as a denial of modern man's bornness. The purpose is to entertain and cultivate what we could call, in analogy to Kant's *transzendentaler Schein* ("transcendental illusion," "transcendental illusory appearance") a *mythologischer Schein*, "mythological illusory appearance."

Furthermore, we could say in more *practical* regards that the function of this type of amplification is to act out the claim that we do not need any long painful *opus*, no labor of the concept, for *making* "'our' gold" (*aurum nostrum*) through numerous acts of negation and sublation (e.g., through processes of putrefaction, fermenting corruption, sublimation, distillation, evaporation of the prime matter), not that slow work which is always undertaken, *if* it is undertaken, with the very real personal risk of maybe never actually arriving at the end product. There is no need for such an opus in this thinking because for it, as I pointed out above, *aurum vulgi* IS (indeed, has all along and without further ado already been) *aurum nostrum*. All that *aurum vulgi*, or any trivial event or behavior for that matter, needs is our renaming it with some (superficially corresponding) mythological name, our conceptually subsuming it under the abstract concept of some "god" or "goddess" or "mythic hero" as an "instance" of it.

It could therefore seem that such an agenda is in the noble service of the gods and the mythic, and wholly for their benefit. *They* seem to be the highest values to which this approach aspires.

But this impression is a product of the "mythological illusory appearance" created by this approach. What this agenda is *actually*, although unwittingly, committed to and *really* serving is precisely the petty, the ordinary, the psychologically banal phenomena of everyday life, the *vulgi* (indeed, maybe even nihilistic) view of reality—in short "the daily" in the sense of the ephemeral, transient, or trivial, in contrast to the dignity and depth of the soul's truths. Again, we can be grateful to Michael Vannoy Adams for inadvertently revealing this underlying commitment to us.

After quoting James Hillman as saying about himself that as a young man he "thought the way to take on wrongs was through politics and journalism" and that *that* had been "where my ambition was," Adams, speaking on his own behalf, tells us that he, too, once aspired to become a journalist. "My ambition was to become a political journalist and to right wrongs by writing about them."[175] He had, as he informs us, indeed majored in journalism and worked as an intern and thereafter as reporter for important newspapers—before he much later became a Jungian analyst because, he says, current events felt superficial to him and "[w]hat appealed to me were ideas, which felt deep."[176]

In itself this personal bit of biographical information would not have to mean much. Not every activity or interest in one's youth must be deeply significant for and reveal the true motivation of a person's work in his mature years. However, we have to keep several things in mind: first, the strategic function that Adams' beginning with this story in his article has and the function of his article as a whole as a panegyric of "newspaper mythology," secondly also his statement that as a Jungian he now feels that even current events can be just as profound as any ideas,[177] thirdly, his trying to interpret mythologically Barrack Obama as well as the economic crisis of 2008, finally the whole wide-spread popular project of psycho-mythology of which Adams is an outstanding exponent. In the light of all these facts, his early ambition to become a *journalist* takes on a deeper significance. It helps us to suddenly realize that still now the deeper driving force behind this whole diacategorial amplification work, not only in him, is journalistic. "Journalistic" in a literal (etymological) sense (not in the everyday sense as referring to a particular profession).

Even though it would be completely wrong to ascribe to the (diacategorial) amplification work the youthful drive mentioned by Hillman and Adams to want to *literally* "right the wrongs of the world," we can nevertheless say that in a metaphorical sense, nay, in an ultimately "metaphysical" sense, its inner motivation is, just as before, still salvational, its implied message a doctrine of salvation, its aim the rescue of the world.[178] Its program is, as we have seen, time and again—and with each amplification always *pars PRO TOTO*—to demonstrate (if only metaphorically by claiming, merely rhetorically) that the modern world as a whole is NOT deserted by the ancient gods, that ordinary everyday life, and that so also the trivial details of

---

[175] Adams, "Obama," p. 291.
[176] Ibid., pp. 291 f.
[177] Ibid., p. 293.
[178] This is what makes it ideological.

each of our lives, HAVE "mythological proportions," and that even current newspaper events ARE just as profound as deep ideas. Salvation, this approach tries to suggest, does not even have to be expected from the future or from afterlife. No, the gods have already now a real presence in our daily life and reality. All that is needed is, we can guess—our mythological "amplification."

The inevitable conclusion that we have to draw about this type of amplificatory or polytheistic psychology is that it is not true psychology at all, not a psychology of soul. Deep down it is psychological *"journalism"*: dedication to *le jour*, to what belongs to the day, a devotion to the petty as that which for this thinking represents the actual soul substance, *however* a devotion to "the petty" in *combination with* the opposite desire, an egoic desire, to gild it with mythological associations so as to make it look like "the Great" (in Jung's sense[179]), like a soul event. "The gods" and the mythic/archetypal rhetoric function as no more than stage scenery, Potemkin villages. Jung once warned of a great danger. "He who is truly and hopelessly little will always drag the revelation of the greater down to the level of his littleness, and will never understand that the day of judgment for his littleness has dawned" (*CW* 9i § 217).[180] This is of course not at all what we find in the type of amplification critiqued here. The danger *it* exemplifies is precisely the opposite. Jung's warning presupposes a situation in which there is in fact a manifestation of the Great. But here there is no such manifestation of the Great. On the contrary, the banal, the ordinary facts of everyday reality, are blown up so as to appear as if they were "the Great."

This is why amplification in the popular "psycho-mythological" sense contents itself with searching for similarities. As we can say with a Kantian distinction, similarities exist, and can be detected, on the level of the *natura ectypa* of phenomena (of their obvious sensual or imaginal appearance, their empirical features). But Jung's amplification

---

[179] On the petty and the Great cf. *CW* 10 § 367 and above, especially section 2.3.8.

[180] Cf. G.W.F. Hegel: "No man is a hero to his valet; not, however, because the man is not a hero, but because the valet—is a valet, whose dealings are with the man, not as a hero, but as one who eats, drinks, and wears clothes, in general, with his individual wants and fancies" (*Phenomenology of Spirit*, tr. A.V. Miller, Oxford [Oxford Univ. Press] 1977, C. (BB.) VI. C. c, p. 404). More or less the same statement occurs in Goethe (in *Wahlverwandtschaften*, II ch. 5).

has to be understood against the background of an entirely different logic, a logic that distinguishes two levels and thus operates with the psychological difference between, to use Kant's terms, the *natura ectypa* and the *natura archetypa*,[181] however in such a way that the former (natura ectypa) is methodologically rejected and ignored so that the latter can emerge for us: so that "... behind the impressions of the daily life—behind the scenes—another picture looms up, covered by a thin veil of actual facts."[182] This is evidenced by the fact that Jung's amplification requires that, when using this method, what one is dealing with in both (or all) items to be compared is precisely strictly one and the same *meaning* or *truth*—on the level of *natura archetypa*, the level of the *other* picture *behind* the impressions of the daily life—rather than merely showing striking similarities *between* the impressions of the daily life (the ectypal) and mythic images (the archetypical in the Kantian sense), even though this "archetypically" same meaning in different texts and in different cultural situations manifests in *ectypally* maybe quite different forms. Similarities, likenesses, are absolutely not enough. What is required is the *sameness* of the "archetypical" meaning or the sameness of the (concrete) Concept, in all the empirical manifestations compared, a sameness which alone guarantees that the items are syncategorial and that the approach is *depth*-psychological rather than operating on the ectypal surface level.

2.3.11 Excursus on emotions and "the numinous" in therapy

There is in Jungian psychotherapy today not only the idea that soul *is* image and that the prime access to soul is via the imaginal, but also another and different widespread tendency to identify the soul with the emotional and/or with "the numinous." Let us leave the numinous aside for a moment and first only concentrate on the conception of the emotional as soul. In our emotions and feelings, sometimes also in our body sensations, so this view goes, we find the soul. Our emotions are our access to depth. Therapy therefore has to be emotion-focused, both concerning dream work and the transference/countertransference relationship. Apropos of dreams,

---

[181] The use of the same word in Kant's "natura archetypa" and in Jung's "archetypes" is possibly a mere coincidence. Kant was, of course, not an archetypalist *avant la lettre*.
[182] C.G. Jung, *The Visions Seminars*, Zürich (Spring Publ.) 1976, p. 8.

patients are invited to feel and say how they experience the various dream images, what feelings and fantasies these images evoke in them. The same applies to the therapists themselves. In working with a dream they, too, try to allow feelings to emerge within themselves, concentrate on them, and take them, just as the patients' expressed feelings, as clues to the meaning of dreams. In dream seminars and supervision sessions, the participants (analysts or analysts-to-be) are likewise asked to go deeply into their feelings incited by the dreams to be discussed or by particular therapeutic situations.

By the same token, emotions and feelings are often seen as the decisive, if not exclusive locus where the actual cure of neurosis and other psychic disorders has to take place. One thinks that in therapy one has to get to the emotional level: this is where the action is supposed to be. However, not only with respect to psychic disorders, but also with respect to the individuation process in the specifically Jungian sense, some Jungian analysts feel that it has to happen on the level of the feelings emerging in the interpersonal relationship between patient and analyst. This interpersonal relationship is then seen as the place where the *mysterium coniunctionis* in the strict alchemical-Jungian sense is supposed to happen as the felt experience of a kind of fusion, of the "pleroma," the "subtle body," or of a "third space" of meaning.

In the foregoing chapters I had already ample occasion to insist on the soul's coldness and on the psychological difference between (the soul's) archetypal truths and (the ego's) emotions. And so it is clear that I cannot accept as truly psychological ones the three convictions mentioned, namely that the major access to dreams is through our emotions, that in therapy one needs to focus on emotions as the essential area in which the cure of psychic disorders takes place, and that the interpersonal relationship between patient and analyst is the locus of the true *coniunctio*. Of course, therapy is a very complex undertaking that does not allow for simple wholesale statements. Every case is different, and in every case there are again many different therapeutic situations that each require their own approach. Nevertheless, once certain distinctions have been made, it is possible to critique the described therapeutic views by way of general guidelines.

The main distinction concerns the terms "feeling" and "emotion." It is a distinction which is complicated by the fact that the first term, "feeling," is often used equivocally for both emotion *and* feeling in the narrower sense as well as by the fact that even apart from any possible confusion with "emotion," "feeling" covers more than one distinct phenomenon (in English "I feel" can even be synonymous with "I think," "my opinion is"). So we should not cling to the words, nor should we restrict the use of one word to only one phenomenon, but rather discriminate the phenomena themselves denoted by the words, regardless of which word happens to be used. Psychology should speak as we speak in the ordinary use of language and not succumb to the scientistic temptation to want to regulate our speaking by creating a fixed purified terminology in which each term always has the same single meaning. I am not a friend of polytheistic psychology, but I certainly stand up for the polysemy and ad-hoc use of the words of the living language, the advantage of which is that it forces *us* to *think* in each case which meaning or which phenomenon is intended, rather than through a standardized, *operationalized* language letting the words relieve us of this work (the "opus" of determining the meaning in each specific statement from within itself).

Of course, in the present context it is both impossible and unnecessary to go into the whole theme of feeling and emotion. Each of them could only adequately be discussed in book-length essays.[183] The aspects that have to concern us here can be identified by starting out from a few quotations taken from a late (27 June 1959) oral impromptu talk Jung gave on feelings in response to questions that were posed to him.[184] Jung says:

> ... it is the great regrettable problem in our culture that we are strangely incapable of realizing our own feelings, that is, to notice [*spüren*, sense] the things that are of concern to us. One sees often that people pass over events or experiences without noticing [*merken*] what actually has happened to them. Because they do not realize at all that they have a feeling [*Gefühlsreaktion*]. Most of the time they merely notice what one calls an affect, an emotion, which goes along with physiological effects. Such as:

---

[183] On emotion cf. for example James Hillman, *Emotion*, London (Routledge and Kegan Paul) 2nd rev. ed. 1962.

[184] C.G. Jung, *Über Gefühle und den Schatten*. Winterthurer Fragestunden. Textbuch, Zürich and Düsseldorf 1999. The following quotations are my translations. I am indebted to Dr. Barbara Hahn for having brought my attention to this publication.

> an intensified activity of the heart, accelerated breathing, phenomena with regard to motor functions; this is what they notice. But when it is a feeling [*Gefühlsreaktion*] they often do not notice it at all because the feeling [*Gefühlsreaktion*] is not accompanied by psycho-physical phenomena. (*op. cit.* p. 12)

Jung goes on to report an experience from the time of his early association experiments. When, in course of investigating the question of how feelings and affects differ, Jung mentioned to his boss Bleuler, who was serving as his test subject, an annoying matter in the clinic that they both knew about, he found that Bleuler showed a clear reaction (a positive psychogalvanic deflection). However, when Jung indirectly alluded to another affair of which he had accidentally become aware, but about which Bleuler thought that nobody else could possibly know of, then no deflection resulted. And when Jung thereafter, through more direct allusion to this affair, let Bleuler see that he, Jung, knew after all about what had happened to him, Bleuler had an enormous deflection. From this Jung concluded that

> When he is alone with himself, he does not know what value this affair has for him, or how much it bothers him. But when he knows that someone else knows about it, then he gets the actual affect. (*ibid.* p. 13)

We notice that Jung here does not make a difference between affect and emotion, but a fundamental difference between emotion and feeling. What he calls feeling is according to him first of all very difficult to become aware of. The feeling that belongs to an experience is normally almost imperceptible. "... I noticed clearly," Jung said about a patient, a philosopher, that "he does not know at all what he has actually experienced or what has happened to him" (p. 14). A feeling requires, if it is to be noticed, either that it is reflected by or via others ("if you experience [something] alone, it is as if it had not really arrived," i.e., come home to you, p. 15) or it requires a particular sensitivity on the part of the subject (be it by nature or through training). Emotions, by contrast, are easily noticed because of their psycho-physical nature or physiological side-effects. In view of the immediate impressiveness of emotions and the rather imperceptible quality of feelings we are here reminded of Thomas Hardy's distinction (apropos of traditional pastimes versus modern revivals) between stolidity, on the one hand,

and excitement and fervor, on the other hand. A feeling is quiet, unobtrusive. Traditional pastimes and rituals, so we could interpret Hardy's observation, are or contain feeling which, however, remains implicit, unconscious, whereas modern revivals or what we call happenings are devoid of feeling, but are all emotion.

The second difference between feeling and emotion is that emotions have, we might say, the character of (minor or major) explosions. They have event character. They come over us, happen within ourselves and to us of their own accord, and are rooted in the organism. They are basically physiological, much like instinctive reactions of animals. One is easily *in the grip* of an emotion, which is why emotions were called *passiones* in Latin and *pathê* in Greek (both terms coming from verbs denoting "to suffer"). We are the *passive* recipients of them. When they happen, *they* are the actual subject, not we. We are *affected* by them. A feeling, by contrast, is, if we follow Jung, fundamentally *cognitive*. It is essentially a realizing, noticing, sensing, feeling by us. It is the realization of "what value something has," of *what* it *is* that has been experienced or has happened. It is sensing or noticing "the *things* that are of concern to us," an awareness of "what it is that happens to" oneself. It is an assessment, and this is also why what Jung had in his typology book termed the "feeling function" was described by him as a rational function, exactly as the "thinking function," whereas the two other orientation functions (sensation and intuition) were irrational functions. This rational cognitive character is what makes both feeling in the sense of the present discussion and the "feeling function" cold, calm, and sober, in striking contrast to the heat and fervor of emotions.

The rational and cognitive character of feeling is also emphasized by the fact that Jung, perhaps surprisingly, connects the word "correct" with it. Feeling thus implies a moment of truth. It is difficult, Jung says, "to have the correct feelings (*die richtigen Empfindungen*)" and necessary, "to register the correct feelings (*die richtigen Gefühle*)" (p. 14), and later he points out that under certain circumstances one is no longer capable "to evaluate (something) correctly" (*richtig zu bewerten*). The attribute of correctness could not possibly be combined either with emotions or with "what *we* feel." Emotions and what *we* feel are irrational. They are the way they happen to be and can merely be noted to exist and to be the way they happen to be. Only in terms of an external value system or with respect to a particular purpose could one say that an emotion or feeling was not the right one, for example not right in the sense of "not socially acceptable," "not practically suitable," or even "neurotic." But what Jung has in mind with his term *richtig* is the correct *perception*, *apperception*, correct grasping, of what an event *actually is* as regards its value, that is, an *adaequatio rei et intellectus*.

It is not that the events or affairs themselves, i.e., the *fact that* they occurred and *what* occurred, is not noticed. Bleuler was certainly fully aware of what had happened to him. What, however, according to Jung he was not aware of was only the feeling, the value that it had for him. It is interesting that Jung repeatedly uses the formulation, "what *actually* has happened" (to him or to people). This shows that he makes a difference between one's knowing *what* has happened and one's knowing what it psychologically *amounts to*, what it means to oneself— or rather to the soul. Jung does not say this, but we probably do not go wrong in stating that what Jung calls "feeling" ultimately is the soul view of events (what events *actually*, in the depths, in truth *are*), in contrast to the external, surface, factual view of them as positive facts. It is indispensable to understand that feeling in this context *does not refer to "what WE feel"* about something, e.g., whether we like it or not, whether it is embarrassing or revolting or upsetting or, conversely, a great joy to us or not, etc. In the case mentioned it is, e.g., to be assumed that Bleuler was very well conscious of, and would have been perfectly able to say, what he felt about that affair that had happened to him. What he was not aware of was, we might say, what *the soul* feels about it. It is true, Jung's wording is, for example, that we are incapable of realizing our own feelings and of sensing the things that are of concern to us. But this must not be misunderstood as referring to what *we* feel about something. We already know that the soul is subjective-objective and not objective in the abstract sense. Realizing our own feelings means being aware of the objective soul value that something has for us. (The same phenomenon may not have this soul's value for others. Nevertheless, "our own feelings," the way that Jung conceives them here, are not merely subjective in the abstract sense, not what *we* feel about it, but what it objectively means to us on the soul level, the soul value it in fact has for us. "What *we* feel about something" is different from both affects or emotions *and* from "our own feeling" as our awareness of what *actually* happened through the event.)

Feeling therefore is an insight into the character or nature of events or experiences. It is, in this sense, objective, a knowing about some reality, specifically about its value, worth, significance aspect, and in this sense has the character of being a *relation* or *statement*. An emotion or affect, by contrast, is exclusively subjective, autistic, enclosed within the individual in whom it happens. An emotion does not *say* anything about the event or phenomenon that caused or triggered it, it only "says" something about what is going on in the human being who has the emotion, much like a fever does not "say" anything, anything about the world, but is only a natural fact from which *we* can conclude something about the personal state of the subject or rather the human organism. The event that occurred may have triggered the emotion, but the emotion itself is only an isolated internal happening in people. Totally self-centered, self-enclosed. And whereas feeling has a *content*, an emotion is contentless. It is only a form or state of a person—an event of agitation, excitation: after all an *e-motion* (a being stirred up out of one's normal state), an energetic tension (which is also why you get the psycho-galvanic deflections), and in more intensive cases a kind of eruption or explosion. Despite the fact that it also has a specific color (joy, pride, embarrassment, disgust, anger, fury, etc.), an emotion is mainly to be seen in quantitative terms.

How is it with "what *we* feel about something"? It has in common with feeling in Jung's sense that we are not the wholly passive recipients of it, but actively do the feeling—assessing—ourselves. But with emotions it shares the quality of being abstractly subjective: self- or ego-centered. If we were willing to attribute a cognitive aspect to them, then we would have to say that what we get to know through them is only aspects of ourselves. Self-experience, self-knowledge, not, however, an awareness of "the *things* that are of concern to us." Here too the events, phenomena, and experiences are no more than opportunities or triggers for finding out "introspectively" what one's own emotional[185] response is and, by extension, what one's specific range

---

[185] "Emotional" here of course in a loose sense.

of feelings, and the range of degrees of their intensity, is, as well as to what one tends to emotionally react in which way.

With the phrase "what *we* feel" we refer to feelings that we *have*, while emotions or affects *have* us. Feeling in the psychological sense, by contrast, cannot be "had" nor do they "have" us. Psychological feeling *is* the (realized = perceived and appreciated) soul value of phenomena.

If we return to the conclusion that Jung drew from his experience with the cited experiment with Bleuler, we see that for Jung that "affair" had objectively, in and of itself, a feeling (worth, value) quality, but one which remained subjectively unfelt by the person to whom it happened and therefore did not *explicitly* become a feeling. This its remaining unfelt and only "implicit" is, according to Jung, due to the extraordinary difficulty, as long as one is alone with one's knowledge of the event, of becoming aware of the feeling quality. But Bleuler's later reaction the moment he became aware that the affair was known to others, namely, the fact that under this new condition the enormous psycho-galvanic deflection occurred, does by no means indicate that now the subject has become able to *feel* the affair. The reaction goes only as far as the occurrence of "the actual *affect*," as Jung himself says, an emotion in other words. The real *feeling* would be something more and something different. The affect proven by the experiment might, but also might not, serve secondarily as an occasion for the subject's also becoming aware of the *feeling*.

After these distinctions and clarifications I can come back to the question of the place of feelings and emotion in therapy and of whether soul is predominantly feelings and emotion. I think we can distinguish at least four different aspects or situations in therapy in which feeling/emotion plays a role.

1. The human level of the relation between the therapist and the patient. It goes without saying that on this level, the human-all-too-human level, the level of both persons as "civil man," feeling on the part of the analyst—in the sense of solidarity with his patient, empathy and a well-meaning, supportive attitude toward him—is very important. Feeling in this sense has to be the underlying atmosphere and spirit of the therapeutic work. But we should be very clear about it that this has nothing to do with psychology. It happens merely on the ordinary human level. It is as ordinary for the consulting room as is polite behavior towards strangers outside the consulting room.

2. In the course of therapy spontaneous emotions may occur. They necessarily have to be attended to. However not necessarily in the sense of cultivating them and taking them *as such* seriously, but rather only as the first immediacy of some implicit content, image, insight. The purpose of the opus in the consulting room is to release the "spirit" from its imprisonment in the physicalness of the matter, here from the emotion. As Jung had stated: "And you always have emotions where you are not adapted. If you are adapted you need no emotion ..."[186]

3. Patients may have *repressed* emotions. For example, a person who had a nasty parent in childhood may, through the defense mechanism of the identification with the aggressor, never have permitted himself the anger and resentment that in fact had wanted to arise in him. In such a situation it is naturally essential to allow these emotions to come to the fore, to express themselves, and this to their full extent. Such patients should get all the emotional support that they need from the therapist to get into real contact with their repressed or avoided feelings. Only once this process has been completed will the work have to continue as indicated under point 2 above.

Similarly patients with severe problems in the area of early attachment and bonding need much therapeutic work in the area of feelings and emotional support. But again, all this is of course not truly psychological work, but work on the same level as discussed above in point 1. Problems due to insufficient mother-child bonding, etc., really belong, as I said before, to the field of human biology in the widest sense, not to psychology. In such cases it is, as far as these specific problems are concerned, not the human soul, but the human animal that has this problem. Nevertheless, even in such cases it is questionable how far an emotion-focused therapy can lead if it is a case of *adult* patients. At some point here, too, truly psychological work will become indispensable. An adult is no longer in the position of the baby or young child that he or she was. Instead of dwelling on feelings, the adult patient has to come to clearly see and understand his deficiencies and learn to *integrate* them so that they cease being open wounds, turn into scars[187] instead, and so that he can go on from there with his life

---

[186] C.G. Jung, *Nietzsche's Zarathustra. Notes of the Seminar Given in 1934–1939*, ed. by James L. Jarrett, vol. 2, Princeton University Press 1988, p. 1497.
[187] Cf. James Hillman, "Puer Wounds and Ulysses's Scar," in: *idem et al., Puer Papers*, Irving, TX (Spring Publications) 1979, pp. 100–128.

without grudge, mourning, and self-pity. He has to cease staying the child who did not get that attachment that ought to have been, the child that believes to have deserved better and lives with the illusionary hope that all will eventually be healed. He needs to become free of these illusions and demands by consciously and explicitly leaving them behind, in order to *be* the adult that he already *is*, without having to make a fuss about what is missing. We all have to learn to take responsibility for our fate: for the wrongs or neglect we experienced, the traumas that happened to us, for the wounds, lacunas, and deficiencies that resulted from our history.

A particular danger of a therapeutic approach systematically oriented towards the emotional and placing its hopes on feeling and empathy is that it may even mislead the therapist to diagnose attachment difficulties due to bad conditions in infancy or traumas in early childhood even in patients where there is actually simply a neurosis, a neurotic *mise-en-scène*. Attachment difficulties in adult patients must of course not always be due to unsuccessful bonding in early childhood. It may also be a neurotic defense. But like sees like. The mind committed to the standpoint of emotion as the true place of soul and informed by attachment theory, which, as we know, catches sight of man only insofar as he is a human animal, will be likely to see early attachment difficulties all the time. And as Shamdasani pointed out, the "malleability of individuals" is such that they are "willing to adopt psychological concepts to view their lives,"[188] in other words, to supply, and thereby corroborate, what according to the therapeutic presupposition is expected. The result may well be a *folie à deux* in the consulting room.

4. What is to be said about that style of therapy in which patients are invited to focus on what they feel for example apropos dreams, to dwell on their emotions and to cultivate those feelings and emotions? This is an invitation to self-indulgence and self-centeredness. It draws us only into ourselves, into the ego-world, the sphere of the human-all-too-human, and into the world of positivity. It constellates the patient exclusively as the "civil man" that he of course also is. Such a therapy teaches him to take himself terribly seriously, as if it were

---

[188] Sonu Shamdasani, *Jung and the Making of Modern Psychology. The Dream of A Science*, Cambridge (Cambridge Univ. Press) 2003, p. 11.

important what *he* thinks and feels. (The same applies of course to the analyst, to what *he* thinks and feels.) But what *we* feel and our emotions are neither here nor there. Rather, a psychotherapy devoted to the soul needs, first, to become aware of the *other picture* that looms up "behind the impressions of the daily life—behind the scenes." What the *soul* says is what needs to be heard in therapy. "It has a say now, not you" (*Letters 2*, p. 532, to Charteris, 9 Jan. 1960). *Not* you! And secondly, such a psychotherapy with soul wants to enable us, both patient and therapist, to distinguish ourselves from ourselves, to gain a distance to ourselves, so as to begin to see ourselves objectively, soberly, detachedly as if from outside, that is to say, *as* objective facts, as givens (given to ourselves), just as are all the other facts of our world, in the spirit of Jung's statement about the "childlike naïveté" of modern man: "He has no objectivity toward himself and cannot yet regard himself as a phenomenon which he finds in existence and with which, for better or worse, he is identical" (*MDR* p. 341). Any concentration on what *we* feel only cocoons us more deeply in ourselves and increases our (*childlike-naïve* sense of) identity with ourselves.

Concerning dream interpretation, concentration on what *we* feel is just as misplaced as free associations which, as Jung insisted, only lead us back to our own complexes. This kind of approach would amount to the cultivation and celebration of the complexes. Where it rules, there, one must think, a notion of soul and of the difference between soul and ego is simply absent. Concerning dreams Jung's "It has a say now, not you!" is of particular relevance. We want to understand the dream, its images, the text as it is written. There has to be a faithful devotion to the dream text in order to try to bring—perhaps—to light what is contained in it. The feeling necessary for dream interpretation is the truly psychological and "professional" feeling discussed above: not what *we* feel about the dream images, but their objective feeling quality, their felt value, their psychological dignity and importance, is what counts. We must not substitute ego feeling and emotion for feeling the *thing* that is of concern and we must not camouflage, through the equivocation inherent in the word feeling, the ersatz that it is. Soul-work is devoted and works on the *matter* with a view to facilitate, through *our* human devotion to it, *its* self-unfolding, the internal dynamic within it, what alchemy called the spirit Mercurius. It wants to release it into its truth. Alchemy distinguished between *aurum vulgi* (the literal gold that the alchemical charlatans promised to make for kings and princes) and *aurum nostrum* (the true alchemists' psychological gold). Devotion to what *we* feel and to our emotions is the sign of one's commitment to the *aurum vulgi*.

Culturally, emotion-focused therapy is the therapeutic parallel to television, advertizing and propaganda, mass sports events, music festivals, the drug culture, etc., which all aim at our excitement and fervor, our feeling *ourselves* intensely, our highs. Sensationalism.

We usually think that what we are doing by introspectively trying to find out what we feel is to finally *discover* our true, previously merely unconscious feelings. But this is a naive belief. Just like active imagination and memory, the concentration on one's feelings is a production process. By one's concentration on "them," those feelings are being fabricated on the spot. Heaven knows whether the exploration of "what we feel" gets us to our "true" feelings that unwittingly existed all along or whether they are merely something that we just now worked ourselves up to and into through this very activity. The soul is uroboric. Such feelings are the results of its own doing.

Jung of course felt that, whereas the method of free association should be criticized as only leading to our subjective complexes, active imagination was a legitimate way that could lead us to the collective unconscious, to the archetypal sphere. But this is an illusion. All such technical practices are methods for the *artificial creation* of contents, images, or feelings, not a sure way to eminent origins, be they archetypal, biographical-historical, or referring to the innermost truth about oneself. "'Psychic reality' is, par excellence, the fabricated real" (Shamdasani, *ibid.*). "The fright and the apparently traumatic effect of the childhood experience are merely staged, but staged in the peculiar way characteristic of hysteria, so that the *mise en scène* appears almost exactly like a reality," Jung, as we heard, had had to realize in the case of hysterical neuroses (*CW* 4 § 364), but the principle of this insight applies much more generally. Memory is productive, not evidential. And so are psychological theories and methods, as I briefly indicated above at the end of point 3 concerning attachment theory. The trouble arises when psychological theories deny their uroboric nature and when their productions are projected out of the uroboros, for example as referring to facts of the literal past.

Quite apart from the concern for *aurum nostrum* and soul-making, a decidedly emotion-focused therapy is also detrimental from a strictly practical-therapeutic point of view. For one thing, it teaches the patient (and us) to make a fuss about himself and about the mishaps and ill fortune in his life. By making him indulge in his resentments, fury, regrets, feelings of misery, inferiority, etc. and to appreciate them as psychologically important, it also teaches him to feel as a victim. "Life was unfair to me." This kind of therapy thus unwittingly tends to send the patient into a trap. The dwelling on one's emotions in such cases is a defense against one's *having to pay the price* for what life has done to oneself. Life was maybe "unfair" to me; I may have had bad starting conditions, cruel parents, traumatic experiences; fate may have dealt me brutal blows—but *so what?* This is psychologically not important. It may be humanly terrible, outrageous, but psychologically it is neither here nor there. By being wronged, insulted, wounded, life presented a bill to *me* that I have to pay. It is essential to realize that it is I (and no-one else) who has to pay the bill for whatever was done to me or whatever I have been deprived of, and it is essential that I finally pay it! Because nobody else can pay this price. What pains me, the blows of fate that happened to me, the insult done to me must psychologically not stay outside, in the form of otherness, as external happenings and doings by others of which I merely happen to be the innocent recipient. I must not try to logically defend myself against and reject them by being angry and finding them revolting.

Anger, fury, the wish for revenge or compensation, etc. are unpsychological, namely (if I may say so) "sociological." These emotions establish and uphold the fantasy of the externality of *interpersonal* transactions between people (or between "life/fate/ God" and me). But there is no "between" between me and my pain. It is utterly mine or rather me. *I* hurt. Where the pain or wound came from is psychologically absolutely irrelevant. What was done to me by others I have to psychically make my very own, part of my self (*this* would be one's paying the price for having been wounded), and without grudge or resentment at that.[189] I have to embrace it as my very own pain, injury, or loss and these as my new inalienable reality. No otherness. This is the only way how I can become free again. Otherwise I will stay caught in the resentment against what happened to me, that is, caught in a *complex*. The flow of life will then be arrested, get stuck (in this area). I have to learn to live with my wounds and deficiencies, to integrate them into my self-definition.

As long as a truly psychological therapy is still concerned with what went wrong in my life in the past, it has to be mainly concerned with the paying of old unpaid bills that the patient has collected. Of course, this is contrary to the mainstream thinking of today. Deep down (or sometimes even consciously) we think that victims ought to be recompensed for what was done to them and that if anybody, then the doers, not the victim, should have to pay the bill. We are in the grip of the (mostly secret, unconscious) dream that the wrong or injury should somehow be undone, that there should be a return to the original state of in-nocence, uninjuredness, of "whole-ness": *heil*, health, although rationally we of course realize that this is impossible. We insist on apologies and remuneration from those who hurt us. In legal and social regards this is appropriate, because there we are concerned with the social arena. But psychologically it is completely wrong. The soul is self-relation. Interpersonal relations cannot appear in psychology. They are not a psychological category.

Those Jungian approaches whose central methodological outlook is such that they focus on the *literal* transference/countertransference emotions and reactions (more or less in a completely personalistic, downright Freudian psychoanalytic sense), but give these so-understood processes out as instances of what Jung in his alchemical psychology worked out as the "psychology of transference" and present them as leading to a true *coniunctio* in the alchemical sense start out from and dwell on what goes on between positively existing people: the social arena within the consulting room. If this is your logical starting point, you cannot possibly arrive at soul. Such approaches likewise produce at best *aurum vulgi*, but pretend that it is *aurum*

---

[189] This is also why forgiving is psychologically so important. It is not only morally or religiously important. It also helps me to be freed from the constraints of my complex.

nostrum. The positive-factual behavior of the two organisms (therapist and patient), namely their egoic emotions and feelings in relation to each other, are directly *identified* with what in alchemy is the soul's background processes taking place between Rex and Regina and precisely *not* the decidedly empirical foreground process of *felt experience*, of the emotional interaction between the positively present analyst and patient. This is an identification merely by naming. The *psychological* level is missed. The actual life of the soul is *reduced* to the process of literal human emotions and relations, stuffed into what *people* feel. Semantically the experiences produced thereby may be completely out of the ordinary. But logically, syntactically they occur on the level of the human-all-too-human. The more complex and logically negative is expressed in the terms of the much simpler level of positive facts, of subjective felt experience or imagination. In the letter about Socrates and his *daimonion* in which Jung said, "'To hell with the Ego-world! Listen to the voice of your *daimonion*. It has a say now, not you'" (*Letters 2*, p. 532, 9 Jan 1960, to Charteris), he later continued: "we still consider his *daimonion* as an individual peculiarity if not worse. Such people, says Buddha, 'after their death reach the wrong way, the bad track, down to the depth, into an infernal world'" (pp. 532f.). The systematic focus on literal transference and countertransference feelings is such a reaching the wrong way, the bad track, namely the way deeper into the subjective psyche and away from the objective soul's truths.

Transference and countertransference feelings within a Jungian analysis only need to be attended to when they *either* make themselves felt in analysis of their own accord *or* when unconscious transference fantasies or emotions conversely interfere with the smooth movement of the therapeutic process. There is a great difference between on principle *basing* one's therapeutic work on the transference relationship, using it as the essential horizon of therapy, on the one hand, and therapeutically attending to transference phenomena as they in fact spontaneously manifest themselves, on the other hand. When patients come with obvious *assumptions* about the therapist, with vehement accusations, with fantasies about his or her private life, with ideas about the therapist's grandiosity, with strong feelings of love or hate towards the therapist, then these can be valuable material for working out together some essential unconscious issues. While such issues might first of all belong to the psychic (only personal) level, it is nevertheless also possible that they have a deeper soul meaning—even if of course only in the context of the *opus parvum*. One important example is when, in the relationship with the therapist, the neurotic soul restages some theme of which it actually, deep down (that is, implicitly), already knows that it is no longer true, but that needs to be dramatically staged once more for the benefit of consciousness and in fact relived and spelled out in all its brutal detail as if it were absolutely real, this for the soul purpose of enabling consciousness *to explicitly depart from it* and in full awareness finally own up to its obsolescence. One always has to *know* what that which is a thing of the past is in order to be able to psychologically leave it behind. Only what is seen in clear daylight and along with everything that it emotionally and practically involves can one truly depart from. And this requires that its obsolescence, on the one hand, and the absurdity of any clinging to the old truth, on the other, has fully been experienced.

The impressiveness of such productive transference phenomena must, however, neither mislead one to see all therapy predominantly in terms of the transference relationship nor to interpret those particular experiences themselves as having the lofty meaning of the alchemical *mysterium coniunctionis*.

Later in his improvised talk "On Feelings" Jung gets to talking about "non-realized primordial experiences" and points to their ambivalent effect. "What, as it were, comes from those primordial ages has a power that pushes its way forward and at the same time pulls backwards. One can withdraw into it. In the case of the mentally ill, for example, this happens that they withdraw, as it were, into the primordial experiences; they are pulled backwards. They even make a point of it, as if this were a special achievement" (p. 21). Then Jung makes a crucial distinction concerning our reaction to such experiences: "It depends on the individual human being whether he goes to the trouble to see these things positively or whether he abandons himself to the impression and the latter pulls him back. It [the impression] can do him just as much harm." Taking a theological example, the idea that "Through the blood of our Lord Jesus Christ we are redeemed of our sins," Jung asks, "What for heaven's sake does this mean?" and laments that on principle nobody thinks about it, which, he thinks, has fatal consequences for people. "Because this is the sort of idea which should lead forward. In reality, however, one simply slides back into the past with them. One is being made unconscious again through them. Because one does not know what these words mean, and because one abandons oneself to the emotional impression [*Gefühlseindruck*]. 'The blood of our Lord Jesus Christ'—this sounds so solemn and so beautifully like Sunday and so religious, so splendidly religious" (p. 22). "For one ought to know what it means. But in this regard there is simply no thinking going on any more. There exists an enormous laziness to think" (p. 23). Jung warns against a state of mind "in which we do not think anything any more and just succumb to absolute suggestion. One becomes suggestible when one does not have conscious thoughts, but only unconscious ones" (pp. 24f.).

Primordial or archetypal experiences and time-honored theological dicta are not our topic here. But the two modes of relating to them that Jung contrasts are highly relevant. The one possibility is that one goes to the trouble of thinking about the motifs that come up, trying to see and understand them "positively," i.e., concretely, as to their specific content and what it really means. This "thinking about" is of course not rationalistic and positivistic thinking, but includes and requires the type of rational, objective feeling discussed above, although Jung does not mention this here. The other possibility is that instead of thinking and feeling the content, one abandons oneself to the emotional impression that the motif makes on oneself, allowing oneself to "succumb to its absolute suggestion." The "emotional impression" is precisely "what *we* feel," what feelings we get, when we hear such dicta. The word "impression" is telling. It shows a direction (from outside into us). The impression does something to us. It impresses itself on us. And its effect is ultimately, according to Jung, that it makes us unconscious again.[190] This type of feeling lulls us into psychological sleep.

The suggestive power of such emotional impressions to take us in is above all due to the fact that they are utterly abstract, only musical; they are about how something "sounds," about the mood they put us into (e.g., "so splendidly religious"). The "third space of meaning," or

---

[190] This is the important topic of "consciousness's becoming unconscious" (*CW* 12 § 563, transl. modif.).

the experience of it, aimed at by certain types of Jungian transference-focused therapy, is probably a case in point: a "space"—completely abstract, fuzzy, vacuous, and unspecific. *But* of course: "subtle body," "pleroma,"and "third space of meaning" all sound "so solemn, so beautifully like Sunday."

What emerges when a patient is invited to explore what *he* feels about this or that dream image is of course usually not "so solemn and splendidly religious." Nevertheless all such subjective feelings and emotions share with the much more lofty "third space of meaning" the totally abstract musical character and the regressive self-abandonment to "emotional impressions."

The other, namely truly psychological kind of feeling, by contrast, requires *our* "taking the trouble" to learn to grasp and appreciate in detail *what* is *really said* and *meant*, our getting down to brass tacks. Feeling as work, effort. And as responsibility (it has to be the *correct* feelings![191]).

Because the last-quoted passages from Jung's text "On Feeling" already introduced the motif of religious dogmatic statements and primordial archetypal experiences, they can serve us as an entry into our second topic, that of the numinous and the sacred.

The term "the numinous" is a neologism created by Rudolf Otto[192] and thus a thoroughly modern, early-20th-century fantasy or construct. During no age prior to Otto did people have (and use) this term (or a corresponding concept), nor have any need for them. Why not? Because one spoke of gods, demons, angels, spirits, fairies, etc., that is to say of really existing forces often (but not always) with person character that were a constituent part of the cosmos, ontological. It is true, the Romans had the term *numen*, on the basis of which Otto coined his own term. It denoted the power or presence of gods and is often seen by scholars as similar in meaning to the word *mana* that comes from a very different cultural region, the South Pacific. But the *numen* (originally meaning Jupiter's "nodding") was merely a quality of gods and not itself the term for a god or a substantial reality. And as a quality or attribute of the gods, it of course presupposed the

---

[191] In the area of "what *we* feel" anything goes. Necessarily so. The only criterion available here is the fact *that* (or whether or not) we feel this or that, whatever it may be.

[192] Tomislav Tribuljak, *Philosophie und Theologie bei Rudolf Otto*, Osijek (Croatia) 2000, p. 228.

existence of gods. Otto, by contrast, conceived of the numinous as an emotional *a priori* in the depth of the psyche, an *a priori* category which may be evoked by certain stimuli, but which, as an *a priori* category, cannot be derived from them.[193]

These briefly described findings suggest that the term "the numinous" became historically possible and or necessary precisely when the real gods and spirits—the divine as objective reality in the world—had disappeared. The gods and spirits of old were very specific, concrete, and substantial. But "the numinous" as well as "the sacred" are abstract-universal concepts. With the change from gods to the numinous, the once upon a time utterly concrete gods, we might say, had (1) evaporated and been condensed into the abstract thinned-down concept of "the numinous" as a mere category, a universal logical form. They had (2) withdrawn from the cosmos into the subjective psyche as its fundamental aptitude to experience according to this *a priori* category. And they had (3) turned from ontological beings into a human emotion, into something irrational. In epistemological regards we could add that Otto thus (4) psychologistically transformed the concept of a Kantian *transcendental a priori* into an emotional *a priori*.

All in all it appears that "the numinous" is a subjectivized, desubstantiated, and worldless substitute, *during* the modern godless age, for what used to be the concrete content of religion. "The numinous" is a concept of the divine that has lost its object, the *Real* that religion used to be about. It is only a feeling or experience in the subject, and thus the invention of the idea of the numinous is a kind of new edition of Schleiermacher's rescue attempt for religion about 120 years before Otto when the loss of God first made itself felt and when religion as a public truth had lost its conviction. Addressing the "Cultured Despisers" of religion and trying to make religion palatable to them again, he had already withdrawn religion from the public sphere (where it was no longer tenable) into the subjective inner of man as the latter's "feeling of his absolute dependence." Otto's notion of "the numinous" as the feeling of our creatureliness seems to hark back to this Schleiermachian idea, although of course on a much more

---

[193] Rudolf Otto, *Das Heilige. Über das Irrationale in der Idee des Göttlichen und sein Verhältnis zum Rationalen*, Breslau 1917, pp. 137–140.

extensive basis of modern concrete scholarly knowledge about the phenomenology of religion than had been available at the time of Schleiermacher. In both cases, the purpose had been to give to religion an unquestionable dignity of its own (a category *a priori*, in the case of Otto; a certain feeling as an anthropological constant, in the case of Schleiermacher) outside and independent of human reason. Emotions and feelings are events, facts. If man is by nature endowed with such religious feelings, then religion has been rendered unassailable for reason. Religion then simply has to be taken the way it is. It does no longer have to account for itself, no more than our genetic make-up and hormones can be considered accountable. They are the way they are. This is their irrationality. The other side of the coin is, however, that religion thereby became one-sided. It had to exclude reason and truth from itself and became worldless.

No doubt, Otto's concepts are, within limits, very useful for the *scientific* study of the phenomenology of religion. But they are of course also a child of their time, expressive of the time at the end of and after World War I, the time of existentialism in philosophy, of expressionism in art and literature, of new secular-religious totalitarian ideologies, like communism, fascism, and nazism. Otto's focus was on the feeling of being *overpowered* by the Wholly Other, by the *mysterium tremendum* and *fascinosum*. Small wonder that Jung, who gladly accepted Otto's concept of numinosity and had himself already in his private experience in typically early-20th century subjectivist style defined God as the *experience* of an irrational, terrible, absolutely overwhelming majesty, would become deeply impressed by the grandiose parades and the highly-emotionalized spirit of the Nazi-era, crediting them with being a manifestation of numinosity, indeed of a god, whom he identified as the ancient Germanic Wotan. If *truth* has been eliminated from the concept of religion, if the emotion is the ultimate criterion left, if overwhelmingness per se and the *tremendum* and *fascinosum* are what ultimately counts, then the Nazi-movement is an excellent candidate for religion. The Nazis had perfected the generally prevailing emotionalizing that is characteristic of the first half of the 20th century. They knew how to mobilize the emotions, how to rouse the masses and make them "succumb to absolute suggestion." They knew how to instill the feeling of being overwhelmed and terrified, just as did other contemporary totalitarian systems. I do not want to connect Otto in any way with the Nazi-movement. But I diagnose a common *spiritus rector* or vortex in all the diverse and independent early-20th century phenomena that abandoned themselves to the emotional, be it in theory, in the sober scientific concept of the numinous as in Otto, or be it in the expressionism in art and literature, or in the high-strung excitedness of the totalitarian political ideologies that, as totalitarian, claim to be a substitute religion.

We have to see through the concept of "the numinous" as ultimately nihilistic. It is truthless and inconsequential. It is defined as just an experience, that is, the event of a feeling. The inference from "the happening of a numinous experience" to "a numinous *reality* as that which is experienced" is fallacious. Experiences per se, whether "numinous" or not, are psychologically utterly irrelevant. The modern notion of "the numinous" itself *testifies to* the end of religion that it wants to prevent.

Jung still honestly and innocently believed in numinous experiences and could—somehow, of course not rationally, but at least experientially—back up his view by his own childhood experiences that he believed provided for him the *immediate* experience of God in his omnipotence and overwhelmingness.[194] For him, the numinous was still something truly serious. And, as I suggested, his experience was in turn backed up by the absolute seriousness of the whole spirit of the age concerning emotion (the elated high-strung spirit of the post-Nietzschean age, the time of World War I and the following two decades), which was characterized by the deadly serious covering over of its fundamental nihilism by heightened emotionality, political activism, and militarism because it did not want to face, and hold its place in, its truth. The concentration on the numinous and on the sacred in some Jungian quarters at the end of the 20th century and the beginning of the 21st century, by contrast, is merely a somewhat silly game. It (along with its game character), too, is of course backed up by the spirit of the age, this time the playful spirit of *medial modernity*.

---

[194] I am referring above all to his Basel cathedral experience during his eleventh year, *MDR* pp. 36–41. "But then came the dim understanding that God could be something terrible" (p. 40). Compare "One must be utterly abandoned to God" (p. 40) with "succumb to absolute suggestion." On this Basel cathedral experience see my "Psychology as Anti-Philosophy: C. G. Jung," in: *Spring 77* (Philosophy and Psychology), June 2007, pp. 11–51.

A lot of hot air. A show for show's sake. The Ego-world. Not *really* serious; only a pretended seriousness. To see the difference let us remember the following. The character of the first half of the 20th century was such that men would still voluntarily go to war, willing to heroically stake their lives for (what they felt was) a great cause with great *pathos*, be it World War I or, for example, the Spanish Civil War. Today nobody in the Western world would voluntarily want to die for any cause. And so one simply enjoys soap bubbles, among them, in certain psychological and New Age circles, "the numinous" and "the sacred."

As to the latter term we should remember that the *real* sacred was relative to the sacrificing cultures that in fact *made* (established) the sacred (*sacrum facere*), and created the sense of the sacred, above all by killing, slaughtering. Sacrificial slaughter was what ultimately authorized and validated the notion of the sacred.[195] The sacred was nothing nice, harmless, lofty, and enjoyable. It was a deadly serious reality. And the sacred was not a subjective feeling or experience, but an objective quality of real places, things, actions, persons. This sense of "sacred" lasted in certain remnants beyond the time of the sacrificing cultures, even way into the 18th century. For example, kings were sacred, which is why a *lèse-majesté* was severely punished, often by the death penalty. If a culture lost its readiness to kill as at least its *ultimate* possibility (which is the case in our modern culture), then all seriousness is gone and "the sacred" is deprived of its foundation. It becomes free-floating. Where it is not used merely as a scholarly tool for understanding historical religious phenomena (as in Rudolf Otto), but is supposed to be an immediate presence, it has become illegitimate, phony. It has taken on mere entertainment value (in a wider sense of the word).

The wish for "the sacred" and "the numinous" in psychology today is an example of a wish for "abandoning oneself to emotional impressions," for indulging in what "*sounds* so solemn and so splendidly religious." It is used for the purpose of self-gratification. But even Jung's own emphasis on the numinous, although it still had some more dignity and cutting edge, nevertheless falls under this his

---

[195] Cf. "Killings," chapter five of my *Soul-Violence*, Collected English Papers vol. III, New Orleans, LA (Spring Journal Books), 2008.

own criticism. When Jung once states that "the approach to the numinous is the real therapy, and inasmuch as you attain to the numinous experience you are released from the curse of pathology" (*Letters* 1, p. 377, to Martin, 20 Aug. 1945), we have to remind him of the fact that the numinous is a nihilistic concept, the concept of an emotional experience without an objective real the experience *of which* it would be. Numinous experiences today are not a locus of soul. Nothing is *healed* by them if one succumbs to their "suggestive power" (cf. *CW* 7 § 269).

In contrast to these egoic feelings and emotions, psychology has to be committed to the fundamentally other Jungian notion of feeling that comes out in Jung's talk about "the *correct* feelings." In other words, psychology has to be committed to trying to feelingly grasp the reality of "the *thing* that is of concern" and thus to a sense of truth—even in the age of medial modernity that dissolves everything into games and shows. The ego can do without truth and substitute emotions and experiences for it. Not so the soul. Psychology is about the soul of the *Real*.

CHAPTER 3

The Phenomenology of the Soul (2): The soul as *subject*, style, and work (soul-making)

3.1 THE OTHERNESS AND ABSENCE OF THE SUBJECT DURING PREMODERN TIMES

In section 2.1.9, "The twofoldness of what we call soul," we became aware that the soul is the—uroboric—unity and difference of (a) its own truths and (b) its own potential to perceive, appreciate, reflect and enact those truths, a unity and difference, moreover, that in Neoplatonic thinking has been expressed in the image of the correspondence of eye and sun, of seeing and shining, we could say: as the internal dialectic of *light*. In the whole part about "the experienced or occurring soul" we were obviously for the most part, although not exclusively, concerned with the objective soul. Now we have to shift our emphasis to the subjective soul, to the soul as that which *knows*,[196] as the *organ* of truth (its own truth) and as the soul-*making* subject (in the sense of the subject that makes that which merely *is* true also *become* true, which is a movement from the

---

[196] Knows in itself, in the soul.

implicit to the explicit). The unity and difference as which the soul phenomenologically shows itself is uroboric inasmuch as the objective, or occurring, soul is also in itself subjective and "made," and not merely a natural, factual, only-objective occurrence. Conversely, we can say, the moments of subjective reception and soul-making are themselves also objective events.

Historically speaking, the subjective aspect of the soul had always been almost exclusively in the foreground of attention. Of the archaic notions that belong here I will only very briefly mention or touch upon a few ideas since they have already been amply discussed by numerous other authors (Erwin Rohde in his *Psyche* [1890 to 1894], Richard Broxton Onians in his *The Origins of European Thought* [1951],[197] C.G. Jung *passim*, James Hillman especially but not only in his *The Dream and the Underworld* [1975],[198] to mention only these few). However, before we come to these ideas, I want to submit a thesis about the origination of such a thing as subjectivity or "I" in prehistoric times, about how it first occurred. It is of course a speculative thesis, since there cannot be any proof for it, but I believe it has some plausibility.

The starting point must have been an I-less condition. The first emergence of an I within this I-less condition must have been momentary and insular, in other words, not a once-and-for-all acquisition. The primordial I or subjectivity was nothing permanent and precisely not a subjective feeling or state. Rather, it is to be assumed that the initial I was the property of particular special situations. The I had event-character, rather than being a constituent part of the "personality" or "psyche" of people. The first reality of subjectivity—so I claim—was the moment of the prehistoric hunter's facing his hunted game and throwing his spear for the kill. This dramatic instant of being face-to-face with an animal to be killed, of the hunter's gazing at the animal and at the same time feeling its gaze upon himself *at the very border between life and death*, feeling himself seen and known (and known *as* the one who is about to kill), *was* the original subjectivity, and it lasted only for as long as

---

[197] Richard Broxton Onians, *The Origins of European Thought about the Body, the Mind, the Soul, the World, Time, and Fate.* Reprint of the 1951(Cambridge, University Press) edition, New York (Arno Press), 1973.

[198] James Hillman, *The Dream and the Underworld*, New York et al. (Harper & Row), 1979.

this absolutely extraordinary, daring, and existential encounter lasted. Once the animal had been killed and once it was a matter of taking it apart for the purpose of eating its meat and utilizing its skin, bones, etc., the moment of "I" was over, too, and the psyche dropped back into the ordinary I-less condition. With respect to childhood Jung spoke similarly of a time "when there is not even a continuous consciousness yet at all, when consciousness consists only of islands which only later grow together into continents."[199]

It is essential to realize that the I that we are here concerned with was (a) something very special, existential, dramatic (occurring only in a life-and-death situation), (b) that it was by no means itself subjective, but rather the quality of an objective event, and (c) that this event was precisely "intersubjective," a relation, a *constellation*, an encounter between Two and not an internal process in the hunter as solitary individual. The constellation, as which the I was, *within* itself unfolded itself into its two sides, the "I" and the "Thou," between which the relation exists (however in such a way that the Thou [i.e., the animal] was at the same time—for the I—also itself an I and the hunter himself also a Thou for this other I.[200] I and Thou are not self-identical entities, but logical concepts uroborically related and reciprocal). Obviously, on account of its only momentary occurrence (a) and objective event character (b), this subjectivity is no more than an *implicit* subjectivity.

It needed a long time of numerous repetitions of such acute moments with the result of a slow *habituation* to them in order for a more stable idea of soul or I to emerge, an idea of soul that now was (at least loosely) attached to each individual human being and no longer dependent on the happening of special events. By getting *accustomed* to the occurrence of the emergence of subjectivity, this "content" could slowly be appropriated by and interiorized into consciousness as consciousness's own idea of personal identity and subjectivity in the sense of a kind of objective *substance* at work in

---

[199] C.G. Jung, *Über Gefühle und den Schatten. Winterthurer Fragestunden*, Textbuch, Zürich and Düsseldorf (Walter) 1999, pp. 75f. (my transl.).
[200] Cf. also my *Tötungen. Gewalt aus der Seele*, Frankfurt et al. (Peter Lang: 1994), chapter "Die Stiftung der Persönlichkeit. Begegnung von Ich und Du." (In English: section "Origination of Personhood. Encounter of I and Thou" of my "Killings," in: W. G., *Soul-Violence. Collected English Papers*, vol. 3, New Orleans, LA (Spring Journal Books: 2008), pp. 224–231.

each person (and thus precisely not really subjectivity *sensu strictiori*): the idea of soul. The most ancient idea of soul is the soul as breath (in the Bible it occurs as the breath of life breathed by God into the nostrils of the human form made of "the dust of the ground," thereby creating Adam).

Very important is also the primitive idea of a "loss of soul," because it is evidence of a rudimentary inkling of subjectivity in the narrower sense, in particular of subjectivity as a (still implicit) *feeling of self*. What is lost (according to the idea of a loss of soul) is in any case "my personal" soul. Jung described this phenomenon as follows.

> The peculiar condition covered by this term is accounted for in the mind of the primitive by the supposition that a soul has gone off, just like a dog that runs away from his master overnight. It is then the task of the medicine-man to fetch the fugitive back. Often the loss occurs suddenly and manifests itself in a general malaise. (*CW* 9i § 213)

Many times the fugitive soul is thought of as a bird, which in one way would be a better image than the dog used by Jung, but of course the dog run away from his master is the better illustration of the idea of loss. Although the idea and experience of a loss of soul shows that—in contrast to the prehistoric hunter's subjectivity that was something that merely *happened* to him and only momentarily—a *concept* of soul as an in principle stable factor must already have existed on this stage of consciousness, Jung connects this phenomenon with the character of primitive consciousness as a consciousness,

> which lacks the firm coherence of our own. We have control of our will power, but the primitive has not. Complicated exercises are needed if he is to pull himself together for any activity that is conscious and intentional and not just emotional and instinctive. Our consciousness is safer and more dependable in this respect ... (*ibid.*)

This statement is of course not politically correct, but nevertheless insightful and correct, its only shortcoming being that the extremes that Jung names for a complex historical development ("primitive" and "we" or, in his next sentence, "civilized man") are too sweeping, too unspecific. Which cultures are primitive in this sense and to what degree in each case at the one end and who really qualifies truly as "civilized man" (or as I would prefer: "modern man") at the other end would have to be seen in detail. But this unspecifity does not detract from the validity of the observed historical difference as such.

However, regardless of the historical difference, the phenomenon itself in our world corresponding to what in primitive societies was termed "loss of soul" is precisely not only to be found in primitive societies. Jung therefore says: "but occasionally something similar can happen to civilized man." We know this condition, too, although we now describe it in different terms, namely no longer in substantiating, mythological, but in psychological terms. And it is this different description of and, correspondingly, different way of *experiencing* the "same" phenomenon that shows that its occurrence in the modern world happens against the backdrop of a fundamentally different psychological situation, namely a situation characterized by the fact that modern man does not merely *have* a *concept* of soul as an objective and in principle stable factor, but knows *himself* to *be* this—normally—stable identity such that he also *exists* on the basis of an actual continuous awareness of the stability of his sense of I and identity (which is the reason why he *is* I, a unitary personality). For modern man this phenomenon is a subjective, strictly *internal* alteration of his fundamentally identical personality, a change of mood or, in severe cases, *his* psychic illness. Having established himself during the early-modern period of Western history (roughly 1500–1800 A.D.) as *subject*, he feels himself, and *in fact* (i.e., in psychological reality) exists, as "substance" (in the philosophical sense) and correspondingly understands a possible "loss of soul" as a mere "accident." In his case, it is not that an independent soul substance mysteriously leaves his body and needs to be recaptured from outside.

The *phenomenology* of this "loss of soul" state, however, is more or less the same in the primitive as in the modern situation. Jung describes it as follows.

> It is a slackening of the tensity of consciousness, which might be compared to a low barometric reading, presaging bad weather. The tonus has given way, and this is felt subjectively as listlessness, moroseness, and depression. One no longer has any wish or courage to face the tasks of the day. ... one no longer has

> any disposable energy. ... The listlessness and paralysis of will
> can go so far that the whole personality falls apart, so to speak,
> and consciousness loses its unity.... (*CW* 9i § 213)

Considering the idea of a loss of soul in the primitive sense, it is interesting that it is precisely only through its loss, its absence, that the soul first makes itself felt. Just as we only become aware of the air around us when it is used up, when we run out of breath, or fear to suffocate, but not when everything is normal, so the soul, when it is "present" (or rather *merely* "*not* lost") is not experienced as such at all. Its "loss" is the first immediacy of an awareness of soul (as a sense of "me")—which is another indication of the soul's negativity. *What* is lost (and what therefore the meaning of soul is here) is the normal tonus, the state of having a normal amount of energy and will-power, and a normal state of "being at one with oneself." Because soul here refers to the loss of a *normal* (precisely not an extraordinary, excessive) degree of energy, it remains normally unnoticed, unreflected. This may seem paradoxical since one would probably expect that such a thing as one's subjectivity, one's sense of "me," in other words, the early form of "I," would by definition have to be conscious. But this is not so. It is precisely taken for granted and *ipso facto* does not count as "soul." The not-lost soul, i.e., one's normal state, does not receive the name of soul. Soul makes itself felt as what it is in its essence only when it is gone or at least threatened—much like, according to early Greek thought, a person's *psychê* came, so to speak, into existence only when it "left" the body at the person's death and had to find its way into Hades, where it dwelled as a shade among all the other shades.

Let me stress this crucial point again in a new way: it would be a completely wrong conclusion to assume that, if what is lost in the loss of soul is the normal sense of oneness with oneself and the intensity of feeling full of energy, then an in fact prevailing sense of oneness with oneself and vigorous presence would also have to be the soul. The presence of this feeling or state does precisely not receive the name soul (neither in the primitive, nor in the Greek, nor, by the way, in the modern situation). Only when "the dog" has run away from his master, only when "the soul bird" has flown away, do the dog and the bird come into being and *are* they the soul in the first place, but not when they are with their master. One's normal psychic condition is precisely referred to by other names, in the Homeric imagination, for example, as *phrenes* (associated with the lungs and breathing) and *thymos* (associated with blood, and thus manifesting as feelings and emotions, particularly as anger and courage, a fighting spirit), and, to mention this only in passing, in the modern situation usually as ego (in obvious contrast to soul).

It is therefore an underdetermination to say that the souls in the underworld *lack* both *phrenes* and *thymos*. The soul in the context of the archaic ideas of a "loss of soul" as well as of the "underworldly soul" does not "lack" anything, the way a person whose legs have been amputated lacks those limbs. Soul IS their *absence* and not anything else. The absence is the whole point. It is the essence and not a mishap. *Psychê* is not, the way the *phrenes* and the *thymos* are, a subsisting substance in its own right. Soul is from the outset an *abstraction* in the literal sense and an abstract *concept* avant la lettre. The *psychê* was precisely not yet psychologized in our modern sense, where "psyche" and "psychic" are usually understood to refer to "what is going on inside people, in each 'me.'" The latter type of psyche was for archaic thinking precisely *not* soul, but, as we have seen, for the early Greeks, for example, *phrenes* and *thymos*. And, as I already pointed out, even for us it is not soul, but the psychic aspect of the ego personality.[201]

The fundamental absence and negativity that I showed to be the essential characteristic of the soul in archaic contexts seems to be contradicted by another, completely different idea of soul. According to the conceptions of archaic "*medicine*" the soul was the liquid in the brain.[202] The brain was not, as for us, the place of thinking. Thinking in olden times was done in the heart or even deeper in the body, in the solar plexus, the belly, not in the brain. The soul in this sense manifested itself in weeping, when the brain liquid forced itself out of the eyes in the form of tears, and it manifested in fingernails and hair which were seen as an outcrop of the soul liquid from the brain in solidified form. This is why fingernail clippings had to be carefully disposed of because if another person would find them they could gain

---

[201] Even here, however, the negativity still makes itself felt inasmuch as what is usually understood by the psychic is especially the *invisible* inner or the "*unconscious*" in contrast to all manifest behavior.

[202] See on this topic, for example, Richard Broxton Onians, *The Origins of European Thought*, Cambridge (University Press) 1951, pp. 108, 115, 234–235.

possession over one's well-being, i.e., one's identity, and use them for bad magic. Also, such practices as scalping have to be understood in terms of hair as the manifestation of a person's soul located in the brain.

In our context these conceptions are astounding. Here we have an idea of soul precisely not as absent, but as a material body substance, "tangible" and demonstrable, as it were. And yet what for us seems to be a contradiction is not one for the symbolic thinking of the archaic mind. To some extent we see the same difference that prevails between *psychê* and *thymos* here, too, namely in the hiddenness of the soul itself as brain fluid and its concrete manifestations in empirical reality in tears and hair. But above all this difference comes most clearly out in the curious Greek type of archaic statue called "herm." It was a statue of Hermes that showed only the head and the phallus whereas the body was not represented, systematically excluded. Its place was taken by a pillar (clearly a negation of the concept of body).

To understand this curious phenomenon, one must know how the procreative act was understood. Just as fingernails and hair, so also the seed had its origin in the brain and traveled through the backbone into the penis. Both brain and penis, no, *phallus*, were those parts of the body that belonged to the soul and precisely not the "biological" body. The act of procreation was not, as for us, a biological event, but fundamentally underworldly ("spiritual" in the sense of spirit-caused). As the liquid in the brain, the soul was the life-substance and thus also the seed, but this life-substance in its turn was not part of life, but otherworldly. The materialized form of the soul thus does not suggest a positive-factual *presence* in life as it does for our biological thinking. It rather shows the presence of an *absence*. And the systematic presentation of the body *as excluded* in the herm through being replaced by the abstract-geometric form of a pillar is evidence of the prevailing notion of the radical difference between, or even mutual exclusiveness of, biological or everyday life and the otherworldliness of the soul. In other words, the same difference that prevails *between* underworldly soul and body we see here projected onto the body itself as the fundamental difference in status between different parts of the body, the brain + phallus, on the one hand, and the body itself in the narrower sense, on the other hand.

Cut-off hair and fingernail clippings had to be carefully protected against magical abuse by others, because as *pars pro toto* they would give those others power over the person's soul. This shows that the materialized soul of the medical imagination, the soul as the brain fluid, represented the first immediacy of the concept of one's personal identity, of a sense of "me." By the same token, inasmuch as the Greek *psychê* in the underworld was a shade, the (to be sure) merely shadowy (bloodless, bodiless, boneless, and this means ultimately: two-dimensional), but nevertheless exact image and likeness (*eidôlon*) of the deceased person, soul also in this very different sense referred to a rudimentary sense of personal identity. The *eidôlon* is what is left when the *phrenes*, the *thymos*, the body, the blood and life are gone: the abstract identity of the person (in the form of a memory image). Soul was not empirical, not phenomenon, not entity or substance, but, as I pointed out, from the outset a *concept* (avant la lettre, that is to say, a concept still appearing in imaginal guise), the *notion* of the deceased person's identity, what was unique about him or her and made it possible to distinguish him or her from others. This concept was that of a person's true, transcendental identity, but, as the term *eidôlon* shows, the identity of the person as he was seen from outside, by others, and not to be confused with an empirical *sense* or *feeling* of identity of that person himself. It had its place in the sphere of *intelligibility*, not in that of felt experience.

(By the same token, the soul as life-breath was also a *concept*. It was, to be sure, metaphorically imagined in the *image* of a breath, but the "life-breath" that was imagined through this image had never been seen or otherwise experienced [except, of course, as the cold air to be felt when there was an apparition of ghosts, i.e., of by definition non-existing beings or un-beings], because it does not exist. It is nothing natural, but of intelligible nature. Contrary to how it was imagined, the factual experience of death was of course not that a breath came out of the dying person's mouth, *leaving* the body as a vaporous substance, but precisely the opposite: that there was no breathing whatsoever any more, that it simply *stopped*. The idea of life-breath was without empirical support, it was a strictly intellectual, *metaphysical* concept added to concrete experience and in contrast to literal breath and breathing.)

3.2 THE SUBJECT AS AN "IT": THE SOUL *SUBSTANCE*

At a later time, in Plato, this notion of the soul as an identical unifying force becomes an explicit thought. According to him, our perceptions and conceptions do not tumble around in us like the Greeks in the Trojan Horse, but they only become a cognition if an identical force turns them into a *unity*.[203] Which name is chosen for this essentially cognitive unity-producing force does not matter, but the name soul offers itself (*Theaitetos* 184 d).

Another aspect of soul in addition to it as unifying force, namely soul as an ethical (and political) force, was already expressed by Plato's teacher Socrates. In the *Apology* (29 d-e) we hear that Socrates, instead of working in his trade as a stonemason, was wont to bother his fellow citizens on the market-place with questions like the following, "Most excellent man, are you who are a citizen of Athens, the greatest of cities and the most famous for wisdom and power, not ashamed to care for the acquisition of wealth and for reputation and honor, when you neither care nor take thought for wisdom and truth and the perfection of your soul?" Soul here meant the strength to leave the traditional supreme values of riches, honor, and family behind. Soul meant the *care for truth and insight*. As far as this turning against worldly values like wealth and honor are concerned, we hear similarly, although from within a different tradition, in the New Testament, "For what is a man profited, if he shall gain the whole world, and lose his own soul?" (Matth. 16:26). The New Testament also connects the care for the soul with a radical turn against the traditional values, laws, and ethnic customs. Thus it questions the absolute significance of the sabbath, of the cult of the dead ("Let the dead bury their dead" Matth. 8:22), and of filial piety ("If any man come to me, and hate not his father, and mother, and wife, and children, and brethren, and sisters, yea, and his own life also, he cannot be my disciple" Luke 14:26).

A third aspect in Plato is that the soul has its origin in the beyond and that as such its progress in life is *anamnesis*. The soul is also imagined as having wings which move us erotically, wanting to *uplift* us beyond the sensible, physical world, to return us to its home, the

---

[203] At the latest with Plato, there is no room any more for a "polytheistic psychology," a psychology stressing multiplicity.

realm of Ideas. Again we see here the negativity of the soul as something transcendental, *meta*-physical.

The idea of a world soul is the fourth aspect to be mentioned from Plato's thinking about soul. Plato proposes a view of the cosmos as a large animal whose "soul" is the impetus and guide of the movements of nature. It follows from this conception that everything that is alive has a soul, even animals and plants. This, the soul as life principle, became a major concept for Aristotle, as briefly mentioned earlier. For him the soul is primarily the *entelechy* of the body, i.e., the form which actualizes itself in the movements and changes of a living organism, or which is that which makes an organism be what it is. In this sense, the Aristotelian notion of soul is, to begin with, essentially tied to the body and its vital functions, which is in open contrast to all that I stressed before about the soul as absence, negativity, and as fundamentally underworldly or *meta*-physical existence. In addition, because soul is tied to the body it also partakes of its stable, continuous existence, its positivity, and the more momentary sense of soul that is characteristic of the special experiences of a "loss of soul" does not have a place in this context.

However, this (the conflict with the idea of the absolute negativity of the soul) applies only to the "vegetative" and "animal" soul aspects, but these two are not the last word about the soul for Aristotle. There is an additional dimension of the soul which comes to the fore only in man: the soul as thought, the mind, *noys*. It is something new and higher that comes "from outside" (*thyrathen*) as an addition to the "vegetative" and "animal" souls (which are both also active in man). This additional soul appears in two forms, as "passive" and as "active mind." Whereas the passive mind is attached to the body, the active mind is without beginning and insusceptible to alteration, i.e., it is everlasting, impassive, unmixed, and ultimately divine. It is the place (or organ) of forms (*topos eidôn*), and in its fully developed form it is the pure and fundamentally unitary intellectivity common to all individuals and ipso facto separable and apart (*chôristos, aney*) from body (Aristotle, *De anima* III, 4, 429 a 26 – 5, 430 a; and I, 1, 403 a 8).

Inasmuch as for Aristotle the soul was for the most part dependent on the body and even as active mind was a supra-personal intellectivity, the notion of a personal immortality of the soul did not seem to be backed up by his philosophy: the lower functions of the soul disappeared with the death of the human being, whereas the higher function was not the individual's personal soul. So it came that after Aristotle there were some who developed the materialistic idea that there could be no immortality of the soul. However, the dominant tradition not only in the later Greek world and in the Christian West, but also with the Arabs, way into the 18th century, held on to the idea of the immortality of the soul, in other words, to the view that the soul can even after death continue to subsist by itself, "apart" from the body—here especially also relying on the Platonic idea of an immaterial, individual, conscious, and intelligent soul (a conception which, a fifth aspect of Plato's ideas concerning the soul, expressed itself particularly in Plato's idea of the transmigration of the soul adopted from ancient Orphic thought and Pindar).

However, as we already learned in chapter 1.1, during the 18th century the skeptical, empiricist critique of the idea of the immortality of the soul increased. The soul as an *identical* point of reference and as the locus, in man, of religion more and more simply lost its power of conviction, a development that led later, during the latter half of the 19th century, to the situation perhaps best articulated in Fr. A. Lange's already discussed demand for a "psychology without soul." The notion of the psyche as what goes on inside people and the sphere of subjectivity slowly took the place of the former idea of soul as a substance that was essentially immortal and found its true fulfillment only in afterlife.

This is a drastic change which broke with an idea that certainly had its origin in prehistoric times and, despite the many transformations that it underwent in the course of its long history concerning its specific interpretations, in its basic substance nevertheless lasted uninterruptedly until the 18th century.

3.3 ENLIGHTENMENT PHILOSOPHY FALSELY BLAMED

It would be a grave mistake to see this change as a result of the intellectual debates of philosophers. We have to reverse our habitual rationalistic causal sequence and derive those debates and all the new philosophical arguments that tended to discredit the notion of soul and to undermine this notion's self-evident power of conviction from a fundamental psychological change in the sense of a waning of the concept of the soul itself. Just as in the case of the death of God, one can only argue away such psychic realities as God and soul if they have already in fact lost their validity. No rational argument can destroy a psychically *real* faith, a *really* felt love, a *real* conviction. Nemo contra "deum" nisi "deus" ipse. Nemo contra "animam" nisi "anima" ipsa. The 17th and 18th century philosophical debates have to be comprehended as the visible *expression* of the radical psychological change occurring in the ground of the soul ("soul" now in my modern psychological sense, not in the sense of the old soul substance) and at the same time as the *vehicle* through which this change realized itself.

If, as Hegel saw it, philosophy is *its* time grasped in thought, philosophical thought always comes after the fact. And as such the new thinking of the Renaissance and Enlightenment philosophers (a) merely articulates, documents the transformation that had been going on in the depths of the soul. It is (b) an essential part of the process through which this change takes place and makes itself explicit. And (c) it has the function of turning psychic fact (i.e., that which a people's faith and feeling as irrational psychic *realities* say and by what notions their mode of being-in-the-world and beliefs are in fact dominated) into psychological insight, of enabling the finite human mind to rationally *account for* the (new) truths in whose thrall it happens to find itself, thereby releasing what merely factually prevails into its truth (its being truth) and bringing it fully home to consciousness— all this very much in the Augustinian[204] spirit of Anselm's Of Canterbury *fides quaerens intellectum* ("faith longing for intellectual understanding") and *Neque enim quaero intelligere ut credam sed credo ut intelligam* ("For I do not seek to understand intellectually so that I might believe, but I believe so that I might understand"). The soul's factual truths want to be integrated into consciousness, into man's own conscious understanding. It is not enough for the soul that a "faith" or "truth" simply prevails in one's life. Man also has to take responsibility for his truths. He has to feel answerable, accountable for his faith and *know* why he has this faith. Only then is it really *his* truth, *his* faith and at the same time really his *truth*. St.

---

[204] See, for example, St. Augustine, *De trinitate* 15,2 (fides quaerit, intellectus invenit); *In Iohannis evangelium tractatus* CXXIV 29,6 (crede ut intellegas).

Augustine even clearly stated that thought has to precede faith (*prius esse cogitare quam credere*)![205]

Otherwise it would be no more than an animal's instinctual certainty. Nietzsche once commented on a type of false explanation, pointing, by way of example, to "women, of a strong constitution, of sterling quality, with the temperament of a cow, who cannot even be shaken by accidents: but they call it their 'trust in God'!—They do not notice that their 'trust in God' is merely the expression of their constitutional robustness—a formulation, not a cause ...."[206] In other words, what from our psychological point of view is actually something "biological" (and thus merely *psychic*) is given a religious (and thus psychological) interpretation. For the soul, however, a so-called faith in the sense of the articulation of a basic constitutional robustness (just as a faith as an irrational event, a natural fact) is irrelevant. "Soul" only begins where a faith takes on the character of *intelligibility*[207] and where the mind has truly made it its own in a process of explicit acquisition.[208]

In accordance with our insight that philosophical thought is merely the articulate expression and intellectual working out of the actual soul movement, we must also emphasize that it is not the "evil" thinkers of the Enlightenment that undermined the traditional notion of soul (and religion), not their *doing*. It is the other way around. The soul (in my sense) conversely used those thinkers to bring about a

---

[205] *De praedestinatione sanctorum*, II.5.

[206] Friedrich Nietzsche, *Die Unschuld des Werdens*, ed. Alfred Baeumler, vol. 1, Stuttgart (Kröners Taschenbuchausgabe vol. 82) 1956, here nr. 953, p. 306f. My transl. The ellipsis is by Nietzsche.

[207] That the notion of the intelligibility of faith and the psychological necessity of turning what is to begin with a mere belief or religious symbol into *comprehended* belief was not even completely alien to Jung may, for example, become apparent from statements of his like the following: "Moreover I seriously wonder whether it is not much more dangerous for the Christian symbols to be made inaccessible to conceptual thought and to be banished to a sphere of unreachable unintelligibility. ... man has the gift of thought that can apply itself to the highest things. The timid defensiveness certain moderns display when it comes to thinking about symbols was certainly not shared by St. Paul or by many of the venerable Church Fathers" (*CW* 11 § 170, transl. modif.). "Indeed, people have for the most part stopped to think about dogma.... There are actually only few Christians ... who think seriously and in the sense of the dogma about it [the Trinity] and would consider this concept a possible subject for thought" (§ 172, transl. modif.). "The trouble with them is that they don't want to think about their own beliefs. ... we ought to think about religious matters ..." (*Letters* 2, p. 335, to Philp, 26 Oct. 1956). See also above Jung's already cited comments apropos the idea, "Through the blood of our Lord Jesus Christ we are redeemed of our sins" (section 2.3.11).

[208] In the archaic situation, initiation processes were the still implicit form of such an explicit acquisition, if I may express myself in these paradoxical terms.

psychological revolution (and, at the same time, to make a revolution that had already long taken place in the depths of the soul articulate for consciousness and intellectually transparent). For a psychological thinking it is as a matter of course the soul itself that turned against itself and undermined its old metaphysical form of realization as the concept of an immortal soul substance. We must overcome the thinking along the tricky escape route of the fallacious adage, "*Omne bonum a deo, omne malum ab homine.*" Jung repeatedly criticized it, but, we must admit, when it was a question of assessing the modern world and Enlightenment thinking he (unwittingly) usually followed it himself; in such contexts he all of a sudden succumbed himself "to the saving delusion that *this* wisdom was good and *that* was bad," to "the artificial sundering of true and false wisdom" (*CW* 9i § 31).[209] Instead we have to comprehend *all great* thinking (in contrast to the personal thoughts of ordinary individuals, which are psychologically neither here nor there) as ultimately the soul's thinking, the historical locus's thinking, and not as people's doing, i.e., not as arbitrary ego-concoctions, even if it indeed rendered the traditional notion of soul obsolete.

Seen from the standpoint of external reflection, Enlightenment philosophy may rightly seem destructive, an undermining influence for all the truths and soul values of traditional religion and thus also for the traditional idea of soul. Purely negative. But from a psychological point of view, negation is itself psychologically indispensable. It is inherent in the soul to negate itself, to sublate itself—in alchemical language: to subject the prime matter ruthlessly to processes of putrefaction, mortification, fermenting corruption, sublimation, distillation, evaporation. Alchemy exposes materials to the acid test. *Omnes superfluitates igne consumuntur.* Alchemy is intrinsically cruel. Not *in order to* be sadistic and to destroy. But in order to change its prime matter from junk into gold by interiorizing it into its mercurial essence, its concept, its truth.

---

[209] Just one example: "It is the fateful misfortune of medical psychotherapy to have originated in an age of enlightenment, when the old cultural possessions became inaccessible through [man's] own fault [*durch Selbstverschulden*]...." (*CW* 10 § 370, transl. modif.). With the word *Selbstverschulden* Jung polemically alludes to, and turns into the opposite, Kant's well-known definition of the Enlightenment as "man's emergence from his self-imposed [or: self-incurred, *selbstverschuldet*] immaturity..." Precisely that which for Kant was the *emergence from* a wrong state due to man's own fault, Jung now presents as the very sin [*Schuld* = guilt].

3.4 THE SOUL'S HOME-COMING. FROM SUBSTANCE TO SUBJECT

If in the history of the soul the soul undermined its own conception of itself as an immortal soul substance and had the notion of the I and of subjectivity take the place of the former, then this is for us the self-display of the fact that the subjectivity, I-character, and sense of personality or individuality (that were from the outset expressed both in the archaic and in the philosophical notion of soul) had now finally come home *to the subject.* As long as the soul had been comprehended as a vaporous soul *substance* that left the body at the person's death (much like blood leaves the body when there is an open wound), the subjectivity was still only an implicit one. No doubt, subjectivity was already intended, articulated, but articulated precisely still as a substance, in other words, as thing-like, ontologized, and as a fundamentally metaphysical, transcendent substance.[210] The traditional soul was precisely not accessible during life. True, one could, during one's life on earth, *take care* of the soul, be it in the sense of the ritualistic cultures, or in the Socratic sense, or in the Christian sense of a pious life and a *cura animarum,* just as one could conversely violate the soul by giving no thought to it, caring instead only for wealth, power, and honor. But even so, the soul itself remained inaccessible: underworldly, otherworldly, or of an ideal nature. Although it *was* indeed the notion *of* I and subjectivity, it did not yet have *the form of* subjectivity, which means conversely that really existing man (the empirical I) was precisely not himself identical with his subjectivity (the soul). The soul was his Other, and it was an It, having the form of an objective substance.

The emergence of subjectivity and the concept of "the I" (instead of "the soul" in the traditional sense) indicates that now the concept of man had in fact become identified with the notion of subjectivity, or, the other way around, that the subjectivity had truly come home to consciousness and was integrated into the very concept of man himself. It was no longer merely something that man "had," the way he has a heart and lungs or blood and hormones. It now had become something that man *was* (*as which* he existed). The notion of

---

[210] I speak of a metaphysical, transcendent substance in contrast to our modern notion of an empirical psyche (i.e., that which is empirically accessible of what is in fact going on in us, what is observably part of the behavior of the organism).

subjectivity had thus finally become explicit, having shed its previous logical form of substance and otherness and instead having now also taken on the *form* of subject.

Of course, we are used to see the I or ego as a kind of opposite of the soul. Early Jung spoke of "the relations between the ego and the unconscious," where the "between" clearly shows that the ego or I and "the unconscious" (Jung's frequent term for "soul") are conceived as two not only distinct but also separate realities, two realities divided by a gulf that is or ought to be bridged through the said "relations." The opposition between soul and I even in the sense of an exclusive "either-or" comes clearly out in certain passages of Jung's, such as in the one already quoted above where, in a particular context, discussing Socrates Jung exclaims, "To hell with the Ego-world! Listen to the voice of your *daimonion*. It has a say now, not you" (*Letters 2*, p. 532, to Charteris, 9 Jan. 1960). Although this construal of soul and I as a mutually exclusive opposition is pretty dominant in Jung's thinking, Jung, especially the later Jung, was also aware of the fact that the I is itself a manifestation of the soul. "The ego [*das Ich*] ... is in fact a highly complex affair full of unfathomable obscurities. Indeed, one could even define it as a *relatively constant personification of the unconscious itself*, or as the Schopenhauerian mirror in which the unconscious becomes aware of its own face" (*CW* 14 § 129). The ego as a personification of the unconscious as a whole! A little later Jung surprises us with the statement that "the alchemists came very close to realizing that the ego [*das Ich*] was the mysteriously elusive arcane substance and the longed-for lapis" (§ 131). The I is itself the arcane substance, the soul! If it was the longed-for lapis, the supreme goal of the whole alchemical opus (and thus of alchemy as such), we also understand that *medieval* alchemy, by unwittingly searching for "the I," within itself in effect *aimed* for its own rendering itself obsolete, for its making itself superfluous, the moment that "the I" (the longed-for lapis) was historically realized. This was the case in early modernity ("Neuzeit"). At any rate, there is a bridge that leads directly from Jung to my thesis that the emergence of subjectivity and the concept of "the I" is the sign that the soul had shed its previous logical form of substance and otherness and taken on the form of subject.

Concerning the insight into the historically late *emergence* of "the I," it may be helpful to remember that the Greeks, for example, did not have a notion of I in an eminent sense. The Greeks certainly had the word I in their language and of course made use of it in everyday speech. They of course also made a difference between body and soul. But the distinction so characteristic of the early modern period between the subjective and the objective, between "the inner" as a world of its own and "external" reality, did not exist. For Aristotle, for example, the science of the soul (*psychê*) is a part of "physics." Emotions like anger and erotic desire, functions like thinking and seeing are cosmic processes, just as rain, thunder, earthquakes, or sunshine are. This is also why affects, somewhat surprisingly, were called *pathê* or *pathêmata* ("what happens to..."), *passiones animae*, *Leiden*schaften, in other words, they were not perceived in terms of the I as its own self-expression, its feelings and desires.

No Greek would in his philosophical thinking have established *man as I* over against *the world as a whole as Non-I*. That this became possible in early-modern philosophy (especially with and since Descartes) is in the last analysis the achievement of Christianity, which put man and his fate into the center of the universe. Christianity is characterized by an anthropocentric character. This is one of the distinguishing marks of the Christian world conception over against the Neoplatonic one. It is true, Neoplatonism also assigned a high metaphysical rank to the human individual. The latter, at least insofar as he was soul and mind, was in Neoplatonic thinking even thought capable of divinization. However, Neoplatonic philosophy would never have placed man in the center of the universe as the ultimate purpose of the whole. Man was no more than one partial phenomenon of the divine workings in the world. But beginning with the Church Fathers, man was seen as the summit of creation and as the purpose and goal of nature. Only on this ground could it happen that centuries later a thinker like Descartes could, in amazing proximity to ideas that can already be found in St. Augustine, establish the *ego cogito* as the foundation (*fundamentum inconcussum*) of philosophy and distinguish between two mutually exclusive substances, the *res cogitans* (a "dwelling within itself"; *inwardness* or *interiority*; the mind, thought) and the *res extensa* (externality; the material world), and that for a number of centuries philosophy, for example explicitly for Kant, the fundamental question of philosophy, in which *all* its other basic questions come to a point, is the question, "What is man?" And in Schelling's philosophy, again a bit later, we find a radical opposition between "transcendental philosophy" and the "philosophy of nature." Such an opposition would have been impossible in the context of Greek thought.

Having mentioned Descartes, I have to address the present-day widespread misconstrual of his thinking as if it were dualistic. Descartes-bashing has become popular, also by some in Jungian psychology. One accuses Descartes of having developed a theory structured by binary opposition, mind—matter, body—soul, subject—object. (The radical opposition in Schelling between transcendental philosophy and the philosophy of nature could of course in much the same way be accused of being dualistic.) This unjustified accusation is based on a superficial reading (if not in many cases merely on hearsay) and ignores the context in which those two substances *res extensa* and *res cogitans* appear, or better: the larger whole into which they are integrated.[211] They are opposites in the specific sense that the one is precisely *not* what the other is and vice versa. As such, and in this specific sense, they are finite. However, both are contained and comprised in God as the *substantia infinita*. God is "the third of the two." Whereas the two finite substances are not only finite over against each other, but also over against the infinite substance, the infinite substance in its turn, as infinite, is *not finite* over against them. Rather, it permeates them through and through. This comes out in the fact that the two finite substances *also* possess a (of course only *relative*) infinity inasmuch as they do not, like two countries, limit each other through bordering on each other, but rather limit each other *only* through the fact that each is nothing else but the *non-being* of the other; the one having its (relative) infinity as one of its objective characteristics (being pure externality: it represents the infinity of outer space), whereas the other is also *for itself* infinite, being pure *ego cogito* or "I dwell within myself." The effect of this interiority within itself is that its relation to the *substantia infinita* necessarily becomes one also *for* the *res cogitans*, in the form of the "innate" *idea Dei*.

Through the infinite substance of God the continuous creation ties both separate finite substances, the representing substance here and the extended substance over there, together into the one

---

[211] In this brief discussion of Descartes I follow Claus-Artur Scheier, in particular his "Medialer Spinozismus" paper read at the Symposium "Geist und Materie" of the Ev. Landeskirche Braunschweig, Goslar, March 3–5, 2008.

knowledge of the system. And on account of this sublatedness of both within the infinite substance it is impossible to play the one against the other in the sense of claiming the one for myself and expelling the other one into absolute otherness. Rather, I (one and the same I) both *am* the thinking substance AND *represent* the other.

By the same token a superficial mind could also construe the opposition of anima and animus in Jungian psychology as a dualism. But both these opposites are ultimately sublated and contained in the soul as syzygy, as *its* internal moments. Only because the soul as syzygy has this internal oppositional structure is it alive, a living process, rather than an ontic (and thus static) entity.

Despite all the different systematic modifications and further differentiations performed in successive steps by the philosophers coming after Descartes, I name only Spinoza, Leibniz, Kant, Fichte, Hegel, the basic unity (that prevented the onto-theo-logical philosophy of the I or subjectivity from falling apart into an unbridgeable duality) continuously prevailed during the early-modern period from Descartes through Hegel. This thinking, just as all earlier thinking, was governed by the (as Jungians we could call it uroboric) logic of the copula or syllogism (*Schluß*) that was capable of logically conjoining (*zusammenschließen*) the opposites with each other. In Hegel the uroboric nature of philosophy becomes especially explicit, for example, when he says: "... the science [= philosophy] exhibits itself as a *circle* returning upon itself, the end being wound back into the beginning, the simple ground, by the mediation; this circle is moreover a *circle of circles*, for each individual member as ensouled by the method is reflected into itself, so that in returning into the beginning it is at the same time the beginning of a new member ..."[212]

In connection with the "loss of soul" idea in primitive cultures Jung had said about primitive consciousness that it

> lacks the firm coherence of our own. We have control of our will power, but the primitive has not. Complicated exercises are needed if he is to pull himself together for any activity that is conscious and intentional and not just emotional and

---

[212] *Hegel's Science of logic*, transl. by A.V. Miller, Atlantic Highlands, NJ (Humanities Paperback Library) 1990, p. 842.

instinctive. Our consciousness is safer and more dependable
in this respect ... (*CW* 9i § 213)

Why does our consciousness have this firm coherence? Why is it
more dependable, a relatively stable I? Why do we have control of our
will power? This is due to the Cartesian *ego cogito*, to the fact that with
Descartes, as I mentioned in ch. 1.1, the sense of I, of subject and
identity, that used to be projected out and away from man into his
soul as an "it" (that he possessed) had become inwardized into
consciousness itself ("... the I, that is to say, the soul through which I
am what I am"[213]). Man himself had explicitly turned into the I on
the psychologically all-important level of the logical definition of man.
This means that from then on his identity was not "out there" in the
soul, in a mere *property* of his that was not reliable inasmuch as it could
also unforeseeably disappear at times of its own accord ("loss of soul").
Now residing in his very definition, in the logic of his being, it was
independent of his changing psychic states. The I maintained itself
psychologically even if *psychically* (in his empirical condition, on the
behavioral level) it was "lost." This new *logic* of "the soul as *ego cogito*"
is what gave consciousness its firm coherence and made it reliable,
dependable. This logic guaranteed, as a principle, the independence
of one's identity or I from circumstance. The I had freed itself from
the natural level, from its immersion ("imprisonment") in the
individual's natural, and thus always contingent, moods, states, and
conditions. The soul had in its consciousness of itself risen above nature
to the level of Concept and turned the *concept* of I, nothing but the
"airy" (logical, intelligible) concept, into the only ground and base
(*fundamentum inconcussum*) of itself. By grounding itself in the
concept, it gave the concept concrete existence and ipso facto
established itself as *the existing concept* (the *ego cogito*). It is this, the
soul's solely relying on the concept (and no longer on anything
imagined as naturally given), which made the I reliable, made it, as
Jung had put it, "safer and more dependable," and gave "us" a "firm
coherence of our own."

Of course, as before I do not wish to present Descartes as the
author of this change, as the cause that brought it about. He did not

---

[213] René Descartes, *Discours de la méthode* IV, 2.

effectuate it. He is only the most obvious example for a general cultural change, a historical transmutation in the logic of the soul, of which Descartes' philosophy is merely one expression, indeed, "symptom"—that expression or symptom that in our context is the most explicit and to the point. It is a soul process (a process in the soul's *opus magnum*) that merely becomes manifest, for example, in the philosophems of the great philosophers (but of course also in many other historical changes in cultural life, in early capitalism, the Reformation, the emancipation of thought from the Church, the invention of perspective in art, etc.). If what this change achieved was the cleansing of the soul (as the *notion of* subject and I) of its substantial and natural character and thus of everything that is not thought, not concept, not *cogito*, such as its cleansing of its dependence on natural psychic states, we see that it is a transformation that clearly follows that principle that the alchemists pictorially described as the freeing of the spirit Mercurius from its imprisonment in the (initially always prevailing) physicalness of the matter, its home-coming from the exile in the imagination (where imagination means the projection out into the natural world as an ontological factor[214]). But we could also describe it, very differently, as the process of the soul's absolute-negative interiorization into itself.

The moment that the formerly only implicit I has become explicit and ipso facto come home to man himself, man has become *born man*, man born out of his previous containment in an enveloping imagined and imaginal soul and in a likewise enveloping natural cosmos imagined as ensouled. Throughout the ages, man had always been dressed in mythical garments, in archetypal roles. In the most general sense he had been a child of gods or God, in a more specific sense he had to be the carrier of a certain (male or female) sexual social identity, and in the most specific senses he had to represent other specific "professional" social roles: he or she *was* the king, a slave, a smith, a peasant, a monk, an executioner, a wife, a virgin, etc. But when he is I, he has his identity in the abstract universal concept of I which does not have any qualitative content or specification. Everybody is I. All imaginal, archetypal contents have fallen off of him (as far as his essence

---

[214] It is relatively irrelevant whether this projection is conceived as a literal or as a merely metaphorical one. In either case the *logical form* of an ontologized or objectual entity is the same.

or identity is concerned), and the roles that he may still have in practical life are no more than external and fundamentally exchangeable, contingent attributes. This is the psychological foundation of modern freedom and liberty.

The soul is no longer "out there." Subjectively this may be experienced as alienation. The psychological difference that formerly existed *between* man and the soul / the natural world / transcendence, now imparts itself on man himself. It is now an internal difference. Man can now gain a distance to himself. He exists now *as* a difference, a duality, a tension: the difference between his more egoic, pragmatic orientation, on the one hand, and his potential of a soulful mode of experiencing and reacting. The soul, having lost its transcendent and substance quality, is now a mode or style in man.

Just prior to modernity, at the very end of the epoch of Western metaphysics, the birth of man (in the sense of a loss of an objectual "absolute" or God "out there" and thus the overcoming of externality as such) had found its full realization and explicit articulation in Hölderlin and Hegel. In them it had come fully home to itself. Following promptings by Spinoza, they had completely *logically* immanentized the absolute, thereby going beyond the observer standpoint that inevitably posits an external absolute and that prevailed in metaphysics from time immemorial and so also in the early-modern period from Descartes up to Kant and Fichte. Hegel performed an absolute-negative inwardization, translating and sublating the entire historical semantics (all the ideas) of the metaphysical tradition into its own syntax or logical form and into the "method" that ensouls the content. It was a move from substance to subject and from the objectual to uroboric movement. With all this, Western metaphysics was brought to its completion and *ipso facto* to its end.

We do not have to go into these fundamental achievements since along with the end of Western metaphysics the realm of absolute-negative inwardness opened up by Hegel was also concluded, that is, closed. Modernity pushed off from it and established a position of a much more radical and absolutely explicit externality and otherness than that of classical metaphysics. The birth of man, which could not be canceled or undone, had to manifest in and as externality. This we will have to turn to as our next topic. The inwardness reached by Hegel

can only find an asylum in that special region within the modern world
that we call psychology and as its special methodological approach.

3.5 MODERNITY (1). THE IRREDUCIBLE EXTERNALITY
AND OTHERNESS OF THE OTHER

Throughout the age of classical metaphysics, up to and including
the time of Hegel and Schelling, thought was informed by the logic
of the copula. It is only in modernity, with the Industrial
Revolution, that the opposites fall absolutely apart. The copula now
turns into a phantasm, the logic of the syllogism (*Schluß*) is succeeded
by the logic of the *tertium non datur*, the uroboric circle is dissolved,
and in its stead we get, for example in the area of production, the
linearity of *serialized* production.

The first thinker in whom this new situation and the *tertium
non datur* became dominant and explicit is Schopenhauer.[215] In §
16 of his *On the fourfold root of the principle of sufficient reason*, he
tells us that

> Our cognizing consciousness, manifesting itself as outer and
> inner Sensibility (receptivity), Understanding, and Reason,
> *falls apart* into subject and object and contains nothing else.
> To be object for the subject and to be our representation are
> the same thing.[216]

Consciousness "falls apart" into the opposites (subject and object)!
And it falls apart into the two opposites without any third capable of
mediating between them (for we hear expressly that it "contains nothing
else"). No copula, no possibility of a conjoining the opposites. The
principle of sufficient reason, "to be sure, connects all representations
of whatever kind with each other [...], but it does not at all connect
these representations with the subject, nor with anything that would

---

[215] For my view of Schopenhauer I above all rely on Claus-Artur Scheier, "Lichter
Punkt und blinder Fleck. Zum Unterschied von moderner und klassischer Rationalität,"
in: *Natura ed artificio in prospettiva europea – Natur und Künstlichkeit in einer europäischen
Perspektive*. Acts of the XXV. international conference of German-Italian Studies, Meran,
October 15–17, 2001, ed. by the Akademie deutsch-italienischer Studien, Roberto
Cotteri director, Meran 2002, pp. 221–236.
[216] Arthur Schopenhauer, *Werke in fünf Bänden*, ed. by Ludger Lütkehaus, Zürich
(Haffmans Verlag) 1991, vol. III, p. 38 f. My transl. and my emphasis. The entire passage
has been emphasized by Schopenhauer.

be neither subject nor object."[217] Here, then, and not in Descartes, we find the unbridgeable difference, the fundamental dissociation, the radical mediation-less dualism between subject and object. The result of this dualism is that the moment that consciousness (as subject) wants to focus upon itself (as its object), its cognition disappears in an "opaque spot," so to speak, in a kind of black hole. The I is "the opaque spot in consciousness, just as the optic nerve's point of entry upon the retina is blind, as the brain itself is completely insensitive, as the body of the sun is dark, and as the eye sees everything except itself."[218] There is nothing to see. Consciousness when turning *to itself* is fundamentally blind. A veritable reflection, consciousness's returning to itself the way it had always been possible during the age of metaphysics (for which the I was precisely the "bright spot" [Schelling[219]] in consciousness[220]), has now become absolutely out of the question.

Small wonder that for Schopenhauer man, at least ordinary man, had to be conceived as *Fabrikwaare der Natur*,[221] nature's factory-made (i.e., mass-produced) goods. (Only "geniuses" are truly unique.) This view about man is a reflection in Schopenhauer's thinking of what at his time was already the prevailing objective logic of serialized industrial production whose products ("commodities") would later be analyzed by Marx in detail along with their inherent "commodities fetishism." If people now, in the modern situation, need to be conceived as mass-produced by nature, they do no longer each have their own immortal soul as their ultimate and inalienable core and absolute treasure, and thus they also do not have, on a religious, "metaphysical," or psychological level, a true identity within themselves. They are exchangeable replicas: *logically* throw-away commodities, sociologically anonymous elements of mass society, politically *Stimmvieh* ("voting

---

[217] *Ibid.*, vol. I, p. 46 (*Die Welt als Wille und Vorstellung* I § 7). My transl.

[218] *Ibid.*, vol. II, p. 570 (*Die Welt als Wille und Vorstellung* II, ch.41). My transl.

[219] F.W.J. Schelling, *System des transzendentalen Idealismus* (1800), in: *Sämmtliche Werke*, ed. by K.F.A. Schelling, Stuttgart and Augsburg 1856-1861, vol. 3, p. 357; *Fernere Darstellungen aus dem System der Philosophie* (1802) *ibid.* vol. 4, p. 391, footnote.

[220] "The mutual opacity of the substances standing in the causal relationship has vanished and become a self-transparent clarity.... ... The Notion when it has developed into a *concrete existence* that is itself free, is none other than the *I* or pure self-consciousness." Hegel, *op. cit.*, pp. 582 and 583.

[221] Arthur Schopenhauer, *op. cit.*, vol. I, p. 255 (*Die Welt als Wille und Vorstellung* I § 36).

fodder")—all this quite independently of what *psychically* their strength of personality, their character may be, and what maturity, education, and capacity of critical judgment they may possess.

In modernity, especially since Feuerbach, the otherness of the Other has become irreducible. I and Thou (just think of Martin Buber or Emmanuel Lévinas) stand vis-à-vis each other in mediation-less opposition. In the human, interpersonal sphere, this mediation-less difference shows concretely, for example, in the unbridgeable difference between guilty perpetrator and innocent victim. "Victimization" and the corresponding notion of "traumatization" is a *logical* problem, an index of the fact that the logic of otherness rules, and thus clearly a problem and distinguishing mark of modernity. In former ages with their totally different logic, the idea of victim in this sense simply did not exist and would have been impossible, although cruelty certainly abounded (slavery, torture, rape, human sacrifices, incredibly brutal forms of punishment). When in antiquity the entire population of a city that had tenaciously defended itself against an ultimately victorious conqueror was sold into slavery by way of punishment, they did not feel "victimized," although they certainly felt miserable. But such a thing was merely seen as bad luck and reacted to with simple sadness, simple pain, not with indignation. Why was this so? Because man was still contained in Nature, in the soul, and thus experienced even terrible blows of fate as part of the *natural* continuous chain of events that was governed by the—uroboric—wheel of *Fortuna*. Nature as well as fate, despite being "other," nevertheless were NOT wholly other, and the otherness that existed between the cruel conqueror and the conquered and enslaved people was, for the soul, likewise not an unbridgeable difference. Both the perpetrator and the "victim," rather than already conceiving each other in terms of the subject-object split, knew themselves to be *moments* of nature that encompassed both. If we go way back to the time of ritualistic sacrificial slaughterings, the killing by the priest did not aim for the annihilation of the wholly Other (the way modern anarchists or terrorists want to eliminate the Other). The so-called victim was also *his own* other. And the latter also did not feel that being killed meant nothing but his destruction. Rather, he knew that in the priest, and along with him in the community for which the priest executed the sacrifice, he had also his own survival and fulfillment (which does not exclude that he felt pain and fear). However, being moderns, being the embodiment of the logic of fundamental otherness, we are hardly able to really get a feel for this, and a congenial understanding.

Once, after having mentioned what he called "Kierkegaardian neurosis," Jung decried, with respect to some people's "relation to God," that it had, "owing to the impoverishment of symbolism, developed into an unbearably exaggerated I-You relationship" (*CW* 9i § 11, transl. modif.). By viewing things this way he showed that he was in principle aware of the problem. Of course, the problem was not really the impoverishment of symbolism. All the symbols were still there. The problem was only that they did not "work" anymore; that they did no longer transport the soul (early Jung might have said "the libido"), away from the pragmatic ego world, to its home country, to its truth (in religious language: to "heaven" or "the beyond"), something they had always done as long as they had been alive. The problem did not lie with the symbols themselves. Rather, it was the deeper one of the disappearance of the *logic* of identity and the copula which alone could have given to the symbols the power of conviction and thus turned them into symbols in the first place. As all those theorists who focus on the imaginal (the semantic), Jung confuses the symptom with the cause.

But apart from this flaw, he is right in attributing the "unbearably exaggerated I-You relationship" to (what expresses itself in) "the impoverishment of symbols," that is, to the lack of *an objective mediating third.* This lack inevitably lets the opposites *fall apart*, leading to an exaggerated personalistic emphasis on I and Thou and to their unbridgeable opposition, and this of course not only in the area of religion. However, despite his general awareness of the problem, owing to the fact that Jung focused on *symbols* or *images*, in other words, entities (instead of the logic, the mercurial spirit, the "element" [logical environment] or "medium," which are absolutely required if symbols are to be animated), Jung's own thinking became also personalistic in his "unbearably exaggerated" concentration on the individual, as I will briefly show in the following. Seeing only the symbols or images and focusing on the abstract individual is, if I may use comparisons from other areas, as if one built locomotives and railway carriages without wasting a thought on the necessity of a rail network, or as if one wanted to grow particular flowers while ignoring the fact that they require a specific kind of environmental conditions, a particular soil and climate.

As deplorable as the exaggerated I-You relationship may be, the fundamental soul-lessness of man and the irreducible otherness of the other together with the easily appearing feeling of victimization and indignation are irrevocably the modern situation, *our* situation, our *truth*. And when present-day's popular psychology sends people on a search for their self, for their wholeness and self-worth, for their "creativity," and for meaning, if not for their personal myth and their god or goddess, it reveals itself as a defensive, counter-factual reaction to our deeply-felt but unadmitted sense of the modern soul's truth that, in the last analysis, namely *psychologically*,[222] we exist as exchangeable "mass-products of nature," as fundamentally *abstract* individuals. Each person, this is the implicit purpose of popular psychology's scheme, is supposed to actively demonstrate through his inner process and his dreams, etc., that he is a "genius" (even if only *en miniature* and of sorts) and as such NOT Schopenhauer's *Fabrikwaare*. But of course, such counter-phobic efforts contrarily precisely manifest and affirm that very underlying truth that they try to deny. The soul's truth is inescapable.

In Jung, too, both the sense of the modern soul's truth and his counter-factual fight against it becomes especially obvious in his "The Symbolic Life," when he describes the psychological status of a certain woman that he had run across in Africa in the following words: "Hers is a life utterly, grotesquely banal, utterly poor, meaningless, with no point in it at all. If she is killed today, nothing has happened, nothing has vanished—because she was nothing!" Nothing but throw-away *Fabrikwaare* obviously. *This* is what is *actually experienced* by Jung, experienced, mind you, not by the ego in him that is blinded by the external appearance, but by the psychologist's penetrating gaze seeing through the external appearance to the psychological essence. *This* diagnostic assessment

---

[222] Although not necessarily *psychically*, subjectively, privately. But of course, our mass-culture and particularly television do their best to bring people even in their private state literally in alignment with the described psychological truth. What *malgré* Schopenhauer biological *nature* does not provide, our industrialized culture achieves, in a perverted sense of the alchemical dictum, *Quod natura relinquit imperfectum, ars perficit.*

describes the psychological phenomenon. *This* is what wants to be seen and integrated into consciousness.

But already Jung's affective and condemnatory tone shows his refusal to become initiated into this (and also personally his) soul truth that is contained in his experience. The defense comes out even more distinctly in what he offers as an antidote. "But if she could say, 'I am the daughter of the Moon. Every night I must help the Moon, my Mother, over the horizon'—ah, that is something else! Then she lives, then her life makes sense ..." (*CW* 18 § 630). He should, of course, have said: "that *would be* something else! Then she *would* live ...." The subjunctive is required to express the irreal, if not absurd, character of this wishful fantasy about a modern, 20th century woman. Jung's whole theory of individuation and of the singular importance of the individual as the one factor on whom the salvation of the world depends (e.g., *CW* 10 § 536) is in denial of the modern soul's truth.

Already the freeing of the concept of subject and I in the sense of cleansing it of its immersion in substantial form and natural qualitative states and thus of everything that is *not* thought had in the early-modern era led to the sharp opposition, in Descartes, of the *res cogitans* and the *res extensa*, an opposition that has often, as I pointed out, been misconstrued as a dualism. But it was only modernity that dissolved the uroboros. Only when the representing I takes itself literally and sets itself mediation-lessly up over against the world or nature is the bond between man and nature irrevocably dissolved.

What in this description sounds totally negative and is also experienced negatively, namely as painful alienation and soul-lessness, from a soul point of view, however, has to be conceived as a step forward in the history of the soul. It means that man has become born man and come of age. He is no longer contained in the womb of Mother Nature as her child. Psychologically, he now has to live *all on his own account*, and, with a metaphor of Jung's, has to sew his garment himself (cf. *CW* 9i § 27) on his own responsibility and risk. The mythic garments that previously had always already been provided for him with unquestionable authority have dropped from him like a snake's old shed skin. Nature and the world have become obsolete (of course only psychologically, not pragmatically). The soul has overcome the world and thus come home to itself.

3.6 MODERNITY (2). FROM "SOUL" AND EARLY-MODERN
I TO "PSYCHOLOGY"

If one would want to blame anyone at all for the dualism between subject and object, thought and matter, mind and body, then it would have to be Schopenhauer and those who followed after him, as we have seen, and certainly not Descartes. But psychology does not blame anybody, because—this is its constituting presupposition, that principle through which alone psychology can *be*—it comprehends what happens *as the soul's own doing*, its acting upon itself, its following its own necessities, and it sees the great artists and thinkers merely as the place where this the soul's acting upon itself occurs and finds its articulation. And above all in this particular case it refrains from blaming. For it knows that this modern situation is the condition a priori of *its own* possibility (the possibility of *psychology* in the modern sense). It needed the obsolescence of soul in the traditional objectual sense and of God as external transcendence, of myth as well as of metaphysics, for psychology to become possible in the first place. The condition of the possibility of psychology is the birth of man, his having been born out of his envelopment in soul. This Jung saw very clearly (see 2.3.5 above).

> Whenever there exists externally a conceptual or ritual form in which all the yearnings and hopes of the soul are absorbed and expressed, that is, for example, a living religion, then the soul is outside and there is no soul problem, just as there is then no unconscious in our sense. It was therefore logical that the discovery of psychology took exclusively place during the last decades, although former centuries possessed enough introspection and intelligence to gain knowledge about psychological facts. [...] The reason for this is that there existed no compelling predicament. [...] It needed the spiritual predicament of our time to force us to discover psychology.
>
> [...] But as soon as he [man] outgrows the periphery of his Western local religion, that is, when his form of religion can no longer contain his life in all its fullness, then the soul begins to become a factor which can no longer be dealt with by the ordinary means. It is for this reason that we today have a psychology that relies on empirical facts and not on articles of

> faith or philosophical postulates, and at the same time I see in
> the fact that we have a psychology a symptom that proves the
> profound convulsions of the general soul. [...] Only in this
> situation, in this *predicament*, do we discover the soul [...]
>
> [...] But no culture before ours felt compelled to take this psychic
> background as such seriously. [...] This distinguishes our time
> from all earlier ones (*CW* 10 §§ 159–161, transl. modif.).

But although Jung saw correctly the historicity of psychology and
that the preconditions for its possibility and for its actual emergence
were the loss of the traditional soul as it expressed itself in myth,
religion, and metaphysics, his view is flawed by his idea that the
emergence of modern psychology amounts to the *discovery of the soul*
and to a first taking seriously of the psychic background as such. This
part of his view expressed here is not tenable, for two reasons. First,
the soul did not need to be "discovered," because the psychic
background had in former ages precisely been taken most if not overly
seriously, much more so than in our time. Secondly, it must be doubted
that *that* which is now taken seriously is *really*, as alleged, the psychic
background, "the soul." I will come to this second point a little later,
in the next section.

The really existing difference between "before" and "today" is a
different one from the way Jung suggested: formerly the form in which
the soul was taken seriously had been that of substantiated thinking.
The soul itself had been a substance, and by the same token the
underworld, Heaven, the soul's eternal life, too, were substantiated,
objectual, and, so to speak, ontologized. And thus it was that the type
of attention paid to the psychic background had the form of religious
convictions, cultic practice and folk customs, of the imagination, or
of a metaphysic of the soul, respectively. Even the soul as Cartesian I,
despite its advancement to the level of the form of concept, had
nevertheless still been conceived as a substance (*res*) from an observer
standpoint. Psychology as a modern field of study is something else.
"Substance" as such is distilled, evaporated. "All that is solid melts
into air," Marx had stated 150 years ago. The historical move from
premodern via early-modern (*neuzeitlich*) to modern is one from
substance via the Cartesian *subject-as-substance* to *subjectivity as form* and
further—and this is the sign of the modern stage—to *form or syntax*

as such, "mediality." For psychology this means that it can today only be the discipline that it is if it is nothing but a particular methodological *procedere*, an approach to (potentially all kinds of) possible experience, a *mode* or *style* of perceiving, reflecting, interpreting, and reacting, a form of consciousness. It is not, the way most sciences are, defined by a *Gegenstandsgebiet*, a special region of reality as its topic, such as by "what goes on inside individuals" in contrast, for example, to what goes on in the natural or political world. (Psychology is not, as Jung rightly called and criticized such a view, a "compartment psychology" [*MDR* p. 145] and does not have a "delimited field" [*CW* 9i § 112]).

But despite this, its fundamental structural closeness to the uroboric stance of Hegel's philosophy, psychology can also not be a continuation of the absolutely inwardized status that metaphysics had reached in the thinking of this philosopher. Hegel's thought was still a form of metaphysics. It came with the claim of being or achieving *true knowing*. As already for Fichte ("Wissenschaftslehre"), philosophy was for Hegel *die Wissenschaft* (science). This is no longer possible for modern psychology. Psychology is no more than one of the possible methodological approaches to what happens and has given up any claim to being or striving for true knowing. Psychology is merely one of the things one can do if one is so inclined. Although the sense of truth is still vital to it, this sense of truth, or its truth itself, is merely internal to it as a methodological guiding principle and aim. Its validity remains enclosed within itself. It does not extend out beyond itself.

The historical move that we are here concerned with is thus a change from soul (as substance) to psychology (as method or logical form). *Psychology* is the successor notion of *soul*. You cannot have both at the same time. As long as there was soul, psychology was not only unnecessary, but even impossible. And conversely, the existence of psychology presupposes the obsolescence of soul. Psychology *is* the sublation of the soul (the soul both as metaphysical individual soul and as the general form of myth, religion, and metaphysics, in which humanity had its soul on a communal level at its different stages of historical development). The relation between psychology and soul is thus not one of subject versus object, scientific discipline versus subject matter to be studied by it. Psychology's distinction does precisely not lie in the fact that it "discovered the soul" and for the first time "takes the psychic background as such seriously." This would still (or again) be a thinking that construes the relation of psychology and soul along the lines of the subject-object dichotomy, establishing psychology as the subject and holding the soul down in the status of psychology's object of study. No, the distinction of psychology is that it *is* the successor to soul, *is* the sublation of soul, the soul's having been inwardized into itself and come home to itself. The former soul as substance, as an "it," has completely gone under—died—*into* its own *concept* (soul had always been the implicit concept of subject, or I, and personal identity), the *logos* of itself ("psycho-logy"), in other words, it has reflected or inwardized itself into the *form* of subject and as such it has *become* psychology (as a *methodological* approach). This transmutation of the soul indicates that it does no longer want to be *anima alba*, naive, innocent soul, but in-itself-reflected soul, sublated soul.

Although there is, I believe, no indication that Jung ever understood the historical process of the soul as one of its going under into psychology, in other words, as a process that rendered "the soul" in its objective sense obsolete (Jung, as we discussed, always seems to have held on to substantiated notions of *the* psyche, *the* soul, *the* unconscious), his understanding of the logic of psychology itself was such that it clearly implied the soul's having died into its concept and thus having transmuted into psychology. This comes out very clearly when he says about psychology that it

> lacks the immense advantage of an Archimedean point such as physics enjoys. ... The psyche ... observes itself and can only translate the psychic back into the psychic. ... There is no medium for psychology to reflect itself in: it can only portray itself in itself, and describe itself. ... [In describing psychic occurrences] (w)e have not removed ourselves in scientific regards to a plane in any way above or besides the psychic process, let alone translated it into another medium. (*CW* 8 § 421, transl. modif.)

> ... psychology inevitably merges with the psychic process itself. It can no longer be distinguished from the latter, and so turns into it. ... it is not, in the deeper sense, an explanation of this process, for no explanation of the psychic can be anything other

> than the living process of the psyche itself. Psychology has to
> sublate itself as a science and therein precisely it reaches its
> scientific goal. Every other science has a point outside of itself;
> not so psychology, whose object is the very subject that produces
> all science. (*ibid.* § 429, transl. modif.)

With this view, Jung's theoretical standpoint has arrived at its summit
(or better said, its nadir): at the standpoint of subjectivity, of subject
come home to itself, and at the uroboric logic of interiority. The psyche
observes *itself—this*, according to Jung, is what *psychology* is. "Psychology
inevitably merges with the psychic process itself"—this presupposes
that the soul itself as substance has gone under into what formerly
might have been the abstract *theory* or *knowledge* or *science* ABOUT the
soul. The soul now has *itself* attained the form of psychology. It
has lost its abstract form as a doctrine *about*,[223] and turned into
method, a method, moreover, which animates the real process in
contrast to a merely subjective method applied from outside to the
real process. Substance has really become subject. Not having the
advantage of an Archimedean point, psychology does not stand as
neutral observer outside and immune vis-à-vis its "object." Instead,
it is itself a priori involved, implicated in what it studies, in what
it *seems* to study *in front of* itself. It finds itself in a uroboric
situation. Psychology has thus been transformed into the fluid,
living self-unfolding of the psychic *process*, the irreducibly *temporal*
process of psychological experience and thought (soul-*making*,
opus), where "temporal process" means that it occurs *as* time, as
history. It cannot construe itself in terms of an antecedently given
reality of the psyche, of timeless archetypal structures, nor comprehend
itself in terms of the fantasy of a supratemporal consciousness-as-such
as neutral observer.

The fact that the soul has died into the life of what it was the
concept of is the reason why in psychology we can use the term soul

---

[223] According to its logical form a scientific doctrine is always construed as the
timeless, fixed truth about the reality it is about, even if empirically it presents itself as
merely hypothetical and thus by definition open to permanent revision. But the revised,
improved, corrected doctrine is in its logical form just as timeless and fixed as the one
of which it is the revision. The difference between *hypothetical* and *dogmatic* is a superficial
one. Hypotheses are only empirically the opposite of dogma, but logically, in their form, the
same. In itself each hypothesis is dogmatic, asserting an "eternal truth." The difference
from explicit dogmas is only that the "eternal truth" that it claims is *as a whole* placed at
the disposal of the process of future experience.

only *either* in historical contexts (as the name of one of our "antiquities") *or* merely as a manner of speaking, sort of tongue-in-cheek (in quotations marks). For psychology there is not such a "thing" as the soul. But for the ease of expressing oneself, the word soul, preferably in quotation marks, may still be used in psychology as a mythologizing *façon de parler* for a (subjective) soulful, psychological approach to phenomena as well as (objectively) for the logical life and dynamic expressing itself in them *for* that soulful approach, which as a soulful one aims at the depth-dimension of phenomena, imaginally speaking, at the "psychic background," or, more adequately expressed, the internal *logic* or *soul*. The moment psychology would in all earnest believe in a subsisting soul, it would have undone itself and become ideological.

By overcoming itself as a subsisting soul substance (be it the underworldly *eidôlon*, the liquid in the brain, or the immortal soul of Christian ages) and distilling, evaporating, itself into the *form* of form (= into psychology as a method), the soul has finally come home to *itself* from its exile in the imagination that had ipso facto located it "out there" in the world of literal substantial (albeit invisible and immaterial) entities (although, of course, an entity hidden *in us*). Despite the fact that even as substantial soul it had already been the *notion* of subjectivity or I and personal identity, it nevertheless had represented this notion only *as* the opposite of "subject," namely in ontological form as substance, as an "it." Now the notion of subjectivity has been interiorized into this imagined substance ("self-application") so that this earlier substantial form (or the form of substance) was completely worked off and released into its truth as subject.

Of course, such an advance is concomitant with, and paid for by, a loss. The soul in the traditional sense had still been something numinous. But having turned into psychology it is—very soberly—nothing but a method or stance. The soul substance of old thus lost its transcendent, otherworldly, as well as futuristic (life-after-death) character and was, as a method to be employed by us at will, fully *immanentized*.[224] This change, furthermore, means that while before

---

[224] "Immanentized" refers to the *logical* movement of inwardizing something into itself, depriving it of all externality (external reference or substance, or first cause, eminent origin). It is not to be understood in a, let us say, religious sense, the way "secularization" is understood: as a kind of amputating the beyond from one's scheme and therefore operating with only the one half left of the former total scheme.

the soul had been a constituent element of an onto-theo-logy that claimed universal validity for itself, it has now become radically relativized: as a method it is not an overall scheme, a doctrine, an ideology, a program, nothing to be believed in and adored, but merely one of many possible methodical approaches; and it is a methodological standpoint that, when it is employed, is soberly employed only now and then and only by those few who are so inclined and only *when* they happen to be so inclined.

Having become psychology, the soul has come down to earth. It has become pragmatic, an instrument, almost in the spirit of Jung's statement that "every spiritual truth [in our case: the soul as substance] is gradually objectified and turns into a ... tool [in our case: a methodical approach] in the hand of man" (*CW* 13 § 302, transl. modif.). Doing psychology does not answer, and does not want to answer, big metaphysical questions and longings. It does not lend itself to a support of the weighty question of or hope for mythic meaning. It does not supply us with a *Weltbild* (world picture). Psychology is a *praxis*, not a *theôria* or *epistêmê* (although its particular *praxis*, I have to add, is the highest form of *praxis*: that of "*theoricieren*" [Paracelsus]). Nothing numinous anymore. No salvational significance of psychology. It does not have, as Jung still thought and many of his followers still pretend, an all-important *mission* for the future of the world. It is *only* something one can do if and when one wants to *and is capable of it*.

For—and this is the other side—instead of being a numinous entity that could possibly be the object of one's ultimate concern and hope (the way formerly one's immortal soul had been people's ultimate concern), psychology is a disciplined practice that requires systematic training and special practical talents (giftedness) that not everybody has. It requires a depth and cultivation of thinking and feeling that enables one to see through to the "psychic background" of the real rather than being taken in by appearances and imaginal likenesses, a mercurial mind which is up to the uroboric dialectic and absolute negativity of the soul's logical life, and, not to be forgotten, the I's clear distance to itself, i.e., *my* distance to myself (the ability to *abstract from* one's personal needs, wishes, preferences, and prejudices).

3.7 REGRESSIVE RESUBSTANTIATION OF THE ALREADY ACHIEVED FORM OF SUBJECT. EGO-PSYCHOLOGY

As we have seen, the move from soul to psychology means the birth of man, where birth also results in our "metaphysical" nakedness. I already talked about the loss that was concomitant with the soul's advance to the standpoint of modernity. "Metaphysically naked" means being without mythical garment or, in Jung's words, being "utterly poor." While in previous ages people *had* gods or a god, the time of this "*having*" is over. If there is an absolute or a "god," then at the point now reached in the history of the soul it will have to be *produced* by human acts and *in* human productions and to be *known* (seen through) to have been humanly produced. In other words, god would no longer be a naturally given, an objectual transcendent entity or power, which also means that the very notion of "god" would have radically altered—if it can still hold its place at all.

But for the time being, why should I be afraid of being—in a "metaphysical" sense—"utterly poor," "being nothing," or being no more than Schopenhauer's *Fabrikwaare der Natur*, i.e., without a soul? Why should I be afraid of being "*Only* fool, *only* poet" (Nietzsche), or rather precisely *not even* poet, since "poet" is, after all, a very lofty title that Nietzsche at least could rightly claim for himself (and which shows him, in contrast to us ordinary people, to have been a "genius" and thus, according to our above insight, precisely not *Fabrikwaare*)? Is not, concerning the subject, the soul's historical move one of *kenôsis*, a relentless being emptied of whatever claim to mythic or divine stature?[225] Of course, as ego (private person, civil man) and on a pragmatic level, I too matter to myself; I too give myself priority in the sense of watching out for my interests. But *psychologically*, in my responsiveness to the soul's present-day truth, I nevertheless

---

[225] Cf. "Just as in Christianity the vow of worldly poverty turned the mind away from the riches of this earth, so spiritual poverty seeks to renounce the false riches of the spirit in order to withdraw not only from the sorry remnants—which today call themselves the Protestant 'church'—of a great past, but also from all the alluring fragrance of the exotic, in order to dwell with oneself alone, where, in the cold light of consciousness, the blank barrenness of the world reaches to the very stars" (*CW* 9i § 29, transl. modif.). Of course we would have to cleanse this statement of all traces of ego volition and decision ("vow," "seeks to," "in order to"), because it is not at all a question of our "withdrawing" or any other doing. It is only and very simply a question of seeing and saying the truth.

know myself to be insignificant. I am *only* me! Or as Jung put it: "I am *only* that!"

Why should I not be able to come down from our high horse, *that* high horse that instilled in Jung, for one, the presumptuous and inflated idea that he should and could have a "symbolic existence in which I am something else, in which I am fulfilling my role, my role as one of the actors in the divine drama of life" (*CW* 18 § 628), in other words, the wish as in olden, long-bygone days to strut about in mythical garments (even if certainly not literally in his external behavior, then at least logically, in his psychological self-definition)? Or why should I not be able to come down from *that* high horse that makes our general public discourse vainly indulge in the inflated ideas of "human rights" and "human dignity"?

To summarily recapitulate the position reached so far: *The* soul of the archaic ancestor cults, of religion, and of metaphysics has in the course of the long history of the soul's logical life—please note the intentional equivocation of the first and the second term "soul"!—transmuted into *psychology*, which is nothing but a methodological approach or style of seeing (and perhaps of being). The formerly objectified notion *of* subjectivity and personal identity has come home to itself, been reflected into itself, so that it now reveals itself truly as subject (the subject that one *is*), rather than object ("the soul" that one *has*). It thereby has attained the form of form and left the form of substance behind.

* * *

Now I have to add to this: Although what I have just described is the truth of our time, *it is not its reality.* The actual general reality is that the subjectivity of the subject has itself precisely been again construed in the same old substantial form and not in the form of form. The emergence of "the subject" made itself felt and was acknowledged alright, but it has generally been taken literally, ontologically, positivistically: as the factually existing empirical human being, as the individual. Psychology has succumbed to the anthropological fallacy by becoming personalistic. And, establishing itself as the theory *about* people's inner, it has also re-established the subject-object dichotomy. In *this* form the subject is seemingly payed tribute to, whereas what in truth happens is that it is successfully checkmated: it turned into *substantiated* and *positivized* subjectivity. Present-day psychology's focus on what goes on in people and on their self-development has to be seen as a long-range *cult effort* whose function it is to defend and celebrate, by way of *simulation*, the old form of substance against the new truth of the soul, and this even while itself already inescapably being *on* the new level of "the subject" that it wants to prevent. Personalistic psychology is, thus, a compromise formation. With its anthropological bias it shows that it is subject to the new form of subject, but in the way it construes the subject (as people, individuals) it regressively holds the subject down in the ontological form of substance.

In Jung, this widespread "personality-cult" comes to its absolute head: in the absolute "importance" he assigns to the individual, in his notion of the Self, in the personalistic view of his program of "individuation," and in his *Red Book* demand that we each should become Christs rather than Christians (what hubris!). The modern positive-factual individual is invited to a *mediation-less* identification with the divine, in fact with the very Mediator himself, with the alchemical vinculum or logical copula! The copula or coniunctio oppositorum is supposed to be an actually *existent* being: me as *Dasein* (Kierkegaard/Heidegger), ontologically; me in my positivity. I am supposed to *be*—exist as—the Christ or the Self (as the coniunctio). What, for a true psychology, would be the task of *psychology*, namely soul-*making* in the sense of learning to *think* psychologically, i.e., to become able to *think* the coniunctio in the way I experience and respond to reality, to think uroborically, this is stuffed into the human being as *its* task. Psychology (a doing or style, approach, discipline) is perverted into "anthropology" (into ongoings within an actual being, a state of this being that is, however, only to be attained in a hoped-for and forever deferred future: realization of the Self). There is a fundamental difference between the idea that I ought to learn to *live as* the *practice* of a mercurial, uroboric thinking, and the idea of my having to become Self. All this quest for the Self and this emphasis on the positive-factual individual is ego-psychology, despite (especially Jung's) explicit devaluation of the ego in favor of the Self and the devaluation of consciousness in favor of the collective unconscious. The much despised (and rightly despised) "ego" (the ego as a *mode* of perceiving, a *style* of thinking, not to be confused with the I) is unwittingly logically the ruling dominant over the (in other regards, and semantically, *decidedly* far less personalistic) "psychology of the collective unconscious."

Some might here of course want to object that Jung does by no means want *us as ego-personalities* to become the Self. Jung himself would have vehemently rejected such an immediate identification of the ego with the Self as inflation and as the opposite of what he had in mind. The Self in his scheme must not be claimed by the ego-personality. It is for Jung a "borderline concept" referring to the *transcendent* wholeness of man, which, as transcendent, is essentially realized in people's *unconscious* as the appearance, in the course of the individuation process, of images of wholeness (mandalas, God-images). But this distinction of two separate regions and, in general, the operating with the notion of something transcendent, is psychologically a structurally neurotic trick. In this way, to be sure, *psychically, empirically* the inflation can be avoided (because I can always dissociate myself as ego-personality and say about the Self: "but it is not me"), but *psychologically* it makes no difference whether I have to *be* the Christ or the Self directly as ego *or* merely in the unconscious. It makes *psychologically* no difference whether the realization of the Self takes place in me as total *human* personality or only in the segregated realm of the *transcendent* unconscious. This distinction is merely an intellectual game. The *logic of identification*, i.e., the hubris, is the same. The mentioned trick merely allows me to play the innocent and thus evade having to pay the price as "civil man" for the real hubris of my claim about myself, my psychological self-definition.[226]

It is sad to see that Jung had to substantiate the coniunctio (the logic of the copula) as the Self, in other words, logically as a "substance," despite the fact that in the case of his theoretical understanding of the nature of psychology we can see that he had, after all, already attained the standpoint of the irrevocable subjectivity of soul-making, the irreducible temporality of process, and the uroboric logic of interiority. Why could he not stay true to it throughout? Why did he have to reserve it for his *theoretische Überlegungen zum Wesen des*

---

[226] The term "Self" cannot escape the fact that it involves one's self-definition.

Psychischen ("theoretical reflections on the nature of the psychic," which is also the title of the essay of his that has been translated into English as "On the Nature of the Psyche," *CW* 8), and to desert it the moment his topic was the psychic process and its telos itself, which meant regressing to the obsolete style of *substantiating* thinking? May it suffice to have raised these questions about Jung here, since the tackling of them does not belong to the topic and task of the present book.

One main form of the regressive resubstantiation of the already achieved form of subject does not happen within psychology, but is what gave and gives rise to (therapeutic) psychology: neurosis. Neurosis is, as it were, *lived, embodied* ego-psychology. Neurosis as a cultural phenomenon was invented during the 19th century. It presupposes the fully developed subjective soul, the I. Before modernity, before the 19th century, neurosis was impossible. The crossing of developmental thresholds and the integration into consciousness of painful events of life or blows of fate could happen relatively smoothly, at times probably also with great difficulties, with suffering or even desperation, but even in such cases without leading to that psychological complication that we call a *neurotic* reaction. In those earlier times man in his self-definition had not yet (fully) been I, which is to say he did not yet have a notion of *self-determination*. The essential determinations *came* to him *as a matter of course* from outside: from the family and clan to which he belonged, from the social corporations of which he was a member, from the government, from his own biological and social process of being transported through the different stages of life, from fate and God. And they came as objective realities. Whether these determinations were welcome or not, man comprehended himself irrevocably as their recipient, above all as the child of God.

The moment that the I has become fully developed, a concept of self-determination permeates man's self-understanding and has turned into a supreme value. The sick soul absolutizes and literalizes this need of self-determination. It does not only instill in us a wish for being self-determined in the social and political arena (democracy), in religious matters and as to one's political, sexual, ideological orientation, etc., i.e., in the pragmatics of life, but also with respect to actually uncontrollable psychological and "metaphysical" issues of one's *essential* being, one's biological development and of fate, i.e., with respect to *truth* as such. The sick soul, the neurotic soul, that spitefully refuses to go along with its own movement and its experience of truth, but wants to be in control of this movement and the truth is the substantiated "the ego." In neurosis the soul's own form of I or subjectivity goes to the head of the soul. It is taken completely literally and is acted out in the positivity of the psyche.

3.8 THE PSYCHOLOGICAL DIFFERENCE WITHIN THE SOUL-AS-SUBJECT

The soul as subject is I. However, the I or subject is within itself the dialectical unity and difference between itself as that function primarily oriented towards "survival" in the most general sense, in other words, the pragmatic, technical I (in the sense of the one side of the subject-object opposition), on the one hand, *and* the internal not-I as the subject of true knowing, the organ of truth and of the syntactical or logical form, on the other. The latter is "not-I" because it is the *objective* subject, *experienced* by the ego-personality as an internal other with an intentionality (and often impelling necessity) of its own. We could also say an autonomous other, however one that despite its otherness is nevertheless also I (me). Whereas the pragmatic or technical I dominates our stance and activities both in everyday life and particularly in science, the other I is what is predominantly, in an eminent sense, at work and productive in artists and thinkers, in the few exceptional great people (and only occasionally and in a rudimentary way in ordinary people). Ultimately it can also be interpreted as the historical locus (the truth of the inner form or logic that really lived life has at a given historical time and place, the truth of the actual mode of being-in-the-world of a community) that stirs as the burrowing spirit Mercurius in them. The I as the internal not-I is thus not self-identical and self-enclosed like an entity, and not enclosed in the human individual. It has its own internal infinity, and, to be sure, an infinity that does not have a *border* to the world,[227] but rather *within itself* extends, and is open, to the community in which it lives, to the historical situation it finds itself in, and to the historical

---

[227] Because, precisely even as Descartes's early-modern *res cogitans*, it is absolute inwardness (an "absolute dwelling within itself").

past it carries within itself (both in sedimented form as its own present real constitution[228] and as memory).

For unborn man still to a large extent enveloped in certain mythical garments, that is, identical with the various roles assigned to him within a given cultural context, the internal difference within I between the I itself and the non-I was not a pronounced one, simply because man in that situation was psychologically still more or less fully *released* into (and enwrapped by) soul, which at that time was a soul that had not yet come home to itself as subjectivity. What I discussed in the previous paragraph became virulent only in the modern situation, the situation of born man, man *emancipated* from the soul as metaphysical entity.

The I as the psychological difference between I and internal not-I must not be identified with the literalized difference in our customary psychology between the ego, on the one hand, and the unconscious, the non-ego, or the Self, on the other. This latter difference is positivized (a logical dissociation). It excludes the moment of unity between the opposites and reifies each. (Erich Neumann's "ego-self axis," while certainly giving expression to the unity between the opposites even reifies, and *ipso facto* undoes, the unity moment itself. We get three things, the ego, the self, and the axis.) We must much rather comprehend the I and the not-I as different styles of knowing and understanding: egoic knowing versus soul knowing. Nevertheless, Jung's emotional outburst cited earlier, "To hell with the Ego-world! Listen to the voice of your *daimonion*. It has a say now, not you" (*Letters 2*, p. 532, to Charteris, 9 Jan. 1960), *if cleansed of* its affect and its personalistic and mythologizing form ("your *daimonion*") and transformed into a sober, but relentless methodological rejection of egoic knowing, remains indispensable for the constitution of soul knowing, the constitution of true psychology.

The dialectical relation that exists between the opposites within the subject means that the soul as subject must be understood to be also one *moment* of itself. The soul is the whole relation (the entire psychological difference, *homo totus*) and at the same time the one *relatum* of this relation or the one moment of this difference, namely the not-I part, the organ of truth and true knowing, in contradistinction

---

[228] The I *is* its history.

to the other moment, the pragmatic I, the egoic type of knowing and understanding. This ambiguity can of course lead to difficulties. It is our job in our psychological work to make it clear to ourselves which "soul" is meant in each specific context, without, however, in our theorizing trying to split the unity of the two for the sake of unambiguity, for example by using two different names. The contradiction and equivocation must not be avoided. It is inherent in the psychological notion of soul.

3.9 THE PSYCHOLOGICAL I

I mentioned in the previous section that the soul as the one moment of itself (itself in the sense of the whole psychological difference) is the organ of truth or the historical locus that stirs as the burrowing spirit Mercurius in the *great* people, in artists and thinkers. But this not-I can have an additional form of realization, namely as the subject of *psychology* or as psychology as a subject. We can call this the psychological I. Whereas the soul that stirs in the great people has event or fact character (it happens to stir of its own accord in this or that person and at this or that moment, or it doesn't make itself felt in him or not at this time; its manifestation is unpredictable), the psychological I is a methodological standpoint, a style of thinking and apperceiving, of interpreting and appreciating, which as such can to some extent be learned and cultivated and even, but only to some extent, be employed or rejected at will. It, too, requires of course a certain aptitude, but it is not reserved for the truly great.

The psychological I is the standpoint of true psychology, the discipline of a soulful approach or reaction to phenomena, (1) in contrast to a soulless, technical, cynical, rationalistic, merely pragmatic approach, (2) in contrast to egoic emotionality, sentimentality, nostalgia, as well as (3) in contrast to an ideology-ridden theory, a subjective wish, need, and quest-driven view of things. Psychology is not in quest of anything. It does not want anything. Inasmuch as the psychological I is the standpoint of true psychology, it is not "my" I, but an *objective* I, *its* (psychology's) I or psychology *as* the I. This is a very important point. I am a psychologist *to the extent that* psychology—its methodological frame of mind—is at work in me. Psychology has to be the subject that is doing the psychologist's seeing, thinking, and feeling, *not* he or she themselves. I already discussed earlier that psychology is the modern form of the former soul. Keeping this in mind we understand that only if psychology is the truly active subject in us is there a possibility that soul-making and awareness or recognition of soul can happen: because only like can know and produce like.

So in psychology we always have to ask ourselves *who* in us experiences. Who is doing the thinking? We know this type of question from Hillman's *Re-Visioning Psychology*. However, his question took the Who? to mean "which God?" This is very different from my "Who?," which is not, like Hillman's, about a *substantiated* third person singular or plural, about god or gods, but really about the first person singular, that is to say, about *my* (human) methodological standpoint. Is what I am doing truly psychology or maybe not at all? As who do I apperceive? As ego—or as "soul"? As civil man, empirical man—or as the psychological standpoint, as psychology?

And this question is not so much merely a question about a fact to be established, but much rather also an invitation or exhortation to *perform* an act, namely the act of self-negation, self-sublation, of departure from myself as conventional I (ego) and civil man, the act of (logically, not positive-factually) going under as civil man. It is in this spirit that I once wrote about psychological discourse: "It has to *be as* the negation of the ego, and the psychologist ... has to speak as one who has long died as ego personality. The art of psychological discourse is to speak as someone already deceased. ... Psychology has to occur in the spirit of logical negativity."[229]

What I described has essential consequences for the conception of the psychological I. It must not be comprehended as an always available part of the personality or a permanent quality of consciousness. The question—"Who? or as who do I apperceive? As ego or as 'soul'?"— must not be taken to imply that we could simply switch from the one to other or that the soul standpoint could simply be switched on. Rather, the psychological I is a product, a result. In order to exist, it has to be *produced*, and produced each time "from scratch," so to speak: soul-*making*. In the sciences we have certain methods and approaches

---

[229] W. Giegerich, *The Soul's Logical Life*, 2ⁿᵈ ed., Frankfurt/Main et al. (Peter Lang) 1999, p. 24.

that one has to learn once and for all and that thereafter merely need to be *applied*. They can, so to speak, be switched on. In psychology this is fundamentally different. Regardless of what topic or matter one's psychological work turns to, no matter what is to be studied psychologically (this dream, this myth, this symptom or neurosis, etc.), in each instance the whole point of the psychological work is to produce the psychological standpoint, the psychological I. This is the goal of the work. The whole purpose of psychology (the psychological *opus*) is to *produce* psychology. Soul-making is psychology-making, and psychology-making is soul-making, i.e., the establishing and further-development, further deepening, of the psychological level in everything one studies. Psychology does not aim for theoretical knowledge about the soul, for a kind of scientific doctrine, new information. The psychological standpoint or perspective is itself that *lapis* that it tries to reach. It is precisely not merely the perspective or method (tool) through which the psychological work is done. Psychology or the psychological I is its own goal, it has its purpose within itself. Here we can remember Jung's already cited statement that "the alchemists came very close to realizing that the ego [*das Ich*] was the mysteriously elusive arcane substance and the longed-for lapis" (*CW* 14 § 131). The goal of psychology is (psychology's) self-production in the spirit of sameness. The goal is not some other outside of itself (not healing, self-development, one's own wholeness and individuation, nor gaining reliable knowledge about the soul). Sameness. No otherness, no external purpose. This is all: giving reality to itself. Proving its (psychology's) existence and proving it only through the deed (*opus*) of fabricating that which it wants to prove as existing.

This means that the psychological I has in itself *opus* and (produced) Work character, it *is* only to the extent that it is *made*. But this in turn means that it exists only in the actual doing, in the performance, to speak in alchemical metaphors: in the adept's ongoing *ars*, in other words, only "momentary." Soul-making is not like building a house. It is more like eating which also does not produce a permanent result. You have to do it again and again, if you want it to happen. The sciences are again different. Scientific methods are the tool for achieving purposes external to themselves. They aim for and produce permanent results (reliable knowledge) independent of the particular way these results were achieved. The insights gained can therefore be generalized and applied to other instances of the same type. In order to use it one does not need to know how exactly penicillin was discovered. Theoretical insights or conclusions last beyond the time and exist outside of the experiments or studies through which they were achieved, and they retain their significance beyond the time of their production (at least until future experiments will disprove or supersede them. But even if they are disproved, they nevertheless last, namely as erroneous hypotheses or opinions in the history of science). Theoretical insights are logically "positive" items; you can transmit them to others in scientific journals or books. But the psychological I is "negative." It is not an item. It comes into being, and exists only, in that mind that actually performs the *opus* of absolute-negative inwardization and exists only for the duration of this inwardization. Whereas *aurum vulgi* can be given as a present to others or can be turned into coins with which you can buy things, *aurum nostrum* cannot be bartered. It IS its own time. If psychology comes up with insights that correspond to scientific knowledge, these are not truly psychological, but at best byproducts, as important and valid that they may be in other (for example, technical) regards.

With each new psychological investigation one always starts out from an external point of view and as civil man, as ordinary consciousness. And each time anew one has to work oneself into whatever happens to be one's prime matter and, by working oneself into its depth, into its interiority (i.e., by going under into the matter), create the *lapis*, the alchemical gold, the tincture: the psychological I. The psychologist has to conquer anew the psychological level for himself each time that he enters into the opus. But if this is so, if the psychological standpoint is the goal and final result of the psychological opus, I seem to have contradicted my starting point: my insistence that from the outset it has to be the psychological I or the soul that has to do the work. However, here we have to keep in mind that the life of the soul is self-contradictory, uroboric, dialectical. That the psychological I needs to be produced as the result of the opus and the fact that it has to be what from the beginning undertakes the opus is not a simple, undialectical contradiction. Rather, we have to realize that the psychologist is only a psychologist to the extent that he is already pregnant with the psychological I from the outset. He as civil man and ordinary consciousness already has to be reached by it, in the grip of it, so that it is the true subject that does the thinking in him, if through the opus he wants to arrive at it. For only unto everyone that hath shall be given. If the psychological I, the alchemical Mercurius, is not the spiritus rector of the work from the start, the Mercurius will not be found. Only like can apperceive and produce like. There is no way from outside psychology into psychology. The psychological level is its own alpha and omega, its beginning and telos. No otherness. But conversely, the Mercurius needs to be *found*. The soul needs to *make* itself. Being pregnant with the psychological I does not mean already having been born as psychological I.

So when before I spoke of "fabricating" the psychological I, this word should not be taken in the sense of ego constructions or concoctions. Rather, we should read this word as referring to the *opus*, which in turn can be understood as the "labor" that is the prerequisite of a birth (and the way in which the birth happens), namely the birth of that which one before was merely pregnant with. A mother does not make the baby, but she nevertheless "pro-duces" the baby that she carried within herself all along. Birth is, as it were, only the *child's* move from "implicit" to "explicit," but this move of the child involves the active labor, and labor pains, of the mother. Soul-making is the soul's or psychology's making itself in the sense of giving birth to itself. But for in fact taking place it also involves and requires our active "labor," our human efforts, our *opus*—what Hegel called the *Anstrengung des Begriffs*, a phrase that has been translated into English as "labor of the concept." This translation allows us to read it in terms of the birth metaphor. It is both the self-unfolding of the concept and the human labor of re-enacting in one's mind and comprehending this self-unfolding.

I will now summarily list in all brevity some of the most important principles and characteristics of the methodological standpoint of psychology, without each time paying attention to the starting-point/result dialectic just discussed. It will be a description of the psychological standpoint *from an external observer standpoint* and thus rather abstract, a talking *about* it. It should not be confused with "the real thing." The real psychological I only shows itself in the actual opus. I will here not need to go into each principle or characteristic at more length because I have discussed those principles numerous times at different occasions in my other works and in part already in other chapters of the present work.

- In looking at phenomena of real life and at texts and images one's presupposition has to be that in them "the soul" is speaking about *itself* (and not about us human beings or anything else in the world) and, furthermore, that there is *nothing behind* this the soul's speaking about itself: no substrate, not a positively existing soul as author, no eminent origin or beginning, nothing antecedently given (like a "primordial mother, the sensory, the natural, the physical" [Hillman]).[230] The speaking or self-display is all there is ("actuosity," immanentism). Production without a producer. And a speaking without external referent. Since it has no external referent, this speaking cannot be compared with a referent as to whether it is adequate (true, correct) or not. The idea of an *adaequatio rei et intellectus* does not make sense here. "... there are still people who believe that a psychoanalyst could be lied to by his patients. But this is quite impossible. Lies are fantasies. And we treat fantasies" (*CW* 4 § 300 fn., transl. modif.). Soul phenomena have to be seen as an *arrangement* (in Alfred Adler's sense), a performance, self-display, a mise en scène. One has to view phenomena as having everything they need within themselves, including their own origin (cause or "author"), their final telos, and their meaning (and "referent"). They *are* their own referent. One has to view them strictly as self-relation, self-representation, self-interpretation. They *are* their own origin and author. Whether true or lies, whether good or bad, enjoyable or despicable like "stinking water," symptoms, and the "massa confusa": they are *causa sui*, and "sufficient unto

---

[230] This negation includes even such "factors" or "dominants" as Jung's archetypes (*if* they are viewed as "factors" in the literal sense of the word) or Hillman's "Gods" and "the imaginal."

[themselves], like the Uroboros, the tail-eater, which is said
to beget, kill, and devour itself" (*CW* 16 § 454). They
within themselves *produce* their own a priori only as their
a posteriori *result.* As such they have their own *inner infinity*
and are in the logical status of *selves,* of individuals.[231]
(Please remember: we are here and in the following points
merely discussing *methodological* presuppositions or
imputations and not making ontological assertions. Only
hypothetically: *if* one wants to do psychology, one has to
view things this way. But nobody is required to do
psychology and view things this way.)

---

[231] Jung (a) substantiated and reified "*the* Self" as a separate archetypal reality and
(b) attributed it to people as each individual's Self. He thought (c) that only through a
long individuation process could the Self—perhaps—be realized and that its experience
was something special. What I am suggesting is the very different idea that being a self
is the (c) inevitable and a priori (a) character or logical form of (b) all manifestations of
soul, all soul phenomena themselves. Only to the extent that also people *are* soul, are
they, too, selves. They don't have a self, they are selves. Something similar applies to the
concept of *wholeness.* Jung viewed wholeness as a goal to be striven for. For me, wholeness
is a methodological *presupposition.* If soul phenomena *are* uroboric, then as a matter of
course they all start out as being in the state of "wholeness." Psychologically, each matter,
each phenomenon has to be placed into and enclosed in the retort. But about the retort
Jung himself said, "As the *vas Hermeticum* of alchemy, it was 'hermetically' sealed (i.e.,
sealed with the sign of Hermes); it had to be made of glass, and had also to be as round
as possible, since it was meant to represent the cosmos [*das Weltall,* the All], in which
the earth was created" (*CW* 13 § 245). This means nothing else than that *for psychology*
each phenomenon is, for the time of its being our subject-matter, a world unto itself,
the *whole* world, the one and only world, the All. This is it! Eachness. The retort, especially
with its hermetic seal, is the image of wholeness by radically excluding the very idea of
anything external, indeed, of externality as such. Jung also quotes alchemists saying,
"Nature is not improved save through its own nature" and "Thus our material cannot
be improved save through itself." And he mentions "the repeated warning of other treatises
not to mix anything from outside with the contents of the Hermetic vessel, because the
lapis 'has everything it needs.'" (*CW* 9ii § 220). Nature "rejoices in its own nature; if it
is joined to another, the work of nature is destroyed" (*CW* 9ii § 244). As with "self" and
"wholeness," so Jung also literalized and ontologized "the individual," identifying this
term with and reserving it for each subsisting human being. This is why he had to construe
"individuation" as the process of people's self-development, whereas psychologically it
should be the "alchemical" process of releasing each prime matter, each soul phenomenon,
into its truth ("improving nature through its own nature," i.e., the move from "implicit"
to "explicit"). In all three cases Jung did not go all the way through with his own concept
of the objective psyche and with the immanentism implied by his own alchemical
teachings, but in the last analysis kept clinging to the substrate personality and thus to
externality. That he tied psychological thinking to the human person as substrate means
that he did not use the *vas Hermeticum!* Psychic phenomena had for him their *ground*
outside themselves in the human being, and this is why "wholeness," "Self," and
"individuation" had to become for his theorizing hard-to-achieve future *goals,* i.e., utopian.

- Viewing things this way means that one sees them *from within* and no longer from outside, from an observer standpoint (This is why Jung rejected the idea of an Archimedean point for psychology.) No vis-à-vis, no immediacy. Psychological work has to follow a logic of sameness. No otherness, no exteriority, that is, nothing outside of any phenomenon (only possibly an internal other, the Other of itself). Practically, for example in psychotherapy, this means that psychology happens when what at first seems to be an other is not viewed as a totally other; when the seeming "facts" of a patient's biography and pathology, etc., (as "predicate") become interiorized into the "(sentence) subject" (= the interiority of the suffering soul) as its self-display. That is to say, the patient's statements, sentences, have to be read as *"analytic judgments"* and not as a "synthetic judgments."[232] Conversely we can say that we enter the sphere of ordinary and scientific world-experience when we read the "predicates" as those of a "synthetic judgment." Because then the predicates (the statements, the phenomena) become "facts" for us that refer to an external referent, in our case, the patient.—One sees here that psychology is a kind of island or oasis within the modern world, an oasis which gives asylum[233] to the ancient metaphysical logic of identity, of the copula, vinculum, ligamentum, or coniunctio, and of the syzygial unity of the unity and difference of the opposites, however asylum only as *reduced to the form and status of a mere methodological approach*, not as an ontology or belief system, not as a worldview or doctrine for mankind at large. Psychology is *sublated* metaphysics, irrevocably *sublated* metaphysics. But also sublated *metaphysics*. Psychology has no higher status and collective significance than has a hobby or

---

[232] I refer here the reader to the more detailed discussion of this topic by Greg Mogenson, "Interiorizing Psychology into Itself," in: W. Giegerich, D.L. Miller, G. Mogenson, *Dialectics & Analytical Psychology*, New Orleans, LA (Spring Journal Books) 2005, pp. 61–75, here esp. pp. 66–71.
[233] Concerning this asylum cf also the last sentence of ch. 3.4.

pastime.[234] Just as hobby and pastime have their place in
the private life of individuals, so psychology has its place
only in the interiority, the hidden recesses, of the
individuals' private soul. When psychology loses this
humility and forgets about this its sublatedness (for
example, by claiming to have an immediate real, "official,"
and public significance for this age and for society at large,
possibly even propagating it as a salvationist scheme for
individuals and the culture at large), it turns into an
ideology,[235] New Age esotericism, pop psychology.
Psychology is the discipline of Mnemosyne. Its tense is the
perfect tense. No future. The owl of Minerva begins its
flight at dusk. This insistence on the sublatedness aspect
is the one caution. The other is: when, conversely,
psychology forgets about its being "metaphysics," it loses
its soul and "*the* soul," turning into Lange's "psychology
without soul."

- But being in this way *within* also implies that our habitual
  object consciousness is overcome. Only from the external
  observer standpoint does what we are concerned with take
  on the logical form of objects or thinglike-ness. Once
  inside, one is within a *speaking*, a living *meaning*, a concept,

---

[234] By saying this I do not wish to deny the obvious fact that there are professional
psychology and the practice of psychotherapy (which, neither for the analyst nor for the
patient is a pastime!). My point is that we must not give to soul-work a higher quasi-
metaphysical, quasi-religious significance, higher than, for example, to one's enjoying a
Bach oratorio. Nor does it have the dignity of *necessity* that industry, banking, commerce
have. It is a luxury, and even more so than the humanities which, other than soul-work,
are not of merely private significance.

[235] When Freud stated that "Drive theory is our mythology" (and with the same
right he could have said the same thing about the Oedipus complex, the "family romance,"
"object-relations," and all sorts of other components of psychoanalytic theory), he
inadvertently admitted that psychoanalysis is in the business of myth-making, ideology-
making, and that the application of psychoanalytic theory in the consulting room is the
project of a ritual cocooning patients in this modern "myth." The same applies to much
of Jungian psychology. The theories of "individuation," of the ego-self axis, of typology,
of the heroic ego, of the terrible one-sidedness of both Christianity and the modern
world in need of being healed by a striving for "wholeness," etc., are, the way they are
used, simply ideologies. And what many Jungians are doing in psychotherapy is to *mindlessly*
act out those theories upon one patient after another willing to be cocooned in a "myth",
as well as, in publications, to act those same theories out in the interpretation of innocent,
helpless symbols, fairy tales, and genuine myths of old.

within a particular manifestation of the sphere of intelligibility. What from outside would show itself as an image object or idea object, reveals itself as itself a priori *being* text, being interpretation (rather than being an object *to be* interpreted). Not a fact of nature, but a certain "statement," "thesis," or "opinion" (about itself), a notion, conception: one of "the soul's" self-interpretations. Psychology tries to interpret *interpretations*.

- The phenomenally appearing meaning or interpretation is alive, is logical life, i.e., a self-moving dynamic "finally," "teleologically" aiming for its full self-unfolding and, through this relentless self-unfolding, for its own exhaustion (and thus ultimately even its own self-overcoming). There is a hidden animating logic at work inside each phenomenon, a "burrowing spirit," alchemy's spirit Mercurius, which, as long as the conscious mind has not entered it or has not, conversely, been truly reached or wounded by it, lies dormant (much like the Kundalini in its initial state), but awakens and comes alive the moment a real contact has been established. *Oportet me adesse.* It needs our dedication, our commitment, our bringing our presence to bear on it.[236] What was implicit in the first immediacy in which a phenomenon, image, or idea originally appeared wants to become explicit, "spelled out" (which, if completely achieved, would at once mean that the life or soul has gone out of it; that *this* phenomenon has become psychologically obsolete, a fact which Jung in his theorizing discussed under the heading of "the death of symbols").

- Psychology must adopt the standpoint of the objective psyche and view phenomena *sub specie* or in terms of the

---

[236] Jung, to be sure, saw this necessity when he demanded that we *enter* our fantasies ("active imagination"), but his solution is sadly deficient. It remains itself a mere fantasy, because this entering is only a semantic one, on the narrative level. As an (imagined) literal act and behavior of entering, it is only a token entering. A real, committed entering, by contrast, would require that it happens as a syntactical one, that is, in the very logic informing consciousness (the logical form of consciousness).

objective psyche and its concerns, we could also say: view
phenomena *from* "the other side" or from within. This
presupposes a translocation away from the ordinarily
prevailing viewpoints. Psychology, in order to *be*, must *have*
left the usual (common-sensical, pragmatic, utilitarian,[237]
emotional, moral, scientific) categories and interests
behind so that it can see things how they are, as Jung put
it, "in Mercurio," in the "archetypal background," in "the
psyche's hinterland," not in empirical-factual reality. Only
in this way does psychology do justice to the psychological
difference that constitutes it. What we have to see in
psychology is "that behind the impressions of the daily
life—behind the scenes—another picture looms up,
covered by a thin veil of actual facts."[238] This other picture
is what psychology has to focus on. The alchemist Dorneus
similarly said, "There is in natural things a certain truth
not seen by the outward eye but perceived by the mind
alone. Of this the philosophers had experience..." (*CW* 11
§ 152 note 47).

• It is clear that this focus requires a certain indirectness,
which I will briefly explain. As a matter of course,
psychology has to concentrate on the empirical
phenomena, on what really shows itself, like the real
pathology, the real symptoms, the real sandplay pictures,
the real dreams, the real great cultural works. But it
concentrates on them as the logically negative expression
or representation of their own internal other, which is the
actual subject-matter that psychology wants to study, their
inner negativity, the soul, the spirit Mercurius. But
psychology cannot study the "Mercurius" directly because
the "Mercurius" does not exist as a positivity in the first
place. It can only be studied indirectly through looking
at how it manifests itself positively in and as empirical

---

[237] This includes all interests and wishes of "the ego," such as those for our survival,
benefit, protection, and consolation. Such interests are, of course, not wrong or bad.
They only must not influence the psychological approach.
[238] C.G. Jung, *The Visions Seminars*, Zürich (Spring Publ.) 1976, p. 8.

phenomena. It is vital for psychology to understand this dialectic. You look at the phenomenal in order to see something else! So you have to truly devote yourself to the phenomenal and yet at the same time *not* intend it as your object. It is an in itself negated focusing on the matter (*ein wegblickendes Hinblicken*, an intently looking at the object that nevertheless, while one solely looks at it, is a looking away). This looking is therefore self-contradictory. It has to be this, because a direct gaze at it would tend to get stuck in the empirical and pragmatic surface appearance of the phenomenon, its merely formalistic-functional or its immediate aesthetic aspects. It would be a seeing with the outward eye and not with the mind. The whole-hearted dedication to a phenomenon requires a stepping-back of the subjective mind, indeed even its going-under (going-under into the phenomenon), so that the true inner substance of the phenomenon (the soul of the real) may come to the fore.

- This translocation also includes the insight that the soul is not about us, about people. For example, not I as civil man must individuate. Individuation in Jung's sense is not people's task (even if, deplorably, Jung usually presented it that way). The subject to undergo individuation is (if we focus on "man") the "archetypal" Purusha, Anthropos, or Adam kadmon, or, less imaginally speaking, the *Concept* of man, the logic of man's self-definition and mode of being-in-the-world. But more generally it is the self-fulfillment of each psychic phenomenon studied, its coming home to itself, its being released into its truth, its concept. Alchemically speaking, it is the freeing of the spirit Mercurius imprisoned in the matter. The move from implicit to explicit. It is a naive and narcissistic mistake to take oneself so seriously as to confuse oneself with the true subject of the soul's life (what or whom it is about). *We* are no more than the stage or place where *it* happens, but where it happens for its own sake, not for ours. The fact that it needs us to acquire a *real* presence in the world and undergo its process of *further-determination* must not go to our heads as if we were meant.

- Doing psychology thus demands also that we have gained a distance from ourselves, have departed from ourselves as ego-personalities. This is a much greater and more real blow to "the naive self-love of men" and the "human megalomania" than what Freud thought (after the Copernican and the Darwinian revolutions) to be "the third and most wounding blow," namely the (alleged) discovery by psychoanalysis that the ego "is not even master in its own house."[239] What Freud referred to is at best a narcissistic wound on the *semantic* level, which is psychologically harmless, indeed irrelevant. But the fact that not we, as human beings, have to experience the individuation process (to stay with this example), but that the *concept* of man is what has to undergo it, is a *logical* or *syntactical* offence that is ipso facto a real psychological wound. And *practically* it means that the psychologist must not allow himself to have a soft spot, a narcissistic tendermindedness, for his own or our collectively cherished ideals, values, and dogmas (that is, for "the ego"; for "the ego" is nothing else but our most precious ideals,

---

[239] See Sigmund Freud, *Introductory Lectures*, no. 18, Standard Edition vol. 15, pp. 284 f. Critically we can say that the insight that the ego is not master in its own house is nothing new, not at all revolutionary. Religious thinking had taught this all along, although of course not in the same Freudian positivistic terms and on the same scientistic basis. Just think of: "For the good that I would I do not: but the evil which I would not, that I do" (Romans 7:19). "For it is God which worketh in you both to will and to do of his good pleasure" (Phil. 2:13). Philosophy likewise had taught that to begin with we tend to be the slaves of our affects and emotions, which is why man's ethical task was to painfully struggle to rise above his dependence in order to thus become a "wise man." There is here no megalomaniac ego for whom the insight that it is not the master in its own house could have been a shocking surprise and "the most wounding blow." For centuries or millennia the traditional ego had grown up with the very insight that Freud now for the first time *sells as* this terrible blow to man's self-love, thereby against appearances precisely for the first time *installing* and *edifying* this fundamentally modern narcissistic ego. Because by presenting this familiar insight as such an unheard-of wound he teaches consciousness to view it all of a sudden as something terribly wrong and ipso facto for the first time creates that majestic unwounded position for which alone this insight could be a terribly humiliating blow. Ostensibly Freud wants to teach us humility, but in truth and unwittingly—on the psychological or syntactical level—he erects the very megalomaniac stance that he ostensibly—on the semantic level—undoes.

interests, and beliefs). Psychology is not for sissies, not for "Beautiful Souls." One has to be able to take it, where "it" here refers to the ruthless truths brought about by the objective *soul movement* or contained in soul phenomena. Ruthless truths as they manifested, for example, in ancient times in cruel rituals like human sacrifices or in more modern times in the fundamental ruptures and losses brought about by scientific and technological progress and the painful collapse of our traditional values and beliefs. And, at least to the extent that one is a psychologist (*not* necessarily, however, to the extent that one is civil man and private individual), one has to firmly, unperturbedly hold one's place vis-à-vis the soul's ruthlessness, allowing the painful soul contents to come home to oneself (as psychologist), to cut into one's flesh, and to transform, redefine, (psychology's) consciousness (rather than protecting psychology's habitual consciousness from them by insisting on one's old values or than "regressively restoring its persona"). Professionalism: no pity and solidarity with the desperate wish of the ego, identified with the *anima alba*, to retain its subjectivism, its innocence, and its aestheticism.

• The particular *procedere* of the psychological approach is an absolute-negative inwardization, a *recursive* progression.[240] It is a relentless movement into the initially hidden ("implicit") depth of the phenomenon at hand via successive logical negations (the self-negations of the phenomenon's first immediacy and its subsequent preliminary appearances) so that what it contains in its depth is made explicit, is brought to light, released into its truth (into its *being* true: "veri-fication"),

---

[240] I will not discuss this here any further since I have given detailed illustrations of this procedure, for example, in my discussion of the Glass-Mountain fairy tale (W. Giegerich, D.L. Miller, G. Mogenson, *Dialectics & Analytical Psychology*, New Orleans, LA [Spring Journal Books] 2005, pp. 9–24), of Heraclitus's dictum about the depth of the soul ("Is the Soul 'Deep'? Entering and Following the Logical Movement of Heraclitus' Fragment 45 (Diels)," now ch. 6 of my *The Soul Always Thinks*, vol. 4 of my Collected English Papers, New Orleans, LA [Spring Journal Books] 2010), and elsewhere.

through its being integrated into consciousness, that is
to say, into consciousness as consciousness's own logical
form, its very constitution.

• The translocation to the viewpoint *sub specie* of the
objective soul is a methodological step, and yet it is not
completely in our hands. To some extent it is *dependent
on one's having been reached by* the soul in the Real,
reached by "the other side." So that a person can be
reached by the soul (in such a way that his or her eyes
are opened to it, in contrast to a merely being reached
by its effects in the form of symptoms), a particular
organ must be present in that person: the organ of
feeling. This is not so common. Of course, emotional
reactions, affective reactions, and feelings are quite
common. But, as we already heard, having feelings and
emotions is something completely different from the
organ of feeling and, of course, also from what Jung
called the feeling function, which is a rational function
and not an emotional outburst or the event of "having
feelings." Many people in psychology speak of feeling
and the feeling function, but they do not know it. Jung
was of the opinion that (a) everybody had a feeling
function, even though in some cases only as an "inferior
function," that is, a merely rudimentary or dormant one
in need of being developed. I do not think so, at least
concerning what I call the organ of feeling: In many
people it is simply absent. Jung also was of the opinion
that (b) the feeling function and the thinking function
mutually exclude each other. Again, while this may be
the case for his concept of them, it is not true for true
thinking and true feeling. Doing psychology requires
that the person who does it does it from a point, a
depth, in which thinking and feeling are one. The
German word *Gemüt* in the older language, and almost
up to recent times, used to denote precisely the unity
of feeling, thinking, and volition, the unity of St.
Augustine's trinity (triunity) of *memoria, intellectus,* and

voluntas.[241] It comprises heart or soul and reason and understanding (*mens, animus*). The *Gemüt* in this sense is the "whole man" (*homo totus*) in his *inwardness*, his inner depth, as his dwelling within himself (in contrast to in the body). The real issue here, of course, is not the *word* "*Gemüt*" itself, but the indifference point, which alone can function as the organ in us to do psychology. "Depth psychology" does not merely mean that it is a psychology that studies *the* depths as its object. Rather, it requires that it be *performed*, not from the level of separate "functions" (in Jung's sense), but from a deeper level, that of the indifference point in which conceptual thought and true feeling go together. The objective soul needs as its counterpart and addressee in the human subject this organ. Only if it were in reality the organ of psychological work could the terrible abstractness prevailing in the psychology as it really exists be overcome, an abstractness that expresses itself in thoughts as deep as a puddle, whose shallowness and murkiness is often merely covered over by a likewise abstract emotionalism devoid of, but given out as, true feeling. This hollow emotionalism comes out most blatantly in the use of hollow power-words such as "the sacred," "the numinous," "the Gods" ....

Here I end my brief outlining of some of the major methodological prerequisites for doing psychology. But I do not want to leave this discussion without pointing out that as far as therapeutic work with actual patients is concerned things are more complicated than presented here because in the practice of therapy we must be *utriusque capax* (capable of both), as alchemy said of the Mercurius. As practicing *therapists* we are not totally identical with the psychologist in ourselves. We must have one leg in psychology and one leg in practical reality, the sphere of the human, all-too-human. We must be able to display a true unadulterated access to soul as well as a practical knowledge of the world (which includes a realistic insight into human nature) and understand the needs of the patient as human being. And, this is most

---

[241] See *Grimm'sches Wörterbuch*, sub voce "Gemüt," vol. 5, col. 3293 ff., here especially col. 3296.

important, we have to *know when it is a question of the one and when of the other*. Some patients are open to soul work right from the beginning or at least at certain times of their analytical work. Some patients, by contrast, do not need much psychology in the true sense of the word. What they need is rather much down-to-earth help, such as real human attention, sympathy, and understanding; an *honest* face-to-face encounter with another human being; guidance through personal crises or difficult life situations, or more generally a kind of philosophical practical wisdom,[242] and so on. Already Jung wisely distinguished four stages (and this also means four possible projects) of psychotherapy, namely *confession, instruction* [Aufklärung], *education*, and *transformation* (*CW* 16 § 122 ff.). Only with Jung's last category would we reach the precincts of psychology proper. So while I do not wish to water down in any way the severe requirements presented above for doing psychology, a psychology *with* soul, I also do not want to absolutize psychology, as if in the consulting room nothing but psychology was permitted. Just as I do not confuse myself as private individual, as "civil man," with the psychologist that (I hope) I am.

---

[242] Marco Heleno Barreto, "'It is something like antique philosophy': Analytical Psychology and Philosophical Practical Wisdom," in: *Spring 77* ("Philosophy & Psychology"), Spring 2007, pp. 79–98.

CHAPTER 4

The Phenomenology of the Soul (3): The two opposite purposes (directions, teleologies) of the soul

Having just mentioned the situation and needs in the consulting room I have to introduce one further crucial distinction which again complicates matters considerably, the distinction between two fundamentally different, indeed opposite, purposes, aims, or directions of the soul's logical life. This distinction is not only of importance in practical psychotherapy, but also with respect to the general theory (or a full understanding) of the nature of the soul as such and its *opus magnum*. In therapy this distinction again requires that we are capable of knowing *when* it is a question of the one direction and *when* of the other.

When we look at psychological phenomenology we can see that there are two very different, even opposite intentionalities, *concerning what "the soul" wants to bring about in humans*, intentionalities that express themselves in the psychologically relevant phenomena and in the soul's life in general. There are the purposes of

INITIATION (*into* soul) as well as REPRESENTATION and CELEBRATION	EMANCIPATION (*from* soul) or INDIVIDUATION and CONSCIOUSNESS
approach in therapy: soul-making (sensu strictiori) final-synthetic approach	*approach in therapy:* alchemical cauterizing reductive-analytical approach

(The expression "reductive-analytical" had been used by Jung to describe above all the Freudian technique and style of interpretation. Here, however, it is used in a more general sense to indicate any sobering approach that brings us down to earth and to ourselves in the sense of the realization "I am *only* that!")

It is clear that the two opposite purposes that the soul has *for us humans* and that are here labeled initiation and emancipation correspond to the two general needs that we ascribed to the soul in our above discussions when we considered it in its own terms, rather than from the human perspective:

The need to be born into the world, to obtain a real, empirical presence in life, to display itself: the soul's *anima* need	The need of the soul's further-determination,[243] the need to overcome and redefine itself: the soul's *animus* need

The first purpose of psychological phenomena (concerning what the soul wants to do to us humans) is to initiate consciousness into the mysteries of the soul's logical life, into the absolute, transcendent; it is the seductive-anima purpose of luring consciousness into the soul's depths, into the unknown, into the otherworldly wisdom of the dead ancestors. The soul here wants to give the absolute and transcendent a real presence in the life of a people. This real presence shows in the cult life of societies, in the myths told, in the regular practice of sending new generations into initiation ceremonies, in recurring feast days, in the building of temples and statues of gods, etc. There is a need on the part of the soul as logical negativity to be symbolized, objectively represented, publicly honored, and celebrated. Jung spoke with respect to this of "the symbolic life,"

---

[243] Jung's equivalent of this is "dreaming the myth onwards": the regressive translation of the soul's animus need into an anima style! Still, in contrast to Hillman Jung had at least a clear awareness of the soul's progression to new statuses of itself.

to which he said that, for example, "the primitive Australians sacrifice [...] two-thirds of their available time—of their lifetime in which they are conscious" (*CW* 18 § 649). Above I pointed out that it is the need of the soul to be born into the world, and that to be born means to be born *as absolutely negative presences*. The fact that sanctuaries were in a *temenos*, as the Greeks called it, in a sacred precinct "cut out" (Greek *temnô*) from the ordinary profane world, may serve as one indication of the absolute negativity of the presence of the holy. What is "cut out" of the realm of the positivity of existence is *ipso facto* logically negative (separated from the sphere of positivity).

The second and very different purpose is that of emancipation precisely from that into which the first purpose initiated or which it celebrated. Jung thus could say: "The aim of individuation is no other one than to free the self of the false wrappings of the persona on the one hand, and of the suggestive power of unconscious images on the other." (*CW* 7 § 269, transl. modif.). What here is aimed at is a dissolution of the *participation mystique*, the unconscious identity (a) with the instincts and drives, (b) with the family, tribe, nation, society, (c) with archetypal or numinous ideas and ideals or, in short, the imaginal, and, last but not least, (d) with oneself! One has to learn to distinguish oneself from the absolute and transcendent, as well as even from oneself, in order to be reduced to the innermost core of one's own being and so truly become the in-dividual that one is. What is here needed is above all one's stepping out of the mythical garments that consist of the collective roles and ideas with which tradition wraps us and then even one's dissolving one's own natural identity with one's self-image or self-definition, that is to say with the whole *unio naturalis*, so as to become able to see oneself objectively, as if from outside: namely as the *hard fact* and "irrational datum" (*CW* 10 § 498) that one is. Individuation means to become *just* oneself, becoming reduced to what one in fact is, knowing that "I am *only* that!" (just "me" in my mythical and metaphysical nakedness). It means learning to face oneself objectively (like an other).[244]

Here the soul does not want to be born *as* absolutely negative presences, as the presence, in consciousness and in cultural life, of a

---

[244] Above I had quoted Jung saying about ordinary man: "He has no objectivity toward himself and cannot yet regard himself as a phenomenon which he finds in existence and with which, for better or worse, he is identical" (*MDR* p. 341).

mythic-imaginal and otherworldly anima-world, as mythological garment in which the world and human existence is cloaked, as projected ideas and cherished values, as gods to be believed in. It wants to be born *out of* itself as anima and into the world *as itself*: as subjectivity, as subjective mind, subjective consciousness as such. Whereas in the former case it was a birth on the semantic level (a rich phenomenology of myths, symbols, and rituals), here it is a birth on the syntactical level or on the level of logical form. This means that the soul wants to come home to *itself* and to human consciousness. It wants to be known as human consciousness itself rather than being only known as and revered as *contents* of consciousness ("projected" into nature, the cosmos: the polytheistic gods, the demons, and nature spirits; or into transcendence, as in metaphysics).

This process of individuation requires the work of trying to make oneself conscious of all the illusions about oneself and life, of one's self-deceptions ("shadow"), and of one's being identified (in the sense of the *unio naturalis*) with one's unconscious assumptions and the presuppositions that one has.

In his paper on "Marriage as a Psychological Relationship" (*CW* 17) already briefly cited above, Jung exemplifies this change by showing the difference between a collective relationship in marriage, one governed by collective ideas and natural needs (like the inner need to establish a family, to have a career in order to provide for one's sustenance), on the one hand, and a truly *individual relationship*, on the other. In the latter case, both people stand psychologically naked vis-à-vis each other, not protected by conventions or rituals, and as persons conscious of themselves.

It is clear that the second purpose has much in common with the goals of that historical movement that we call The Enlightenment. This is why I also introduced the term "emancipation" which is, as far as I can tell, not Jung's *term*. But as we have seen, Jung does comprehend individuation as aiming for a freeing, an emancipation from the soul, the soul both as the "wrappings of the persona" and as the imaginal or mythic with its enormous suggestive power. *Contra naturam* means here: against what—in a *psychological* sense—is nature: namely the values and treasures of tradition, the conventional, the familiar. In a sense individuation is *subversive*! Initiation, by contrast, is that process by which the traditions of the ancestors are revived and rejuvenated again and again and thereby prevented from becoming sterile, meaningless routines. Initiations help to fill the conventional forms and contents of a society's cultic life and mythological ideas projected out into the cosmos with new deep and living meaning by establishing a deep *personal* connection of the individual to them. If it were not for the fact that initiations mainly occur in cultures without writing I would say: only they (initiations) help to provide the spirit for the dead letters (cf. in this context those fairytales where a dragon prevents access to the fountain of life...). Initiation thus means to follow the path of (psychological) "nature," to sustain the tradition, to allow oneself to succumb to the suggestive power of the mythic images and be enwrapped by them, to dream the myth further, to uphold the projection.

On the level of modernity, for psychology, initiation must not be confused with the time-honored cultural institutions of this name. Initiation now means one's being initiated through one's absolute-negatively interiorizing the phenomenon one is dealing with into itself and thus releasing it into its spirit and truth. This is how today, how in psychology, the dead letter can come alive with spirit, how the spirit Mercurius can be freed from its imprisonment in the physicalness, literalness of "the matter."

Through the connection of the second soul purpose, that of "emancipation" and an increase of consciousness, on the one hand, with the aims of the Enlightenment, on the other hand, we are led to an awareness of an inherent need in the soul for historical development, its own further-determination. The Enlightenment is, after several forerunners in earlier history, above all a period in the early-modern era (roughly 1500–1800 A.D.) and had the function of undermining those aspects of tradition that initiation was about. Traditional societies are relatively stable. They do change, too, but more accidentally; cultural change is not the purpose of the soul in them; on the contrary, as I just pointed out, initiation serves the purpose of sustaining the prevailing tradition. By contrast, the purpose of emancipation and an increase of consciousness directly *aims* for change. It catapults consciousness to higher[245] stages and statuses of itself.

---

[245] "Higher" not in a spatial sense, but in the sense of higher degrees of refinement, sublimation, distillation, as in alchemical thinking, which at the same time means "deeper" into itself, into its concept and truth.

Above we discussed the difference between the soul and *human* concerns. Now we see that the purpose of "emancipation" implies the effort to raise the human concerns to full consciousness and to *free them from the soul*. In a way, the soul now appears as an enemy. This is so because it is often incompatible with what our humanness demands of us or because it even poses a threat to it. One striking example of this might be the fact that in archaic times, when people were pretty much enwrapped in, taken in by, and permeated by, the soul, when, in other words, *as* I's they were to a large degree simply identical with the promptings and needs of the soul, so that it was quite natural ("instinctive") for them to faithfully follow (and execute, enact) those soul needs, sacrificial killings of animals and even of humans were customary, which for us would be intolerable and revolting. So it is necessary for modern man to distance himself from the soul, to dissolve the previous unconscious identity with it, the *participation mystique* and *unio naturalis*, and to establish himself vis-à-vis the soul concerns.

And yet I also claimed that "emancipation" was one of the purposes of the soul itself. This contradiction needs to be understood in terms of the soul's internal dialectic, a dialectic which is already expressed in the Axiom of Nature by Pseudo-Democritus frequently quoted by Jung (e.g., *CW* 16 § 469): "Nature rejoices in nature, nature conquers nature, nature rules over nature" (Ἡ φύσις τῇ φύσει τέρπεται, καὶ ἡ φύσις τὴν φύσιν νικᾷ, καὶ ἡ φύσις τὴν φύσιν κρατεῖ). We already know that the soul is self-relation; that it is itself the origin or cause of whatever is done to itself and, furthermore, that "Nature is not improved save through its own nature" and "our material cannot be improved save through itself" (*CW* 9ii § 220). The soul works upon itself. This means in the case we have here in mind that the soul within itself needs to distance itself from itself, maybe in order to possibly at a later date arrive at a new unity with itself on a "higher" (or "lower," "deeper," more "fundamental") level. The purpose of emancipation *from* the soul is itself a soul purpose! The work *against* nature ("contra naturam") is in itself a work *by* or *in the spirit* of nature. Or "soul-making" (now in the wider sense) can under certain historical conditions, conditions as they seem to be given in the Western world and especially in modernity, paradoxically take the form of emancipation from soul. Emancipation from soul does not mean absolute defection from soul, because this emancipation from soul conversely occurs only within soul.

Emancipation in the sense of "individuation," freeing oneself from illusions, facing oneself objectively, is nowadays a psychological *task* of the individual, which is one reason why we now have the institution of psychotherapy. But emancipation is also a historical process that has already taken place so that we find ourselves objectively in the accomplished situation of emancipation (emancipatedness) as a fact. It is a world condition, the condition of psychologically *born* man. This means that it is an objective logical status of modern Man as such, a truth that we as individuals inevitably find ourselves in—*regardless of* our personal attitudes or the stage reached by us in our subjective psychic or mental development and *regardless of* whether we like it and know it or not. I want to comment briefly on this objective general status in contrast to the status of unborn man.

Jung insisted that "The individual, however, as an irrational datum, is the true and authentic carrier of reality, the *concrete* man..." (*CW* 10 § 498). The individual as the ultimate reality. This is the decidedly modern view, the view of born man. The individual comes first; society, the nation, the universal are secondary results of a union or association, or of abstractions. This thinking is already at the basis of Rousseau's "social contract." Perhaps, maybe, one could even on the ancient mythological and metaphysical stages of consciousness have agreed with Jung that, as he said several times, "man and his soul, the individual, is the only real carrier of life" (e.g., *Letters 2*, p. 286, to Böhler, 8 January 1956). But certainly not that the individual is the only carrier of *reality*. True and authentic reality lay under those conditions in the general, the universal, in Mother Nature or, later, in the Platonic Ideas, in essences, in the Neoplatonic One, in God. Man as individual was merely a part or exponent of and contained in a larger unity, a "piece" of the greater, higher reality of all-encompassing nature. Only nature had the status of substance and thus full-fledged reality, whereas the human individual (as well as all individual entities) were ultimately accidents. In medieval Christian times, the individual human being as a creature of God was contained in nature as the created world, which in turn was contained in God as the ultimate reality and substance.

Because in archaic times the individual had the status of accident, it was possible to sacrificially slaughter human beings, just as in antiquity it was not seen as a problem that people were kept as slaves and that during the medieval and, to some extent, early-modern periods people could be subjected to torture, to most cruel forms of death punishment, or be burned at the stake. And throughout the ages, nobody saw anything wrong with men's having to die in war by the thousands. The individual as such did not count. Not even in Christian times, during which, however, the individual *soul*, that is, the otherworldly transcendent part of man, already counted. But the higher purpose of the rescue of the immortal soul could precisely require that the human individual, Jung's "the *concrete* man," had to be burned at the stake if he or she was considered a heretic or witch. In contrast to Jung's "man and his soul, the individual," the individual *was* not his soul, but he was enwrapped in his soul, contained in it, or, conversely, the immortal soul was felt to be imprisoned in him as finite body, and with respect to his soul as his true substance he as human individual had only the said status of accident.

I already quoted Jung's insight that it is something peculiar that in our time the soul is on the side of the inner. "There are peoples and epochs where it [the soul] is outside, peoples and epochs that are unpsychological.... Whenever there exists externally a conceptual or ritual form in which all the yearnings and hopes of the soul are absorbed and expressed, that is, for example, a living religion, then the soul is outside..." (*CW* 10 §§ 158 f., transl. modif.). Apart from the erroneous idea of personalistic psychology that what is "on the side of the inner" is the soul, Jung's insight about former times and about the difference between them and our modern situation is crucial. The *soul* is always "outside," all around us and around everything, because it is the syntax or logic of life, and "inside" it is only in the sense and to the extent that as such it also permeates us and everything in our world. But it is not only religion at large in which people in former times had their soul, as Jung suggested. Also as individual people they were enwrapped in soul in particular ways.

This shows in the fact that they were subsumed under concepts, universal concepts. The king *was* king, the virgin *was* virgin, the widow *was* widow, an illegitimate child *was* a bastard. The Universals came first. People had to *live* and *be* the role, office, or status that was assigned to them or in which they found themselves. A virgin was not first a girl and person who happened to be a virgin. A slave was not first of all a human individual and then also a slave. The public roles and statuses were substances. In *them*, people had their identity and self, their soul, not in themselves. Onians[246] has shown how in early Greek antiquity (and elsewhere) the *substantial identification* of a human being with a role or office conferred on him was performed by means of a *telos*, a literal band, crown, laurel wreath, a slave's iron collar, a ring. "The kingship is a band put about a person, who thus becomes king."[247] The band binds the person inescapably, we could almost say imprisons him in the role. "Telos" was also an invisible bond that fate, old age, indeed death put over a person and enveloped him or her, which underlines the inescapability. From here we understand what it means that the Man of archaic times and antiquity was essentially a natural being contained and embedded in nature. It must by no means reductively be understood in biological terms, as a dependence on literal nature in the modern sense (which of course also existed). It rather means this fundamental inescapably being bound in a pre-given order, both the "naturally" given order of fate, birth, death, etc., and the culturally given order of general concepts as true substances.

Because man had his identity and self in the roles that he had to embody, it is clear that during those times (archaic times, classical antiquity, the Middle Ages, early modernity [the time up to around 1800]) it was out of the question that anybody could have attempted to search in himself for hidden causes of his personality and his behavior; that people could have tried to understand the dispositions of the self of an adult individual in terms of the person's early childhood experiences; that one would have searched for "one's true self" and "one's identity"; that one would have tried to find out what "one's true feelings" are. One's own self was not enigmatic: one lived it out openly in one's public roles and offices, in the universal concepts underlying these roles.

---

[246] Richard Broxton Onians, *The Origins of European Thought about the Body, the Mind, the Soul, the World, Time, and Fate.* Reprint of the 1951(Cambridge, University Press) edition, New York (Arno Press) 1973.

[247] *Ibid.*, p. 377.

And, for example, in the Middle Ages, the "mythic garment" of those roles in which one was enwrapped was also frequently made publically visible in the literal garments or symbols worn by people. Just think of the beginning of *Julius Caesar*:

> Hence! home, you idle creatures, get you home:
> Is this a holiday? what! know you not,
> Being mechanical, you ought not walk
> Upon a labouring day without the sign
> Of your profession?

Similarly, in many places people were in church seated according to their status, the married women, the maidens and unmarried women, the married men, the unmarried young men, the children—each of these groups in their own pews. As I said, the concept came first.

Modern man's emancipation from soul is concretely seen in the full-fledged separation of the person from the office or role he or she may have. The individual comes first. It is substantial. It is now the role, by contrast, which is in the status of accident. Concepts have lost their substantiality (substantial reality). The (psychological) birth of man (i.e., birth out of the soul) means the redefinition of man as autonomous individual. Man is no longer seen, does objectively no longer see himself, as contained in a larger whole, be it as a piece of nature as in the ancient world or be it as a creature of God as in the Middle Ages. Instead he now possesses human dignity and human rights. This is why Jung was able to say that the individual is the only carrier of reality. Man possesses human dignity and human rights just like that, without any ritual act, without any baptism or the like, a ritual that would *bestow* this dignity on him for the first time the way the putting of the "band of kingship" on a person, the crowning, anointing, investiture, and enthronization, *made* this person king and a carrier of majesty. A fundamental reversal of universal and individual as far as the sense of reality is concerned. Each individual precisely *as* "civil man" and in his positivity (Jung: as "irrational datum") now possesses human dignity by birth, *as* the naked biological organism that he is, indeed even already as zygote, in other words, as a natural being and in his singular individuality. And he possesses it inalienably.

Equipped with this inalienable dignity the human individual IS now the true and ultimate substance, whereas "human dignity" is his attribute and property that consequently also disappears with the death of the person and the decomposition of the body in its positivity. "Human dignity" is fundamentally secular, worldly, earthly (despite the fact that *historically* it is the secularization of the Christian high estimation of the individual as *imago dei*). By contrast, it had been the inalienable quality of the soul that as spirit it was indestructible, immortal, an entelechy. Indeed, in order to become fully released into its own the soul needed to be freed from the body and everything earthly as the finite and perishable part of man. The mythic soul had had its place in the underworld, the Christian and metaphysical soul likewise in the afterlife, in Heaven (or Hell). The essential outlook of man was toward the (not secular, innerworldly, but metaphysical) future. Life on earth was only the place where man had to be deeply concerned about the salvation of his soul and its everlasting life. The soul had and found its full reality only in God.

"Human dignity," by contrast, is always already given, and from the outset given in final and complete form. It cannot be diminished or increased. We cannot possibly lose it. No matter how undignified, wretched, evil our behavior, attitude, or condition may be, we, as positive facts, are totally identical with our "human dignity." It is so to speak "behind" me, my ground and *a priori*, and something which I possess in the form of a privilege and claim that is in principle enforceable here on earth before human courts. And the most dignified, creative, intelligent, humane, moral man does not have one gram more "human dignity" than anybody else. Pre-modern man *had* a soul as his immortal part (which required a permanent *cura animae*), but modern man *is* his "human dignity." As the possessor of "human rights" the modern individual IS defined as "empirical civil man" or "ego." To be ego is his essence.

The moment this has become the case myth, metaphysics, gods, and God have become impossible.[248] The time of soul is irrevocably

---

[248] "For the first time since the dawn of history we have succeeded in swallowing the whole primordial animatedness of nature into ourselves. Not only did the gods step, or rather were they dragged, down from their heavenly planetary houses.... Now, for the first time, we are living in a nature bereft of soul and gods [*in einer entseelten und entgötterten Natur*]" (*CW* 10 § 431, transl. modif.). It is a fallacy to think, as Jung did and many Jungians do, that you could simply reverse the order and *within* ourselves rediscover the same (the gods or God) that once upon a time had been *out there*. It is incredibly naive

over. It is delusional to try, in the context of an empirical psychology, to impute a *soul* to modern man by means of the mystifying invention of "the inner," "the unconscious" as the "soul's" hiding-place (*if* "soul" is to still have its concrete meaning). A personal soul and "human dignity" cannot coexist. One cannot be positivistic and metaphysical at the same time. One cannot be equipped with "human dignity" (as modern man inevitably is) and yet claim to have a soul. The former is, after all, the secularized, positivized, and "swallowed" successor concept to the latter. The physical body in its positivity has snatched and claimed the former soul for *itself*, pocketed and appropriated it, and the result of this sequestration by the body is "human dignity." This makes the concept of "human dignity" structurally analogous to that of "the unconscious." The latter, in the sense of Jung's "collective unconscious," is likewise a sunken, "swallowed," and secularized former cultural reality, however, not that of the soul (as the true substance and subject of man), but of the *semantics* of the whole wealth of *essential* (mythic, religious, metaphysical) conceptions.

But "human dignity" is also incompatible with soul in the cultural and semantic sense: because the autonomous individual, as the carrier of "human dignity" or, in Jung's terms, as the only "true and authentic carrier of reality," is only autonomous if and to the extent that it is metaphysically naked, and irrevocably so, whereas "soul" in the cultural, semantic sense means that one is cloaked in substantial concepts (roles) as in "mythic garments." Autonomy is not a ready-made. It requires the continuous work of a stripping off piece by piece of whatever concept that modern man shows himself to be *still* cloaked

and the psychologistic *prôton pseudos* to think that if "the stars [= the gods] have fallen from heaven," one could simply "rediscover the gods as psychic factors, that is, as archetypes of the unconscious" (cf. *CW* 9i § 50). A mere change of location, not a psychological, alchemical change of the character or inner constitution of "the matter" itself! Psychologically it is, as it were, a kind of "regressive restoration of the persona" (persona here as man's mythic garment). One smuggles the old form of consciousness, *its* old categories, into the totally new situation. The concept and reality of gods stands or falls on the logic of man's containment within a divine firmament. "Gods" are not like a piece of furniture that stays what it was regardless of whether you move it from the upper story to the cellar or not. Gods are not self-identical objects, things. The place "up there," in heaven, is part of what makes gods be gods. Once heaven as a spiritual reality is gone and now absolute-negative interiority is the soul's new self-definition, the very concept of god has become obsolete. Once this fall of the stars noted by Jung has happened, "all things are become new" (2 Cor. 5:17), and our theorizing has to go back to first base, to *discover* the *concepts* and *categories* appropriate for the new situation from within itself.

in despite all previous emancipation efforts, the work of more and more literally *laying bare* "human dignity" as *the* core of modern man *in* its nothingness or contentlessness: as no more than a *claim.*

The emancipation from the soul or the birth of man, which crystallizes and has its clearest expression in modern man's self-definition in terms of "human dignity," is an achievement of modernity, but it was prepared by many individual steps from the Middle Ages onwards (the acquisition of freedom of cities, of burghers, of universities, of the bourgeoisie, religious freedom, liberation from absolute rulers, etc.[249]). By the time of the Renaissance and even more so the period of the Enlightenment, man had already on a cultural level objectively established the concept of himself as autonomous on account of his mind, and in a few great individuals this newly acquired cultural idea had also already subjectively become a lived reality, while the mass of people were still far away from it. Greatness had been required in order to be an autonomous mind, and the autonomy had to be an actual life form, it had to be practically performed, as sort of factually "acted out" behavior and an independence of mind. Now, however, each ordinary individual is by definition autonomous man, simply on account of his human dignity, even if empirical-factually (ontically, psychically) he may quite obviously be governed by heteronomy (by trends, fads, public opinion, peer group pressure, etc., or by his own emotions and desires). Autonomy, as the emancipation from soul, has become ontological.

Until the middle of the last century, there was still one single role or universal concept that people carried as a mythic garment, one small remainder of soul in the old sense. It was the role of being "male" or "female." In this area, the individual was still, and still had to be, truly *identical* with the concept of masculinity or femininity, respectively. It was until then objectively a priori known and unquestionable what "masculine," "man" and what "feminine," "woman" meant and how a man and a woman had to be. The roles of the sexes were therefore the last remainder of really *lived* myth. (Myth, let us remember, is not a theory about ..., not an interpretation or opinion. Myth means: factual identity of concept and lived life; the unquestioned living a concept

---

[249] See for example Günther Mensching, *Das Allgemeine und das Besondere. Der Ursprung des modernen Denkens im Mittelalter,* Stuttgart (Metzler) 1992.

as an unquestionable truth). But since then, this mythic garment has also been taken off, and so now each individual is free to find out for himself or herself what sexual role they want to play and to try out different roles at different stages of their lives at their own discretion. Here, as in all other regards, man is now "man for himself" and up to his own devices: autonomous. The freedom from soul is total today—*with one single exception: neurosis.*

In contrast to psychotic delusions which are interpretations, assertions, or beliefs, in other words, something mental, noetic, neurosis means an immediate *identity* "in the flesh" of the neurotic person with some neurotic concept without interposition of any mental process. This concept is absolutely and immediately embodied, lived—absolutely compelling, an emotional, almost physical fact. Usually it is precisely not believed in. It simply rules. The neurotic person IS the hysterical behavior displayed by him or her, IS the depression, and the phobically feared spider IS a terrible threat, just like in olden times a king WAS majesty in a concrete substantial sense.

However, because neurosis is the (soul's objective) simulation of a mythic garment *under the conditions of born man* and his complete and irrevocable emancipation from soul—as witnessed by man's possessing human dignity—neurosis precisely has to, and can only, show itself as something truly neurotic, as sick and without that dignity it is supposed to have. This makes a few reflections about neurosis and its purpose in the soul's life necessary.

In our time it is above all neurosis, as a veritable soul phenomenon (i.e., a product of the soul, its own work, rather than a result caused by external events or circumstances), which requires for its "healing" the soul's emancipation *from* the soul. This being so, and for the reasons I sketched out above, it would be a serious therapeutic mistake to approach a neurosis, *if* it indeed is a real neurosis, with the traditional idea of soul-making in the sense of an imaginal psychology, to respond to it with an attempt to find out "Who? Which God?" manifests in it, or to lead the neurotic pathology back (*epistrophê*) to myths or archetypes. When Jung said, "Neurosis is intimately bound up with the problem of our time and really represents an unsuccessful attempt on the part of the individual to solve the general problem in his own person" (*CW* 7 § 18), he needs to be contradicted. No, no. Provided that it is a real neurosis, it is really sick, without any redeeming value, and precisely not a (*merely unsuccessful*) attempt at healing the prevailing problem (be it general or personal). It is a manifestation and product of the *sick* soul (see 2.2.1 and 2.3.2 above). Likewise, when Jung says: "The main interest of my work is not concerned with the treatment of neurosis but rather with the approach to the numinous. But the fact is that the approach to the numinous is the real therapy, and inasmuch as you attain to the numinous experience you are released from the curse of pathology" (*Letters* 1, p. 377, to Martin, 20 Aug. 1945[250]), we need to contradict and say that in this way one would precisely do the neurosis's bidding. It would be a neurosis-*syntonic* approach in which the therapist would "ride the same hobby-horse"[251] as the neurosis.

It is of course Jung's prerogative not mainly to be concerned with the treatment of neurosis. I have no problem with that. But to offer the numinous as a cure from the curse of neurotic pathology is not acceptable, and viewing neurosis as a result of (as caused by) the "lack of meaning" in our time is itself a neurotic explanation of neurosis. Nobody needs to become *neurotic* because of a lack of meaning. This conception shows that he who thinks this way has no understanding of the specific nature and reality of neurosis, no *concept*, or only a muddled one, of what makes neurosis *neurotic*.

On the contrary, we can surmise that the invention of neurosis as a cultural phenomenon during the 19th century (and the soul's thus, surprisingly, taking on the form of *sick soul*) happened for the sole purpose of forcing itself (the soul) to *explicitly* emancipate itself from itself. Neurosis is, briefly put, (a) the soul's—stubborn, spiteful—insistence on simulating and celebrating the standpoint of a "mythic" *identity* of concept AND real individual, or of a kind of *metaphysic* (in the form of an absolute principle, namely "The Absolute")—*at the historical time* when the soul has already experienced, and definitively knows, that the times of metaphysic and of myth are once and for all over (*this is*, as I pointed out, what makes it *neurotic*[252]). But (b) neurosis is also the obvious *representation* of this celebration *as sick*, as phony,

---

[250] In the German edition the date of this letter is the 28th of August.
[251] Cf. *CW* 10 § 362.
[252] Unsuccessful attempts at solving the general problem of the age in which one lives are not neurotic. They are simply failures.

disgusting, silly, stupid, pathological—at any rate untrue. Everyone can see it, and the neurotic person painfully feels it. And so, I submit, the soul invented neurosis for itself both as *incentive* and as a kind of *springboard* to push off from. For the soul it is obviously not enough to simply (easily, "just like that") *outgrow* metaphysics in a natural developmental process (metaphysics as the historical successor to myth), which would be no more than an "implicit" overcoming of it. It has to actively, systematically, in detail and in full awareness *work off* its own fascination and infatuation with the metaphysical, the mythic, the numinous, and the suggestive power of the imaginal— *through* pulling itself out of its neurosis, *really* stepping out of it and leaving it behind as the nothing that it is. The soul needs to concretely, as a hard-core reality, *put before itself* once more that from which its natural development has already long removed it, and to give it a new artificial presence so that it (the soul) is forced to also psychologically, explicitly depart from it. Only then is the departure psychologically real because only then has the full price been paid for the departure from the previous stage of consciousness, and paid for in cash, namely in real pain and the systematic labor of the concept.

It is the soul that becomes neurotic, and by the same token it is the soul that needs to overcome its neurosis. But it can only overcome it by actively involving and employing the consciousness of the human *person* in whom the neurosis lives itself out. Human consciousness, that is to say, the human person's strictly analytical, conceptual thought (his or her uncompromisingly seeing through and critiquing the neuroticness of the soul's perverse *mise en scène* in all its practical details) is indispensable for it to become possible that the soul can push off from its own neurosis and be truly freed of it. Why? For at first this assertion seems surprising. After all, is it not all the soul's doing and its own need to overcome the neurosis produced by itself? If so, why is there this need for the human person's comprehension? The reason is that the very purpose of this whole undertaking is that—within objectively already irrevocably born man—now also the soul itself emancipates itself from itself, is *born out* of its cocoonment within itself (within itself as myth, religion, the imaginal, metaphysics, etc.), and thus becomes not only factually, but also explicitly and *for itself* a born soul. But the born soul is born *as* human consciousness and its infinite *interiority*.

Myth was, we heard as much, essentially cosmic, all around us. It was, as we nowadays say, "projected." Man was enwrapped in mythic garments, in narratives and images about a world animated by gods, spirits, fairies, and goblins as well as in concepts (roles, offices, statuses). The soul at the time of unborn man was fundamentally outside and public. It formed, as already millennia ago the Orphics realized, a cave, the world egg. The I was enclosed within. Human existence—the island or garden of the human, all-too-human—had its limited place, and took place, only within this "egg." It was enclosed by it on all sides. At later stages of the soul's historical development, religion and metaphysics likewise created, or represented, a world of meaning all around man. *That* soul that in addition to *man's* emancipation from it has also been *born out of itself*, by contrast, means—maybe paradoxically—that it has precisely come home to itself, returned to itself, namely by having realized itself as absolute-negative *inwardness*: having acquired the form or status of inwardness as its form of existence. This is not the (literal, in itself external) inwardness in man, not traditional psychology's "the unconscious," but the inwardness in itself, absolute interiority.

I said that the soul can only overcome neurosis by actively involving and employing the consciousness of the human *person* in whom the neurosis lives itself out. But now I have to modify this statement. Although this involvement of the neurotic person is indispensable if this person wants to be freed from his or her neurosis, the neurosis is not aimed at the individual neurotic, is not created by the soul for his or her becoming initiated in soul as absolute-negative interiority. The true subject that neurosis is aimed at is psychology, and the *person* whose consciousness needs to get actively involved is really the psychologist. Not the individual neuroses, but neurosis at large, the cultural phenomenon or "institution" of neurosis in modernity, is the psychopomp that on a cultural level and in psychology as a discipline has the function of bringing about the explicit birth of the soul out of itself.

But returning from here to the topic of the treatment of neurotic patients, after what I said it is clear that if one offers to the neurotic soul the imaginal or the numinous, its *neurotic* tendency will, to its (the neurotic soul's) delight, only be supported, because the imaginal and the numinous are only another guise of the neurotic soul's "The Absolute." And on top of it they are seemingly a much more dignified (even if less "real" and powerful, more vaporized) version that, as ideology, can *without* obvious symptoms be entertained by persons. In this way the neurosis, which heretofore had been totally immersed down here in the real individual ("in his own person"), has been kicked upstairs, elevated to the lofty level of theory or ideology, but precisely not dissolved. On the contrary, it has been cemented and legitimized because to the extent that the psychological ideology actually works for the person who suffered from the neurosis, the neurotic symptoms become superfluous. Naturally so, because the move to ideology (here to "myths," "the Gods," "the imaginal," etc., just as, more personalistically, to "the Oedipus complex," etc.) is a move from "in his own person" (the place of the neurotic pathology) and from the fundamentally unintelligible positive factuality of neurotic symptoms *to* the fundamentally general, universal level of *intelligibility* (grand concepts). At the same time, the previously obvious offensiveness of the neurosis has been successfully concealed in a belief-system whose offensiveness is now only (only?) an intellectual one. The concealment succeeds by placing the *semantic* aspect of the ideology absolutely in the foreground (its contents are time-honored myths, etc., and as such indeed absolutely inoffensive, more than that, truly respectable) so that its syntactical character (ideology as "false consciousness" [Marx] and ideologizing as mystification) must not be noticed.

Concerning the daily work in the consulting room, what I pointed out here is not to be taken abstractly as the one and only recipe for the therapies of cases of neurosis to be pedantically followed. Even if a patient comes into analysis because of a neurosis, there may nevertheless also be certain phenomena, for example, individual dreams, which need an imaginal approach: an attempt by analyst and patient to go along with what shows itself into its depth in the spirit of soul-making and inwardization. Conversely, in cases in which soul-making in the traditional sense may be the predominant direction to be taken, there will also be moments when caustic analytical work is necessary. There are many different situations in each actual therapy. The point is not that *this* case needs the cauterizing approach and the *that* case a soul-making approach. Rather, the question always is what this individual phenomenon or situation here and now needs. Eachness. This is why we need to discern the spirits, learn to know when it is time for the one and when for the other approach. For this, the feeling function is required, an "instinct," as it were, that lets us sense what the soul needs: whether it wants us in this specific instance to resistancelessly follow it into its depth or whether what it presents us with it presents for the sole purpose that conversely we have something to push off from. There is no technical sign that could decide for us and would relieve us of having to come forward with our own judgment on our own risk in each situation, vis-à-vis each soul phenomenon.

After this last chapter forced us to narrow down our focus upon individual neuroses and the therapeutic work in the consulting room, I do not want to close this book about the question *What Is Soul?* without reminding the reader again of the whole range of our foregoing explorations and of Jung's express warning that "It is [only] the smallest part of the psyche, and in particular of the unconscious, that presents itself in the medical consulting room."[253]

---

[253] *Letters 2*, p. 307, 17 June 1956, to Nelson.

Index

from implicit to explicit, 53, 70, 188, 258, 273, 278, 304, 306, 309, 311, 332
from mythos to logos, 164
from ontology to logic, 20
fugitive stag (*see also*: soul, fugitive), 81
further-determination, *see* historical progression

G

Gadamer, Hans-Georg, 73, 224
Gebser, Jean, 120
Gehrts, Heino, 169
Gemüt, 314
general faith, generality, 33-35, 39, 116, 136, 147, 201
genius/human person relation, 127, 128
ghost in the machine, 21, 23
Giegerich, Wolfgang, 7, 60-62, 66, 118, 137, 145, 147, 178, 184, 254, 255, 259, 301, 307, 313
God, 8, 10, 13, 23, 46, 55, 77, 125, 137, 162, 164, 173, 198, 199, 215, 221, 252-254, 260, 269, 270, 275, 278, 279, 283, 286, 297, 312, 323, 326-328
god, goddess, 97, 161, 162, 179, 195, 204, 213, 220, 221, 225, 226, 228, 231, 251, 253, 284, 293, 301
gods, 8, 52, 57, 58, 63, 65, 77-79, 84, 91, 117-119, 136, 141, 160-164, 185, 186, 192, 195, 198, 199, 202, 209, 213, 215, 217-223, 225, 227-233, 251, 252, 278, 293, 301, 305, 315, 318, 320, 327, 328, 333, 334
rhetoric / jargon of gods, 220, 221
Goethe, Johann Wolfgang von, 20, 95, 109, 124, 149, 186, 205, 219, 233
"manifest mystery", 152
made by his poems, 95, 96, 184
great dream, 187

great, the (vs. the petty or ordinary), 10, 40, 63, 64, 66, 169, 171, 173, 174, 184, 189, 190, 195-202, 233, 271, 278, 286, 298, 300, 310, 329

H

habituation, getting accustomed, 183, 192, 259
Hades, 14
Hardy, Thomas, 121, 128, 237, 238
Haydn, Joseph, 229
Heaven and Earth (mythol.), 123, 149
Hegel, G.W.F., 10-12, 31, 41, 42, 62, 116, 125, 126, 128, 131, 133, 152, 153, 169, 192, 201, 202, 233, 269, 276, 279-281, 288, 304
Heidegger, Martin, 39, 67, 123, 295
Heraclitus, 12, 59, 74, 125, 151, 152, 313
herm: head and phallus, 264
Hillman, James, 1, 6, 57, 62, 77, 78, 81, 87, 107, 163, 217, 231, 232, 236, 242, 258, 301, 305, 318
historical locus, 10, 42, 43, 58, 73, 174, 187, 188, 197, 204, 209, 271, 298, 300
historical progression, further-determination (*see also*: *opus magnum*; pushing off), 35, 72, 186, 198, 199, 203, 230, 318, 321
history, sunken, *see under*: unconscious, the
Hobbes, Thomas, 8
Hofmannsthal, Hugo von
"Letter of Lord Chandos", 64
Homer, 14, 51, 58, 95
homo totus, 100, 143, 158, 173, 299, 315
human-all-too-human, the, 15, 89, 92, 99, 102, 109, 111, 132, 135, 136, 144, 146, 149, 154, 156, 161, 177, 189, 190, 199, 216, 222, 241, 315

P

Paris, Ginette, 117, 214-216, 218, 222, 225
participation mystique, 171, 319, 322
passiones animae, 274
pathê or *pathêmata*, 274
paying the price for one's wounds, 246, 247
personhood, human, derivation of, 185
personification, 24
Petrarch, 178, 193
Pharaoh, 52, 186, 213
phenomena (*see also*: soul phenomena)
    as triggers, 240
    have nothing behind themselves, 84, 305
    in themselves linguistic, 93
    mean themselves, 82
    only one true (higher-level) phenomenon in modernity, 209
    sublation of the many into one, 164
philosophy, 8, 10, 12, 27, 43, 44, 76, 77, 79, 84, 86, 180, 193, 195, 202, 253, 268, 274-276, 278, 288, 312
    articulation of the truth of the age, 10, 269, 270
phonemes, 53
phrenes, 263, 265
Pindar, 268
Plato, 12, 31, 44, 73, 94, 179, 192, 266-268
pleroma, 235, 251
Plotinus, 124, 149
poet, as "author"?, 95
Poimandres, 109
political correctness, 24
polytheistic psychology, 165, 209, 217-220, 228, 233, 236, 266
Poncelet, Abbé, 97
positivism, 23

practical gain vs. blessedness, 125-128
pregnancy (of the mind), 38, 171, 304
production without a producer (*cf.* dance without a dancer), 44, 45
progress, *see*: historical progression
Proklos, 31
Pseudo-Democritus, 322
psyche (*see also*: soul; psychic, the), 16
    part of human biology, 156
psychê, 31, 35, 51, 121, 262-265, 274
psychic images, our being enwrapped in, 65, 74-76, 134, 299, 321, 322, 324, 326, 333
psychic, the, vs. the psychological, 77, 85, 86, 99, 101-105, 109-111, 126, 139, 140, 144, 146, 147, 149, 156, 160, 163, 166, 208, 215, 219, 249, 263, 270
psychological difference, 35, 54, 80, 81, 101-104, 109, 111, 123, 127, 129-131, 144, 146, 148, 149, 151, 162, 163, 176, 189, 190, 217, 219, 234, 235, 279, 298-300, 310
    the new psychological difference, 149
psychological novel, 103, 108, 203
psychological relationship, 320
"psychologically true", as reduced sense of truth, 143
psychologist, must have died as ego personality, 301
psychology
    acted out, 1
    as a historical discipline, 141
    as a subject, 300, 304
    as *Ersatz* for soul, 140
    as human biology (ethology), 100
    as journalism, 231-233
    as methodological *procedere*, 288-290, 292, 294, 299-301, 304, 306, 307, 313
    as sublated metaphysics, 307

as the "I" or subject, 300
autonomous mind/soul, 6, 7, 14,
    25, 32, 44, 58, 59, 68, 70, 76,
    84, 329
"behind the impressions of the
    daily life", 234, 244, 310
compartmentalized, 17
interprets *interpretations*, 309
Jung's alchemical, 101, 247
made possible by loss of symbols,
    141, 182
meaning of the word "p.," 16
needs giftedness and feeling
    function, 206, 292
needs subtler intelligence, 85
no Archimedean point, 289, 290,
    307
not a science, 20, 22
not concerned with life, 13
not only *with* soul but also *of* soul,
    77
of the unconscious, 3
piecemeal engineering, 2
possible only through loss of soul,
    182, 286
possible only through loss of
    symbols, 286
self-negation, self-sublation, 104,
    106
soul-lessness built into its
    definition, 22
successor of soul, 288, 289
"the soul": figurative speech, 24,
    291
true psychology, 2, 22, 58, 105,
    107, 108, 120, 142, 185, 228,
    233, 295, 299, 300
views events as the soul's own
    doing, 286
vs. the humanities, 76, 77

with / without soul, 5, 7, 14, 15,
    17, 19, 21, 22, 24, 26, 76, 223,
    268, 308, 316
pushing off (*see also*: historical
    progression), 29, 30, 43, 49, 50, 53,
    56, 61, 67-70, 72, 73, 90, 104,
    105, 142, 166, 217, 279, 332, 335
putrefaction, 42, 231, 271

Q

Quintaes, Marcus, 62

R

reduction, reductive, 48, 54, 98, 101,
    105, 127, 147, 159, 210, 215, 318,
    325
referent, external, 40, 82, 83, 86, 305,
    307
religion, 5, 9, 10, 13, 14, 25, 43, 77,
    86, 114, 140, 143, 148, 161, 178,
    182, 208, 209, 218, 227, 252-254,
    268, 270, 271, 283, 286-288, 294,
    324, 332, 333
representation / celebration of soul
    truths, 91, 124, 125, 128, 136,
    153, 165, 177, 178, 181, 196, 229,
    318, 331
reversal, 127, 183-186, 195, 268, 326
    reversal of our causal sequence, 186
Rex, Regina, 101, 248
right means, right man, right moment,
    220
Rimbaud, as "author"?, 95
rituals, 122, 123, 125, 128, 238
    as celebration of the soul's truth,
    125
Robinson Crusoe, 38
Rohde, Erwin, 258
Rousseau, Jean-Jacques, 9, 323

For Product Safety Concerns and Information please contact our EU
representative GPSR@taylorandfrancis.com
Taylor & Francis Verlag GmbH, Kaufingerstraße 24, 80331 München, Germany

www.ingramcontent.com/pod-product-compliance
Lightning Source LLC
Chambersburg PA
CBHW070546270326
41926CB00013B/2223